Macmillan/McGraw-Hill READING

Contributors

The Princeton Review, Time Magazine, Accelerated Reader

The Princeton Review is not
affiliated with Princeton
University or ETS.

learning through listening

Students with print disabilities may be eligible to obtain an accessible, audio version
of the pupil edition of this textbook. Please call Recording for the Blind & Dyslexic at
1-800-221-4792 for complete information.

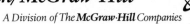

A Division of The **McGraw·Hill** Companies

Published by Macmillan/McGraw-Hill, a division of The McGraw-Hill Companies, Inc., Two Penn Plaza, NY, NY 10121

Printed in the United States of America

ISBN 0-02-188571-0/5

　5 6 7 8 9　058/043　04 03 02

Macmillan/McGraw-Hill READING

Authors

James Flood

Jan E. Hasbrouck

James V. Hoffman

Diane Lapp

Donna Lubcker

Angela Shelf Medearis

Scott Paris

Steven Stahl

Josefina Villamil Tinajero

Karen D. Wood

Macmillan McGraw-Hill

New York   Farmington

UNIT 1

TIME OF MY LIFE

Árbol de limón/Lemon Tree 16
A Poem in Spanish and English by Jennifer Clement,
translated by Consuelo de Aerenlund

Stories in Art 18

READING STRATEGY A Special Gift 19
PROBLEM AND SOLUTION

The Wise Old Woman 20
A Japanese Folk Tale retold by Yoshiko Uchida,
illustrated by Martin Springett
Story Questions and Activities 40
Study Skills: Use Parts of a Book 42
LANGUAGE ARTS CONNECTION
Test Power 43

Stories in Art 44

READING STRATEGY The Mysterious Boat 45
STORY ELEMENTS

The Voyage of the *Dawn Treader* 46
A Fantasy Adventure from the book by C. S. Lewis,
illustrated by Amy Hill
Story Questions and Activities 62
Study Skills: Use a Glossary 64
SOCIAL STUDIES CONNECTION
Test Power 65

Stories in Art 66

READING STRATEGY **Stephen Hawking: An Extraordinary Man** 67
CAUSE AND EFFECT

Wilma Unlimited 68
A Biographical Story by Kathleen Krull,
illustrated by David Diaz

    Story Questions and Activities 90
    Study Skills: Use an Index 92
    SOCIAL STUDIES CONNECTION
    Test Power 93

Stories in Art 94

READING STRATEGY **Max Finds the *Fox*** 95
STORY ELEMENTS

The Wreck of the *Zephyr* 96
A Fantasy written and illustrated
by Chris Van Allsburg

    Story Questions and Activities 120
    Study Skills: Use a Table of Contents
    and Headings 122
    LANGUAGE ARTS CONNECTION
    Test Power 123

Stories in Art 124

READING STRATEGY **Hurricane Andrew** 125
CAUSE AND EFFECT

TIME FOR KIDS **Tornadoes!** 126
A Science Article from TIME FOR KIDS

    Story Questions and Activities 130
    Study Skills: Read a Bibliography 132
    LANGUAGE ARTS/SCIENCE CONNECTION
    Test Power 133

Knoxville, Tennessee 134
A Poem by Nikki Giovanni

🌐 **Reading Social Studies** 732

UNIT 2

Building Bridges

Oranges 136
A Poem by Jean Little

Stories in Art 138
READING STRATEGY **Tanya Plays the Piano** 139
MAKE PREDICTIONS

The Gold Coin 140
A Central American Tale written by Alma Flor Ada,
translated from the Spanish by Bernice Randall,
illustrated by Neil Waldman
Story Questions and Activities 162
Study Skills: Use a Dictionary 164
LANGUAGE ARTS CONNECTION
Test Power 165

Stories in Art 166
READING STRATEGY **The Transcontinental Railroad** 167
FACT AND NONFACT

John Henry 168
A Tall Tale retold by Julius Lester,
illustrated by Jerry Pinkney
Story Questions and Activities 196
Study Skills: Use the Internet 198
SOCIAL STUDIES CONNECTION
Test Power 199

6

Stories in Art..**200**

READING STRATEGY **Kids Helping Kids**..................................**201**
MAIN IDEA

It's Our World, Too!..............................**202**
Two Biographical Sketches from the book
by Phillip Hoose, illustrated by Robert Roper
    Story Questions and Activities **218**
    Study Skills: Use a Telephone Directory **220**
      SOCIAL STUDIES CONNECTION
    Test Power **221**

Stories in Art..**222**

READING STRATEGY **A Meeting with a Star**..........................**223**
MAKE PREDICTIONS

Dear Mr. Henshaw..............................**224**
Realistic Fiction from the novel by Beverly Cleary,
illustrated by R. J. Shay
    Story Questions and Activities **238**
    Study Skills: Use an Encyclopedia Index.............**240**
      SOCIAL STUDIES CONNECTION
    Test Power **241**

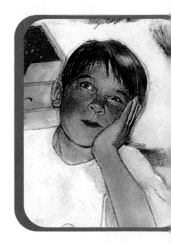

Stories in Art..**242**

**Williamsburg, Virginia: A Restored
Colonial Town** **243**
MAIN IDEA

TIME FOR KIDS **Digging Up the Past** **244**
A Social Studies Article from TIME FOR KIDS
    Story Questions and Activities **248**
    Study Skills: Conduct an Interview....................**250**
      LANGUAGE ARTS CONNECTION
    Test Power **251**

I Hear America Singing **252**
A Poem by Walt Whitman

Reading Science **738**

UNIT 3

iMAGINE THAT!!

The Sidewalk Racer, or On the Skateboard ... 254
A Poem by Lillian Morrison

Stories in Art.. 256

READING STRATEGY The Spelling Bee 257
STEPS IN A PROCESS

The Marble Champ 258
A Short Story from the book *Baseball in April*
by Gary Soto, illustrated by Ken Spengler

Story Questions and Activities 270

Study Skills: Follow Instructions 272
SOCIAL STUDIES CONNECTION

Test Power 273

Stories in Art.. 274

READING STRATEGY Fooling the Hungry Tiger......................... 275
SEQUENCE OF EVENTS

The Paper Dragon 276
A Fantasy by Marguerite W. Davol,
illustrated by Robert Sabuda

Story Questions and Activities 304

Study Skills: Use a Graph............................. 306
MATH CONNECTION

Test Power 307

8

Stories in Art.. 308

READING STRATEGY Remembering Franklin Delano
Roosevelt 309
STEPS IN A PROCESS

Grandma Essie's Covered Wagon.......... 310
A Biographical Story by David Williams,
illustrated by Wiktor Sadowski

Story Questions and Activities 336
Study Skills: Use a Time Line 338
SOCIAL STUDIES CONNECTION
Test Power 339

Stories in Art.. 340

READING STRATEGY Jacob Lawrence: Art as History 341
AUTHOR'S PURPOSE, POINT OF VIEW

**Going Back Home:
An Artist Returns to the South** 342
A Biographical Story interpreted and written
by Toyomi Igus, based on the illustrations of Michele Wood

Story Questions and Activities 368
Study Skills: Read a Family Tree 370
SOCIAL STUDIES CONNECTION
Test Power 371

Stories in Art.. 372

READING STRATEGY The Vietnam Memorial: A Dream
Becomes Reality 373
SEQUENCE OF EVENTS

TIME FOR KIDS **A Mountain of a Monument**................. 374
A Social Studies Article from TIME FOR KIDS

Story Questions and Activities 378
Study Skills: Use Scale Drawings 380
MATH CONNECTION
Test Power 381

To Dark Eyes Dreaming 382
A Poem by Zilpha Keatley Snyder

NEWS Reading Media 744

UNIT 4

Investigate!

First Flight **384**
A Poem by Frank Richards

Stories in Art **386**

READING
STRATEGY **The Pest** **387**
        JUDGMENTS AND DECISIONS

Carlos and the Skunk **388**
Realistic Fiction by Jan Romero Stevens,
illustrated by Jeanne Arnold

   Story Questions and Activities **404**
   Study Skills: Read a Diagram **406**
            SOCIAL STUDIES CONNECTION
   Test Power **407**

Stories in Art **408**

READING
STRATEGY **Woolly Mammoth Found** **409**
        IMPORTANT AND UNIMPORTANT INFORMATION

How to Think Like a Scientist **410**
Science Nonfiction by Stephen P. Kramer,
illustrated by Kim Behm

   Story Questions and Activities **428**
   Study Skills: Use an Outline **430**
            LANGUAGE ARTS/SCIENCE CONNECTION
   Test Power **431**

Stories in Art.. **432**

READING STRATEGY **Komodo Dragons**............................. **433**
    FACT AND NONFACT

An Island Scrapbook.................................. **434**
Science Nonfiction written and illustrated
by Virginia Wright Frieroon
    Story Questions and Activities.................... **460**
    Study Skills: Read an Observation Chart............ **462**
        SCIENCE CONNECTION
    Test Power.. **463**

Stories in Art.. **464**

READING STRATEGY **A Perfect Storm**.............................. **465**
    JUDGMENTS AND DECISIONS

The Big Storm.. **466**
A Science Book written and illustrated
by Bruce Hiscock
    Story Questions and Activities.................... **488**
    Study Skills: Read a Weather Map.................. **490**
        SCIENCE CONNECTION
    Test Power.. **491**

Stories in Art.. **492**

READING STRATEGY **Sacajawea**.................................... **493**
    FACT AND NONFACT

TIME FOR KIDS **Catching Up with Lewis and Clark**....... **494**
A Social Studies Article from TIME FOR KIDS
    Story Questions and Activities.................... **498**
    Study Skills: Use a Map.......................... **500**
        SOCIAL STUDIES CONNECTION
    Test Power.. **501**

Early Spring.. **502**
A Poem by Shonto Begay

Reading Research.................................. **748**

11

UNIT 5

Bright Ideas

To Make a Prairie **504**
A Poem by Emily Dickinson

Stories in Art **506**

READING STRATEGY **The Riddle of the Sphinx** **507**
COMPARE AND CONTRAST

The Riddle **508**
An Old Catalan Story retold by Adele Vernon,
illustrated by Robert Rayevsky and Vladimir Radunsky

Story Questions and Activities **528**
Study Skills: Follow Directions **530**
SOCIAL STUDIES CONNECTION

Test Power **531**

Stories in Art **532**

READING STRATEGY **The Oak Island Treasure** **533**
AUTHOR'S PURPOSE, POINT OF VIEW

Life in Flatland **534**
Mathematical Fiction from *Flatland* by Edwin Abbott,
illustrated by Wallace Keller

Story Questions and Activities **550**
Study Skills: Read Signs **552**
SOCIAL STUDIES CONNECTION

Test Power **553**

Stories in Art 554

READING STRATEGY The Leopard and His Spots 555
PROBLEM AND SOLUTION

Tonweya and the Eagles 556
A Lakota Indian Tale from the book
by Rosebud Yellow Robe,
illustrated by Richard Red Owl

Story Questions and Activities 576
Study Skills: Read a News Article 578
SOCIAL STUDIES CONNECTION

Test Power 579

Stories in Art 580

READING STRATEGY King Toll and His Bridges 581
COMPARE AND CONTRAST

Breaker's Bridge 582
A Chinese Folk Tale from *The Rainbow People*
by Laurence Yep, illustrated by David Wisniewski

Story Questions and Activities 598
Study Skills: Read a Help-Wanted Ad 600
SOCIAL STUDIES CONNECTION

Test Power 601

Stories in Art 602

READING STRATEGY Save Our Air! 603
PROBLEM AND SOLUTION

TIME FOR KIDS **Cleaning Up America's Air** 604
A Science Article from TIME FOR KIDS

Story Questions and Activities 608
Study Skills: Read an Editorial 610
SCIENCE CONNECTION

Test Power 611

Philbert Phlurk 612
A Poem by Jack Prelutsky

Reading Online Resources 752

UNIT 6

CROSSROADS

Paper I...**614**
A Poem by Carl Sandburg

Stories in Art..**616**

READING STRATEGY **Frederick Douglass Chooses Home**..........**617**
     JUDGMENTS AND DECISIONS

Amistad Rising: A Story of Freedom...**618**
Historical Fiction written by Veronica Chambers,
illustrated by Paul Lee
  Story Questions and Activities.......................**644**
  Study Skills: Use the Card Catalog....................**646**
    LANGUAGE ARTS CONNECTION
  Test Power...**647**

Stories in Art..**648**

READING STRATEGY **A Real History Class**..........................**649**
    IDENTIFY CAUSE AND EFFECT

Rip Van Winkle..**650**
A Play based on the classic tale by Washington Irving,
dramatized by Adele Thane, illustrated by Gary Kelley
  Story Questions and Activities.......................**670**
  Study Skills: Use an Online Library Catalog.........**672**
    LANGUAGE ARTS CONNECTION
  Test Power...**673**

READING STRATEGY Stories in Art..674

A Letter Home 675
SEQUENCE OF EVENTS

The Sea Maidens of Japan 676
Realistic Fiction by Lili Bell,
illustrated by Erin McGonigle Brammer
Story Questions and Activities 694
Study Skills: Choose Reference Sources 696
LANGUAGE ARTS CONNECTION
Test Power 697

READING STRATEGY Stories in Art..698

Lizzie Stanton Speaks Out......................699
JUDGMENTS AND DECISIONS

The Silent Lobby 700
Historical Fiction from *The Big Book for Peace*
by Mildred Pitts Walter, illustrated by Gil Ashby
Story Questions and Activities........................714
Study Skills: Use the Library.........................716
SOCIAL STUDIES CONNECTION
Test Power 717

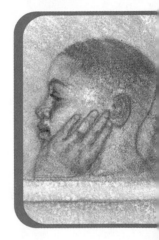

READING STRATEGY Stories in Art...718

Nature's Giants..719
SEQUENCE OF EVENTS

Amazon Alert! 720
A Science Article from TIME FOR KIDS
Story Questions and Activities........................724
Study Skills: Use an Encyclopedia 726
LANGUAGE ARTS CONNECTION
Test Power 727

Frederick Douglass 1817–1895......................728
A Poem by Langston Hughes

How To **Reading Directions** 756

Glossary..760

TIME OF MY LIFE

Árbol de limón

Si te subes a un árbol de limón
siente la corteza
con tus rodillas y pies,
huele sus flores blancas,
talla las hojas
entre tus manos.
Recuerda,
el árbol es mayor que tú
y tal vez encuentres cuentos
entre sus ramas.

by Jennifer Clement

Lemon Tree

If you climb a lemon tree
feel the bark
under your knees and feet,
smell the white flowers,
rub the leaves in your hands.
Remember,
the tree is older than you are
and you might find stories
in its branches.

Translated by
Consuelo de Aerenlund

Stories in Art

Have you ever heard the saying
"A picture is worth a thousand words"?
Sometimes a picture can tell a story—
with characters, a setting, and events
that present problems and solutions.

Look at this painting of the court of
Alexander the Great. What do you think
is happening? Who are the people in
the painting? Why is the man standing
before the king?

Imagine that you are at the court. What
problem might you present to the king?
What answer might he give to solve it?

Court of Alexander the Great Manuscripts
British Library, London

18

lexandre
fist suptu
eusement
mettir en
sepulture
les gens de guerre quil auoit
perdu en chassant le roy daire
et distribua · XIIII · marz

aux aultres compaignones
de son armee dont la pluspt
des cheuaulx fut perdue · et
meismes ceulx qui demoure
rent par la payne et grant
challeur se mofondirent ·
Toute la peine quon auoit
deuant assamblee de la cite

Problem and Solution

Develop a strategy for identifying problems and solutions.

1 **Read the beginning of the story** to identify the main character's problem.

2 **Restate the problem** in your own words.

3 **Identify the actions** the character takes to solve the problem.

4 **Read the ending of the story** to determine if and how the problem was solved.

5 **Evaluate the solution.** Was this a good way to solve the problem? Why?

A Special Gift

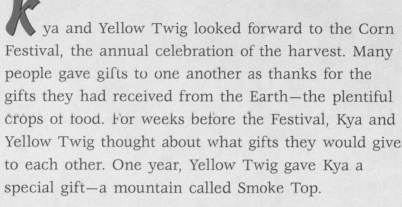

Kya and Yellow Twig looked forward to the Corn Festival, the annual celebration of the harvest. Many people gave gifts to one another as thanks for the gifts they had received from the Earth—the plentiful crops of food. For weeks before the Festival, Kya and Yellow Twig thought about what gifts they would give to each other. One year, Yellow Twig gave Kya a special gift—a mountain called Smoke Top.

"What a fine gift," Kya said. She understood that the gift was special because it was not hers alone. A mountain belonged to everyone. Now it was time to give a gift back to Yellow Twig.

"What should I give my good friend?" Kya asked Noga, her grandmother.

"Give her something that is special to you," Noga said. "What is special?"

"I like stars," Kya said.

Early that night Kya found a special star. But when Yellow Twig arrived later, the star was gone! It had moved to a different place in the sky. "Where is my gift?" Yellow Twig asked.

"I'll have it for you tomorrow night," Kya said. But the next night the same thing happened. The star was gone!

Finally, Kya went to Noga. "Silly child," Noga said. "Didn't you know that stars travel in the night sky? Only one star stays in its place. That is the North Star." Noga pointed to the star in the sky.

"It's very beautiful," Kya said.

The next night, Kya gave the North Star to Yellow Twig. "What a fine gift," Yellow Twig said. "Now I will always have something to remind me of our friendship!" she said.

Meet Yoshiko Uchida

Yoshiko Uchida was born in 1912. She grew up in northern California during the Great Depresion of the 1930s. Uchida started writing stories when she was ten years old, and she never stopped. She also kept a journal as a child. She saved all her journals, which turned out to be important to her career as a writer. These journals helped her remember experiences from her childhood that she might otherwise have forgotten.

As a child of Japanese immigrants to the United States, all of Yoshiko Uchida's stories are about Japanese culture or the Japanese-American experience. Through her stories, she hoped to share with her younger readers her pride in her Japanese heritage.

The Wise Old Woman was Yoshiko Uchida's last book for young people before her death in 1992. The story takes place in a small village in ancient Japan. There, an old woman proves she is wise by teaching a lesson to a young lord. It is a lesson about youth and age from which we can all learn.

The Wise Old Woman

retold by
Yoshiko Uchida
illustrated by
Martin Springett

Long ago in the wooded hills of Japan, a young farmer and his aged mother lived in a village ruled by a cruel young lord.

"Anyone over seventy is no longer useful," the lord declared, "and must be taken into the mountains and left to die."

When the young farmer's mother reached the dreaded age, he could not bear to think of what he must do. But his mother spoke the words he could not say.

"It is time now for you to take me into the mountains," she said softly.

So, early the next morning, the farmer lifted his mother to his back and reluctantly set off up the steep mountain path.

Up and up he climbed—until the trees hid the sun, and the path was gone, until he could no longer hear the birds, but only the sound of the wind shivering through the trees.

On and on he climbed. But soon he heard his mother breaking off small twigs from the trees they passed.

"I'm marking the path for you, my son," she said, "so you will not lose your way going home."

The young farmer could bear it no longer.

Mother, I cannot leave you behind in the mountains," he said. "We are going home together, and I will never, ever leave you."

And so, in the dark shadows of night, the farmer carried his mother back home. He dug a deep cave beneath the kitchen, and from that day, the old woman lived in this secret room, spinning and weaving. In this way two years passed, and no one in the village knew of the farmer's secret.

hen one day, three fierce warriors in full armor galloped into the small village like a sudden mountain storm.

"We come from the mighty Lord Higa to warn you," they shouted to the young lord. "When three suns have set and three moons have risen, he will come to conquer your village."

The cruel young lord was not very brave. "Please," he begged, "I will do anything if you will spare me."

"Lord Higa knows no mercy," the warriors thundered, "but he does respect a clever mind. Solve the three impossible tasks written upon this scroll and you and your village will be saved."

Then, tossing the scroll at the young lord, they galloped off as quickly as they had come.

F irst, make a coil of rope out of ashes," the young lord read.
"Second, run a single thread through the length of a crooked
log. And third, make a drum that sounds without being
beaten."

The young lord quickly gathered the six wisest people of
his village and ordered them to solve the impossible tasks.
They put their heads together and pondered through the night.
But when the stars had vanished and the roosters began to
crow, they still had no answers for the young lord.

They hurried to the village shrine and sounded the giant
bronze bell. "Help us," they pleaded to the gods.
But the gods remained silent.

They went next to seek the clever badger of the forest, for
they knew that animals are sometimes wiser than men.

"Surely, you can help us," they said eagerly.

But the badger only shook his head. "As clever as I am,"
he said, "I see no way to solve such impossible tasks as these."

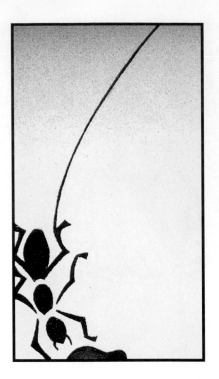

When the six wise people returned to the young lord without any answers, he exploded in anger.

"You are all stupid fools!" he shouted, and he threw them into his darkest dungeon. Then he posted a sign in the village square offering a bag of gold to anyone who could help him.

The young farmer hurried home to tell his mother about the impossible tasks and Lord Higa's threat. "What are we to do?" he asked sadly. "We will soon be conquered by yet another cruel lord."

The old woman thought carefully and then asked her son to bring her a coil of rope, a crooked log with a hole running through the length of it, and a small hand drum. When the farmer had done as she asked, she set to work.

First, she soaked the coil of rope in salt water and dried it well. Then, setting a match to it, she let it burn. But it did not crumble. It held its shape.

"There," she said. "This is your rope of ash."

Next she put a little honey at one end of the crooked log, and at the other, she placed an ant with a silk thread tied to it. The farmer watched in amazement as the tiny ant wound its way through the hole to get to the honey, taking the silk thread with it. And the second task was done.

Finally, the old woman opened one side of the small hand drum and sealed a bumblebee inside. As the bee beat itself against the sides of the drum trying to escape, the drum sounded without being beaten. And the third task was done.

When the farmer presented the three completed tasks to the young lord, he was astonished. "Surely a young man such as you could not be wiser than the wisest people of our village," he said. "Tell me, what person of wisdom helped you solve these impossible tasks?"

The young farmer could not lie, and he told the lord how he had kept his mother hidden for the past two years. "It is she who solved each of your tasks and saved our village from Lord Higa," he explained.

The farmer waited to be thrown into the dungeon for disobeying the lord. But instead of being angry, the young lord was silent and thoughtful.

"I have been wrong," he said at last. "Never again will I send our old people into the mountains to die. Henceforth they will be treated with respect and honor, and will share with us the wisdom of their years."

Whereupon the young lord freed everyone in his dungeon. Next he summoned the old woman and gave her three bags of gold for saving the village.

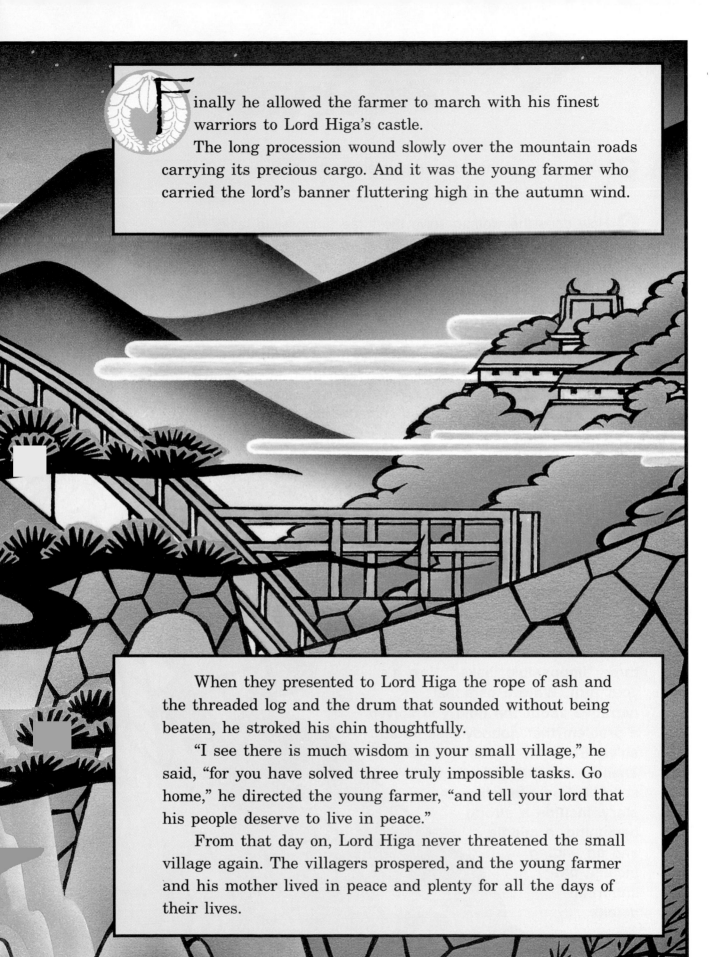

inally he allowed the farmer to march with his finest warriors to Lord Higa's castle.

The long procession wound slowly over the mountain roads carrying its precious cargo. And it was the young farmer who carried the lord's banner fluttering high in the autumn wind.

When they presented to Lord Higa the rope of ash and the threaded log and the drum that sounded without being beaten, he stroked his chin thoughtfully.

"I see there is much wisdom in your small village," he said, "for you have solved three truly impossible tasks. Go home," he directed the young farmer, "and tell your lord that his people deserve to live in peace."

From that day on, Lord Higa never threatened the small village again. The villagers prospered, and the young farmer and his mother lived in peace and plenty for all the days of their lives.

1 What is the young farmer's problem at the beginning of the story?

2 How does the woman solve the three "impossible tasks"?

3 What makes you think that the old woman is wise?

4 What values is this story trying to teach?

5 Compare this story with another story in which a character solves a riddle or a problem and saves a whole town. The other story could be *The Pied Piper of Hamelin* or the story in *Hans Brinker* of the little Dutch boy and the dike. Focus your comparison on how the main character uses problem solving.

Write a Personal Narrative

The wise old woman in the story found a way to solve the three "impossible tasks." Now it's your turn. Write a personal narrative about the time you solved a problem that nobody else could solve. State the problem clearly. Then show what you did to solve it. Use *I* to tell your story. Include a strong beginning, a middle, and an ending. Include only important details.

Do a Science Experiment

Find a simple science experiment, such as floating a toothpick on top of water. Then try the experiment. After you have done it, learn how the experiment works. Challenge someone else to try it. Then have that person explain it.

Make a Fact Sheet

What happens when a bee stings you? Do army ants really march? Can locusts block out the sun? Make a list of interesting questions about insects. Then look in an encyclopedia or a science book to discover the answers. Use the questions and answers to make a fact sheet of amazing insect facts.

Find Out More

The story of the wise old woman took place in Japan long ago. What do you know about the history of Japan? Start by looking in an encyclopedia. Then choose a topic. Your topic might be about Japanese shoguns, like Lord Higa. Share what you learn with a partner, a small group, or the class.

Use Parts of a Book

The title page and the table of contents are in the front of a book. The **title page** tells the name of the book, the author, the publisher, and the place where it was published. The **table of contents** lists the units or chapters and the selections. It gives the page number on which each of these begins.

The **glossary** is at the back of the book. It is like a small dictionary. The glossary gives the meaning of some words as they are used in the book. It also tells how to pronounce these words. Like the glossary, the **index** is arranged in alphabetical order. It is a listing of all the topics and names in the book.

TABLE OF CONTENTS

Chapter 1 .... Page 2
Chapter 2 .... Page 12
Chapter 3 .... Page 32
Chapter 4 .... Page 40
Chapter 5 .... Page 53

The Magic Hat
by Kevin Dempsey

Millbrook Press
Millbrook, IL

Glossary

A
Armour A covering, usually metal, worn to protect the body. The knight wore heavy *armour.*

INDEX

J
Japan, 11, 30, 42-44
Johnson, Lyndon Baines, 140-145
Journal, 5, 7, 93
Journeys, 25, 160

Use the sample parts of a book to answer these questions.

1 Where would you look to find the name of the book and the author?

2 Where would you look to find the page on which a chapter begins?

3 In which part of the book would you look to find out what the word *pagoda* means?

4 Where would you look if you wanted to find out if a book had a certain topic?

5 How does knowing the parts of a book save you time?

TEST POWER

DIRECTIONS

Read the sample story. Then read each question about the story.

SAMPLE

The Special Quarter

As Susan walked home, she saw her neighbor, Mr. Edwards, in front of his house. At his feet were several bags of groceries.

"May I help you?" Susan asked.

Mr. Edwards nodded. Susan quickly picked up the bags and carried them in for him.

"Thank you so much," said Mr. Edwards. "Please, take this for your trouble." Between his fingers, he held a shiny quarter.

"Thanks," said Susan. But as she reached out to take the coin, Mr. Edwards closed his hand. When he opened it again, the coin was gone! Susan looked up at him with surprise.

"Where did it go?" she asked.

Mr. Edwards smiled and waved his hand in the air. "Here it is!" he said, and he pulled the coin from behind Susan's ear!

"Wow," Susan said, "that was neat! Let me know anytime that you need help with your groceries."

1   Why did Mr. Edwards give Susan a quarter?

   A   for being so patient

   B   for listening to his jokes

   C   for teaching him a new trick

   D   for helping him out

2   How did Susan feel when the quarter disappeared?

   F   Worried

   G   Amazed

   H   Disappointed

   J   Lonesome

Stories *in Art*

Cliffs of the Upper Colorado River, Wyoming Territory
by Thomas Moran, 1882
National Museum of American Art, Washington, DC

Just as a writer uses vivid words, so a painter uses color and brush strokes to describe a setting and characters.

Look at this setting. What is the main impression you get? How does the artist show you that a storm is brewing? What mood do the dark splotches of color and sweeping brush strokes create? How do the people feel in this setting? Why do you think so?

Close your eyes. What do you remember about the painting? Why?

Story Elements

Develop a strategy for understanding character and setting.

1 **Look at the photograph.** What clues does it give about where the story takes place?

2 **Identify character and setting.** Find out who the characters are and where the story takes place.

3 **Find details** that tell about the characters' thoughts and actions.

4 **Picture the characters** in the setting. What are the characters doing, and why?

5 **Talk about character and setting.** How does the setting affect Andrea's actions?

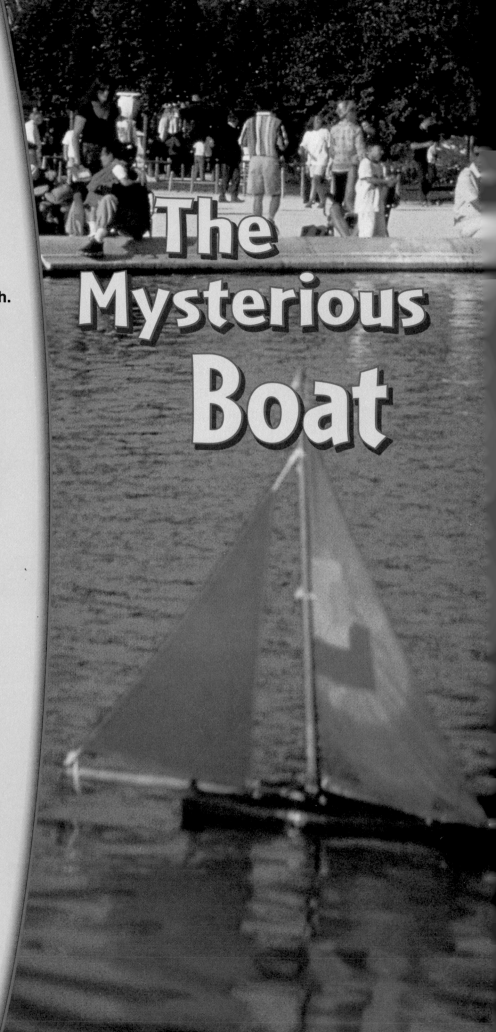

The Mysterious Boat

June 9, 2003

Dear Grandpa,

You'll never believe what happened today. I took the model sailboat that you sent me for my birthday to a park near our house. The park has a small pond with a bronze fountain shaped like a whale in its center.

When I got there, I saw about five boats already in the water. One boy had a remote-controlled boat that kept going in circles because he couldn't figure out how to make it go straight!

I put my boat in the water just as the wind started picking up. The sails filled, and the boat started moving across the pond. The wind blew harder. My boat was heading straight for the fountain! I was worried that the boat might sink if it collided with the whale. And then the weirdest thing happened. I thought I heard a tiny voice shout, "Watch out!" Suddenly the boat changed course. It turned away from the fountain and toward the other side of the pond. If I didn't know better, I would say that somebody had turned the miniature ship's wheel. But that's ridiculous, right?

Where did you say you got the boat? I can tell it's really old. Is that why it has such a strange name—*The Echo*? It seems like a really good name for my sailboat.

Love,

Andrea

THE VOYAGE OF THE DAWN TREADER

By C.S. Lewis

Illustrated by Amy Hill

Cousin Eustace is a rather whiny and annoying boy. Unfortunately, Lucy and Edmund Pevensie must spend the entire summer at his house. They would much rather be in the enchanted land of Narnia, which they have visited twice before.

The land of Narnia is one of literature's most unforgettable places. And the means of getting there are— like Narnia itself—magical, mysterious, and entirely unexpected.

47

The story begins on an afternoon when Edmund and Lucy were stealing a few precious minutes alone together. And of course they were talking about Narnia, which was the name of their own private and secret country. Most of us, I suppose, have a secret country but for us it is only an imaginary country. Edmund and Lucy were luckier than other people in that respect. Their secret country was real. They had already visited it twice; not in a game or a dream, but in reality. They had got there of course by magic, which is the only way of getting to Narnia. And a promise, or very nearly a promise, had been made them in Narnia itself that they would some day get back. You may imagine that they talked about it a good deal, when they got the chance.

They were in Lucy's room, sitting on the edge of her bed and looking at a picture on the opposite wall. It was the only picture in the house that they liked. Aunt Alberta didn't like it at all (that was why it was put away in a little back room upstairs), but she couldn't get rid of it because it had been a wedding present from someone she did not want to offend.

It was a picture of a ship—a ship sailing nearly straight towards you. Her prow was gilded and shaped like the head of a dragon with wide open mouth. She had only one mast and one large, square sail which was a rich purple. The sides of the ship—what you could see of them where the gilded wings of the dragon ended—were green. She had just run up to the top of one glorious blue wave, and the nearer slope of that wave came down towards you, with streaks and bubbles on it. She was obviously running fast before a gay wind, listing over a little on her port side. (By the way, if you are going to read this story at all, and if you don't know already, you had better get it into your head that the left of a ship when you are looking ahead, is *port,* and the right is *starboard*.) All the sunlight fell on her from that side, and the water on that side was full of greens and purples. On the other, it was darker blue from the shadow of the ship.

"The question is," said Edmund, "whether it doesn't make things worse, *looking* at a Narnian ship when you can't get there."

"Even looking is better than nothing," said Lucy "And she is such a very Narnian ship."

"Still playing your old game?" said Eustace Clarence, who had been listening outside the door and now came grinning into the room. Last year, when he had been staying with the Pevensies, he had managed to hear them all talking of Narnia and he loved teasing them about it. He thought of course that they were making it all up; and as he was quite incapable of making anything up himself, he did not approve of that.

"You're not wanted here," said Edmund curtly.

"I'm trying to think of a limerick," said Eustace. "Something like this:

"Some kids who played games about Narnia
Got gradually balmier and balmier—"

"Well, *Narnia* and *balmier* don't rhyme, to begin with," said Lucy.

"It's an assonance," said Eustace.

"Don't ask him what an assy-thingummy is," said Edmund. "He's only longing to be asked. Say nothing and perhaps he'll go away."

Most boys, on meeting a reception like this, would either have cleared out or flared up. Eustace did neither. He just hung about grinning, and presently began talking again.

"Do you like that picture?" he asked.

"For Heaven's sake don't let him get started about Art and all that," said Edmund hurriedly, but Lucy, who was very truthful, had already said, "Yes, I do. I like it very much."

"It's a rotten picture," said Eustace.

"You won't see it if you step outside," said Edmund.

"Why do you like it?" said Eustace to Lucy.

"Well, for one thing," said Lucy, "I like it because the ship looks as if it was really moving. And the water looks as if it was really wet. And the waves look as if they were really going up and down."

Of course Eustace knew lots of answers to this, but he didn't say anything. The reason was that at that very moment he looked at the waves and saw that they did look very much indeed as if they were going up and down. He had only once been in a ship (and then only as far as the Isle of Wight) and had been horribly seasick. The look of the waves in the picture made him feel sick again. He turned rather green and tried another look. And then all three children were staring with open mouths.

What they were seeing may be hard to believe when you read it in print, but it was almost as hard to believe when you saw it happening. The things in the picture were moving. It didn't look at all like a cinema either; the colours were too real and clean and out-of-door for that. Down went the prow of the ship into the wave and up went a great shock of spray. And then up went the wave behind her, and her stern and her deck became visible for the first time, and then disappeared as the next wave came to meet her and her bows went up again. At the same moment an exercise book which had been lying beside Edmund on the bed flapped, rose and sailed through the air to the wall behind him, and Lucy felt all her hair whipping round her face as it does on a windy day. And this was a windy day; but the wind was blowing out of the picture towards them. And suddenly with the wind came the noises—the swishing of waves and the slap of water against the ship's sides and the creaking and the over-all high, steady roar of air and water. But it was the smell, the wild, briny smell, which really convinced Lucy that she was not dreaming.

"Stop it," came Eustace's voice, squeaky with fright and bad temper. "It's some silly trick you two are playing. Stop it. I'll tell Alberta—ow!"

The other two were much more accustomed to adventures, but, just exactly as Eustace Clarence said "Ow," they both said "Ow" too. The reason was that a great cold, salt splash had broken right out of the frame and they were breathless from the smack of it, besides being wet through.

"I'll smash the rotten thing," cried Eustace; and then several things happened at the same time. Eustace rushed towards the picture. Edmund, who knew something about magic, sprang after him, warning him to look out and not to be a fool. Lucy grabbed at him from the other side and was dragged forward. And by this time either they had grown much smaller or the picture had grown bigger. Eustace jumped to try to pull it off the wall and found himself standing on the frame; in front of him was not glass but real sea, and wind and waves rushing up to the frame as they might to a rock. He lost his head and clutched at the other two who had jumped up beside him. There was a second of struggling and shouting, and just as they thought they had got their balance a great blue roller surged up round them, swept them off their feet, and drew them down into the sea. Eustace's despairing cry suddenly ended as the water got into his mouth.

Lucy thanked her stars that she had worked hard at her swimming last summer term. It is true that she would have got on much better if she had used a slower stroke, and also that the water felt a great deal colder than it had looked while it was only a picture. Still, she kept her head and kicked her shoes off, as everyone ought to do who falls into deep water in their clothes. She even kept her mouth shut and her eyes open. They were still quite near the ship; she saw its green side towering high above them, and people looking at her from the

deck. Then, as one might have expected, Eustace clutched at her in a panic and down they both went.

When they came up again she saw a white figure diving off the ship's side. Edmund was close beside her now, treading water, and had caught the arms of the howling Eustace. Then someone else, whose face was vaguely familiar, slipped an arm under her from the other side. There was a lot of shouting going on from the ship, heads crowding together above the bulwarks, ropes being thrown. Edmund and the stranger were fastening ropes round her. After that followed what seemed a very long delay during which her face got blue and her teeth began chattering. In reality the delay was not very long; they were waiting till the moment when she could be got on board the ship without being dashed against its side. Even with all their best endeavours she had a bruised knee when she finally stood, dripping and shivering, on the deck.

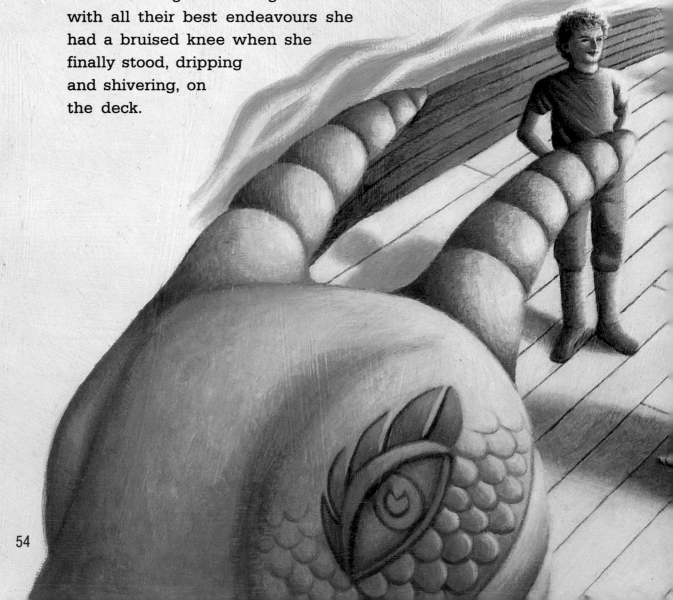

After her Edmund was heaved up, and then the miserable Eustace. Last of all came the stranger—a golden-headed boy some years older than herself.

"Ca—Ca—Caspian!" gasped Lucy as soon as she had breath enough. For Caspian it was; Caspian, the boy king of Narnia whom they had helped to set on the throne during their last visit. Immediately Edmund recognised him too. All three shook hands and clapped one another on the back with great delight.

"But who is your friend?" said Caspian almost at once, turning to Eustace with his cheerful smile. But Eustace was crying much harder than any boy of his age has a right to cry when nothing worse than a wetting has happened to him, and would only yell out, "Let me go. Let me go back. I don't *like* it."

"Let you go?" said Caspian. "But where?"

Eustace rushed to the ship's side, as if he expected to see the picture frame hanging above the sea, and perhaps a glimpse of Lucy's bedroom. What he saw was blue waves flecked with foam, and paler blue sky, both spreading without a break to the horizon. Perhaps we can hardly blame him if his heart sank. He was promptly sick.

"Hey! Rynelf," said Caspian to one of the sailors. "Bring spiced wine for their Majesties. You'll need something to warm you after that dip." He called Edmund and Lucy their Majesties because they and Peter and Susan had all been kings and queens of Narnia long before his time. Narnian time flows differently from ours. If you spent a hundred years in Narnia, you would still come back to our world at the very same hour of the very same day on which you left. And then, if you went back to Narnia after spending a week here, you might find that a thousand Narnian years had passed, or only a day, or no time at all. You never know till you get there. Consequently, when the Pevensie children had returned to Narnia last time for their second visit, it was (for the Narnians) as if King Arthur came back to Britain as some people say he will. And I say the sooner the better.

Rynelf returned with the spiced wine steaming in a flagon and four silver cups. It was just what one wanted, and as Lucy and Edmund sipped it they could feel the warmth going right down to their toes. But Eustace made faces and spluttered and spat it out and was sick again and began to cry again and asked if they hadn't any Plumptree's Vitaminised Nerve Food and could it be made with distilled water and anyway he insisted on being put ashore at the next station.

"This is a merry shipmate you've brought us, Brother," whispered Caspian to Edmund with a chuckle; but before he could say anything more Eustace burst out again.

"Oh! Ugh! What on earth's *that!* Take it away, the horrid thing."

He really had some excuse this time for feeling a little surprised. Something very curious indeed had come out of the cabin in the poop and was slowly approaching them. You might call it—and indeed it was—a Mouse. But then it was a Mouse on its hind legs and stood about two feet high. A thin band of gold passed round its head under one ear and over the other and in this was stuck a long crimson feather. (As the Mouse's fur was very dark, almost black, the effect was bold and striking.) Its left paw rested on the hilt of a sword very nearly as long as its tail. Its balance, as it paced gravely along the swaying deck, was perfect, and its manners courtly. Lucy and Edmund recognised it at once—Reepicheep, the most valiant of all the Talking Beasts of Narnia and the Chief Mouse. It had won undying glory in the second Battle of Beruna. Lucy longed, as she had always done, to take Reepicheep up in her arms and cuddle him. But this, as she well knew, was a pleasure she could never have: it would have offended him deeply. Instead, she went down on one knee to talk to him.

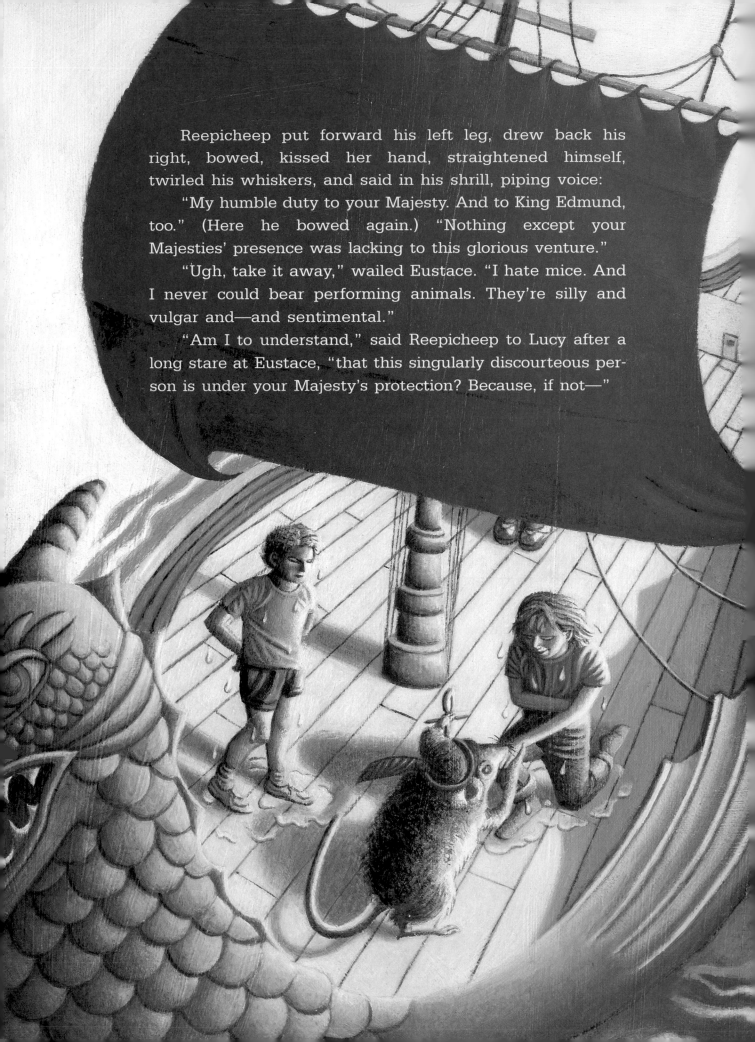

Reepicheep put forward his left leg, drew back his right, bowed, kissed her hand, straightened himself, twirled his whiskers, and said in his shrill, piping voice:

"My humble duty to your Majesty. And to King Edmund, too." (Here he bowed again.) "Nothing except your Majesties' presence was lacking to this glorious venture."

"Ugh, take it away," wailed Eustace. "I hate mice. And I never could bear performing animals. They're silly and vulgar and—and sentimental."

"Am I to understand," said Reepicheep to Lucy after a long stare at Eustace, "that this singularly discourteous person is under your Majesty's protection? Because, if not—"

At this moment Lucy and Edmund both sneezed.

"What a fool I am to keep you all standing here in your wet things," said Caspian. "Come on below and get changed. I'll give you my cabin of course, Lucy, but I'm afraid we have no women's clothes on board. You'll have to make do with some of mine. Lead the way, Reepicheep, like a good fellow."

"To the convenience of a lady," said Reepicheep, "even a question of honour must give way—at least for the moment—" and here he looked very hard at Eustace. But Caspian hustled them on and in a few minutes Lucy found herself passing through the door into the stern cabin. She fell in love with it at once—the three square windows that looked out on the blue, swirling water astern, the low cushioned benches round three sides of the table, the swinging silver lamp overhead (Dwarfs' work, she knew at once by its exquisite delicacy) and the flat gold image of Aslan the Lion on the forward wall above the door. All this she took in in a flash, for Caspian immediately opened a door on the starboard side, and said, "This'll be your room, Lucy. I'll just get some dry things for myself"—he was rummaging in one of the lockers while he spoke—"and then leave you to change. If you'll fling your wet things outside the door I'll get them taken to the galley to be dried."

Lucy found herself as much at home as if she had been in Caspian's cabin for weeks, and the motion of the ship did not worry her, for in the old days when she had been a queen in Narnia she had done a good deal of voyaging. The cabin was very tiny but bright with painted panels (all birds and beasts and crimson dragons and vines) and spotlessly clean. Caspian's clothes were too big for her, but she could manage. His shoes, sandals and sea-boots were hopelessly large but she did not mind going barefoot on board ship. When she had finished dressing she looked out of her window at the water rushing past and took a long deep breath. She felt quite sure they were in for a lovely time.

This is only one exciting adventure that Lucy, Edmund, and Eustace experience with their friends in the land of Narnia. You can join them on a voyage of the imagination that leads to magical lands and enchanted happenings when you read the series of books called The Chronicles of Narnia.

Meet
C.S. LEWIS

C. S. Lewis grew up with rows and rows of books in every room of his family's house. These books full of stories spurred his imagination. As a child, he created his own stories of an "Animal-Land" inhabited by dressed animals and knights in armor.

When Lewis grew up, he started writing about the adventures of four brave children in a magic land. He planned just one book, *The Lion, the Witch and the Wardrobe,* but he went on to add six more books to his *Chronicles of Narnia.* In these books, which can be read in any order, the saga of Narnia is told through tales of adventure filled with fantastic creatures.

In *The Magician's Nephew,* Lewis tells how the passage between earth and Narnia was created: A tree grown from the magical Narnia apple blew over, and its wood was used to build a wardrobe. Through this wardrobe, the children first enter Narnia, where they help the lord-lion Aslan fight the powers of evil.

Lewis advised one young girl who had written to him, "Write about what really interests you, whether it is real or imaginary things." Following his own advice, Lewis created an entire world for readers.

Story Questions & Activities

1 What is Narnia?

2 Why do Lucy and Edmund think that the imaginary journey to the boat is worth the bumpy, wet, and wavy conditions?

3 What makes Narnia "one of literature's most unforgettable places"? Explain.

4 How would you summarize this selection?

5 How does the painting on Lucy's wall compare with the painting on page 44? Which makes you use your imagination more? Which seems more real to you? Why?

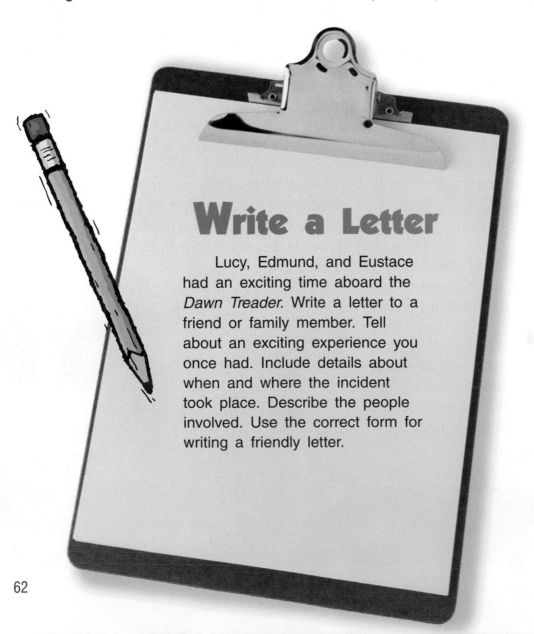

Write a Letter

Lucy, Edmund, and Eustace had an exciting time aboard the *Dawn Treader*. Write a letter to a friend or family member. Tell about an exciting experience you once had. Include details about when and where the incident took place. Describe the people involved. Use the correct form for writing a friendly letter.

Draw a Picture

Eustace does not know how to use his imagination. Help him by drawing a picture of how you see the ship and the raging sea in the story. Show details that you imagine are in the story but are not pictured in the illustrations.

Freewrite

Choose a painting or a photograph that you like. After spending a few minutes looking at every detail, write what would happen if you entered the world of that picture. Let your imagination take you by the hand. Write about what comes to mind. Remember: In imaginary countries, anything is possible.

Find Out More

In the story, the ship is an old-fashioned sailing vessel. What other kinds of ships would be good for adventures? How would a Viking ship, for example, aid a Viking adventure? Look in an encyclopedia or in a book about ships. Use what you learn to compare how certain ships could aid certain types of adventures.

Use a Glossary

The writer uses some words in the story that you may not know. You may have seen some of these words, like *prow* or *stern*, but you may not know what they mean. You may also not know how to pronounce them. For help, you can turn to the glossary.

The **glossary** is at the back of the book. It is like a small dictionary but lists only important words from the stories. The glossary tells what the words mean as they are used in the book. It also tells you how to pronounce them. Sometimes a glossary will show how to use the word in a sentence. It may also give other important information about the word. The **main entries** in the glossary are listed in alphabetical order. Like a dictionary, **guide words** at the top of the page tell you the first and last words on that page.

prow/stern —— guide words   main entry   definition

prow The front part of a boat or ship; bow. ———
The *prow* of the ship cut through the waves. —— example sentence
    prow (prou) *noun, plural* **prows**.

S

    squirm To turn or twist the body. The child *squirmed* in her seat.
    squirm (skwûrm) *verb,* **squirmed, squirming**.   verb forms

stern The rear part of a boat or ship. The sailor stood at the
stern of the ship and waved good-bye.
    stern (stûrn) *noun, plural* **sterns**.   part of speech   pronunciation

Use the sample glossary to answer these questions.

1 What is the meaning of *stern?*

2 How do you pronounce the word *prow?*

3 Is *prows* singular or plural?

4 What part of speech is the word *squirm?*

5 How could looking up words in a glossary help you understand a story?

TEST POWER

Test Tip

Read each answer choice slowly and carefully!

DIRECTIONS

Read the sample story. Then read each question about the story.

SAMPLE

Hampton and the Light Box

Hampton believed that if he left a box open during the day and closed it before nightfall, light would be trapped inside.

His sister, Danielle, tried to <u>discourage</u> this foolish idea. She did not believe that light could be trapped in such a way.

"I made a box that will trap light," Hampton said proudly to Danielle. "Do you want to see it?" he asked her.

Danielle could not help being curious about Hampton's invention and was eager to see what it looked like. Hampton brought a small black box into the room and set it on the table.

Hampton left the box open all day, and closed it at sunset. That night, he invited Danielle to watch as he opened the box. But when he lifted the lid, there was nothing inside.

"Well," said Danielle, trying to make him feel better, "perhaps the light has already gone out—it's nighttime." They both laughed at her joke.

1   In this passage, the word <u>discourage</u> means —

   A convince someone to do something

   B try to get someone not to do something

   C ask someone to help you

   D tell someone about a new invention

2   Why did Hampton make his box?

   F To try to trap light

   G To show his sister how to catch a bug

   H Because he was curious about the dark

   J For a project for his science class

Like artists and their tools, sports photographers use their cameras to capture the speed and determination of runners as they try to win a race.

Look at this photograph. What can you tell about it? How does the photographer show you that the athletes are determined to win? What causes someone to want to be a winner? What effect does winning have on the athlete?

Look at the photograph again. Which runner do you think will win? How will the losers feel? How would you feel if you were running in this race?

Jesse Owens at the Berlin Olympics, 1936
United Press International

Cause and Effect

Develop a strategy for identifying cause-and-effect relationships.

1 **Pay attention** to what happens and why it happens.

2 **Look for clue words** that signal cause-and-effect relationships, such as *because* or *in order to.*

3 **Separate causes from their effects.** An effect tells what happened. A cause tells why it happened.

4 **Watch for a chain of events.** One cause may lead to an effect. That effect becomes the cause of another effect, and so on.

Stephen Hawking

An Extraordinary Man

Even as a young student in England, Stephen Hawking was brilliant in science. He decided to study physics and astronomy in hopes of understanding the very existence of the universe.

Hawking went on to receive numerous awards, medals, and prizes for his scientific work and teaching. In 1995 his book *A Brief History of Time* became a best-seller.

These achievements would be remarkable for anyone, but for Stephen Hawking, they are incredible. That's because he developed a very rare disease that, over a period of years, has left him unable to move, speak, or breathe on his own.

Hawking refused to give in to his condition. In order to communicate, he learned to spell out words, letter by letter, by raising his eyebrows when someone pointed to the correct letter on a card. He then began to communicate through a complex computer speech program operated by head or eye movement.

Despite his physical challenges, Stephen Hawking proved himself to be one of the most brilliant scientists of his time. Because of his discoveries, our knowledge of the universe has increased in ways we are only beginning to understand.

Meet Kathleen Krull

When she was growing up in the suburbs of Chicago, Kathleen Krull thought books were the most important thing in the world. For a time she worked in a library. After a while she was fired. The reason: She was reading on the job instead of working!

Krull has devoted her working life to books. As an adult, she has worked both as a children's book editor and as a book reviewer. She has also written many books for young people, including mysteries, biographies, and books about music.

Krull's books reflect the things in which she is most interested. In addition to music and reading, these things include World War II and strong women. *Wilma Unlimited* is the story of Wilma Rudolph, who was the world's fastest woman runner. Rudolph is one of the strong women Kathleen Krull admires.

Meet David Diaz

David Diaz is an award-winning illustrator. He has worked for newspapers, magazines, and corporations. In addition, he has illustrated many books for young readers. In 1995, Diaz won the important Caldecott Medal for the first book he ever illustrated, *Smoky Night*, written by Eve Bunting.

Wilma Unlimited is a favorite with the artist. The illustrations in the book combine dramatic paintings with photographic backgrounds to create an unusual style. In fact, Diaz's illustrations are quite complicated. He believes there is "no need to 'draw down' to a younger audience."

Wilma Unlimited

How Wilma Rudolph Became the World's Fastest Woman

Written by Kathleen Krull
Illustrated by David Diaz

No one expected such a tiny girl to have a first birthday. In Clarksville, Tennessee, in 1940, life for a baby who weighed just over four pounds at birth was sure to be limited.

But most babies didn't have nineteen older brothers and sisters to watch over them. Most babies didn't have a mother who knew home remedies and a father who worked several jobs.

Most babies weren't Wilma Rudolph.

Wilma did celebrate her first birthday, and everyone noticed that as soon as this girl could walk, she ran or jumped instead.

She worried people, though—she was always so small and sickly. If a brother or sister had a cold, she got double pneumonia. If one of them had measles, Wilma got measles, too, plus mumps and chicken pox.

Her mother always nursed her at home. Doctors were a luxury for the Rudolph family, and anyway, only one doctor in Clarksville would treat black people.

Just before Wilma turned five, she got sicker than ever. Her sisters and brothers heaped all the family's blankets on her, trying to keep her warm.

During that sickness, Wilma's left leg twisted inward, and she couldn't move it back. Not even Wilma's mother knew what was wrong.

The doctor came to see her then. Besides scarlet fever, he said, Wilma had also been stricken with polio. In those days, most children who got polio either died or were permanently crippled. There was no cure.

The news spread around Clarksville: Wilma, that lively girl, would never walk again.

But Wilma kept moving any way she could. By hopping on one foot, she could get herself around the house, to the outhouse in the backyard, and even, on Sundays, to church.

Wilma's mother urged her on. Mrs. Rudolph had plenty to do—cooking, cleaning, sewing patterned flour sacks into clothes for her children, now twenty-two in all. Yet twice every week, she and Wilma took the bus to the nearest hospital that would treat black patients, some fifty miles away in Nashville. They rode together in the back, the only place blacks were allowed to sit.

Doctors and nurses at the hospital helped Wilma do exercises to make her paralyzed leg stronger. At home, Wilma practiced them constantly, even when it hurt.

To Wilma, what hurt most was that the local school wouldn't let her attend because she couldn't walk. Tearful and lonely, she watched her brothers and sisters run off to school each day, leaving her behind. Finally, tired of crying all the time, she decided she had to fight back—somehow.

ilma worked so hard at her exercises that the doctors decided she was ready for a heavy steel brace. With the brace supporting her leg, she didn't have to hop anymore. School was possible at last.

But it wasn't the happy place she had imagined. Her classmates made fun of her brace. During playground games she could only sit on the sidelines, twitchy with impatience. She studied the other kids for hours—memorizing moves, watching the ball zoom through the rim of the bushel basket they used as a hoop.

Wilma fought the sadness by doing more leg exercises. Her family always cheered her on, and Wilma did everything she could to keep them from worrying about her. At times her leg really did seem to be getting stronger. Other times it just hurt.

One Sunday, on her way to church, Wilma felt especially good. She and her family had always found strength in their faith, and church was Wilma's favorite place in the world. Everyone she knew would be there—talking and laughing, praying and singing. It would be just the place to try the bravest thing she had ever done.

She hung back while people filled the old building. Standing alone, the sound of hymns coloring the air, she unbuckled her heavy brace and set it by the church's front door. Taking a deep breath, she moved one foot in front of the other, her knees trembling violently. She took her mind off her knees by concentrating on taking another breath, and then another.

Whispers rippled throughout the gathering: Wilma Rudolph was *walking*. Row by row, heads turned toward her as she walked alone down the aisle. Her large family, all her family's friends, everyone from school—each person stared wide-eyed. The singing never stopped; it seemed to burst right through the walls and into the trees. Finally, Wilma reached a seat in the front and began singing too, her smile triumphant.

Wilma practiced walking as often as she could after that, and when she was twelve years old, she was able to take off the brace for good. She and her mother realized she could get along without it, so one memorable day, they wrapped the hated brace in a box and mailed it back to the hospital.

As soon as Wilma sent that box away, she knew her life was beginning all over again.

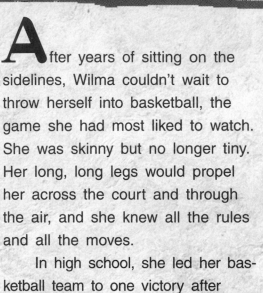

After years of sitting on the sidelines, Wilma couldn't wait to throw herself into basketball, the game she had most liked to watch. She was skinny but no longer tiny. Her long, long legs would propel her across the court and through the air, and she knew all the rules and all the moves.

In high school, she led her basketball team to one victory after another. Eventually, she took the team all the way to the Tennessee state championships. There, to everyone's astonishment, her team lost.

Wilma had become accustomed to winning. Now she slumped on the bench, all the liveliness knocked out of her.

But at the game that day was a college coach. He admired Wilma's basketball playing but was especially impressed by the way she ran. He wanted her for his track-and-field team.

With his help, Wilma won a full athletic scholarship to Tennessee State University. She was the first member of her family to go to college.

Eight years after she mailed her brace away, Wilma's long legs and years of hard work carried her thousands of miles from Clarksville, Tennessee. The summer of 1960 she arrived in Rome, Italy, to represent the United States at the Olympic Games—as a runner.

Just participating in the Olympics was a deeply personal victory for Wilma, but her chances of winning a race were limited. Simply walking in Rome's shimmering heat was a chore, and athletes from other countries had run faster races than Wilma ever had. Women weren't thought to run very well, anyway; track-and-field was considered a sport for men. And the pressure from the public was intense—for the first time ever, the Olympics would be shown on television, and all the athletes knew that more than one hundred million people would be watching. Worst of all, Wilma had twisted her ankle just after she arrived in Rome. It was still swollen and painful on the day of her first race.

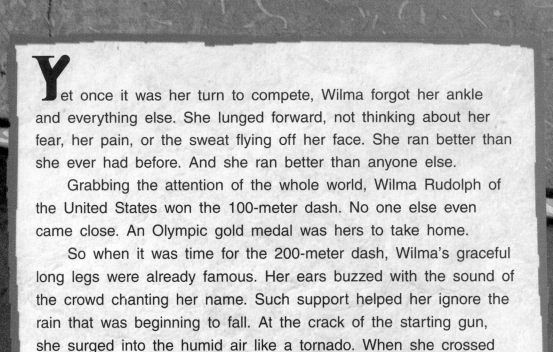

Yet once it was her turn to compete, Wilma forgot her ankle and everything else. She lunged forward, not thinking about her fear, her pain, or the sweat flying off her face. She ran better than she ever had before. And she ran better than anyone else.

Grabbing the attention of the whole world, Wilma Rudolph of the United States won the 100-meter dash. No one else even came close. An Olympic gold medal was hers to take home.

So when it was time for the 200-meter dash, Wilma's graceful long legs were already famous. Her ears buzzed with the sound of the crowd chanting her name. Such support helped her ignore the rain that was beginning to fall. At the crack of the starting gun, she surged into the humid air like a tornado. When she crossed the finish line, she had done it again. She finished far ahead of everyone else. She had earned her second gold medal. Wet and breathless, Wilma was exhilarated by the double triumph. The crowd went wild.

The 400-meter relay race was yet to come. Wilma's team faced the toughest competition of all. And as the fourth and final runner on her team, it was Wilma who had to cross the finish line.

Wilma's teammates ran well, passed the baton smoothly, and kept the team in first place. Wilma readied herself for the dash to the finish line as her third teammate ran toward her. She reached back for the baton—and nearly dropped it. As she tried to recover from the fumble, two other runners sped past her. Wilma and her team were suddenly in third place.

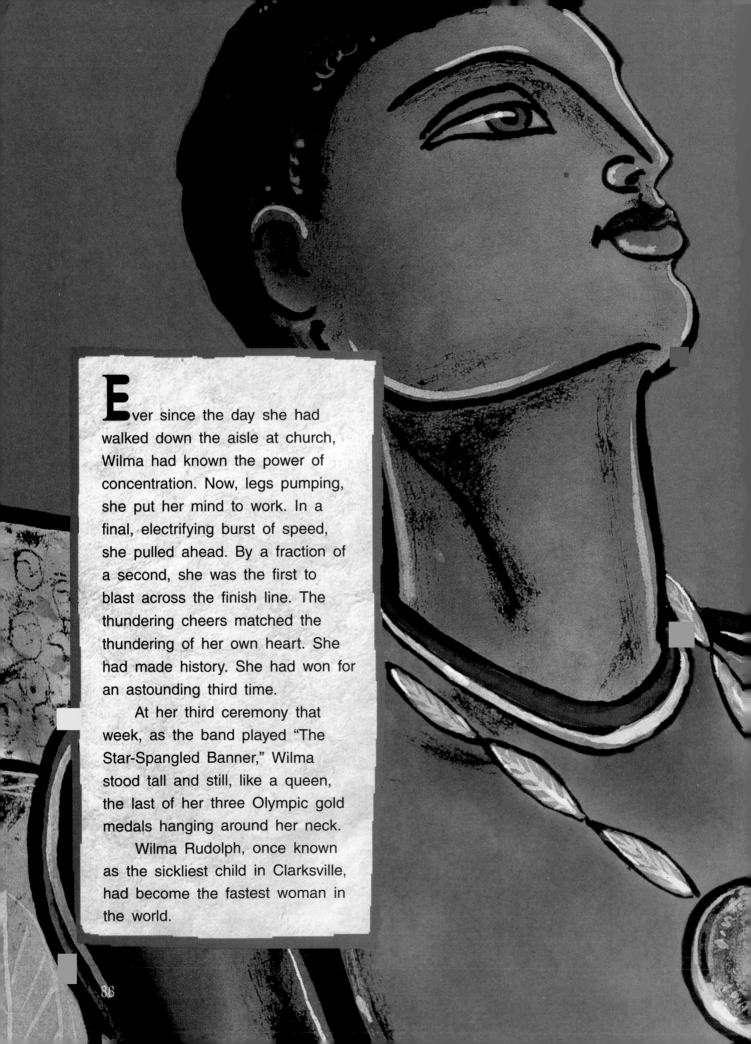

Ever since the day she had walked down the aisle at church, Wilma had known the power of concentration. Now, legs pumping, she put her mind to work. In a final, electrifying burst of speed, she pulled ahead. By a fraction of a second, she was the first to blast across the finish line. The thundering cheers matched the thundering of her own heart. She had made history. She had won for an astounding third time.

At her third ceremony that week, as the band played "The Star-Spangled Banner," Wilma stood tall and still, like a queen, the last of her three Olympic gold medals hanging around her neck.

Wilma Rudolph, once known as the sickliest child in Clarksville, had become the fastest woman in the world.

Author's Note

Wilma Rudolph became, at age twenty, the first American woman to win three gold medals at a single Olympics. When she returned home from Rome, her family was waiting for her, and so was all of Clarksville, Tennessee. The huge parade and banquet held in her honor were the first events in the town's history to include both blacks and whites.

During the time of Wilma's childhood in the 1940s, polio, also known as infantile paralysis, was the world's most dreaded disease. A cure for it was not found until 1955. By then it had killed or crippled 357,000 Americans, mostly children—only 50,000 fewer than the number of Americans who had died in World War II.

After she retired from her career as a runner in 1962, Wilma became a second-grade teacher and a high school coach. She remained a much-admired celebrity, but to prove that there was more to her than just running, she started a company called Wilma Unlimited that gave her opportunities to travel, lecture, and support causes she believed in. Later she founded the nonprofit Wilma Rudolph Foundation to nurture young athletes and to teach them that they, too, can succeed despite all odds against them. The story of all she overcame in order to win at the Olympics has inspired thousands of young athletes, especially women.

Wilma Rudolph died in 1994.

Story Questions & Activities

1 What caused Wilma Rudolph to lose the use of her leg?

2 How did polio make Wilma fight back?

3 What made Wilma Rudolph a winner?

4 What is the main idea of this true story?

5 Suppose that Wilma Rudolph could step into the photograph on page 66. What one question do you think she would ask the winner of the race? What question might he ask her?

Write a Speech

Wilma Rudolph achieved her goals against all odds. What about you? Choose one important goal that you have achieved, and write a short speech about it. Explain how you accomplished your goal and what happened as a result.

Create an Ad

Just before Wilma turned five, she was stricken with polio. Today, people are vaccinated against this disease and many others. Write and design an ad that will persuade parents to have their children vaccinated against certain diseases. Use persuasive words to get across your message.

Make a Poster

Wilma Rudolph was a track-and-field star— a runner in the Olympic games. Yet there are many more summer and winter Olympic events, such as diving, skiing, and figure skating. Draw a poster for a future Olympics. Create a work of art that shows the city where the games could be held, or one or more of the athletes, or Olympic events. Write a slogan that will get people to come to the games.

Find Out More

Wilma Rudolph made history at the 1960 Olympic games by winning three gold medals. What do you know about the Olympics? When and where did they first begin? Start by looking in an encyclopedia or in a book about the Olympics. Use what you learn to compare the Olympic games in ancient Greece with today's modern Olympics.

Use an Index

Suppose that you are reading a book about Wilma Rudolph. You want to find information about the races she won in the Olympic games. Where would you look in the book to find this information quickly? You could look in the index. The **index** is in the back of the book. It lists all the topics in the book in alphabetical order. Next to each topic are one or more numbers. These numbers tell you the pages on which you will find the information on your topic.

Basketball, 15
Church, 12, 13, 24–25
Clarksville, Tennessee, 6, 7, 8, 17, 21
Nashville, Tennessee, 9
Olympic Games, 17–21
Polio, 8
Rome, Italy, 17–21
School, 10, 11
Tennessee State University, 16

Use the sample index to answer these questions.

1 Where would you find information about the Olympic Games?

2 On which page would you look to find out what polio is?

3 Where would you find information about Wilma's early school experience?

4 Between which two entries would you find an entry on Nashville, Tennessee?

5 How can an index help you locate information quickly?

TEST POWER

DIRECTIONS

Read the sample story. Then read each question about the story.

SAMPLE

Fossils of the Present

Mary Thompson presented this recipe to her class. She informed her peers that the directions should be followed exactly. She warned that the "fossil" dough would not turn out correctly if the recipe were to be <u>altered</u>.

Gather together these items:
a mixing bowl; 1 cup coffee grounds; 1/2 cup cold coffee; 1 cup flour; 1/2 cup salt; round cookie cutter; waxed paper; and small objects to press into dough.

Here are the steps to follow:
1) Mix the coffee grounds, cold coffee, salt, and flour until the mixture becomes dough-like.
2) Knead the dough. Then flatten it onto the waxed paper.
3) Cut circles of dough large enough to fit your small objects, or "fossils."
4) Press the objects firmly onto the dough and then carefully remove the objects. Now you have fossil imprints!

1 The word <u>altered</u> in this passage means —

  A stirred

  B impressed

  C changed

  D kneaded

2 Which of these should be done first?

  F Add 1 cup of flour to the mixture.

  G Flatten the dough onto waxed paper.

  H Press small objects firmly into the dough.

  J Cut small circles in the dough.

Dad's Coming by Winslow Homer, 1873

Collection of Mr. and Mrs. Paul Mellon

This painting shows a mother and her children waiting for Dad to return home from a sea voyage.

What expression has the artist shown on the mother's face? Why is the boy looking out to sea? What do you think would happen if he saw his father's ship approaching land?

What can you tell about the setting? How does the artist show a calm day? How do the characters contrast with the calm setting? How does the painting make you feel?

Story Elements

Develop a strategy for understanding characters and setting in a story.

1 **Look at the pictures** to get an idea of the characters and setting.

2 **Read the first** paragraph. Find out who the characters are and where they are.

3 **Look for details** that tell about what the characters think, say, and do.

4 **Think of what** you know about animal behavior. Does it help you to understand what Max the parrot does?

5 **State in** your own words who the characters are and why they act as they do.

Max Finds the *Fox*

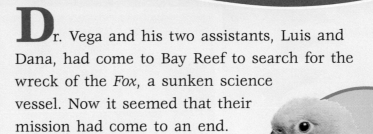

Dr. Vega and his two assistants, Luis and Dana, had come to Bay Reef to search for the wreck of the *Fox*, a sunken science vessel. Now it seemed that their mission had come to an end.

Perched inside his cage, Max the parrot shook his wings. "Happy boy!" Max croaked.

Max had also been on board the *Fox* five years ago when it sank. No lives were lost, but important data had been on board. Dr. Vega hoped to find that data to complete his own research.

"We need supplies," Dr. Vega said. "Dana, call Port Jeffers."

Suddenly, Max got very upset. "Port Jeffers! Mayday!" croaked Max. "Mayday!"

Max was usually calm. What had upset him so much? Dana wondered. Was it something Dr. Vega had just said?

Dana tested her theory. "Supplies?" she said to Max. Max did nothing. "Port Jeffers?" she said.

Max flapped wildly at the words *Port Jeffers*. "Mayday! Mayday!" he cried.

Luis and Dana looked at each other, then at Dr. Vega. All three of them had the same idea: the *Fox* hadn't sunk near Bay Reef after all. The *Fox* must have gone down near Port Jeffers!

The search team headed toward Port Jeffers. After a few unsuccessful dives, they finally found the sunken *Fox* lying on its side.

They knew that Max was the one to thank. He had known where the *Fox* was all along.

The Wreck of the Zephyr

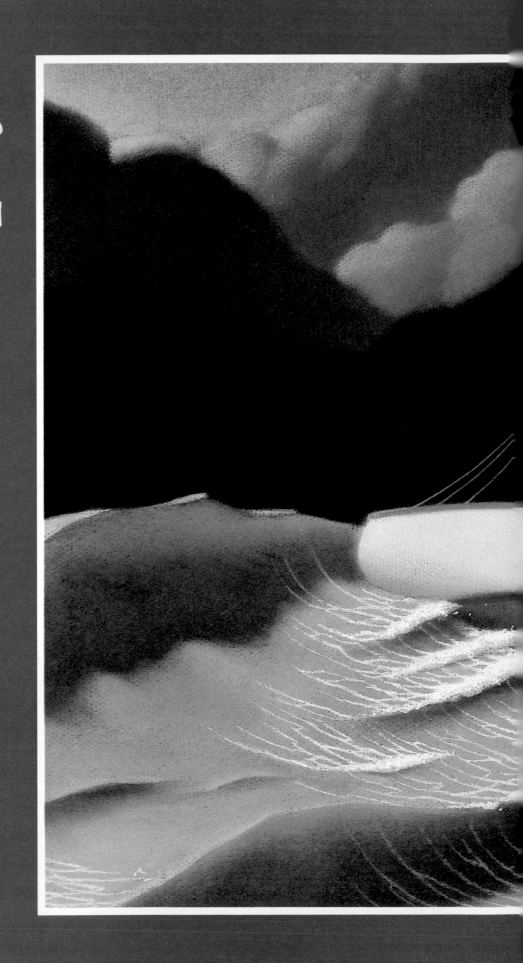

Once, while traveling along the seashore, I stopped at a small fishing village. After eating lunch, I decided to take a walk. I followed a path out of the village, uphill to some cliffs high above the sea. At the edge of these cliffs was a most unusual sight—the wreck of a small sailboat.

An old man was sitting among the broken timbers, smoking a pipe. He seemed to be reading my mind when he said, "Odd, isn't it?"

"Yes," I answered. "How did it get here?"

"Waves carried it up during a storm."

"Really?" I said. "It doesn't seem the waves could ever get that high."

The old man smiled. "Well, there is another story." He invited me to have a seat and listen to his strange tale.

"In our village, years ago," he said, "there was a boy who could sail a boat better than any man in the harbor. He could find a breeze over the flattest sea. When dark clouds kept other boats at anchor, the boy would sail out, ready to prove to the villagers, to the sea itself, how great a sailor he was.

"One morning, under an ominous sky, he prepared to take his boat, the *Zephyr,* out to sea. A fisherman warned the boy to stay in port. Already a strong wind was blowing. 'I'm not afraid,' the boy said, 'because I'm the greatest sailor there is.' The fisherman pointed to a sea gull gliding overhead. 'There's the only sailor who can go out on a day like this.' The boy just laughed as he hoisted his sails into a blustery wind.

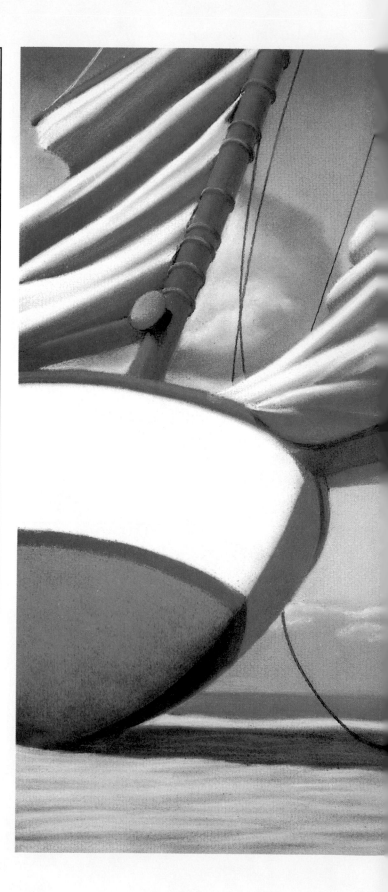

"The wind whistled in the rigging as the *Zephyr* pounded her way through the water. The sky grew black and the waves rose up like mountains. The boy struggled to keep his boat from going over. Suddenly a gust of wind caught the sail. The boom swung around and hit the boy's head. He fell to the cockpit floor and did not move.

"When the boy opened his eyes, he found himself lying on a beach. The *Zephyr* rested behind him, carried there by the storm. The boat was far from the water's edge. The tide would not carry it back to sea. The boy set out to look for help.

"He walked for a long time and was surprised that he didn't recognize the shoreline. He climbed a hill, expecting to see something familiar, but what he saw instead was a strange and unbelievable sight. Before him were two boats, sailing high above the water. Astonished, he watched them glide by. Then a third sailed past, towing the *Zephyr*. The boats entered a bay that was bordered by a large village. There they left the *Zephyr*.

"The boy made his way down to the harbor, to the dock where his boat was tied. He met a sailor who smiled when he saw the boy. Pointing to the *Zephyr* he asked, 'Yours?' The boy nodded. The sailor said they almost never saw strangers on their island. It was surrounded by a treacherous reef. The *Zephyr* must have been carried over the reef by the storm. He told the boy that, later, they would take him and the *Zephyr* back over the reef. But the boy said he would not leave until he learned to sail above the waves. The sailor told him it took years to learn to sail like that. 'Besides,' he said, 'the *Zephyr* does not have the right sails.' The boy insisted. He pleaded with the sailor.

"Finally the sailor said he would try to teach him if the boy promised to leave the next morning. The boy agreed. The sailor went to a shed and got a new set of sails.

"All afternoon they sailed back and forth across the bay. Sometimes the sailor took the tiller, and the boat would magically begin to lift out of the water. But when the boy tried, he could not catch the wind that made boats fly.

"When the sun went down they went back to the harbor. They dropped anchor and a fisherman rowed them to shore. 'In the morning,' the sailor said, 'we'll put your own sails back on the *Zephyr* and send you home.' He took the boy to his house, and the sailor's wife fed them oyster stew.

"After dinner the sailor played the concertina. He sang a song about a man named Samuel Blue, who, long ago, tried to sail his boat over land and crashed:

'For the wind o'er land's ne'er steady nor true,
   an' all men that sail there'll meet Samuel Blue.'

"When he was done with his song, the sailor sent the boy to bed. But the boy could not sleep. He knew he could fly his boat if he had another chance. He waited until the sailor and his wife were asleep, then he quietly dressed and went to the harbor. As he rowed out to the *Zephyr,* the boy felt the light evening wind grow stronger and colder.

"Under a full moon, he sailed the *Zephyr* into the bay. He tried to remember everything the sailor had told him. He tried to feel the wind pulling his boat forward, lifting it up. Then, suddenly, the boy felt the *Zephyr* begin to shake. The sound of the water rushing past the hull grew louder. The air filled with spray as the boat sliced through the waves. The bow slowly began to lift. Higher and higher the *Zephyr* rose out of the water, then finally broke free. The sound of rushing water stopped. There was only the sound of wind in the sails. The *Zephyr* was flying.

"Using the stars to guide him, the boy set a course for home. The wind blew very hard, churning the sea below. But that did not matter to the *Zephyr* as she glided through the night sky. When clouds blocked the boy's view of the stars, he trimmed the sails and climbed higher. Surely the men of the island never dared fly so high. Now the boy was certain he was truly the greatest sailor of all.

"He steered well. Before the night was over, he saw the moonlit spire of the church at the edge of his village. As he drew closer to land, an idea took hold of him. He would sail over the village and ring the *Zephyr*'s bell. Then everyone would see him and know that he was the greatest sailor. He flew over the tree-topped cliffs of the shore, but as he reached the church the *Zephyr* began to fall.

"The wind had shifted. The boy pulled as hard as he could on the tiller, but it did no good. The wind shifted again. He steered for the open sea, but the trees at the cliff's edge stood between him and the water. At first there was just the rustle of leaves brushing the hull. Then the air was filled with the sound of breaking branches and ripping sails. The boat fell to the ground. And here she sits today."

"A remarkable tale," I said, as the old man stopped to relight his pipe. "What happened to the boy?"

"He broke his leg that night. Of course, no one believed his story about flying boats. It was easier for them to believe that he was lost in the storm and thrown up here by the waves." The old man laughed.

"No sir, the boy never amounted to much. People thought he was crazy. He just took odd jobs around the harbor. Most of the time he was out sailing, searching for that island and a new set of sails."

A light breeze blew through the trees. The old man looked up. "Wind coming," he said. "I've got some sailing to do." He picked up a cane, and I watched as he limped slowly toward the harbor.

Van Allsburg holding a scene from his book
The Polar Express

Chris Van Allsburg is probably one of the most successful book illustrators in the United States—yet he almost didn't become an illustrator at all. As a child, he loved to draw and was good at it. But by the time he went to college, he wanted to be a lawyer. His talent won out. He took one drawing class "as a lark," and a year later he began serious study to become a professional artist.

His first book, *The Garden of Abdul Gasazi,* won eight book awards, and his second book, *Jumanji,* won a Caldecott Medal, the top award given for children's book illustration. A 1985 book, *The Polar Express,* won another Caldecott Medal—making Van Allsburg the first artist ever to win two.

Part of Van Allsburg's success may have to do with his idea of what an artist should be. "To me, the artist's role is as a magician who can make strange things happen," he explains. "The opportunity to create a small world between two pieces of cardboard . . . is exciting and rewarding." He has turned this fascination into books and illustrations that are both weird and wonderful. In *Jumanji,* a jungle board game comes to life—with frightening results. In the award-winning *The Wreck of the Zephyr,* you saw how Van Allsburg's "magic" turned a simple sailboat into something marvelous to behold.

Story Questions & Activities

1. Who is the main character of the story?

2. How is the setting important to the story?

3. How do you know that this story is not true?

4. The narrator is telling this story to a traveler. How does that make "The Wreck of the Zephyr" a story within a story?

5. Imagine that the boy in the story could give advice about sailing to the boy in the painting on page 94. What advice do you think he would give?

Write a Journal Entry

Imagine that you are the boy sailor in the story. You are keeping a sailor's log of your "flying" adventure. Write a journal entry that tells about your experience. Include details that describe the setting. Tell how you felt about sailing the *Zephyr*.

120

Make a Sailboat

A sailboat plays a major part in this story. Make a sailboat. Get a bar of soap that floats, a pencil, and paper or thin cardboard for the sails. Cut out a triangular sail from the paper or cardboard. Fasten the sail to the tip of your pencil. Insert the pencil firmly into the middle of the bar. Now float your boat on water and blow the sail. What happens if you blow from different directions? If you make the sail bigger? Note your findings.

Draw a Sailing Vessel

Artists, such as Winslow Homer, have often chosen sailboats as subjects. Look at pictures of sailing vessels in a museum or the library. Then draw your own picture. It could be a simple sailboat for one person or a mighty sailing vessel with many sails. Make your drawing accurate. Write a caption that tells the kind of sailboat it is.

Find Out More

For many centuries, sailing boats were the most efficient way to cross the sea. Today, sailing is a popular sport. Read about sailing in an encyclopedia or find a book or magazine about sailing. Choose a sailing topic, such as the history of sailing, the age of clipper ships, or yacht racing. Report your findings to a small group of classmates.

Use a Table of Contents and Headings

"The Wreck of the *Zephyr*" is just one story in your pupil book. As you know, larger books like this one often have a table of contents. A **table of contents** is in the front of the book. It gives you a list of the book's units, chapters, and selections. It also lists the page on which each of these begins. A chapter or selection in the book may have a heading. **Headings** are words or phrases at the beginning of a section that tell what that section is about.

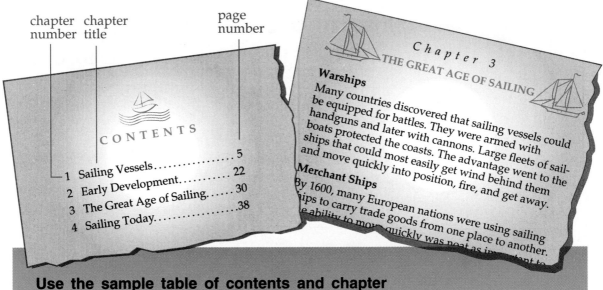

chapter number chapter title page number

CONTENTS

1 Sailing Vessels................ 5
2 Early Development........... 22
3 The Great Age of Sailing...... 30
4 Sailing Today................. 38

Chapter 3
THE GREAT AGE OF SAILING

Warships
Many countries discovered that sailing vessels could be equipped for battles. They were armed with handguns and later with cannons. Large fleets of sailboats protected the coasts. The advantage went to the ships that could most easily get wind behind them and move quickly into position, fire, and get away.

Merchant Ships
By 1600, many European nations were using sailing ships to carry trade goods from one place to another. The ability to mov quickly was not as important to

Use the sample table of contents and chapter headings to answer these questions.

1 How many chapters are there in the book?

2 What is the title of Chapter 2?

3 On which page does Chapter 4 begin?

4 What is the second section of Chapter 3 about?

5 Why is it a good idea to check the table of contents before reading a book?

TEST POWER

DIRECTIONS

Read the sample story. Then read each question about the story.

SAMPLE

Who ruined the cake?

Reed examined the entire recipe book before deciding to bake a lemon cake for dessert. With his mother's assistance, Reed mixed the sugar and butter in the electric mixing bowl. He then added flour, spices, and lemon juice. He even tasted a little bit of batter. He predicted that the cake would turn out deliciously.

When the cake began to bake, the entire house filled with the sweet smell of lemon. After the cake was done baking, Reed's mother set it aside to let it cool.

Reed went to get the cake once it had cooled <u>sufficiently</u> for it to be frosted. He couldn't believe his eyes. The center of the cake was completely gone, and there were crumbs everywhere. He looked up to see a bird looking at him from the windowsill. Reed had found who ruined his cake!

1 Who ate the center of the cake?

  A Reed

  B Reed's mother

  C A bird

  D A cake burglar

2 The word <u>sufficiently</u> in this passage means —

  F too little

  G often

  H later

  J enough

Did you answer both questions correctly? Tell how.

The Great Wave of Kanagawa by Katsushika Hokusai

Like a mystery story or a scary movie, an artist can build suspense by showing that something is about to happen.

Look at this picture. How is the artist creating suspense? How do you think the rowers feel? What is causing them to row so quickly? What effect will the crashing wave have on them? Will they reach safety? What do you think?

Look at the picture again. Do you feel drawn into the artist's work? Explain.

Cause and Effect

Develop a strategy for identifying cause-and-effect relationships.

1 **Pay attention** to what happens and why it happens.

2 **Look for clue words,** that signal a cause-and-effect relationship, such as *because* or *since*.

3 **Separate causes from effects.** An *effect* tells what happened. A *cause* tells why it happened.

4 **Look for more than one effect** from a cause. What were the effects of Hurricane Andrew?

Hurricane ANDREW

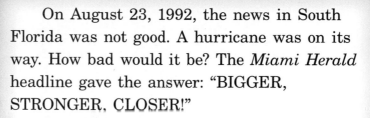

On August 23, 1992, the news in South Florida was not good. A hurricane was on its way. How bad would it be? The *Miami Herald* headline gave the answer: "BIGGER, STRONGER, CLOSER!"

Some people began packing up to leave, but most Floridians stayed. These people would get more than they had bargained for.

Although Andrew wasn't a particularly large hurricane, it struck with a fierceness no one had expected. On a scale of 1–5, Andrew rated a 4 as it charged ashore. What Andrew lacked in size, it made up for in fury.

Slamming into Florida at 3 A.M. on August 24, Andrew's winds destroyed entire neighborhoods. Winds at landfall gusted at up to 180 mph. In the town of Homestead, 80% of the houses were torn to pieces, and 7,500 families were left homeless. Boats and cars were tossed around like toys.

By the time it was over, 50,000 homes had been destroyed, and 175,000 people were left homeless. An estimated 25 billion dollars of damage had been done. And worst of all, 41 people lost their lives.

Would South Florida ever recover? Within days, people began to repair the damage. Buildings were rebuilt, and communities came back together.

Perhaps most importantly, people learned from Hurricane Andrew. After the storm, many building code laws were changed. Now when a fierce storm approaches, Florida knows what to do to be prepared.

TIME
FOR KIDS
SPECIAL REPORT

Tornadoes!

Tracking nature's most powerful storms

Tornado Watch

Tracking twisters is a real science

COVER: DON LLOYD/WEATHERSTOCK;
RIGHT: HOWARD BLUESTEIN/PHOTO RESEARCHERS; FAR RIGHT:PHIL DEGGINGER

The chase was on. Mark Askelson was riding in a truck. Danger was rushing closer and closer: a swirling, angry tornado. Askelson had to get to safety. But it wasn't time for him to get out of the storm's way—yet.

First he had to drop tools in the path of the tornado. The tools would measure the storm's temperature and strength. Askelson positioned the tools and then quickly found safety.

Askelson works for the National Severe Storms Laboratory in Norman, Oklahoma. He studies tornadoes to figure out when and where they will hit. With that information, scientists can give people warning. "That's our goal: to answer scientific questions about tornadoes so that we can help save people's lives," says Askelson.

Tornadoes are nature's most powerful storms. They can produce winds that blow at speeds of 300 miles an hour. That's the fastest wind on Earth. With all that wind comes a lot of noise. People have said that a tornado sounds like a rushing train. When a tornado strikes, it can cause serious damage and death.

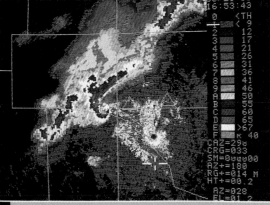

The National Severe Storms Laboratory uses radar to track tornadoes.

Scientists place instruments in the path of an oncoming tornado. Then they will race to safety.

Tornado chasers like Askelson use computers, satellites, and other instruments to detect and track tornadoes. These tools have made predictions more reliable than in the past and have saved many lives. Unfortunately, however, tornadoes are still not easy to predict. And since it takes only five to 10 minutes for a twister to form, people in a storm's path can't always get an early warning.

Even though tornadoes can happen anywhere and at any time, most tornadoes take place in spring and summer. That's when colder air most frequently mixes with warmer air, creating the conditions needed for a twister to form.

Tornadoes most often occur in places where the land is flat. "Tornado Alley" includes Texas, Oklahoma, Missouri, Nebraska, Kansas, and Iowa—the states where tornadoes are most common.

DAVE MARTIN–AP; OPPOSITE PAGE: ILLUSTRATION FOR TIME FOR KIDS BY ALEX REARDON

A twister crashed through this Nashville church in 1998.

Watch or Warning?

Many people don't know the difference between a tornado watch and a tornado warning. But the difference could save your life. The National Weather Service issues a tornado watch when weather conditions are right for a tornado. If this happens, keep your radio or TV on and listen for further news—or a tornado warning.

A tornado warning is issued when a twister has actually been spotted or picked up on radar. When you hear a tornado warning, be prepared to head to safety—fast!

128

Based on an article in *TIME FOR KIDS*.

Twisters are so powerful that they can pick up cars, trees, and boulders. They can rip the roof off any house in their path. In 1931, a train in Minnesota was lifted from its tracks, carried through the air, and set down 80 feet away. Amazingly, only one of the 170 people on board was killed.

Rodney Stanford of Nashville, Tennessee, saw a twister tear through a football stadium. "Parts of the stadium were being tossed around like Popsicle sticks," he said. "I've never seen anything like it."

Scientists are a long way from knowing how to stop tornadoes and how to avoid the destruction they cause. But they're closer than ever to understanding how and why they form (*see below*). Says Askelson: "We're moving toward a time when we'll be able to give people hours of notice before a storm hits." Those hours will save lives.

FIND OUT MORE
Visit our website:
www.mhschool.com/reading

*inter*NET
CONNECTION

How a Tornado Forms

A giant storm system made of moisture and wind is called a supercell. It is formed when a mass of warm air crashes into a mass of cooler air. The crash sometimes causes the wind to start spinning and form a tornado. The center of a tornado is called a vortex. Most tornadoes are dark gray or black from the dust and dirt they suck up from the ground. Sometimes they are reddish or yellowish, if that's the color of the dirt they've picked up.

WARM AIR

COLD AIR

Story Questions & Activities

1. What causes a tornado?

2. What effect can a tornado have on people and property?

3. What makes tracking a tornado a "real science"?

4. What is the main idea of this selection?

5. How are the scientists who study tornadoes like the main characters in the stories in this unit?

Write an Eyewitness Account

Scientists have watched many tornadoes. They have also taken many pictures of them. Imagine that you have taken one of the photographs in this article. Write an eyewitness account of what you saw.

Make a List

Tornadoes are most common in the central part of the United States, but they can happen anywhere. Learn what to do during a tornado watch. Look in an encyclopedia, or find a book about severe storms. Make a list of rules to follow if a tornado is coming. Make the list into a poster for your room at home.

Read the Clouds

Because tornadoes form quickly, it is almost impossible to predict where and when they will occur. However, you can predict weather patterns if you know how to read the clouds. Find out what the different kinds of clouds look like and the kind of weather they forecast. Share your information with your classmates.

Find Out More

This article tells you how a tornado forms. It even gives you a diagram. Find out what causes another kind of storm, such as a hurricane. First, choose the storm. Then look in an encyclopedia or a science book. Draw a diagram to illustrate what happens.

131

Read a Bibliography

Authors of nonfiction often want to let readers know where they got their information. That's why many books and articles include a **bibliography** at the end. The bibliography lists books, magazine articles, and other sources that the author used. The sources are arranged alphabetically by author. Bibliographies also tell readers where to find out more about the same subject.

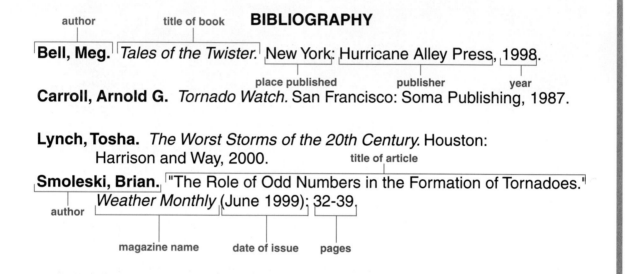

Use the bibliography to answer these questions.

1. Is *Tornado Watch* a book or a magazine? How do you know?

2. On what pages of *Weather Monthly* would you find "The Role of Odd Numbers in the Formation of Tornadoes"?

3. Where was *Tales of the Twister* published?

4. Which of these sources would you look at if you wanted to read about a terrible snowstorm?

5. Why is a bibliography important?

TEST POWER

DIRECTIONS
Read the sample story. Then read each question about the story.

SAMPLE

The Burglar

Grant was baby-sitting next door when he noticed a rustling outside the window. It sounded as though someone were trying to break into the house.

In the event of an emergency, Grant was instructed to call his father right away. Grant picked up the phone and immediately called his father, who was just next door. When his father answered the phone, Grant whispered, "Can you come over here right away? There's a noise outside, and I think a burglar might be trying to break in!"

Several tense minutes passed, and the rustling continued until it stopped as suddenly as it had started. Then there was a knock at the door. Grant inched his way toward the door and quietly asked, "Who's there?"

"Grant, it's Dad," his father said. "I found your burglar."

Grant opened the door. There was his father and a tabby cat!

1 This passage is mostly about —

   A a boy who calls his father for advice

   B a boy who mistakes a cat for a burglar

   C a man who brings a cat for a visit

   D a knock at the door that scares Grant

2 How did Grant probably feel when he saw the tabby cat?

   F Relieved

   G Scared

   H Obedient

   J Patient

133

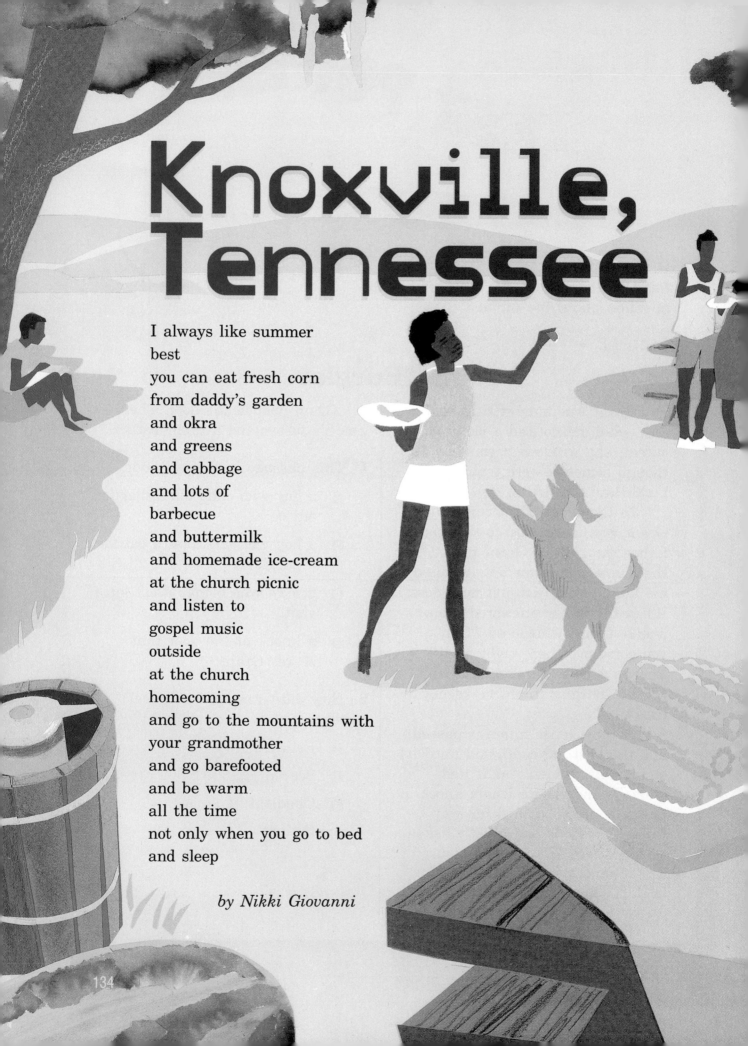

Knoxville, Tennessee

I always like summer
best
you can eat fresh corn
from daddy's garden
and okra
and greens
and cabbage
and lots of
barbecue
and buttermilk
and homemade ice-cream
at the church picnic
and listen to
gospel music
outside
at the church
homecoming
and go to the mountains with
your grandmother
and go barefooted
and be warm
all the time
not only when you go to bed
and sleep

by Nikki Giovanni

Building Bridges

Oranges

I peel oranges neatly.
The sections come apart cleanly, perfectly, in my hands.

When Emily peels an orange, she tears holes in it.
Juice squirts in all directions.

"Kate," she says, "I don't know how you do it!"

Emily is my best friend.
I hope she never learns how to peel oranges.

by Jean Little

Stories in Art

The Underground Railroad by Charles T. Webber, 1893

In the 1800s, some people fought slavery by helping enslaved people escape on the Underground Railroad. This was not a real railroad but a network of secret routes to the North.

Look at this painting of the Underground Railroad. What can you tell about it? Who are the people helping others? Why are they helping them? Where are the people going? What do you think will happen once they get there?

If this painting suddenly came to life, what would you tell the "conductors" on the Underground Railroad? Do you think that the people escaping will find a better life? Explain your prediction.

Make Predictions

Develop strategies for making, confirming, and revising predictions.

1 **Read the title** and first paragraph. Use these clues to make a prediction about the story.

2 **Pay attention to what the characters say and do.** Based on what you know about people, what do you think Tanya will do?

3 **Read to find out** if your prediction was correct.

4 **Check and revise your predictions.** Was the ending different from what you had predicted?

Tanya Plays the Piano

I am going to be a concert pianist when I grow up. But first, I have to be able to play in front of people.

My mom suggested I head over to the senior citizens center. She read in the community newspaper that a baby grand piano had been donated to the center. So off I went.

I almost forgot about being nervous when I saw the piano. It was made of smooth, dark wood, and its white keys popped out at me like pearls.

Part of me wanted to run away, but a voice inside of me whispered, "This is your chance."

I walked across the bright room. People were chatting over coffee and cake, reading, and playing checkers. One man was sitting by himself, staring out the window.

I closed my eyes and pretended I was at home. I started to play a soft tune. The group near me stopped chatting. Then I switched to something livelier. The checkers group moved closer.

The man by the window pulled out a harmonica. "Do you mind?" he asked. Then he started to play along.

Did I *mind?* From the very first note, I could tell he was terrific!

We played for over an hour – blues, jazz, pop, you name it. Other folks joined in, clapping their hands and humming.

By the time I left, I had forgotten all about being afraid. And no one had known the man by the window could play the harmonica, either. He told me he had been afraid, too.

Can you imagine *that?*

Meet
Alma Flor Ada

"Most of my stories I told aloud before I ever wrote them down," says Alma Flor Ada. "And it was other people listening and other people being interested that gave me a motivation to write them."

Listening to other people's stories has also influenced Ada's writing. *The Gold Coin* is based in part on a story her grandfather told her when she was about fifteen. In the story, a rich man had to choose between going away to save his fortune or staying with his dying wife. That man was Alma Flor Ada's grandfather—and he told her he never regretted choosing to stay with his wife. "[Money] should never rule your life," he told her.

Alma Flor Ada grew up in Cuba and today lives in California, where she is a professor of multicultural education at the University of San Francisco. She has written many children's books published in Mexico, Peru, Argentina, and Spain.

THE GOLD COIN

by Alma Flor Ada

illustrated by Neil Waldman

translated from the Spanish by Bernice Randall

Juan had been a thief for many years. Because he did his stealing by night, his skin had become pale and sickly. Because he spent his time either hiding or sneaking about, his body had become shriveled and bent. And because he had neither friend nor relative to make him smile, his face was always twisted into an angry frown.

One night, drawn by a light shining through the trees, Juan came upon a hut. He crept up to the door and through a crack saw an old woman sitting at a plain, wooden table.

What was that shining in her hand? Juan wondered. He could not believe his eyes: It was a gold coin. Then he heard the woman say to herself, "I must be the richest person in the world."

Juan decided instantly that all the woman's gold must be his. He thought that the easiest thing to do was to watch until the woman left. Juan hid in the bushes and huddled under his poncho, waiting for the right moment to enter the hut.

Juan was half asleep when he heard knocking at the door and the sound of insistent voices. A few minutes later, he saw the woman, wrapped in a black cloak, leave the hut with two men at her side.

Here's my chance! Juan thought. And, forcing open a window, he climbed into the empty hut.

He looked about eagerly for the gold. He looked under the bed. It wasn't there. He looked in the cupboard. It wasn't there, either. Where could it be? Close to despair, Juan tore away some beams supporting the thatch roof.

Finally, he gave up. There was simply no gold in the hut.

All I can do, he thought, is to find the old woman and make her tell me where she's hidden it.

So he set out along the path that she and her two companions had taken.

It was daylight by the time Juan reached the river. The countryside had been deserted, but here, along the riverbank, were two huts. Nearby, a man and his son were hard at work, hoeing potatoes.

It had been a long, long time since Juan had spoken to another human being. Yet his desire to find the woman was so strong that he went up to the farmers and asked, in a hoarse, raspy voice, "Have you seen a short, gray-haired woman, wearing a black cloak?"

"Oh, you must be looking for Doña Josefa," the young boy said. "Yes, we've seen her. We went to fetch her this morning, because my grandfather had another attack of—"

"Where is she now?" Juan broke in.

"She is long gone," said the father with a smile. "Some people from across the river came looking for her, because someone in their family is sick."

"How can I get across the river?" Juan asked anxiously.

"Only by boat," the boy answered. "We'll row you across later, if you'd like." Then turning back to his work, he added, "But first we must finish digging up the potatoes."

The thief muttered, "Thanks." But he quickly grew impatient. He grabbed a hoe and began to help the pair of farmers. The sooner we finish, the sooner we'll get across the river, he thought. And the sooner I'll get to my gold!

It was dusk when they finally laid down their hoes. The soil had been turned, and the wicker baskets were brimming with potatoes.

"Now can you row me across?" Juan asked the father anxiously.

"Certainly," the man said. "But let's eat supper first."

Juan had forgotten the taste of a home-cooked meal and the pleasure that comes from sharing it with others. As he sopped up the last of the stew with a chunk of dark bread, memories of other meals came back to him from far away and long ago.

By the light of the moon, father and son guided their boat across the river.

"What a wonderful healer Doña Josefa is!" the boy told Juan. "All she had to do to make Abuelo better was give him a cup of her special tea."

"Yes, and not only that," his father added, "she brought him a gold coin."

Juan was stunned. It was one thing for Doña Josefa to go around helping people. But how could she go around handing out gold coins—*his gold coins?*

When the threesome finally reached the other side of the river, they saw a young man sitting outside his hut.

"This fellow is looking for Doña Josefa," the father said, pointing to Juan.

"Oh, she left some time ago," the young man said.

"Where to?" Juan asked tensely.

"Over to the other side of the mountain," the young man replied, pointing to the vague outline of mountains in the night sky.

"How did she get there?" Juan asked, trying to hide his impatience.

"By horse," the young man answered. "They came on horseback to get her because someone had broken his leg."

"Well, then, I need a horse, too," Juan said urgently.

"Tomorrow," the young man replied softly. "Perhaps I can take you tomorrow, maybe the next day. First I must finish harvesting the corn."

So Juan spent the next day in the fields, bathed in sweat from sunup to sundown.

Yet each ear of corn that he picked seemed to bring him closer to his treasure. And later that evening, when he helped the young man husk several ears so they could boil them for supper, the yellow kernels glittered like gold coins.

While they were eating, Juan thought about Doña Josefa. Why, he wondered, would someone who said she was the world's richest woman spend her time taking care of every sick person for miles around?

The following day, the two set off at dawn. Juan could not recall when he last had noticed the beauty of the sunrise. He felt strangely moved by the sight of the mountains, barely lit by the faint rays of the morning sun.

As they neared the foothills, the young man said, "I'm not surprised you're looking for Doña Josefa. The whole countryside needs her. I went for her because my wife had been running a high fever. In no time at all, Doña Josefa had her on the road to recovery. And what's more, my friend, she brought her a gold coin!"

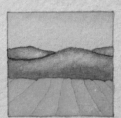

Juan groaned inwardly. To think that someone could hand out gold so freely! What a strange woman Doña Josefa is, Juan thought. Not only is she willing to help one person after another, but she doesn't mind traveling all over the countryside to do it!

"Well, my friend," said the young man finally, "this is where I must leave you. But you don't have far to walk. See that house over there? It belongs to the man who broke his leg."

The young man stretched out his hand to say good-bye. Juan stared at it for a moment. It had been a long, long time since the thief had shaken hands with anyone. Slowly, he pulled out a hand from under his poncho. When his companion grasped it firmly in his own, Juan felt suddenly warmed, as if by the rays of the sun.

But after he thanked the young man, Juan ran down the road. He was still eager to catch up with Doña Josefa. When he reached the house, a woman and a child were stepping down from a wagon.

"Have you seen Doña Josefa?" Juan asked.

"We've just taken her to Don Teodosio's," the woman said. "His wife is sick, you know—"

"How do I get there?" Juan broke in. "I've got to see her."

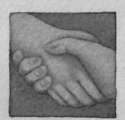

"It's too far to walk," the woman said amiably. "If you'd like, I'll take you there tomorrow. But first I must gather my squash and beans."

So Juan spent yet another long day in the fields. Working beneath the summer sun, Juan noticed that his skin had begun to tan. And although he had to stoop down to pick the squash, he found that he could now stretch his body. His back had begun to straighten, too.

Later, when the little girl took him by the hand to show him a family of rabbits burrowed under a fallen tree, Juan's face broke into a smile. It had been a long, long time since Juan had smiled.

Yet his thoughts kept coming back to the gold.

The following day, the wagon carrying Juan and the woman lumbered along a road lined with coffee fields.

The woman said, "I don't know what we would have done without Doña Josefa. I sent my daughter to our neighbor's house, who then brought Doña Josefa on horseback. She set my husband's leg and then showed me how to brew a special tea to lessen the pain."

Getting no reply, she went on. "And, as if that weren't enough, she brought him a gold coin. Can you imagine such a thing?"

Juan could only sigh. No doubt about it, he thought, Doña Josefa is someone special. But Juan didn't know whether to be happy that Doña Josefa had so much gold she could freely hand it out, or angry for her having already given so much of it away.

When they finally reached Don Teodosio's house, Doña Josefa was already gone. But here, too, there was work that needed to be done. . . .

Juan stayed to help with the coffee harvest. As he picked the red berries, he gazed up from time to time at the trees that grew, row upon row, along the hillsides. What a calm, peaceful place this is! he thought.

The next morning, Juan was up at daybreak. Bathed in the soft, dawn light, the mountains seemed to smile at him. When Don Teodosio offered him a lift on horseback, Juan found it difficult to have to say good-bye.

"What a good woman Doña Josefa is!" Don Teodosio said, as they rode down the hill toward the sugarcane fields. "The minute she heard about my wife being sick, she came with her special herbs. And as if that weren't enough, she brought my wife a gold coin!"

In the stifling heat, the kind that often signals the approach of a storm, Juan simply sighed and mopped his brow. The pair continued riding for several hours in silence.

Juan then realized he was back in familiar territory, for they were now on the stretch of road he had traveled only a week ago—though how much longer it now seemed to him. He jumped off Don Teodosio's horse and broke into a run.

This time the gold would not escape him! But he had to move quickly, so he could find shelter before the storm broke.

Out of breath, Juan finally reached Doña Josefa's hut. She was standing by the door, shaking her head slowly as she surveyed the ransacked house.

"So I've caught up with you at last!" Juan shouted, startling the old woman. "Where's the gold?"

"The gold coin?" Doña Josefa said, surprised and looking at Juan intently. "Have you come for the gold coin? I've been trying hard to give it to someone who might need it," Doña Josefa said. "First to an old man who had just gotten over a bad attack. Then to a young woman who had been running a fever. Then to a man with a broken leg. And finally to Don Teodosio's wife. But none of them would take it. They all said, 'Keep it. There must be someone who needs it more.'"

Juan did not say a word.

"You must be the one who needs it," Doña Josefa said.

She took the coin out of her pocket and handed it to him. Juan stared at the coin, speechless.

At that moment a young girl appeared, her long braid bouncing as she ran. "Hurry, Doña Josefa, please!" she said breathlessly. "My mother is all alone, and the baby is due any minute."

"Of course, dear," Doña Josefa replied. But as she glanced up at the sky, she saw nothing but black clouds. The storm was nearly upon them. Doña Josefa sighed deeply.

"But how can I leave now? Look at my house! I don't know what has happened to the roof. The storm will wash the whole place away!"

And there was a deep sadness in her voice.

Juan took in the child's frightened eyes, Doña Josefa's sad, distressed face, and the ransacked hut.

"Go ahead, Doña Josefa," he said. "Don't worry about your house. I'll see that the roof is back in shape, good as new."

The woman nodded gratefully, drew her cloak about her shoulders, and took the child by the hand. As she turned to leave, Juan held out his hand.

"Here, take this," he said, giving her the gold coin. "I'm sure the newborn will need it more than I."

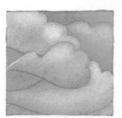

Story Questions & Activities

1 What is Juan like at the beginning of the story?

2 Why did or didn't you expect Juan to give back the coin at the end of the story?

3 What makes Juan realize that stealing is wrong?

4 This selection is based on a true story that the writer's grandfather told her. The theme of that story is that money should never rule your life. How is that theme also the main point of this story?

5 Imagine that Doña Josefa became part of the painting on page 138. Why do you think she might help these people escape to freedom?

Write an Advice Column

Imagine that Juan spent the rest of his life helping people to lead honest lives. Pretend you are Juan. Write an advice column to a student who is thinking of telling a lie. Persuade the student to see that lying is wrong. Give three good reasons.

Make a Map

Juan travels the countryside looking for Doña Josefa and the gold coin. Make a map of Juan's journey, beginning and ending with Doña Josefa's hut. Use posterboard or construction paper, and include clues from the story in your map. Be sure to draw mountains, a river, fields, and other features of nature that Juan sees along the way. Include a compass rose, a map key, and a map scale.

Plan a Menu

Juan realizes that it has been a long time since he has had a home-cooked meal. Plan a menu for your family's dinner. Choose food from the five basic food groups. Then design a menu. Use construction paper. Include an appetizer, a main course, and a healthy dessert.

Find Out More

Doña Josefa hands Juan the gold coin at the end of the story. How much money do you think it is worth? When did people start using gold as money? Why was it used? Look up the history of money in an encyclopedia. Use this fascinating history to make a time line of money.

163

Use a Dictionary

Doña Josefa uses special herbs to help her sick patients. What is an *herb*? How do you say this word? Is the *h* silent? Where would you go to find this information? A dictionary could give you the answer.

A **dictionary** gives the pronunciation and meaning of a word. It also has a pronunciation key to help you sound out the word. A dictionary tells you the word's part of speech, and may show you how to use the word in a sentence. Look at the sample pronunciation key and the entry word in the dictionary below.

Pronunciation   Part of speech

Main entry — **herb** *(ûrb, hûrb) noun* — **1.** any plant part that is used for flavor in cooking, or in making medicines or perfumes and cosmetics: Example sentence: *She used an herb in cooking.*
Definitions — **2.** any flowering plant that does not form a woody stem, but instead dies down to the ground at the end of each growing season.

herb

Use the sample dictionary to answer these questions.

1 How many meanings does the dictionary give for the word *herb*?

2 What are the two ways to pronounce *herb*?

3 What is the meaning of *herb* as it is used in the example sentence?

4 What part of speech is the word *herb*?

5 How can you use a dictionary to find the meaning and pronunciation of a word you don't know?

TEST POWER

Test Tip

Always read the directions carefully.

DIRECTIONS

Read the sample story. Then read each question about the story.

SAMPLE

Charles Learns Something New

"It sounds as if Samantha's house is no fun," Charles complained. "She doesn't have a TV, video games, or a computer."

Charles's father, Tom, looked at Samantha's father, Miguel. Miguel and Tom were friends from their college days. Now Miguel and his family lived in a small town in Guatemala. They had come to visit Charles and Tom for a few days.

"You know," Miguel said to Charles, "when I was growing up, my pueblo didn't have electricity. At night, we had to use kerosene lamps to light our house. Even now, we don't have a TV or a computer at home. Samantha and her brother invent their own games."

"Samantha must be happy to be here where she can play video games, then," Charles exclaimed.

"Well," replied Miguel, "when we first arrived, she watched TV and played video games, but I think she has found that the games she makes are often more creative than what she sees on TV. Why don't you ask her to show you some of her games?"

1 The word pueblo in this story means —

A village

B game

C telephone

D radio

2 You can tell from the passage that —

F Tom likes making games to play by himself

G Charles thinks that playing video games is fun

H Guatemala can be a very warm place in which to live

J Samantha misses her home in Guatemala

165

Stories in Art

Like legends, which mix fact with fiction, some of the most interesting art makes you wonder which people and events in a picture could be real.

Look at the painting. What do you notice right away? Is it the children? The clouds? The giant? Why is the giant painted so lightly? Is it to show that he may exist only in the children's imagination? Why aren't the children running away? Is it because they cannot decide whether the giant is real? Explain what you think.

Clouds sometimes play tricks on your eyes. What shapes have you seen clouds form? How did you know that the shape you were seeing was only a cloud?

The Giant by N.C. Wyeth, 1923

166

Fact and Nonfact

Develop a strategy for distinguishing between fact and nonfact.

1. **Remember that** a fact is something that can be proved.

2. **Think about each statement.** Read the details. Can the details be proved? If the answer is yes, the statement is a fact.

3. **Find statements** that cannot be proven true or false.

4. **What statements** in this story are not facts? How do you know?

The Transcontinental Railroad

In 1838, Congress was asked for money to help build a railroad. The transcontinental railroad would link the eastern and western United States.

It would be like "trying to build a railroad to the moon," Congress said.

Thirty-one years later, a spike made of gold was hammered into a track laid at Promontory Point, Utah. Two great railroads, the Union Pacific and the Central Pacific, had done what seemed impossible.

Workers had laid 1,700 miles of track over mountains, across deserts and plains to link the eastern and western United

States. Now cattle, gold, and food from the West could be shipped to the East; clothing, machines, and manufactured goods could flow west. What had taken months by covered wagon or ship would now take only days.

The country celebrated from coast to coast. But like all great events, it meant change.

More people began moving west. Towns rose where there had been only prairie before. Native Americans, who had depended on the buffalo for their way of life, could no longer follow the great herds across the plains. With the railroad, their way of life ended forever.

Still, the railroad meant progress. Without it, products, services, and ideas could never have spread throughout the country as rapidly as they did.

The transcontinental railroad is completed, May 10, 1869.

Meet Julius Lester

Julius Lester was born in St. Louis, Missouri, and raised in the Middle West and the South. Today, he is a college professor. He is also a writer of poetry, novels, nonfiction books, and articles for newspapers and magazines. Some of his most important writing has been about slavery.

"I write," Lester says, "because the lives of all of us are stories. If enough of those stories are told, then perhaps we will begin to see that our lives are the same story. The differences are merely in the details."

Meet Jerry Pinkney

Jerry Pinkney has illustrated several books by Julius Lester. About his artwork Pinkney says, "I'd rather sit and draw than do almost anything else." That is exactly what he has done, with amazing success. Many of Pinkney's books, including *John Henry*, have won important awards.

JOHN HENRY

by Julius Lester

pictures by
Jerry Pinkney

You have probably never heard of John Henry. Or maybe you heard about him but don't know the ins and outs of his comings and goings. Well, that's why I'm going to tell you about him.

When John Henry was born, birds came from everywhere to see him. The bears and panthers and moose and deer and rabbits and squirrels and even a unicorn came out of the woods to see him. And instead of the sun tending to his business and going to bed, it was peeping out from behind the moon's skirts trying to get a glimpse of the new baby.

Before long the mama and papa come out on the porch to show off their brand-new baby. The birds "oooooohed" and the animals "aaaaaaahed" at how handsome the baby was.

Somewhere in the middle of one of the "ooooooohs," or maybe it was on the backside of one of the "aaaaaaahs," that baby jumped out of his mama's arms and started growing.

He grew and he grew and he grew. He grew until his head and shoulders busted through the roof which was over the porch. John Henry thought that was the funniest thing in the world. He laughed so loud, the sun got scared. It scurried from behind the moon's skirts and went to bed, which is where it should've been all the while.

The next morning John Henry was up at sunrise. The sun wasn't. He was tired and had decided to sleep in. John Henry wasn't going to have none of that. He hollered up into the sky, "Get up from there! I got things to do and I need light to do 'em by."

The sun yawned, washed its face, flossed and brushed its teeth, and hurried up over the horizon.

That day John Henry helped his papa rebuild the porch he had busted through, added a wing onto the house with an indoor swimming pool and one of them jacutzis. After lunch he chopped down an acre of trees and split them into fireplace logs and still had time for a nap before supper.

The next day John Henry went to town. He met up with the meanest man in the state, Ferret-Faced Freddy, sitting on his big white horse. You know what he was doing? He was thinking of mean things to do. Ferret-Faced Freddy was so mean, he cried if he had a nice thought.

John Henry said, "Freddy, I'll make you a bet. Let's have a race. You on your horse. Me on my legs. If you and your horse win, you can work me as hard as you want for a whole year. If I win, you have to be nice for a year."

Ferret-Faced Freddy laughed an evil laugh. "It's a deal, John Henry." His voice sounded like bat wings on tombstones.

175

The next morning folks lined up all along the way the
race would go. John Henry was ready. Ferret-Faced Freddy
and his horse were ready.

BANG! The race was on.

My great-granddaddy's brother's cousin's sister-in-law's
uncle's aunt was there that morning. She said everybody
saw Ferret-Faced Freddy ride by on his big white horse and

they were sho' 'nuf moving. Didn't nobody see John Henry. That's because he was so fast, the wind was out of breath trying to keep up with him. When Ferret-Faced Freddy crossed the finish line, John Henry was already on the other side, sitting in a rocking chair and drinking a soda mom.

After that Ferret-Faced Freddy was so nice, everybody called him Frederick the Friendly.

John Henry decided it was
time for him to go on down the big
road. He went home and told his
mama and daddy good-bye.

His daddy said, "You got to
have something to make your way
in the world with, Son. These
belonged to your granddaddy."
And he gave him two twenty-
pound sledgehammers with four-
foot handles made of whale bone.

A day or so later, John Henry
saw a crew building a road. At
least, that's what they were doing
until they came on a boulder right
smack-dab where the road was
supposed to go. This was no ordinary boulder. It was as hard as
anger and so big around, it took
half a week for a tall man to walk
from one side to the other.

John Henry offered to lend them a hand.

"That's all right. We'll put some dynamite to it."

John Henry smiled to himself. "Whatever you say."

The road crew planted dynamite all around the rock and set it off.

KERBOOM BLAMMITY-BLAMMITY BOOMBOOM BANGBOOMBANG!!!

That dynamite made so much racket, the Almighty looked over the parapets of Heaven and hollered, "It's getting too noisy down there." The dynamite kicked up so much dirt and dust, it got dark. The moon thought night had caught her napping and she hurried out so fast, she almost bumped into the sun who was still climbing the steep hill toward noontime.

When all the commotion from the dynamite was over, the road crew was amazed. The boulder was still there. In fact, the dynamite hadn't knocked even a chip off it.

The crew didn't know what to do. Then they heard a rumbling noise. They looked around. It was John Henry, laughing. He said, "If you gentlemen would give me a little room, I got some work to do."

"Don't see how you can do what dynamite couldn't," said the boss of the crew.

John Henry chuckled. "Just watch me." He swung one of his hammers round and round his head. It made such a wind that leaves blew off the trees and birds fell out of the sky.

RINGGGGGG!

The hammer hit the boulder. That boulder shivered like you do on a cold winter morning when it looks like the school bus is never going to come.

RINGGGGGG!

The boulder shivered like the morning when freedom came to the slaves.

John Henry picked up his other hammer. He swung one hammer in a circle over his head. As soon as it hit the rock—RINGGGG!—the hammer in his left hand started to make a circle and—RINGGGG! Soon the RINGGGG! of one hammer followed the RINGGGG! of the other one so closely, it sounded like they were falling at the same time.

RINGGGG! RINGGGG!
RINGGGG! RINGGGG!

Chips and dust were flying from the boulder so fast that John Henry vanished from sight. But you could still hear his hammers—RINGGGG! RINGGGG!

The air seemed to be dancing to the rhythm of his hammers. The boss of the road crew looked up. His mouth dropped open. He pointed into the sky.

There, in the air above the boulder, was a rainbow. John Henry was swinging the hammers so fast, he was making a rainbow around his shoulders. It was shining and shimmering in the dust and grit like hope that never dies. John Henry started singing:

I got a rainbow
RINGGGG! RINGGGG!
Tied round my shoulder
RINGGGG! RINGGGG!
It ain't gon' rain,
No, it ain't gon' rain.
RINGGGG! RINGGGG!

John Henry sang and he hammered and the air danced and the rainbow shimmered and the earth shook and rolled from the blows of the hammer. Finally it was quiet. Slowly the dust cleared.

Folks could not believe their eyes. The boulder was gone. In its place was the prettiest and straightest road they had ever seen. Not only had John Henry pulverized the boulder into pebbles, he had finished building the road.

In the distance where the new road connected to the main one, the road crew saw John Henry waving good-bye, a hammer on each shoulder, the rainbow draped around him like love.

John Henry went on his way. He had heard that any man good with a hammer could find work building the Chesapeake and Ohio Railroad through West Virginia. That was where he had been going when he stopped to build the road.

The next day John Henry arrived at the railroad. However, work had stopped. The railroad tracks had to go through a mountain, and such a mountain. Next to it even John Henry felt small.

But a worker told John Henry about a new machine they were going to use to tunnel through the mountain. It was called a steam drill. "It can hammer faster and harder than ten men and it never has to stop and rest."

The next day the boss arrived with the steam drill. John Henry said to him, "Let's have a contest. Your steam drill against me and my hammers."

The man laughed. "I've heard you're the best there ever was, John Henry. But even you can't outhammer a machine."

"Let's find out," John Henry answered.

Boss shrugged. "Don't make me no never mind. You start on the other side of the mountain. I'll start the steam drill over here. Whoever gets to the middle first is the winner."

189

The next morning all was still. The birds weren't singing and the roosters weren't crowing. When the sun didn't hear the rooster, he wondered if something was wrong. So he rose a couple of minutes early to see.

What he saw was a mountain as big as hurt feelings. On one side was a big machine hooked up to hoses. It was belching smoke and steam. As the machine attacked the mountain, rocks and dirt and underbrush flew into the air. On the other side was John Henry. Next to the mountain he didn't look much bigger than a wish that wasn't going to come true.

He had a twenty-pound hammer in each hand and muscles hard as wisdom in each arm. As he swung them through the air, they shone like silver, and when the hammers hit the rock, they rang like gold. Before long, tongues of fire leaped out with each blow.

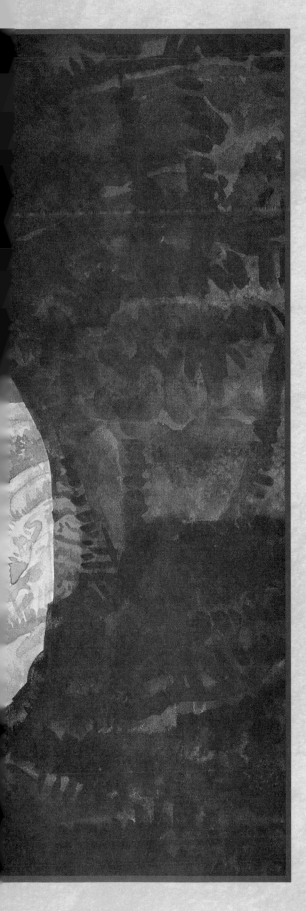

On the other side the boss of the steam drill felt the mountain shudder. He got scared and hollered, "I believe this mountain is caving in!"

From the darkness inside the mountain came a deep voice: "It's just my hammers sucking wind. Just my hammers sucking wind." There wasn't enough room inside the tunnel for the rainbow, so it wrapped itself around the mountain on the side where John Henry was.

All through the night John Henry and the steam drill went at it. In the light from the tongues of fire shooting out of the tunnel from John Henry's hammer blows, folks could see the rainbow wrapped around the mountain like a shawl.

The sun came up extra early the next morning to see who was winning. Just as it did, John Henry broke through and met the steam drill. The boss of the steam drill was flabbergasted. John Henry had come a mile and a quarter. The steam drill had only come a quarter.

Folks were cheering and yelling, "John Henry! John Henry!"

John Henry walked out of the tunnel into the sunlight, raised his arms over his head, a hammer in each hand. The rainbow slid off the mountain and around his shoulders.

With a smile John Henry's eyes closed, and slowly he fell to the ground. John Henry was dead. He had hammered so hard and so fast and so long that his big heart had burst.

Everybody was silent for a minute. Then came the sound of soft crying. Some said it came from the moon. Another one said she saw the sun shed a tear.

Then something strange happened. Afterward folks swore the rainbow whispered it. I don't know. But whether it was a whisper or a thought, everyone had the same knowing at the same moment: "Dying ain't important. Everybody does that. What matters is how well you do your living."

First one person started clapping. Then another, and another. Soon everybody was clapping.

The next morning the sun got everybody up early to say good-bye to John Henry. They put him on a flatbed railroad car, and the train made its way slowly out of the mountains. All along the way folks lined both sides of the track, and they were cheering and shouting through their tears:

"John Henry! John Henry!"

John Henry's body was taken to Washington, D.C.

Some say he was buried on the White House lawn late one night while the President and the Mrs. President was asleep.

I don't know about none of that. What I do know is this: If you walk by the White House late at night, stand real still, and listen real closely, folks say you just might hear a deep voice singing:

I got a rainbow
RINGGGG! RINGGGG!
Tied round my shoulder
RINGGGG! RINGGGG!
It ain't gon' rain,
No, it ain't gon' rain.
RINGGGG! RINGGGG!

1 What deeds does John Henry do in the story?

2 Which deeds could the real John Henry have done? Which deeds couldn't he have done? Why?

3 Tall tales exaggerate the lives and deeds of American folk heroes. What makes "John Henry" a tall tale? Explain.

4 What is the story of John Henry mostly about?

5 Imagine that John Henry dared the giant in the painting on page 166 to enter a contest against him. What kind of contest could it be? Who do you think would win? Why?

Write a Public-service Announcement

John Henry would be a big help to any local government. Write a public-service announcement for a local television station to persuade people to vote for John Henry for mayor. State his fantastic accomplishments. Give examples.

Write a Song

Have you ever heard one of the songs about John Henry? The writer said that he based his story on one of these folk songs. Now plan your own American folk song. Listen to songs about John Henry or another American folk hero, such as Davy Crockett. Tell the story of your hero in your song. Be sure to sing his or her praises.

Draw a Comic Strip

Everywhere John Henry went he helped people. He cleared a boulder so a road could be built. He hammered a tunnel through a mountain so the railroad could pass. Draw a comic strip to show one of the events from the story. Include characters and dialogue.

Find Out More

In the story, John Henry dies after he hammers through a mountain to lay tracks for the Chesapeake and Ohio Railroad. When were the first railroads built in this country? What parts of the country did they connect? How did they change the United States? Start by checking in your social studies textbook. Then look in an encyclopedia or on the Internet to find information about early railroads. Create a railroad time line with classmates.

197

Use the Internet

Suppose that you wanted to find information about Abraham Lincoln. You could start by checking the **Internet**. To use the Internet, you need a tool called a **search engine**. A search engine allows you to search for **World Wide Web** pages containing the information you need. For example, if you want to know more about Abraham Lincoln, you can type in his name and click the *search* button. The search engine will then explore the Internet for Abraham Lincoln **websites**. These are pages containing information about him.

FIND IT!

`Abraham Lincoln` `Search`

- **Abraham Lincoln for Primary Children** - Here's a web-based activity about Abraham Lincoln for young children. –*http://siec.k12.in.us/~west/project/lincoln/index.html*
- **Lincoln's Gettysburg Address** - Abraham Lincoln's Gettysburg Address on November 19, 1863 at Gettysburg in Pennsylvania. –*http://www.crwflags.com/gettysburg.html*
- **Abraham Lincoln** - Genealogy of Abraham Lincoln, 1809-1865. –*http://www.my-ged.com/db/page/longacre/04434*

Use the sample Internet information to answer these questions.

1 Which website will lead you to a children's version of the life of Abraham Lincoln?

2 What key words would you type in if you wanted to learn about Abraham Lincoln as President?

3 Is there a website where you can find a family history, or genealogy, for Abraham Lincoln? How could you get into that website?

4 If you wanted to read what Abraham Lincoln said in his famous Gettysburg Address, which website would you visit?

5 How can the Internet help you find information?

TEST POWER

DIRECTIONS

Read the sample story. Then read each question about the story.

SAMPLE

How do spiders use their webs?

Although there are many different types of spiders, most spiders have at least one thing in common—they use their webs to catch their food.

Orb-weaver spiders make webs that look like a bicycle wheel. When a stuck bug tries to escape, the web shakes, and the orb-weaver knows that it has its prey in its web.

Trapdoor spiders use their teeth to dig tunnels in the ground. Then they spin soft silk around the walls and opening. They cut out a piece for a door, but leave one side attached so that the door swings open and shut. When these spiders hear an insect walking over the doorway, they leap out and grab it.

The funnel-web spider hides in the bottom of its web, which is shaped like a funnel. The top part of the web spreads out like a sheet. When an insect lands on the sheet, the spider runs out of the funnel and grabs it.

1 The Trapdoor spider leaves one side of the door attached so that

   A the insect can come inside

   B the rain doesn't come in

   C it can grab its food quickly

   D the web covers the ground

2 Which is a FACT in this passage?

   F All spiders make the same kind of web.

   G The orb-weaver spider makes the strongest and largest web.

   H Funnel-web spiders hide in the bottom part of their web.

   J Trapdoor spiders use their legs to dig tunnels in the ground.

Did you reread the story to get all the facts? Explain.

Stories in Art

This mural is filled with motion. Notice how the painter uses color, light, and balance in his artwork to show movement.

~

Look at this mural. Notice the details. How does the artist give you the feeling of workers hard at work in a shipyard? If this mural were an essay, what would be its main idea?

~

Look at the painting again. What shapes does the artist use? What other details do you notice? How does the artist use the mural to show something he feels strongly about?

City Building,
from *America Today*, 1930
by Thomas Hart Benton
Collection, AXA Financial, Inc. through its subsidiary
The Equitable Life Assurance Society of the U.S.

Main Idea

Develop a strategy for finding the main idea and supporting details.

1 **Read the title.** What clues does the title give you about the article?

2 **Read the facts and examples.** This will help you figure out the main thing that is being said.

3 **Look for supporting details.** What details relate to the main idea?

4 **Ask yourself: What is the main idea** the author wants to express? Then state the main idea in your own words.

Kids Helping Kids

Bart Szczech is a young man who spends his time doing good things for others. When Bart read about the wars and disasters that children in other countries experienced, he knew he wanted to do something to help them. So he started a group to help young people all around the world.

Bart's organization is called Kids Helping Kids in Crisis or KHKIC. It raises money to buy medical supplies, food, beds, and clothes for children in need all over the world. It also raises money to help kids in the United States who are ill.

Bart Szczech and Sean Colon at the KHKIC information booth.

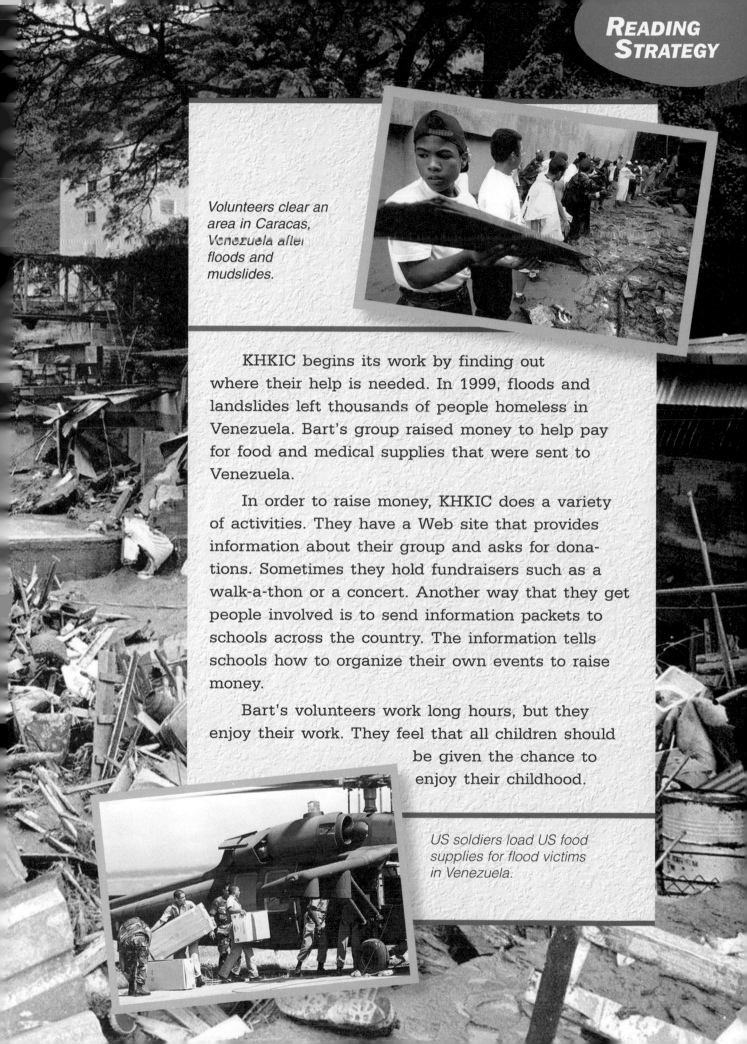

Volunteers clear an area in Caracas, Venezuela after floods and mudslides.

KHKIC begins its work by finding out where their help is needed. In 1999, floods and landslides left thousands of people homeless in Venezuela. Bart's group raised money to help pay for food and medical supplies that were sent to Venezuela.

In order to raise money, KHKIC does a variety of activities. They have a Web site that provides information about their group and asks for donations. Sometimes they hold fundraisers such as a walk-a-thon or a concert. Another way that they get people involved is to send information packets to schools across the country. The information tells schools how to organize their own events to raise money.

Bart's volunteers work long hours, but they enjoy their work. They feel that all children should be given the chance to enjoy their childhood.

US soldiers load US food supplies for flood victims in Venezuela.

It's Our

World, Too!

Stories of Young People Who Are Making a Difference

by Phillip Hoose

Justin Lebo

Since he was ten, Justin Lebo, fourteen, of Paterson, New Jersey, has been building bicycles out of used parts he finds from old junkers. When he finishes, he gives them away to kids who are homeless or sick. He plows most of his allowance into the project and often works on nights and weekends. Why does he do it? The answer is surprising. "In part," he says, "I do it for myself."

Something about the battered old bicycle at the garage sale caught ten-year-old Justin Lebo's eye. What a wreck! It was like looking at a few big bones in the dust and trying to figure out what kind of dinosaur they had once belonged to.

It was a BMX bike with a twenty-inch frame. Its original color was buried beneath five or six coats of gunky paint. Now it showed up as sort of a rusted red. Everything—the grips, the pedals, the brakes, the seat, the spokes—were bent or broken, twisted and rusted. Justin stood back as if he were inspecting a painting for sale at an auction. Then he made his final judgment: perfect.

Justin talked the owner down to $6.50 and asked his mother, Diane, to help him load the bike into the back of their car.

When he got it home, he wheeled the junker into the garage and showed it proudly to his father. "Will you help me fix it up?" he asked. Justin's hobby was bike racing, a passion the two of them shared. Their garage barely had room for the car anymore.

It was more like a bike shop. Tires and frames hung from hooks on the ceiling, and bike wrenches dangled from the walls.

After every race, Justin and his father would adjust the brakes and realign the wheels of his two racing bikes. This was a lot of work, since Justin raced flat out, challenging every gear and part to perform to its fullest. He had learned to handle almost every repair his father could and maybe even a few things he couldn't. When Justin got really stuck, he went to see Mel, the owner of the best bike shop in town. Mel let him hang out and watch, and he even grunted a few syllables of advice from between the spokes of a wheel now and then.

"It is by spending one's self that one becomes rich."

Sarah Bernhardt

Now Justin and his father cleared out a work space in the garage and put the old junker up on a rack. They poured alcohol on the frame and rubbed until the old paint began to yield, layer by layer. They replaced the broken pedal, tightened down a new seat, and restored the grips. In about a week, it looked brand new.

Justin wheeled it out of the garage, leapt aboard, and started off around the block. He stood up and mashed down on the pedals, straining for speed. It was a good, steady ride, but not much of a thrill compared to his racers.

Soon he forgot about the bike. But the very next week, he bought another junker at a yard sale and fixed it up, too. After a while it bothered him that he wasn't really using either bike. Then he realized that what he loved about the old bikes wasn't riding them: it was the challenge of making something new and useful out of something old and broken.

Justin wondered what he should do with them. They were just taking up space in the garage. He

remembered that when he was younger, he used to live near a large brick building called the Kilbarchan Home for Boys. It was a place for boys whose parents couldn't care for them for one reason or another.

He found "Kilbarchan" in the phone book and called the director, who said the boys would be thrilled to get two bicycles. The next day when Justin and his mother unloaded the bikes at the home, two boys raced out to greet them. They leapt aboard the bikes and started tooling around the semicircular driveway, doing wheelies and pirouettes, laughing and shouting.

The Lebos watched them for a while, then started to climb into their car to go home. The boys cried after them, "Wait a minute! You forgot your bikes!" Justin explained that the bikes were for them to keep.

"They were so happy," Justin remembers. "It was like they couldn't believe it. It made me feel good just to see them happy."

On the way home, Justin was silent. His mother assumed he was lost in a feeling of satisfaction. But he was thinking about what would happen once those bikes got wheeled inside and everyone saw them. How would all those kids decide who got the bikes? Two bikes could cause more trouble than they would solve. Actually, they hadn't been that hard to build. It was fun. Maybe he could do more. . . .

"Mom," Justin said as they turned onto their street, "I've got an idea. I'm going to make a bike for every boy at Kilbarchan for Christmas." Diane Lebo looked at Justin out of the corner of her eye. She had rarely seen him so determined.

When they got home, Justin called Kilbarchan to find out how many boys lived there. There were twenty-one. It was already June. He had six months to make nineteen bikes. That was almost a bike a week. Justin called the home back to tell them of his plan. "I could tell they didn't think I could do it," Justin remembers. "I knew I could."

"It just snowballed."

Justin knew his best chance was to build bikes almost the way GM or Ford builds cars: in an assembly line. He would start with frames from three-speed, twenty-four-inch BMX bicycles. They were common bikes, and all the parts were interchangeable. If he could find enough decent frames, he could take parts off broken bikes and fasten them onto the good frames. He figured it would take three or four junkers to produce enough parts to make one good bike. That meant sixty to eighty bikes. Where would he get them?

Garage sales seemed to be the only hope. It was June, and there would be garage sales all summer long. But even if he could find that many bikes, how could he ever pay for them? That was hundreds of dollars.

He went to his parents with a proposal. "When Justin was younger, say five or six," says his mother, "he used to give some of his allowance away to help others in need. His father and I would donate a dollar for every dollar Justin donated. So he asked us if it could be like the old days, if we'd match every dollar he put into buying old bikes. We said yes."

Justin and his mother spent most of June and July hunting for cheap bikes at garage sales and thrift shops. They would haul the bikes home, and Justin would start stripping them down in the yard.

Justin Lebo, who has built hundreds of bikes and given them away to kids who are orphaned, ill, or homeless.

But by the beginning of August, he had managed to make only ten bikes. Summer vacation was almost over, and school and homework would soon cut into his time. Garage sales would dry up when it got colder, and Justin was out of money. Still, he was determined to find a way.

At the end of August, Justin got a break. A neighbor wrote a letter to the local newspaper describing Justin's project, and an editor thought it would make a good story. One day a reporter entered the Lebo garage. Stepping gingerly through the tires and frames that covered the floor, she found a boy with cut fingers and dirty nails, banging a seat onto a frame. His clothes were covered with grease. In her admiring article about a boy who was devoting his summer to help kids he didn't even know, she said Justin needed bikes and money, and she printed his home phone number.

Overnight, everything changed. "There must have been a hundred calls," Justin says. "People would call me up and ask me to come over and pick up their old bike. Or I'd be working in the garage, and a station wagon would pull up. The driver would leave a couple of bikes by the curb. It just snowballed."

By the start of school, the garage was overflowing with BMX frames. Pyramids of pedals and seats rose in the corners. Soon bike parts filled a toolshed in the backyard and then spilled out into the small yard itself, wearing away the lawn.

More and more writers and television and radio reporters called for interviews. Each time he told his story, Justin asked for bikes and money. "The first few interviews were fun," Justin says, "but it reached a point where I really didn't like doing them. The publicity was necessary, though. I had to keep doing interviews to get the donations I needed."

By the time school opened, he was working on ten bikes at a time. There were so many calls now that he was beginning to refuse offers that weren't the exact bikes he needed.

As checks came pouring in, Justin's money problems disappeared. He set up a bank account and began to make bulk orders of common parts

> "I don't think you can ever really do anything to help anybody else if it doesn't make you happy."
>
> Justin Lebo

208

from Mel's bike shop. Mel seemed delighted to see him. Sometimes, if Justin brought a bike by the shop, Mel would help him fix it. When Justin tried to talk him into a lower price for big orders, Mel smiled and gave in. He respected another good businessman. They became friends.

"Why do you do it?"

The week before Christmas Justin delivered the last of the twenty-one bikes to Kilbarchan. Once again, the boys poured out of the home and leapt aboard the bikes, tearing around the snow.

And once again, their joy inspired Justin. They reminded him how important bikes were to him. Wheels meant freedom. He thought how much more the freedom to ride must mean to boys like these who had so little freedom in their lives. He decided to keep on building.

"First I made eleven bikes for the children in a foster home my mother told me about. Then I made bikes for all the women in a battered women's shelter. Then I made ten little bikes and tricycles for the kids in a home for children with AIDS. Then I made twenty-three bikes for the Paterson Housing Coalition."

In the four years since he started, Justin Lebo has made between 150 and 200 bikes

and given them all away. He has been careful to leave time for his homework, his friends, his coin collection, his new interest in marine biology, and of course his own bikes.

Reporters and interviewers have asked Justin Lebo the same question over and over: "Why do you do it?" The question seems to make him uncomfortable. It's as if they want him to say what a great person he is. Their stories always make him seem like a saint, which he knows he isn't. "Sure it's nice of me to make the bikes," he says, "because I don't have to. But I want to. In part, I do it for myself. I don't think you can ever really do anything to help anybody else if it doesn't make you happy.

"Once I overheard a kid who got one of my bikes say, 'A bike is like a book; it opens up a whole new world.' That's how I feel, too. It made me happy to know that kid felt that way. That's why I do it."

Dwaina Brooks

On Friday nights, Dwaina Brooks, eleven, and as many as twenty-six of her friends and relatives, turn her mother's kitchen into a meal factory for the homeless of Dallas. With the radio set to 100.3—the rap station—and with mayonnaise up to their elbows, they have produced as many as three hundred meals in a night.

*E*ach morning on her way to school, Dwaina Brooks saw the line of men and women outside a homeless shelter and soup kitchen in Dallas. Many looked cold and sleepy. Sometimes one man stood in the street carrying a sign that said, "I Will Work for Food to Feed My Children." No one ever stopped to talk to him. How could they just pass him by?

At school, her fourth-grade class was doing a unit on homelessness. Once a week, students telephoned a shelter and talked with someone who was staying there. Dwaina would ask the person on the other end of the phone, "How'd you wind up on the streets?" "Do you want to be there?" "What did you do before?" She listened carefully.

Most people's lives had been going along okay, and then something bad had happened. They got fired. The family broke up. They couldn't make a rent payment.

Always she asked, "What do you

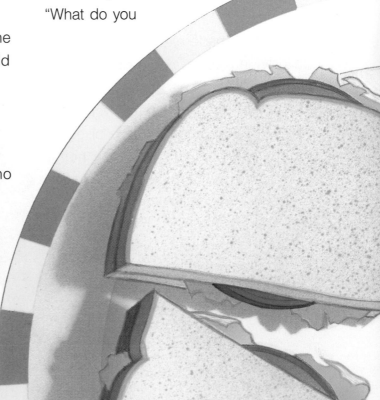

need?" The answer was always "a home," or "a job." It never seemed as though she could do much more than keep sending her lunch money to the shelter. Then one afternoon, Dwaina talked with a young man who had been without a home for a long time.

"What do you need?" she asked him.

"I need a job and a permanent home," he replied.

"Well, I can't give you that," she answered impatiently. "I don't have a job either. Don't you need anything else?"

"Yeah. I would love a really good meal again."

"Well, now," said Dwaina, brightening. "I *can* cook."

> "*Even when she was a baby, Dwaina couldn't stand to see anyone hurt . . .*"
>
> Gail Brooks

Why not?

Dwaina tore into the house that night after school and found her mother, Gail. As usual, she was in the kitchen. "Mama," she said. "I need you to help me fix some stuff to take down to that shelter we call at school. Let's make up as much as we can. Sandwiches and chicken. Let's get everyone to do it. C'mon."

Gail Brooks looked at her daughter. All of her children were generous, but Dwaina had always been a little different. Even when she was a baby, Dwaina couldn't stand to see anyone hurt or left out. If she only took one doll to bed with her, pretty soon she would start wondering if all the others felt bad. The next morning, there would be a bed full of dolls and Dwaina on the floor.

Make food for the homeless? Well, why not? They decided to prepare meals on Friday night. They spent the next three days shopping and preparing. Counting Dwaina's lunch money, which she decided to donate to the cause, they figured they had about sixty dollars to spend. Their challenge was how to make that stretch into as many meals as possible.

Coupons helped cut the prices for sandwich wrapping, cookies, and mayonnaise. Dwaina's uncle got them discount lunch meats from the store where he used to work. Thursday night was bargain night at the bakery in nearby Lancaster. They drove away with six big loaves of day-old bread for $1.78. "Mama, do you think anyone at the shelter will really eat day-old bread?" Dwaina asked. "We eat it," Gail replied. "If it don't kill us, it won't kill them."

The baker gave them twenty free boxes, too, when he heard how they would be used. Dwaina's aunts and uncles brought over huge sacks of chips and big bottles of salad dressing.

When Dwaina got home from school on Friday, the stage was set. Her mother's table was covered with a plastic cloth. The plastic gloves from the dime store were laid out. Mountains of ham, turkey, and cheese were at one end. Two rows of bread went from one end of the table to the other. They looked like piano keys. A huge jar of mayonnaise was open and ready.

Dwaina's sisters, Stephanie, sixteen, and Crystal, nine, already had aprons tied around their waists. Dwaina turned on the radio, and they all formed an assembly line and dug in. Gail threw chicken into three skillets and got them all going at once. Dwaina slapped meat on open slices of bread and covered them with mayo. Crystal wrapped sandwiches and stuffed sacks. Dwaina looked on proudly as the corner of the kitchen began to fill up with sacks. It looked like a lot of meals.

It was after ten when the last sack was stuffed. The kitchen looked like a tornado had ripped through it. They placed 105 carefully wrapped meals in the bakery boxes, loaded them in the Oldsmobile, and headed downtown.

When they got to the shelter, two men came out to the street and helped carry in the boxes. Dwaina set down her first box and looked around the shelter. It was a big, open room with beds along the walls. It was dark, but some men were up front in a lighted area drinking coffee. She wondered if the man who had said he wanted a good meal was still living there. If he was, she thought with pride, he sure enough would have a treat tomorrow.

"Who'll be there?"

After that, nearly every Friday night for a year, Dwaina and her mother and

whatever sisters were around made food for shelters in Dallas. At first they took the food to the shelters themselves, but then their church volunteered to make the deliveries for them.

Always, Dwaina wanted to make more meals. That shelter had hundreds of people; she and her mom alone probably weren't feeding half of them. One Friday evening, she had an idea: she knew where she could get some extra help, and lots of it, too.

The following Monday, she asked her fifth-grade teacher, Mr. Frost, if she could speak to the class while he took roll. Dwaina had been the class leader since the first day of school, when she had told a group of loud boys to shut up so she could hear her teacher. She could be tough or funny or kind. She always seemed to know exactly what would move them.

Now Dwaina smacked both hands on her desk hard to get their attention and stood up. She pushed her glasses up onto her forehead and glared at them for a moment, hands on hips, as if she were about to lecture them:

"Okay, y'all," she began. "We've been reading about the homeless in class, and I can tell you that for some reason it's getting worse and worse." Her eyes swept around the room. "Now, my mama and I been makin' sandwiches this year till we got mayonnaise up to our elbows and we can't make enough. Why should we be up till midnight every Friday night when y'all ain't doin' a thing? Now, listen. I want you to come to my house this Friday night and help. Who'll be there?"

Twenty-three hands went up. When Dwaina excitedly reported this to her mother, Gail Brooks nearly passed out. "Twenty-three kids? Plus *our* family?" "Yeah, Mama, isn't it great! Think how many meals we can make!"

Dwaina Brooks, who organized her family and friends to feed homeless people in Dallas.

Dwaina and Gail advised each participating family about where to get food cheaply. They made a central list of who would bring what and taped it to the refrigerator. All that week, parents drove boxes of food to the Brooks's small house. At school, the kids made bigger and bigger plans each day. Making food for the shelter was shaping up to be the social event of the year.

"Why don't y'all stay over?" asked Dwaina.

"I'll bring popcorn!" said Claire.

"I got a Hammer tape," said Qiana.

"What about boys?" said Christopher. "Can we sleep over, too?"

"Sorry," came a chorus of girls. "Oh, maybe on the kitchen floor."

The next Friday night, twenty-eight people crowded into the Brooks kitchen. They set up one of the world's longest assembly lines, kicked the radio onto 100.3 FM-JAMZ—the rap station—wrapped towels around their waists, and started in. By midnight, the boxes were filled with more than three hundred sacks.

In a little more than two years, Dwaina Brooks, now in sixth grade, has organized several thousand meals for unfortunate people in the Dallas area. She and her mother and the classmates who sometimes still join in have perfected the art of helping others and having fun at the same time. They do it by doing something they already love to do: cooking and putting meals together.

Dwaina hopes to become a doctor and open her own clinic someday, but she thinks it's crazy to wait till then to start caring for others. "Kids should get going," she says. "There aren't enough jobs out there, especially for people without diplomas. Not even at McDonald's. We should try to help. If we don't act, there will be more and more homeless people. Each of us should have some kind of concern in our hearts for other people. And we owe it, too: there isn't a one of us who hasn't been helped by someone."

Meet
Phillip Hoose

Phillip Hoose got the idea for *It's Our World, Too!* from his daughter Hannah. She and some classmates held an art sale at their elementary school in Portland, Maine. They sold their own drawings and paintings. The money raised went to a homeless shelter. Hoose says, "Their good work gave me an idea for a book. Why not look all around the world for great stories of young people reaching out, making a difference, trying to help others?"

Hoose spent the next year searching for young people working for positive change. He ended up talking with over a hundred young activists.

When Hoose is not writing, he himself also works to change the world. He raises money for a group that tries to save prairies, swamps, marshes, and forests from being destroyed.

Story Questions & Activities

1. What do Justin Lebo and Dwaina Brooks do to help people?

2. How does knowing the facts help you understand how Justin and Dwaina are making a difference?

3. Why do you think Justin and Dwaina help others?

4. What is the main idea of this selection?

5. Compare Dwaina Brooks with Doña Josefa in the story "The Gold Coin." How does each make a difference in her community? If they could meet, what kind of organization might they start together?

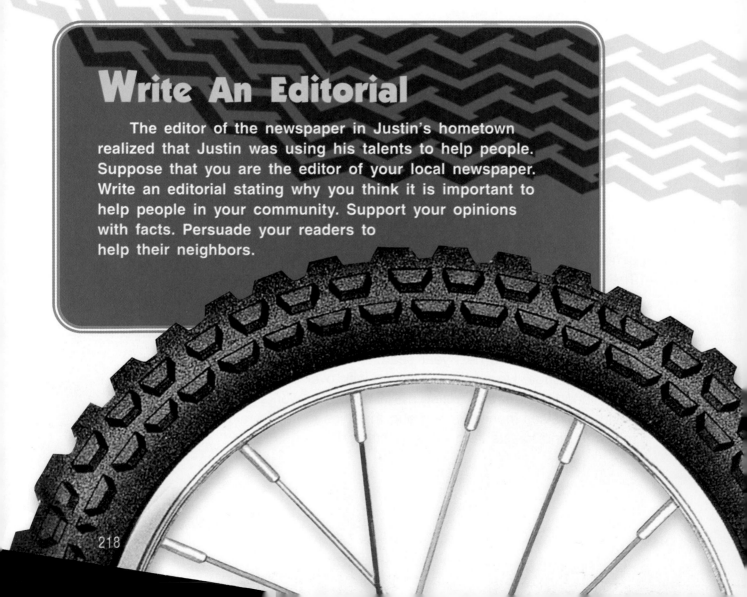

Write An Editorial

The editor of the newspaper in Justin's hometown realized that Justin was using his talents to help people. Suppose that you are the editor of your local newspaper. Write an editorial stating why you think it is important to help people in your community. Support your opinions with facts. Persuade your readers to help their neighbors.

Make a Poster

Justin made bicycles for orphaned, sick, or homeless children. Now it's your turn. Make a bicycle safety poster that he could share with those children. Use posterboard and markers to create your poster. Include the importance of wearing a helmet, as well as the rules cyclists should follow.

Create Word Problems

Justin fixed more than 150 bicycles. Determine how much you think it cost him to fix each bike. Use your own numbers—for example, cost of frame, $6.50; cost of paint, $3.25; cost of parts, $1.70, and other costs, $.45—for a total of $11.90 for each bicycle. Write four word problems using your numbers.

Find Out More

In the story, Dwaina's class is doing a unit on homelessness. Some students begin by calling shelters to get more information. How do people in your community help the homeless? Start by looking in a telephone directory for organizations that help homeless people. Contact churches and community centers. Speak with parents or teachers about ways your school or community can help the homeless.

219

Use a Telephone Directory

Do you remember how Justin finds out how to contact the Kilbarchan Home for Boys? He used a **telephone directory**. Most telephone directories have these three parts.

- **White Pages** list names in alphabetical order with addresses and telephone numbers. Some white pages may also have gray pages for business listings.
- **Yellow Pages** list businesses in alphabetical order by specialty, or type.
- **Blue Pages** list local, state, and federal government services.

PERMITS and
LICENSES..................................245-2277
POLICE HEADQUARTERS
100 S. Hughey Ave.
EMERGENCY 911
NON-EMERGENCY...................245-2525
SOCIAL SERVICES...................245-6565

BROOKS A 51 Court St 633-4815
BL 182 Lake Rd 639-2138
Carol 43 Randall Rd 639-4931
Gail 65 Centre Rd 633-6076
Harold 39 Moss Circle 633-5117
.................................675-9987

Loco Motion
135 Fairbanks............798-3177

Mel's Bike Shop
108 Waymore Circle...798-2133

Paterson Cycles
618 Mills Rd..............798-2400

Use the telephone directory to answer these questions.

1 People at the Homeless Shelter want to thank Dwaina and her mother for the meals. What can they use to find her number?

2 Dwaina and her friends want to find out about other shelters in their area. They look in the Blue Pages. What department should they call?

3 Suppose that Justin had to get a permit to repair bicycles. Which part of the Telephone Directory should he look in?

4 To find the phone number of Mel's Bike Shop, where would you look?

5 Why do you think businesses may be listed in both the Yellow and White pages?

TEST POWER

Test Tip

Read all the answer choices.
Then pick the best one.

DIRECTIONS

Read the sample story. Then read each question about the story.

SAMPLE

Jocelyn's Wet Feet

Jocelyn's neighbor had a beautiful garden of flowers. When Jocelyn stood close to the fence, she could smell the flowers' sweet <u>fragrance</u> in the air.

But when she stood close to the fence, she was likely to get her feet wet. Her neighbor left his sprinkler running nearly all the time, and the water collected at the fence to make a big puddle. Jocelyn loved smelling the flowers, but she didn't always like getting her feet wet.

One day, Jocelyn had a great idea. She would put rocks down on her side of the fence. She would be able to stand on them to keep her feet dry, and she could keep on smelling the flowers.

1 The word <u>fragrance</u> in this passage means —

A wetness

B odor

C rain

D sunshine

2 How does Jocelyn feel about the flowers?

F She enjoys them.

G She dislikes them.

H They annoy her.

J They make her concerned.

Why are these answers the best choices?

221

Stories in Art

This picture of a California highway is a special kind of collage. Notice that the artist uses his artwork to let you see something in a new way.

❧

Look at this picture. How is the sky unusual? What has the artist done to create this effect? How do the broken sky and blurred picture make you think that something is going to happen? What might that be?

❧

Look at this picture again. How is it more effective than a regular photograph? How does the artist make you feel as if you are riding down the highway? What do you think will happen at the end of the road?

detail of *Pearblossom Hwy.,*
11-18th April 1986
by David Hockney, 1986

222

Make Predictions

Develop a strategy for making, confirming, and revising predictions.

1. **Use the title** and illustration to help you predict what might happen in the selection.

2. **Pay attention** to the main characters' words and actions.

3. **As you read,** ask: What might happen next? Why do I think so?

4. **Read to see** if your predictions were correct.

5. **Revise predictions,** if necessary, and make new ones. Were the events in the story different from what you had predicted?

223

A Meeting with a Star

Hilary Hahn

*M*y name is Tina Dawson. I am not a musical star, but I practice my violin regularly, and I am improving. My best friend, Maria, and I play in a youth orchestra. I hope to play with a symphony someday.

My heroine is the violinist Hilary Hahn. When she was still a teenager, she began traveling around the world giving concerts. I've listened to her recordings and read her postcards on her Web site. She wrote about playing at Carnegie Hall in New York City. She seems really nice. I've always wanted to meet her.

On my eleventh birthday, Mom greeted me after school with an envelope. "Open it," she said, smiling. Inside were tickets to hear Hilary Hahn! I could not believe it! I immediately invited Maria. We could hardly wait!

The concert was awesome! I especially liked hearing Hilary play a concerto by J. S. Bach. Her fingers just flew!

After the applause, the conductor said, "Hilary will be happy to greet the audience after the concert."

As I shook Hilary's hand afterward and told her how much I had enjoyed her playing, Maria whispered, "Tina, genius just might be contagious!"

I haven't become a genius yet, but I have been inspired to practice more. It was a meeting I will never forget.

Dear Mr.

Henshaw

by Beverly Cleary
illustrated by R. J. Shay

Leigh Botts wants to be a famous author someday. He's been corresponding with his favorite author, Boyd Henshaw, who suggests that he keep a diary. Through his diary, Leigh learns a lot about himself and about the many changes going on in his life. Leigh's in a new school in a new town. He isn't finding it easy to make friends, and on top of that, someone keeps stealing things from his lunchbag. One day he rigs up a burglar alarm for a lunchbox, and it really works!

Leigh's parents are divorced, and he really misses his father, who drives a truck cross-country and is on the road most of the time. When he calls his father unexpectedly one day, he is about to take another boy and his mother out for pizza. Leigh worries that his father might remarry.

He also has other things on his mind. There's a Young Writers' contest at his school, and the prize will be lunch with a "Famous Author." Leigh is hoping to win.

Tuesday, March 20

Yesterday Miss Neely, the librarian, asked if I had written anything for the Young Writers' Yearbook, because all writing had to be turned in by tomorrow. When I told her I hadn't, she said I still had twenty-four hours and why didn't I get busy? So I did, because I really would like to meet a Famous Author. My story about the ten-foot wax man went into the wastebasket. Next I tried to start a story called *The Great Lunchbox Mystery,* but I couldn't seem to turn my lunchbox experience into a story because I don't know who the thief (thieves) was (were), and I don't want to know.

Finally I dashed off a description of the time I rode
with my father when he was trucking the load of grapes
down Highway 152 through Pacheco Pass to a winery.
I put in things like the signs that said STEEP GRADE, TRUCKS
USE LOW GEAR and how Dad down-shifted and how skillful
he was handling a long, heavy load on the curves. I put
in about the hawks on the telephone wires and about that
high peak where Black Bart's lookout used to watch for
travelers coming through the pass so he could signal to
Black Bart to rob them, and how the leaves on the trees
along the stream at the bottom of the pass were turning
yellow and how good tons of grapes smelled in the sun.
I left out the part about the waitresses and the video
games. Then I copied the whole thing over in case neat-
ness counts and gave it to Miss Neely.

Saturday, March 24

Mom said I had to invite Barry over to our house for
supper because I have been going to his house after
school so often. We had been working on a burglar alarm
for his room which we finally got to work with some help
from a library book.

I wasn't sure Barry would like to come to our house
which is so small compared to his, but he accepted when
I invited him.

Mom cooked a casserole full of good things like ground
beef, chilies, tortillas, tomatoes and cheese. Barry said he
really liked eating at our house because he got tired of eating with a bunch of little sisters waving spoons and drum-
sticks. That made me happy. It helps to have a friend.

Barry says his burglar alarm still works. The trouble is,
his little sisters think it's fun to open his door to set it off.
Then they giggle and hide. This was driving his mother
crazy, so he finally had to disconnect it. We all laughed
about this. Barry and I felt good about making something
that worked even if he can't use it.

Beep! Beep! Beep! Beep!

WARNING!
BURGLAR
ALARM

My friend, Barry.

from My Scrapebook

Barry saw the sign on my door that said KEEP OUT MOM THAT MEANS YOU. He asked if my Mom really stays out of my room. I said, "Sure, if I keep things picked up." Mom is not a snoop.

Barry said he wished he could have a room nobody ever went into. I was glad Barry didn't ask to use the bathroom. Maybe I'll start scrubbing off the mildew after all.

Sunday, March 25

I keep thinking about Dad and how lonely he sounded and wondering what happened to the pizza boy. I don't like to think about Dad being lonesome, but I don't like to think about the pizza boy cheering him up either.

Tonight at supper (beans and franks) I got up my courage to ask Mom if she thought Dad would get married again. She thought awhile and then said, "I don't see how he could afford to. He has big payments to make on the truck, and the price of diesel oil goes up all the time, and when people can't afford to build houses or buy cars, he won't be hauling lumber or cars."

I thought this over. I know that a license for a truck like his costs over a thousand dollars a year. "But he always sends my support payments," I said, "even if he is late sometimes."

"Yes, he does that," agreed my mother. "Your father isn't a bad man by any means."

Suddenly I was mad and disgusted with the whole thing. "Then why don't you two get married again?" I guess I wasn't very nice about the way I said it.

Mom looked me straight in the eye. "Because your father will never grow up," she said. I knew that was all she would ever say about it.

Tomorrow they give out the Young Writers' Yearbook! Maybe I will be lucky and get to go have lunch with the Famous Author.

Today wasn't the greatest day of my life. When our class went to the library, I saw a stack of Yearbooks and could hardly wait for Miss Neely to hand them out. When I finally got mine and opened it to the first page, there was a monster story, and I saw I hadn't won first prize. I kept turning. I didn't win second prize which went to a poem, and I didn't win third or fourth prize, either. Then I turned another page and saw Honorable Mention and under it:

A DAY ON DAD'S RIG
by
Leigh M. Botts

There was my title with my name under it in print, even if it was mimeographed print. I can't say I wasn't disappointed because I hadn't won a prize, I was. I was really disappointed about not getting to meet the mysterious Famous Author, but I liked seeing my name in print.

Some kids were mad because they didn't win or even get something printed. They said they wouldn't ever try to write again which I think is pretty dumb. I have heard that real authors sometimes have their books turned down. I figure you win some, you lose some.

Then Miss Neely announced that the Famous Author the winners would get to have lunch with was Angela Badger. The girls were more excited than the boys because Angela Badger writes mostly about girls with problems like big feet or pimples or something. I would still like to meet her because she is, as they say, a real live author, and I've never met a real live author. I am glad Mr. Henshaw isn't the author because then I would *really* be disappointed that I didn't get to meet him.

230

Friday, March 30

Today turned out to be exciting. In the middle of second period Miss Neely called me out of class and asked if I would like to go have lunch with Angela Badger. I said, "Sure, how come?"

Miss Neely explained that the teachers discovered that the winning poem had been copied out of a book and wasn't original so the girl who submitted it would not be allowed to go and would I like to go in her place? Would I!

Miss Neely telephoned Mom at work for permission and I gave my lunch to Barry because my lunches are better than his. The other winners were all dressed up, but I didn't care. I have noticed that authors like Mr. Henshaw usually wear old plaid shirts in the pictures on the back of their books. My shirt is just as old as his, so I knew it was OK.

Miss Neely drove us in her own car to the Holiday Inn, where some other librarians and their winners were waiting in the lobby. Then Angela Badger arrived with Mr. Badger, and we were all led into the dining room which was pretty crowded. One of the librarians who was a sort of Super Librarian told the winners to sit at a long table with a sign that said Reserved. Angela Badger sat in the middle and some of the girls pushed to sit beside her. I sat across from her. Super Librarian explained that we could choose our lunch from the salad bar. Then all the librarians went off and sat at a table with Mr. Badger.

There I was face to face with a real live author who seemed like a nice lady, plump with wild hair, and I couldn't think of a thing to say because I hadn't read her books. Some girls told her how much they loved her books, but some of the boys and girls were too shy to say anything. Nothing seemed to happen until Mrs. Badger said, "Why don't we all go help ourselves to lunch at the salad bar?"

What a mess! Some people didn't understand about salad bars, but Mrs. Badger led the way and we helped ourselves to lettuce and bean salad and potato salad and all the usual stuff they lay out on salad bars. A few of the younger kids were too short to reach anything but the bowls on the first rows. They weren't doing too well until Mrs. Badger helped them out. Getting lunch took a long time, longer than in a school cafeteria, and when we carried our plates back to our table, people at other tables ducked and dodged as if they expected us to dump our lunches on their heads. All one boy had on his plate was a piece of lettuce and a slice of tomato because he thought he was going to get to go back for roast beef and fried chicken. We had to straighten him out and explain that all we got was salad. He turned red and went back for more salad.

"A Day On Dad's Rig"

by

Leigh M. Botts

I was still trying to think of something interesting to say to Mrs. Badger while I chased garbanzo beans around my plate with a fork. A couple of girls did all the talking, telling Mrs. Badger how they wanted to write books exactly like hers. The other librarians were busy talking and laughing with Mr. Badger who seemed to be a lot of fun.

Mrs. Badger tried to get some of the shy people to say something without much luck, and I still couldn't think of anything to say to a lady who wrote books about girls with big feet or pimples. Finally Mrs. Badger looked straight at me and asked, "What did you write for the Yearbook?"

I felt myself turn red and answered, "Just something about a ride on a truck."

"Oh!" said Mrs. Badger. "So you're the author of *A Day on Dad's Rig!*"

Everyone was quiet. None of us had known the real live author would have read what we had written, but she had and she remembered my title.

A Mess!

HONORABLE MENTION
Young writer's yearbook
This is to certify that

Leigh M. Botts

completed with honors a written story about a personal experience
and is to be congratulated for an assignment well done.

Teacher

Author

234

"I just got honorable mention," I said, but I was thinking, She called me an author. *A real live author called me an author.*

"What difference does that make?" asked Mrs. Badger. "Judges never agree. I happened to like *A Day on Dad's Rig* because it was written by a boy who wrote honestly about something he knew and had strong feelings about. You made me feel what it was like to ride down a steep grade with tons of grapes behind me."

"But I couldn't make it into a story," I said, feeling a whole lot braver.

"Who cares?" said Mrs. Badger with a wave of her hand. She's the kind of person who wears rings on her forefingers. "What do you expect? The ability to write stories comes later, when you have lived longer and have more understanding. *A Day on Dad's Rig* was splendid work for a boy your age. You wrote like *you,* and you did not try to imitate someone else. This is one mark of a good writer. Keep it up."

I noticed a couple of girls who had been saying they wanted to write books exactly like Angela Badger exchange embarrassed looks.

"Gee, thanks," was all I could say. The waitress began to plunk down dishes of ice cream. Everyone got over being shy and began to ask Mrs. Badger if she wrote in pencil or on the typewriter and did she ever have books rejected and were her characters real people and did she ever have pimples when she was a girl like the girl in her book and what did it feel like to be a famous author?

I didn't think answers to those questions were very important, but I did have one question I wanted to ask which I finally managed to get in at the last minute when Mrs. Badger was autographing some books people had brought.

"Mrs. Badger," I said, "did you ever meet Boyd Henshaw?"

"Why, yes," she said, scribbling away in someone's book. "I once met him at a meeting of librarians where we were on the same program."

"What's he like?" I asked over the head of a girl crowding up with her book.

"He's a very nice young man with a wicked twinkle in his eye," she answered. I think I have known that since the time he answered my questions when Miss Martinez made us write to an author.

On the ride home everybody was chattering about Mrs. Badger this, and Mrs. Badger that. I didn't want to talk. I just wanted to think. A real live author had called *me* an author. A real live author had told me to keep it up. Mom was proud of me when I told her.

Meet Beverly Cleary

In 1982, Beverly Cleary received several letters from boys who had read her books. "Please," they suggested, "write a book about a boy whose parents are divorced." As she thought about this, she began to get ideas. She overheard a remark about a father who forgot to call his son as promised. She learned about a student who had rigged up a burglar alarm for his lunchbox. These bits and pieces went into the book. Cleary says, *"Dear Mr. Henshaw* was a most satisfying book to write. It seemed almost to write itself."

Surprisingly, Cleary was a poor reader when she began school. By the third grade, however, she had learned to read and to love books. In fact, her school librarian suggested that Cleary write children's books when she grew up. Cleary liked the idea but didn't write her first book until many years later. When she and her husband moved into a new house, they found several packages of blank paper in a closet. Her husband gave her a pencil sharpener, and she began to write. Her first book, *Henry Huggins,* was an instant success, as was its sequel, *Henry and Beezus*. Cleary has won many awards for her writing, including two Newbery Honor Awards for her books about a girl named Ramona and a Newbery Medal for *Dear Mr. Henshaw*.

Story Questions & Activities

1 What special event does Leigh Botts want to attend?

2 Why is Leigh's story so important to him?

3 What makes Leigh a good writer? Explain.

4 Which events in the story turned out as you expected? Which events were the opposite of what you thought would happen?

5 Imagine that Leigh is writing in his journal about the picture on page 222. What do you think it would remind him of? What would he say?

Write a Letter

Beverly Cleary says that she wrote *Dear Mr. Henshaw* because several boys had written her letters asking her to "write a book about a boy whose parents are divorced." Write a letter to your favorite author. Try to persuade him or her to write a book about a subject that is important to you. Convince the writer that many students your age would want to read the book.

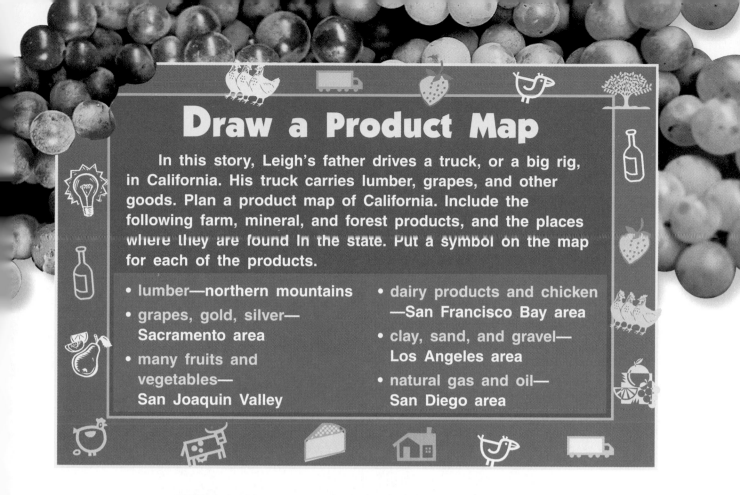

Draw a Product Map

In this story, Leigh's father drives a truck, or a big rig, in California. His truck carries lumber, grapes, and other goods. Plan a product map of California. Include the following farm, mineral, and forest products, and the places where they are found in the state. Put a symbol on the map for each of the products.

- lumber—northern mountains
- grapes, gold, silver— Sacramento area
- many fruits and vegetables— San Joaquin Valley

- dairy products and chicken —San Francisco Bay area
- clay, sand, and gravel— Los Angeles area
- natural gas and oil— San Diego area

Make a Poster

Leigh and his friend Barry invent a burglar alarm that uses a battery, a light switch, and a doorbell. Brainstorm a list of inventions with a group of your classmates. Choose one and make a poster to show how to use it.

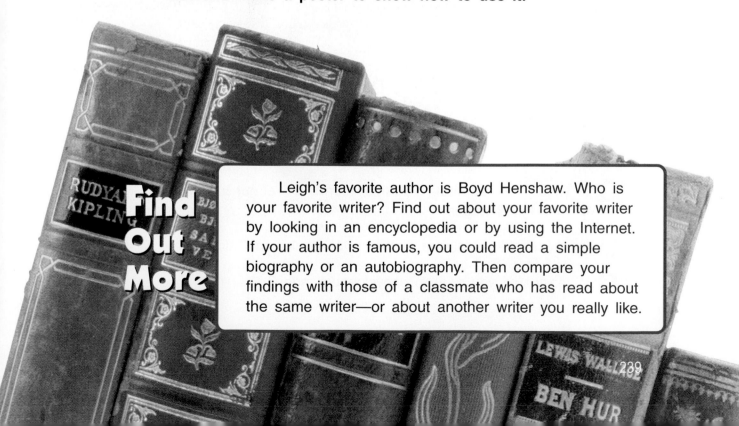

Find Out More

Leigh's favorite author is Boyd Henshaw. Who is your favorite writer? Find out about your favorite writer by looking in an encyclopedia or by using the Internet. If your author is famous, you could read a simple biography or an autobiography. Then compare your findings with those of a classmate who has read about the same writer—or about another writer you really like.

Use an Encyclopedia Index

Where would you look to find a topic quickly in an encyclopedia? You could check the **encyclopedia index**. The index is the last book in the set of encyclopedias.

Look at the sample entries below from an encyclopedia index. Notice the capital letter after the main entry. It is the letter *C*. This means that you will find articles and information about California, for example, in the *C* volume. Keep in mind that some encyclopedias are arranged by volume numbers only, not by letters. After the colon (:) in the **entries**, you will find the page number on which the information appears.

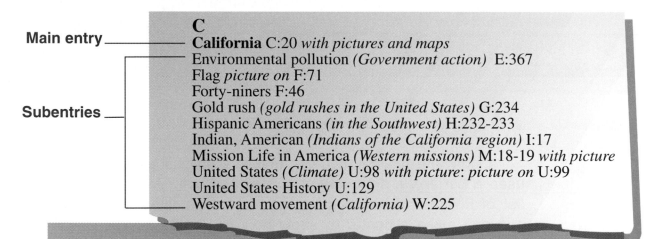

Main entry

Subentries

C

California C:20 *with pictures and maps*
Environmental pollution *(Government action)* E:367
Flag *picture on* F:71
Forty-niners F:46
Gold rush *(gold rushes in the United States)* G:234
Hispanic Americans *(in the Southwest)* H:232-233
Indian, American *(Indians of the California region)* I:17
Mission Life in America *(Western missions)* M:18-19 *with picture*
United States *(Climate)* U:98 *with picture: picture on* U:99
United States History U:129
Westward movement *(California)* W:225

Use the sample entries from an encyclopedia index to answer these questions.

1 On which page does the encyclopedia article about California begin?

2 Does the article about California show maps of the state? How do you know?

3 In which volume would you find information about the climate of the United States?

4 Where might you find a picture of a mission in California?

5 When would you use an encyclopedia index?

TEST POWER

Test Tip

Look in the story for clues about the character's feelings.

DIRECTIONS

Read the sample story. Then read each question about the story.

SAMPLE

Angelo's Accident

Madeline had been home only a few minutes when the phone rang.

She picked up the receiver. "Hello," she said.

"Hi, Madeline. This is Mr. Lee. While your brother, Angelo, was here at Judo lessons, he stepped on a rusty nail in the locker room. Do you know if he has had a tetanus shot recently?"

At first, the news of the incident was a shock to Madeline. She quickly regained her composure, though, and said, "Hold on and I'll check." She told her mother what had happened. Her mother went into her office and looked in the cabinet for the children's medical records. She pulled out Angelo's file and went back to the phone.

"Mr. Lee?" she said. "This is Angelo's mother. His records <u>indicate</u> that he had a tetanus shot last year. He should be all set."

1   In this passage, the word <u>indicate</u> means —

A   keep

B   ask

C   show

D   try

2   How did Madeline feel when she first heard that her brother had stepped on a nail?

F   helpful

G   worried

H   happy

J   bored

Stories in Art

These rows of life-size terra-cotta soldiers were discovered in the tomb of China's first emperor. Today, more than 7,000 clay soldiers and horses have been uncovered.

Look at the scene in the photograph. What can you tell about it? Notice the details. Why do you think the Chinese emperor wanted so many soldiers in his tomb? How do you think the archaeologists felt when they uncovered this "find"?

Look at the photograph again. How would you state its main idea?

Terra-cotta Soldiers, **circa 220** B.C.
Qin Shi Huangdi Tomb, Bingmayong, Xian, China

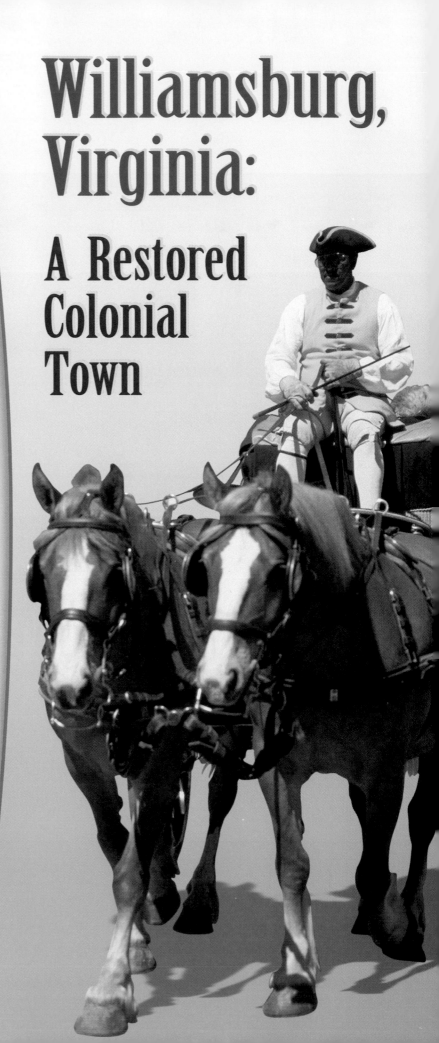

Williamsburg, Virginia:
A Restored Colonial Town

READING STRATEGY

Main Idea

Develop a strategy for finding the main idea and supporting details.

1 **Read the title and subtitle.** How do they help you focus your reading?

2 **Look at the facts** and examples. What do most of them tell about? Can you figure out the main idea from this?

3 **Look for details that support the main idea.** Which details answer *who, what, why, when,* and *where?*

4 **Study the time line.** How do details on the time line support the main idea?

5 **State the main idea in your own words.** Ask yourself: What is the most important idea I learned from this article?

243

The Capitol Building in Williamsburg, Virginia

YEAR	EVENT
1698–1699	English Colonial government moves to Williamsburg
1704–1705	Capitol building completed
1759	George Washington takes seat
1765	Patrick Henry speaks there
1779	Building is last used as a capitol
1832	East Wing burns
1928	Reconstruction begins

Williamsburg, Virginia, is a town with an important history. Before the American Revolution, Virginia was England's most powerful colony. Williamsburg was its capital. In this famous city, George Washington and Thomas Jefferson planned the future of the United States.

In 1780, the capital of Virginia moved to Richmond. Williamsburg was now a quiet county seat.

Then, when Dr. Goodwin moved to town in 1903, the future of Williamsburg brightened. Goodwin loved history, and he had a great idea. He wanted to restore the colonial city and preserve its history. John D. Rockefeller, one of the world's richest people, agreed to pay for the project.

Teams of historians, architects, and builders were hired. They restored libraries, churches, meeting halls, and homes.

Today, Williamsburg is a living history museum, recreating a town where teachers, lawyers, merchants, and craftspeople lived with their families. The townspeople are really actors wearing costumes. Three million people visit Williamsburg each year. They glimpse colonial life and walk in the footsteps of our colonial ancestors.

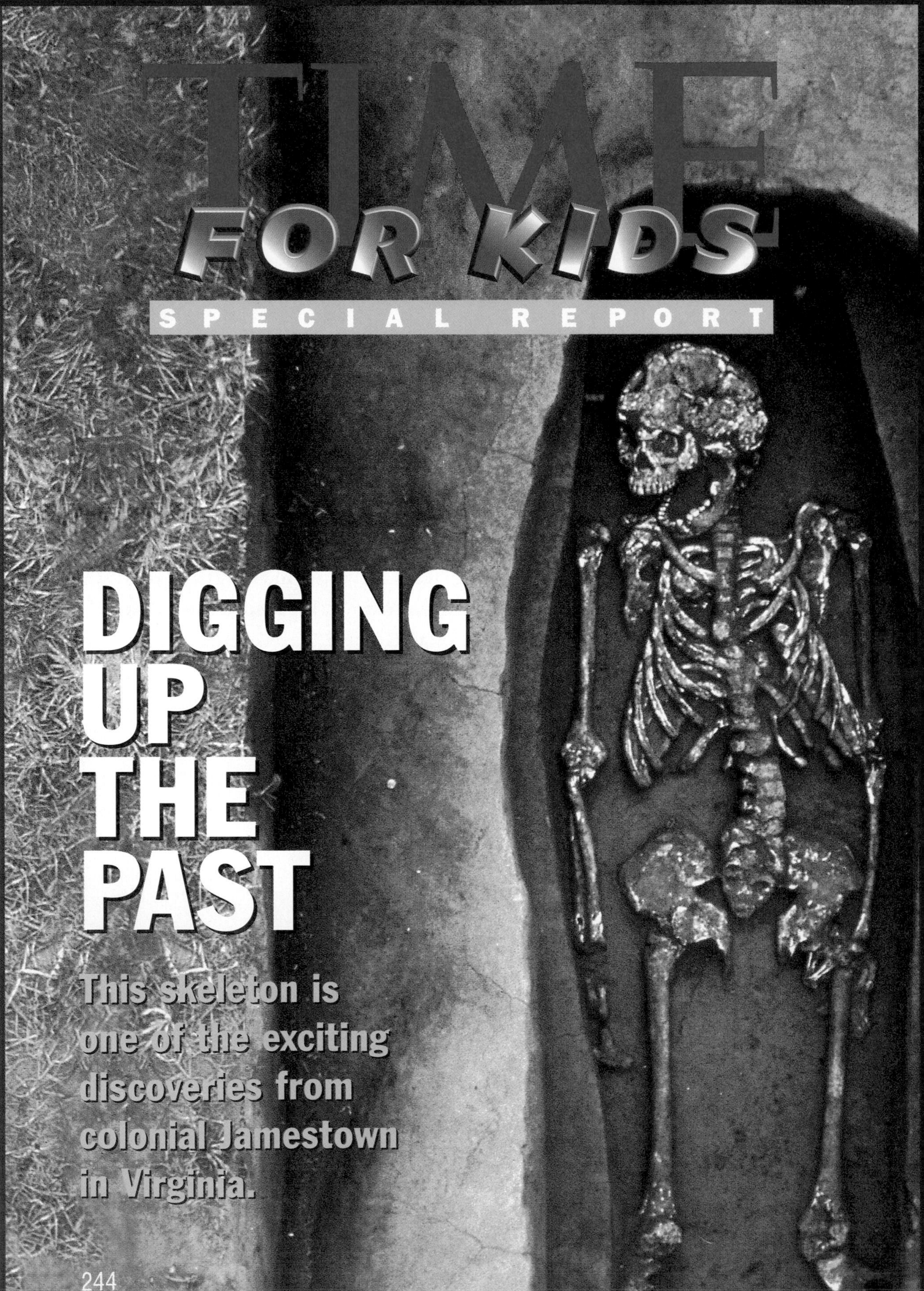

TIME FOR KIDS

SPECIAL REPORT

DIGGING UP THE PAST

This skeleton is one of the exciting discoveries from colonial Jamestown in Virginia.

Rediscovering Jamestown

New finds show what life was like for America's first English settlers

Brent Smith, 9, of Houston, Texas, cannot take his eyes off the skeleton. Lying in a glass case at the National Geographic Society in Washington, D.C., the skeleton—with a bullet in its right leg—is a mystery. "I just need to know what happened to this guy," says Brent. "What was his name? How did he die?"

That's what historians are wondering, too. The skeleton is nearly 400 years old. It was found in Jamestown, Virginia, site of the first permanent English settlement in America. For years, people thought that the old fort there had been washed away by the James River. But new discoveries, including this skeleton, coins, candlesticks, armor, and arrowheads, prove that the fort and its clues to colonial life are buried under the soil.

Visitors to Jamestown National Park in Virginia can watch archaeologists search for buried treasures at the colonists' original fort.

A model shows how the 1607 fort once looked.

245

Copper pennies like these were probably traded between the settlers and Native Americans.

A family crest on this brass ring (right), links it to William Strachey, secretary of the colony in 1610.

A CITY THAT WASN'T BUILT TO LAST

On May 13, 1607, a ship carrying 104 men and boys from England arrived in Virginia. They named their settlement Jamestown, after Britain's King James. The soil and climate seemed just right for a new home.

The colonists built a triangle-shaped fort along the river to protect themselves from the Spanish and the Native Americans. Over the next few years, disease, starvation, and attacks by the Powhatan tribe killed many settlers.

In those early days, Jamestown was Virginia's capital. Then after a fire destroyed some important buildings there in 1698, the state capital was moved to Williamsburg. Eventually Jamestown began to disappear above ground.

DUSTING OFF HISTORY

But what about underground? In April 1994, archaeologist Bill Kelso and others discovered an interesting spot.

Settlers seem to have tossed garbage, including fish bones and waste iron, into pits like this one at the fort site.

246

OPPOSITE PAGE And JOHN SMITH: ASSOCIATION FOR THE PRESERVATION OF VIRGINIA ANTIQUITIES; POCAHONTAS: VIRGINIA HISTORICAL SOCIETY

"There was a piece of ground, shaped like a triangle, that no one had ever put a shovel into," Kelso recalled.

Kelso and his team soon found bits of pottery that could only have been from the 1607 fort. "That first day, we knew we had found it!"

Since then, archaeologists have uncovered more than 180,000 artifacts from the early 1600s, including beads, keys, and toys. And only a fraction of the fort's grounds have been explored! "We don't dig things up, we uncover them," says Kelso. The process requires care: "You just can't hurry it up."

CLUES TO COLONIAL LIFE

The discoveries are giving scientists and historians the best picture ever of how early colonists lived. Pistols, knives, and armor tell the story of a violent time. And skeletons give clues to how these people died.

Archaeologists will continue their search for several more years. They hope to come up with more answers for kids like Brent Smith. He looks one last time at the skeleton and says, "Wow! I really like knowing what happened 400 years ago!"

FIND OUT MORE
Visit our website:
www.mhschool.com/reading

*inter*NET
CONNECTION

Pocahontas and Captain John Smith

Everyone knows the tale of how Pocahontas rescued Captain John Smith from her father, Chief Powhatan. But is it true? No one can say. What's certain is that Pocahontas came to like the English settlers after they kidnapped her to use as a bargaining chip with the chief. She learned English, was renamed Rebecca, and wed farmer John Rolfe in 1614.

In 1616, Pocahontas and Rolfe toured England with their infant son, Thomas. Pocahontas delighted King James and was treated like a princess. But just before the family was to return to Virginia, she fell ill and died. She is buried in England.

Based on an article in *TIME FOR KIDS*.

Story Questions & Activities

1. What happened in Virginia on May 13, 1607?

2. What is being discovered at the Jamestown settlement?

3. Why is the rediscovery of Jamestown important?

4. What is the main idea of this selection?

5. Imagine that one of the archaeologists rediscovering Jamestown has just stepped into the picture on page 242. How would he compare this find with the one at Jamestown?

Write a Plan

It costs a lot of money to send archaeologists on a "dig." Travel, tools, and workers are expensive. Imagine that you are an archaeologist. Choose a place you would like to "uncover," such as Atlantis or an Egyptian pharaoh's tomb. Write a plan for your project, and give a list of possible expenses. Try to persuade the United States government to pay for your "dig." Give three good reasons.

Make a List

Imagine that 400 years from now a group of archaeologists "uncover" your school. What artifacts will they find? Make a list of artifacts left behind, such as pens, notebooks, chalkboards, and computers. Next to each item on your list, explain what it tells about you, your classmates, your school, or your community.

Create a Glossary

This selection uses special vocabulary, such as *settlement, historian, artifacts,* and *dig.* What do these words mean? What other words might archaeologists use in uncovering secrets from the past? Use these words to create your own glossary. Go through the selection and choose other special vocabulary words. List the words in alphabetical order. Then give the pronunciation and meaning, the part of speech, and an example sentence for each word. Use a dictionary or the glossary in the back of this book to guide you.

Find Out More

Jamestown was the first successful English settlement in North America. What made this colony successful? Who helped the settlers survive? How did the colonists get along with the Powhatan, the Native Americans in the area? Start by looking in your social studies textbook. Then use an encyclopedia or the Internet to find out more information about Jamestown, the Powhatan, Pocahontas, or John Smith. Use the information to create a diorama, or shadow box, of the early Jamestown settlement.

STUDY SKILLS

Conduct an Interview

One way to get information about someone is to interview them. Suppose you were going to interview Pocahontas. What questions would you ask? Like a letter or a dialogue, an **interview** follows a pattern of questions and answers. Here are some ways you can prepare for an interview.

- Decide the questions you will ask beforehand.
- Make note cards of the main questions.

Then follow these speaking and listening guidelines.

SPEAKING AND LISTENING GUIDELINES:
An Interview
- State the purpose of the interview clearly.
- Be polite. Ask questions simply and directly.
- Listen closely to the answers and take notes about them.
- Ask questions to get more information about an answer.

Use the information about interviewing to answer these questions.

1 Why is it important to know something about the person you are interviewing before the interview?

2 Why should you write down the questions you will ask?

3 Why do you need to take notes during the interview?

4 Why are good speaking and listening skills important during an interview?

5 What kind of information can you get from an interview that you cannot get from a book or another source?

250

TEST POWER

DIRECTIONS

Read the sample story. Then read each question about the story.

SAMPLE

Bicycle for Sale!

Arthur was leafing through the classified section of the morning newspaper when he saw an ad that caught his attention. He read it twice before he called over his mother.

"Mom, this is what I've been waiting for," he said excitedly.

Arthur's mother looked over his shoulder. "Let's call them right now. This sounds exactly like what you had in mind," she said.

ARTICLES FOR SALE

BICYCLE FOR SALE! MUST SELL IMMEDIATELY!
Fire-engine red mountain bike in mint condition. New tires, new seat, 10-speed, state-of-the-art handlebar brakes. Perfect for dirt trails, mountain paths, or cruising on rocky terrain. Only two years old. Comes with a warranty. Price negotiable. Call now! Talk to Mike at 555-1212

MOUNTAIN BICYCLE FOR SALE

1 The author gives you enough information to conclude that —

A Arthur was looking for a new bicycle

B Arthur's mother thought that he should have a faster bike

C Arthur often read the newspaper

D Arthur wanted to buy a new sled

2 According to the advertisement, this bicycle is mainly for —

F riding to school

G riding on rough trails

H riding on smooth surfaces

J riding on the sidewalk

I HEAR AMERICA SINGING

I hear America singing, the varied carols I hear,

Those of mechanics, each one singing his as it should be
blithe and strong,

The carpenter singing his as he measures his plank or beam,

The mason singing his as he makes ready for work, or
leaves off work,

The boatman singing what belongs to him in his boat, the
deckhand singing on the steamboat deck,

The shoemaker singing as he sits on his bench, the hatter
singing as he stands,

The wood-cutter's song, the ploughboy's on his way in the
morning, or at noon intermission or at sundown,

The delicious singing of the mother, or of the young wife
at work, or of the girl sewing and washing,

Each singing what belongs to him or her and to none else,

The day what belongs to the day—at night the party of
young fellows, robust, friendly,

Singing with open mouths their strong melodious songs.

by Walt Whitman

253

iMAGiNE THAT!

THE SIDEWALK RACER OR – ON THE SKATEBOARD

Skimming
  an asphalt sea
    I swerve, I curve, I
      sway, I speed to whirring
    sound an inch above the
    ground; I'm the sailor
   and the sail, I'm the
  driver and the wheel
I'm the one and only
  single engine
    human auto
      mobile.

by Lillian Morrison

Stories in Art

Sculptures Reno, Nevada

Sculptors create sculpture from almost anything—scraps of wood, metal, and other "found objects." They even create sculptures from scraps of old cars!

Look at these sculptures. What do they remind you of? Do you think the cars were there before the sculptor started working? How do you think he made these sculptures? What did he do first? Next? Last?

What can you create from the materials around you? How can you join them together to make a sculpture? What steps would you follow as sculptors do?

Steps in a Process

Develop a strategy for identifying steps in a process.

1 **Read the title** and beginning of the story. What is the story about?

2 **Identify what process** is being described.

3 **Look for clue words,** such as *first, now,* and *after,* to help you understand the order of steps.

4 **Check your understanding** as you read. Ask yourself: Could I follow these steps?

5 **Use your own words** to retell the order of steps.

The Spelling Bee

Peter walked through the door. He looked unhappy.

"What's wrong?" his sister Emily asked.

"We have a spelling bee on Friday. I know most of the words, but I get nervous in front of the class."

"That used to happen to me, but I learned how to stay calm."

"Really? How? Will you teach me?"

"Sure, but it's a lot of work. First, stand up. Now imagine you're in front of the class."

Peter did as he was told. Right away he could feel his stomach tighten and twist.

Emily looked at Peter's word list. "Spell *pleasant*," she said. Right after that, she made a funny face at him by squinting her eyes and puffing out her cheeks and lips.

Peter laughed. "P-l-e-a-s-a-n-t," he said.

"Very good," Emily said. She continued down the word list. After each word, she made a face. Peter's stomach ache disappeared.

Friday came, and Peter knew he was ready. He stood in front of the class and heard his teacher say, "Peter, spell *pleasant*." He imagined Emily with her puffed-out cheeks and turned-up nose. Instantly, his nervousness vanished. He smiled, spelled the word correctly, and thought that he just might win!

the MARBLE

by Gary Soto

CHAMP

illustrated by Ken Spengler

Lupe Medrano, a shy girl who spoke in whispers, was the school's spelling bee champion, winner of the reading contest at the public library three summers in a row, blue ribbon awardee in the science fair, the top student at her piano recital, and the playground grand champion in chess. She was a straight-A student and—not counting kindergarten, when she had been stung by a wasp—never missed one day of elementary school. She had received a small trophy for this honor and had been congratulated by the mayor.

But though Lupe had a razor-sharp mind, she could not make her body, no matter how much she tried, run as fast as the other girls'. She begged her body to move faster, but could never beat anyone in the fifty-yard dash.

The truth was that Lupe was no good in sports. She could not catch a pop-up or figure out in which direction to kick the soccer ball. One time she kicked the ball at her own goal and scored a point for the other team. She was no good at baseball or basketball either, and even had a hard time making a hula hoop stay on her hips.

It wasn't until last year, when she was eleven years old, that she learned how to ride a bike. And even then she had to use training wheels. She could walk in the swimming pool but couldn't swim, and chanced roller skating only when her father held her hand.

"I'll never be good at sports," she fumed one rainy day as she lay on her bed gazing at the shelf her father had made to hold her awards. "I wish I could win something, anything, even marbles."

At the word "marbles," she sat up. "That's it. Maybe I could be good at playing marbles." She hopped out of bed and rummaged through the closet until she found a can full of her brother's marbles. She poured the rich glass treasure on her bed and picked five of the most beautiful marbles.

She smoothed her bedspread and practiced shooting, softly at first so that her aim would be accurate. The marble rolled from her thumb and clicked against the targeted marble. But the target wouldn't budge. She tried

"She poured the rich glass treasure on her bed..."

"...the bedspread was slowing the marbles."

again and again. Her aim became accurate, but the power from her thumb made the marble move only an inch or two. Then she realized that the bedspread was slowing the marbles. She also had to admit that her thumb was weaker than the neck of a newborn chick.

She looked out the window. The rain was letting up, but the ground was too muddy to play. She sat cross-legged on the bed, rolling her five marbles between her palms. Yes, she thought, I could play marbles, and marbles is a sport. At that moment she realized that she had only two weeks to practice. The playground championship, the same one her brother had entered the previous year, was coming up. She had a lot to do.

To strengthen her wrists, she decided to do twenty push-ups on her fingertips, five at a time. "One, two, three . . ." she groaned. By the end of the first set she was breathing hard, and her muscles burned from exhaustion. She did one more set and decided that was enough push-ups for the first day.

She squeezed a rubber eraser one hundred times, hoping it would strengthen her thumb. This seemed to work because the next day her thumb was sore. She could hardly hold a marble in her hand, let alone send it flying with power. So Lupe rested that day and listened to her brother, who gave her tips on how to shoot: get low, aim with one eye, and place one knuckle on the ground.

"Think 'eye and thumb' and let it rip!" he said.

After school the next day she left her homework in her backpack and practiced three hours straight, taking time only to eat a candy bar for energy. With a popsicle stick, she drew an odd-shaped circle and tossed in four marbles. She used her shooter, a milky agate with hypnotic swirls, to blast them. Her thumb *had* become stronger.

After practice, she squeezed the eraser for an hour. She ate dinner with her left hand to spare her shooting hand and said nothing to her parents about her dreams of athletic glory.

Practice, practice, practice. Squeeze, squeeze, squeeze. Lupe got better and beat her brother and Alfonso, a neighbor kid who was supposed to be a champ.

"Man, she's bad!" Alfonso said. "She can beat the other girls for sure. I think."

The weeks passed quickly. Lupe worked so hard that one day, while she was drying dishes, her mother asked why her thumb was swollen.

"It's muscle," Lupe explained. "I've been practicing for the marbles championship."

"You, honey?" Her mother knew Lupe was no good at sports.

"Yeah. I beat Alfonso, and he's pretty good."

That night, over dinner, Mrs. Medrano said, "Honey, you should see Lupe's thumb."

"Huh?" Mr. Medrano said, wiping his mouth and looking at his daughter.

"Show your father."

"Do I have to?" an embarrassed Lupe asked.

"Go on, show your father."

Reluctantly, Lupe raised her hand and flexed her thumb. You could see the muscle.

The father put down his fork and asked, "What happened?"

"Dad, I've been working out. I've been squeezing an eraser."

"Why?"

"I'm going to enter the marbles championship."

Her father looked at her mother and then back at his daughter. "When is it, honey?"

"This Saturday. Can you come?"

The father had been planning to play racquetball with a friend Saturday, but he said he would be there. He knew his daughter thought she was no good at sports and he wanted to encourage her. He even rigged some lights in the backyard so she could practice after dark. He squatted with one knee on the ground, entranced by the sight of his daughter easily beating her brother.

"…Lupe raised her hand and flexed her thumb."

The day of the championship began with a cold blustery sky. The sun was a silvery light behind slate clouds.

"I hope it clears up," her father said, rubbing his hands together as he returned from getting the newspaper. They ate breakfast, paced nervously around the house waiting for 10:00 to arrive, and walked the two blocks to the playground (though Mr. Medrano wanted to drive so Lupe wouldn't get tired). She signed up and was assigned her first match on baseball diamond number three.

Lupe, walking between her brother and her father, shook from the cold, not nerves. She took off her mittens, and everyone stared at her thumb. Someone asked, "How can you play with a broken thumb?" Lupe smiled and said nothing.

She beat her first opponent easily, and felt sorry for the girl because she didn't have anyone to cheer for her. Except for her sack of marbles, she was all alone. Lupe invited the girl, whose name was Rachel, to stay with them. She smiled and said, "OK." The four of them walked to a card table in the middle of the outfield, where Lupe was assigned another opponent.

She also beat this girl, a fifth-grader named Yolanda, and asked her to join their group. They proceeded to more matches and more wins, and soon there was a crowd of people following Lupe to the finals to play a girl in a baseball cap. This girl seemed dead serious. She never even looked at Lupe.

"I don't know, Dad, she looks tough."

Rachel hugged Lupe and said, "Go get her."

"You can do it," her father encouraged. "Just think of the marbles, not the girl, and let your thumb do the work."

The other girl broke first and earned one marble. She missed her next shot, and Lupe, one eye closed, her thumb quivering with energy, blasted two marbles out of the circle but missed her next shot. Her opponent earned two more before missing. She stamped her foot and said

"It was now six to six..."

"Shoot!" The score was three to two in favor of Miss Baseball Cap.

The referee stopped the game. "Back up, please, give them room," he shouted. Onlookers had gathered too tightly around the players.

Lupe then earned three marbles and was set to get her fourth when a gust of wind blew dust in her eyes and she missed badly. Her opponent quickly scored two marbles, tying the game, and moved ahead six to five on a lucky shot. Then she missed, and Lupe, whose eyes felt scratchy when she blinked, relied on instinct and thumb muscle to score the tying point. It was now six to six, with only three marbles left. Lupe blew her nose and studied the angles. She dropped to one knee, steadied her hand, and shot so hard she cracked two marbles from the circle. She was the winner!

"I did it!" Lupe said under her breath. She rose from her knees, which hurt from bending all day, and hugged her father. He hugged her back and smiled.

Everyone clapped, except Miss Baseball Cap, who made a face and stared at the ground. Lupe told her she was a great player, and they shook hands. A newspaper photographer took pictures of the two girls standing shoulder-to-shoulder, with Lupe holding the bigger trophy.

Lupe then played the winner of the boys' division, and after a poor start beat him eleven to four. She blasted the marbles, shattering one into sparkling slivers of glass. Her opponent looked on glumly as Lupe did what she did best—win!

"... she displayed her trophies..."

The head referee and the President of the Fresno Marble Association stood with Lupe as she displayed her trophies for the newspaper photographer. Lupe shook hands with everyone, including a dog who had come over to see what the commotion was all about.

That night, the family went out for pizza and set the two trophies on the table for everyone in the restaurant to see. People came up to congratulate Lupe, and she felt a little embarrassed, but her father said the trophies belonged there.

Back home, in the privacy of her bedroom, she placed the trophies on her shelf and was happy. She had always earned honors because of her brains, but winning in sports was a new experience. She thanked her tired thumb. "You did it, thumb. You made me champion." As its reward, Lupe went to the bathroom, filled the bathroom sink with warm water, and let her thumb swim and splash as it pleased. Then she climbed into bed and drifted into a hard-won sleep.

meet Gary Soto

Gary Soto grew up in Fresno, California—the town where "The Marble Champ" takes place—in the agricultural Central Valley. Many of the other stories in his book *Baseball in April and Other Stories* are also based on his youth and Mexican heritage. In simple, realistic language, he tells how it feels to grow up Chicano in California. Soto has also begun making short films based on his stories.

Though he hopes his work speaks to everybody, Soto has a specific audience in mind. "My target is Mexican children," he says. "It's really to make them feel that their story is as important as anyone else's story."

Story Questions & Activities

1. What does Lupe do to become good at marbles?

2. What makes marbles a good sport for Lupe?

3. How would you apply this saying to the story: "Practice makes perfect"? Explain.

4. What would you say in a summary of this story?

5. Suppose that Lupe could meet Wilma Rudolph in "Wilma Unlimited." Do you think they would agree on a strategy for winning? Why or why not?

Write Instructions

Lupe prepared to become the marble champ by practicing and by following the instructions that explained the game. Now think of your favorite game or sport. Write the instructions that will explain how to play it. Be sure to include a diagram to illustrate the steps.

Draw a Pie Graph

At one point in the marbles championship, the score stood six to six. Later, Lupe played the winner of the boys' division and beat him eleven to four. Most sports or games involve numbers. Choose a team of a sport you enjoy and find out their winning or losing percentages. Divide the number of games won (or lost) by the total number of games played. For example, if a team played 50 games and won 32, you would write 32/50, or 64 percent. Draw a pie graph to illustrate the percentages.

Observe the Laws of Motion

What happens when an object is acted upon by a force? The object moves. Place marbles on a level table and blow on them. Your breath is a force that makes the marbles roll. The marbles will not move if no force is applied. Observe other objects to see what makes them move.

Find Out More

The game of marbles is not new. In fact, it has been around for centuries. Find out how this game, or another ancient game, started and how it has changed over the years. What are the rules for different games of marbles? Use an encyclopedia or another book and share your findings with a partner.

Follow Instructions

Instructions for a game explain how to play, step-by-step. Read instructions carefully. Don't leave out any steps, or you might not be able to do the next one! Instructions for playing jacks are below.

Like marbles, the game of jacks is played in different forms throughout the world. In Brazil, children play a game called *Cinco Marias*. Children in Zimbabwe know the game as *Iguni*, while in Tibet, it is called *Abhadhö*.

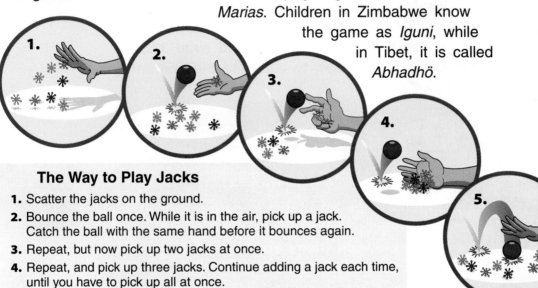

The Way to Play Jacks

1. Scatter the jacks on the ground.
2. Bounce the ball once. While it is in the air, pick up a jack. Catch the ball with the same hand before it bounces again.
3. Repeat, but now pick up two jacks at once.
4. Repeat, and pick up three jacks. Continue adding a jack each time, until you have to pick up all at once.
5. If the ball bounces twice before you pick up your jacks, then your turn is over and the next player starts.

Use the instructions to answer these questions.

1 How many jacks do you pick up at the beginning?

2 Which hand should you use to pick up the jacks?

3 How many times is the ball allowed to bounce?

4 When does the next player get his or her turn?

5 If you only had the pictures from the instructions, not the words, do you think you could still learn to play jacks? Explain.

TEST POWER

DIRECTIONS

Read the sample story. Then read each question about the story.

SAMPLE

Melanie's First Poem

"I can't believe it!" Melanie exclaimed.

Melanie had entered the school poetry contest and had won! The poem she wrote was about a girl named Julie, whom she had met when her parents had taken her to the ocean for their summer vacation. She and Julie had become good friends. They swam together, built sandcastles, and told each other stories.

Before they went home, Melanie and Julie had exchanged addresses. Although their homes were far apart, their <u>correspondence</u> made them feel close to each other. They wrote letters to each other every other week.

Melanie had never written a poem before. But her teacher had reassured her by saying, "Write down what you feel." Melanie had done just that. She wrote about her vacation and her new friend.

1 You can tell from the passage that <u>correspondence</u> is —

  A making sandcastles

  B writing letters

  C telling stories

  D going on vacation

2 Melanie was surprised that she won the contest because —

  F her poem was not well written

  G she didn't like her poem

  H it was a strange poem

  J it was her first poem

Stories in Art

What happens when you walk into a movie theater in the middle of a movie? You get only part of the story.

Look at the painting. What makes you think you have come in in the middle? What happened before the girl started writing this letter? How do you know this isn't her first try? What will she do when she finishes her letter? Do you think she will read it again and revise it? Why?

Study the details of the painting. How does the artist use dabs of color? What mood do his colors create? How does the girl feel about writing this letter? What makes you think so?

Girl Writing by Pierre Bonnard, 1908
The Barnes Foundation, Merion, Pennsylvania

READING STRATEGY

Sequence of Events

Develop a strategy for determining the sequence of events.

1. **Look for clue words,** such as *first, then,* and *after,* to help you understand the order of events in time.

2. **Ask yourself questions** as you read: What happened first? What happened next?

4. **Check your understanding** as you read. Reread any parts that confused you.

5. **Retell** the order of events in your own words. Why is the order of the events important to understanding the story?

Fooling the

275

Hungry Tiger

Once, long ago, some children were walking near a large forest. As they went by, they heard a voice. The voice sounded so kind that Abu, the youngest of them, ran into the forest.

"Oh no!" the others cried. "Abu was tricked by the hungry Tiger!"

Zakir said, "We have to save Abu. First we must let Abu know about the hole in Tiger's fence by the palm tree. Next, we'll distract Tiger so Abu can make his escape."

"How will we tell Abu?" asked the others.

"We'll send a coded message," Zakir replied.

These children had a secret code they all knew. The number 1 was *a*, 2 was *b*, and so on. They wrote this message on a sheet of paper: 8-15-12-5   2-25   16-1-12-13 20-18-5-5. After that, they folded it into a paper airplane.

The children then crept close to Tiger's house. They threw the paper airplane, but Tiger grabbed it. "Ha!" he cried. "A message! But what does it say?" He looked at the terrified Abu. "Read it to me!" Tiger commanded.

Abu read the coded message. "It says happy birthday," Abu lied.

"How odd!" Tiger said. "It's not my birthday." Suddenly, there was a great clatter on the roof. Tiger ran up to look, and when he did, Abu ran for the tree, found the hole, and escaped. Up on the roof, Tiger found only coconuts and rocks.

Meet Marguerite W. Davol

Marguerite W. Davol has been around children and books all her life. Children have taught her a lot over the years about what makes a good book. "And I am still learning!" she says. Davol writes for children of all ages. She has also written articles about her travels in Central and South America.

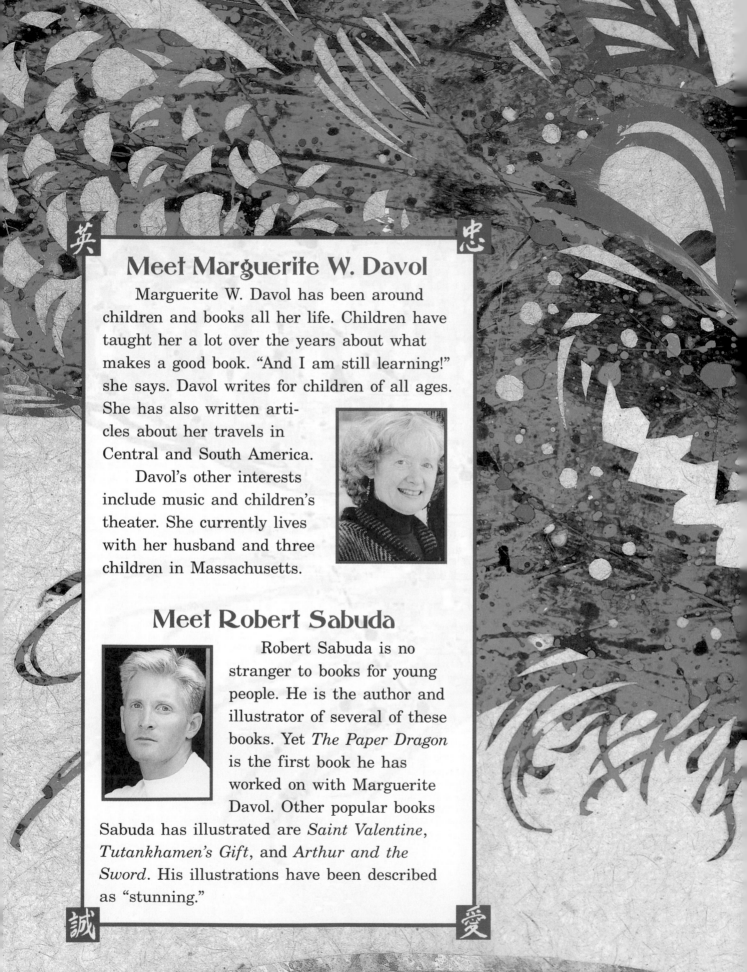

Davol's other interests include music and children's theater. She currently lives with her husband and three children in Massachusetts.

Meet Robert Sabuda

Robert Sabuda is no stranger to books for young people. He is the author and illustrator of several of these books. Yet *The Paper Dragon* is the first book he has worked on with Marguerite Davol. Other popular books Sabuda has illustrated are *Saint Valentine*, *Tutankhamen's Gift*, and *Arthur and the Sword*. His illustrations have been described as "stunning."

The Paper Dragon

Written by Marguerite W. Davol
Illustrated by Robert Sabuda

Long, long ago, there lived a humble artist named Mi Fei. Between each day's sunrise and sunset, Mi Fei would dip his narrow brushes in colored inks and paint on paper scrolls. He loved to paint the glorious past—scenes of the gods and their festivals, portraits of great heroes and their deeds. People from far beyond his village came to buy Mi Fei's scrolls so they could learn about their gods and heroes as one would learn from books.

But the artist cared nothing for the fame his paintings
brought him. He was a simple man, content to live and work
in his own village. When children crowded his windows to
watch him paint, Mi Fei would call to them, "Come in!" When
neighbors appeared at his door, he put his brushes aside,
ready to listen to their latest tale of triumph or woe. Mi Fei
was happy, surrounded by people he loved.

One morning, Mi Fei's work was interrupted by shouts outside his window. "A messenger! A messenger!" people cried as they ran past. Brush in hand, Mi Fei rushed to join his neighbors in the village square. The messenger, Mu Wang, brought distressing news.

"The great dragon of Lung Mountain, Sui Jen, has awakened from its hundred years' sleep and is loose upon the land," the messenger gasped. "Its huge legs have trampled rice fields into mud, and the winds created by its lashing tail have uprooted the mulberry trees, destroying the silkworms. Sui Jen's fiery breath has scorched the tea leaves on the bushes. Villages everywhere are in ruins.

"Someone must face the dragon," Mu Wang warned the crowd. "Someone must convince it to sleep once more, or your village, too, will be crushed under the weight of Sui Jen."

281

The frightened people murmured among themselves. Was anyone in their village brave enough and clever enough to confront a dragon? One by one, they turned to Mi Fei. "You know all about gods and heroes," one of the villagers said. "Surely you can find a way to stop Sui Jen."

Mi Fei shook his head. "I am no hero," he protested, "only a simple artist who paints the past. All I know of heroic deeds has been told to me by others!" But the villagers crowded around him, pleading for his help. Looking into their worried faces, he knew he could not refuse.

The next morning Mi Fei tucked some rice cakes into his pack, along with brushes, paper, and ink. He bundled up his painted scrolls to bring him comfort. Knowing he might never see friends and neighbors again, Mi Fei looked around his beloved village one last time. Then he sadly set off for Lung Mountain.

Through valleys and across streams Mi Fei walked, stopping only to pick a few berries to eat or to quench his thirst at a spring. After many hours, he reached Lung Mountain. Mi Fei stared upward. Smoke and flames billowed from the mountaintop, and enormous rocks bounced down the steep slopes. Mi Fei was frightened, but up, up he climbed, until he stood at Lung Mountain's peak. Thick mist swirled around him.

285

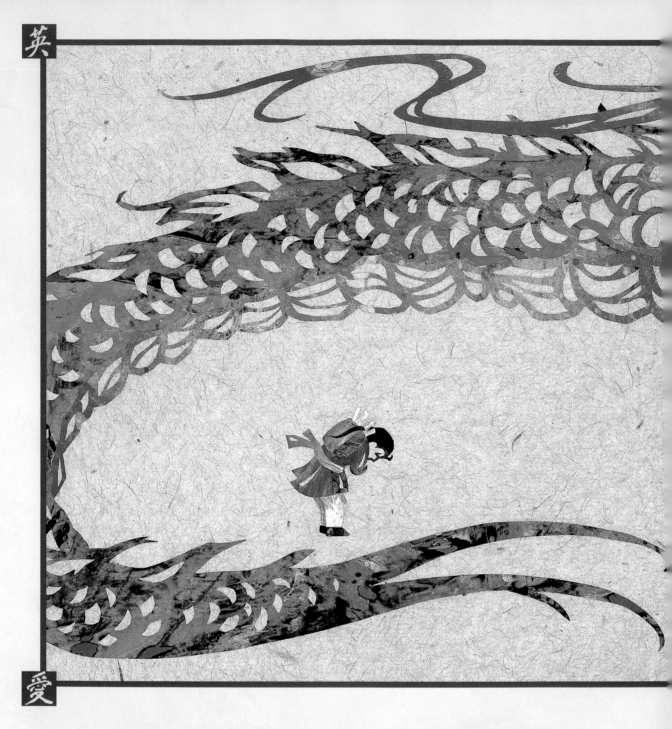

Then through the mist, with a rumbling roar so loud Mi Fei thought his head would burst, the dragon appeared. "Hah, who dares to disturb Sui Jen, the source of fire, the heart of the mountain?"

Mi Fei trembled. He turned to run away from the terrifying sight. But the worried faces of the villagers filled his mind and Mi Fei turned back to face the dragon. He bowed low and managed to say, "I am Mi Fei, a humble painter of scrolls."

Bright fire spurted from the dragon's nostrils, hot on Mi Fei's face. The wind from its lashing tail nearly blew him off his feet, but somehow Mi Fei was able to stand his ground.

"Please, Sui Jen, the villages below are in ruins. You have scorched the tea leaves and trampled the rice, leaving nothing for people to eat or drink. You have uprooted the mulberry trees and the silkworms are dying, leaving nothing for people to wear or sell. I beg of you, return to your sleep of a hundred years."

287

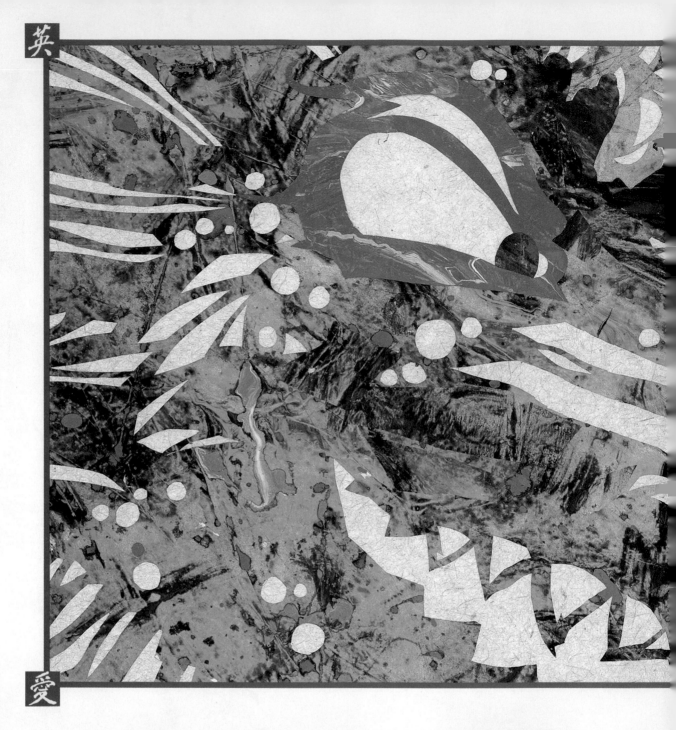

Huge scales glistened as the dragon coiled itself into a tight circle. Its red eyes glowed. "Hah, Mi Fei, know that before I return to my ageless slumber, someone must perform three tasks. Until then," thundered the dragon, its forked tongue flicking in and out, "I must prowl the countryside, trampling and burning all in my path."

Mi Fei sighed. Could a simple artist stop Sui Jen's devastation? His voice very small, Mi Fei asked the dragon, "What . . . what are the three tasks?"

Sui Jen's terrible teeth clicked once, twice. "First tell me, Mi Fei," the beast said, "what is the most important thing your people have created?"

The artist answered without thinking. "Paper," he said. "The paper on which I paint my scenes."

"Paper? Indeed!" The dragon howled with laughter. "The first task, then, is to bring me fire—wrapped in paper. Go. Do this before sunset or I must devour you."

Mi Fei crouched behind a large rock, seeking shelter from the dragon. He shook his head. "How can I carry out Sui Jen's task?" he said to himself. "Impossible! I was foolish to say paper, important as it is to me, instead of brass. Or tin. But paper . . . "

Mi Fei looked down at the bundle of scrolls he had carried from his village. People far and wide learn of their history

from my paper scrolls, he thought. Perhaps knowing about the
past can help me find answers for the present.

Mi Fei unrolled one scroll after another, looking at each of
them carefully. On one scroll, he had painted a celebration of
light, the Festival of the First Full Moon. Mi Fei smiled as he
examined the scene. Then he took out his small knife and cut
the paper scroll, folding and fashioning it into a different shape.

Before the sun slid from sight, Mi Fei returned to face
Sui Jen. Although nervous so close to the dragon, he took a
candle stump from his pack and lit the wick from Sui Jen's
fiery breath. Mi Fei placed the burning candle inside the
paper lantern he had made. The dragon laughed and the
flame in its nostrils died to a wisp of smoke. Mi Fei knew he
had succeeded.

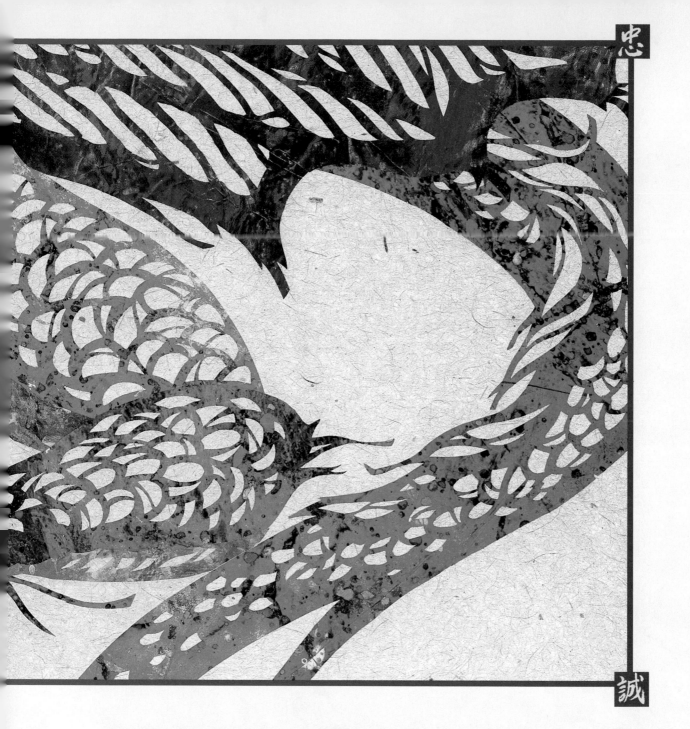

But then Sui Jen began to whip its heavy tail back and forth so violently that the clouds in the sky were swept away. "Your second task is to bring me the wind captured by paper," the dragon roared. "Do this before noon tomorrow or I must devour you."

Mi Fei slept very little that night. He had solved the first task, but the second seemed far more difficult. "Can my scrolls help me again?" he asked himself over and over. In morning's orange glow, he again unrolled his scrolls, one after another. Mi Fei stared at one, a hero's rescue of a beautiful princess lost in the hot desert, then nodded. Quickly he took out his small knife and cut the paper scroll, folding and fashioning it into a new shape.

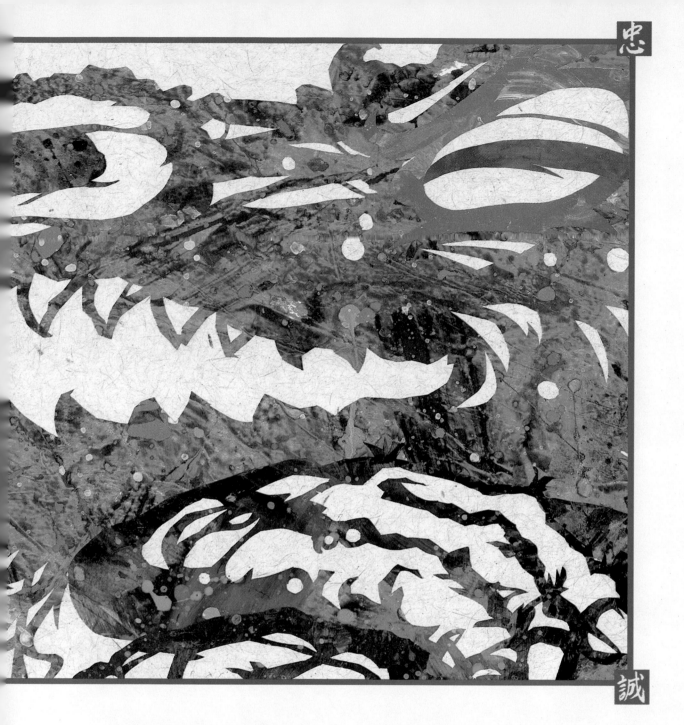

Mi Fei found the dragon resting, its eyes closed. He
approached the scaly beast and, with the folded paper, began
to fan its face. The wind captured in the fan tickled Sui Jen.
Opening its eyes, the dragon laughed once more and lazily
uncoiled its massive tail. Mi Fei knew he had succeeded again.

But almost instantly, Sui Jen opened its red eyes wide and
bellowed, "Your third task is to bring me the strongest thing
in the world carried in paper. Do this before sundown or I
must devour you."

Mi Fei hurried back to the shelter of the rock. "The strongest thing in the world," he repeated. "Is it Sui Jen? Or the rock I now lean against? What huge, heavy thing can be carried in paper?"

His scrolls had saved him twice and Mi Fei once again unrolled each one, searching for an answer. But no matter how hard he looked, this time not one of the scrolls offered Mi Fei a solution. He set them aside, disheartened. "Surely Sui Jen will devour me at sundown," he said.

Resigned, Mi Fei reached into his pack and took out his brushes, paper, and inks. He began to paint, certain that it would be for the last time. But he did not paint scenes of gods or heroes. Instead, Mi Fei painted what was closest to his heart, what he cherished most. He began to paint the people of his village—young and old, men, women, and children.

Mi Fei worked until the sun arced low in the west, then wearily laid his brushes aside.

He looked at the familiar world he had re-created, the faces of friends and neighbors he loved. Words began to crowd his head, take shape, and become a poem. Mi Fei picked up his brush and made the poem a part of his painting.

When he had finished, Mi Fei looked for a long time at
what he had created. Then he smiled and nodded. He knew
what he would do. This time Mi Fei did not cut the paper or
fold it into a new shape. Instead, he carefully rolled up the
scroll and tied it with a red ribbon.

Once more Mi Fei trudged along the narrow mountain
path. The enormous beast lay waiting, its great length coiled
around and around the mountaintop. Opening its wide mouth
lined with pointed yellow teeth, the dragon said, "Well, am I
to eat you for dinner?"

Mi Fei held out the picture he had created and said in a
clear, firm voice:

        Love can move mountains,
        Stretch the sky, calm the sea.
        Love brings light and life.

When he had finished, Mi Fei looked into Sui Jen's eyes. He was astonished to see that the dragon was shrinking. In a whisper rather than a roar, Sui Jen said, "Thank You, Mi Fei. You have found the way for me to sleep once more. Truly, the strongest thing in the world is love."

With that, the dragon became smaller and smaller until, with a flip of its tail, Sui Jen disappeared. In its place, Mi Fei found a small paper dragon. He carefully placed it within the scroll to take back to his village.

For the rest of his long life, Mi Fei
continued to paint the gods and their festivals,
to portray the exploits of great heroes. He continued to paint
portraits of the villagers he knew and loved. But whatever he
painted, he always drew a small dragon in one corner to remind
everyone of the strongest thing in the world.

What the Chinese Characters Stand for

 Courage   Loyalty   Love   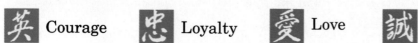 Sincerity

303

Story Questions & Activities

1 How does Mi Fei learn of the dragon?

2 Why do the villagers ask Mi Fei to help them?

3 What makes Mi Fei a true artist? Explain.

4 What is the order of events in this story?

5 Suppose that Mi Fei could meet the girl in the painting on page 274. Do you think that they would both agree that paper is the most important thing that people have created? Explain your reasons.

Write a Comic Strip

Create a comic strip that shows a way to handle a dragon. Use the story of Mi Fei and Sui Jen, or come up with your own method. Each frame should show a step in the process. Use speech balloons for dialogue.

Make a Poster

Sui Jen asks Mi Fei, "What is the most important thing your people have created?" Without thinking, the artist answers, "Paper." Keep track of all the paper you use in a week at school. Think about all the trees needed to make all that paper. Make a poster that shows others why recycling paper is so important.

Draw a Scroll

The artist Mi Fei would dip his narrow brushes in colored inks and paint on paper scrolls. He loved to paint scenes of the past, including portraits of heroes and their deeds. Now it's your turn. Choose a scene from history. Make a scroll that will make the past come alive.

Find Out More

Mi Fei says that his people created paper. Start by checking in an encyclopedia. Find out more about how the Chinese invented the modern process of making paper more than 2,000 years ago. Use your findings to prepare an oral report.

STUDY SKILLS

Use a Graph

The people of Mi Fei's village would be better prepared if they knew when Sui Jen the dragon might come down from his mountain. A **graph** can show patterns that will help you make predictions. What could the villagers learn from the line graph below? Assume the graph shows a typical week.

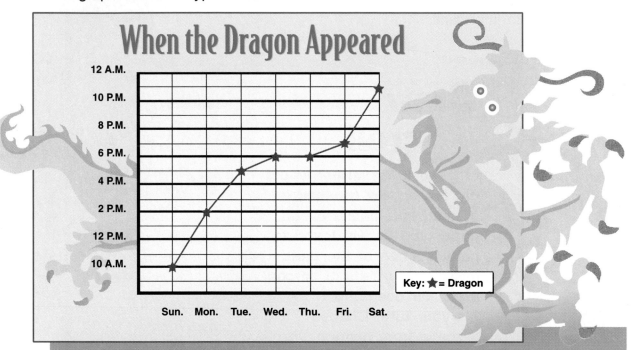

Use the graph to answer these questions.

1 When is the earliest time that the dragon was seen?

2 At what time was the dragon seen on Tuesday?

3 If some villagers have to go out either early next Thursday morning or early next Thursday evening, when should they go? Why?

4 Why do you think Sui Jen comes out at the times he does?

5 What other information would be helpful on this graph?

TEST POWER

DIRECTIONS

Read the sample story. Then read each question about the story.

SAMPLE

Icarus and the Magic Wings

The story of Daedalus and Icarus is a Greek myth. The story says that Daedalus was a great inventor who always wanted to fly like the birds. He and his son Icarus decided to build wings by using wax to attach feathers to wooden frames.

When they completed their wings, Daedalus and Icarus put their wings onto their arms. Daedalus said, "Son, we must be careful not to fly too high. There are many hidden dangers that we do not know about."

Daedalus flew forward, never daring to fly too high. Icarus, however, was excited about his wonderful wings. He flew straight upward, trying to touch the sun. As Icarus came close to the sun, the heat melted the wax that held the feathers to the frames. Icarus' wings broke apart, and he fell into the sea.

1 What is the main idea of this passage?

   A Icarus did not listen and flew too close to the sun.

   B Icarus invented something that allowed him to touch the sun.

   C Daedalus and Icarus were high-flying birds.

   D The thing Daedalus wanted most was to build paper wings.

2 Which is an OPINION in this passage?

   F Daedalus built wings.

   G Icarus flew upward.

   H Icarus liked his wings.

   J Icarus' wings broke.

Stories in Art

The artist who painted this picture used a story about a knight told long ago. He also used a painting process that is 500 years old.

Look at the picture. The artist made sketches first before painting. Then he drew the picture on canvas and painted it brown and white. After that step, he applied the colors and the details. What do you think of the result? Does the process work to tell an old story? Explain your reasons.

Look at the painting again. Who are the children? Why did the knight help them cross the river? Where could the children be going?

Sir Isumbras at the Ford
by Sir John Everett Millais
Lady Lever Gallery, Port Sunlight, England

Steps in a Process

Develop a strategy for identifying steps in a process.

1 **Read the title.** What is the letter about?

2 **Identify the process.** What process is being described?

3 **Look for clue words,** such as, *first, next,* and *when* to help you understand the order of events.

4 **Check your understanding.** Ask yourself: Can I describe the steps Roosevelt took to help our country?

5 **Retell the order** of steps in your own words. Be sure you include each step.

Remembering Franklin Delano Roosevelt

April 15, 1945

Dear Elizabeth,

You recently asked me why I was so upset when I heard that President Roosevelt had died. Perhaps you are too young to remember when he first took office twelve years ago. For many Americans, however, F.D.R. offered hope when there was little to be found.

When Roosevelt was first elected, our country was in the midst of the Great Depression. Many people had lost their savings, their homes, and their jobs.

Just after taking office, F.D.R. began a series of "fireside chats" over the radio that helped to calm the country. As he talked, the President made us believe that things could improve.

First, F.D.R. focused on banks. He helped to create a more stable banking system. Next, he helped the nation's farmers. His programs allowed them to better manage their crops and lands. After that, F.D.R. focused on industry. His policies helped small businesses.

America's hard times weren't over, but F.D.R. gave us the courage and strength to go on. He told us right from the start that "we have nothing to fear but fear itself." He was a wise leader, and I will miss him greatly.

With love,
Grandpa

GRANDMA ESSIE'S COVERED WAGON

by **DAVID WILLIAMS** • illustrated by **WIKTOR SADOWSKI**

I was born in a log cabin near Duenweg, Missouri, almost ninety years ago. There were six kids in our family—Stella, Opal, Kenneth, me, Jack, and Violet—and we lived in two little rooms. Papa worked as a hired hand, which didn't pay enough for us to buy nice things. But we didn't know any different and were happy—we had no idea Papa dreamed of something more.

apa saved his money, then decided to go west and farm
wheat. "There's lots of rich land in Kansas," he said, and soon we
were all dreaming. Papa bought a frame wagon that farmers had
used to haul crops. He bent wooden stays from one side to the
other, nailed them down to form hoops, and stretched a white
canvas over. As he worked, we watched our covered wagon rise,
a magic ship that could take us anywhere.

Inside, Papa built shelves and Mama put in a little monkey
stove. We loaded the wagon with all our clothes and blankets,
and Kenneth hooked four mules to the front. Our calf, Molly, who
was so gentle we kids used her for a pony, was tied to the back
along with the milk cow. At last we were off to see the world.

312

Mama had made quilts, rugs, and comforts for everyone to sit on, and she rode with Violet on her lap. Opal, who was pregnant and got sick some of the time, sat between her husband, Arthur, and Stella. Kenneth rode up front with Papa. Jack and I rode wherever we felt like. Sometimes when we were restless, we'd even jump out and trot behind the wagon. We'd throw dirt clods at each other or ride Molly. There were lots of wild things outside—wolves, coyotes, foxes—but if they scared us, we'd just jump back inside and be safe.

We traveled through Kansas on dust and rock roads that went on forever. Sometimes we'd pass little farms and Mama'd buy eggs. She'd make pancakes in the morning out of scratch and brew Papa's coffee in a blue granite percolator. In the evenings we'd eat lots and lots of potatoes.

There were nights we never made it to a town and had to sleep on the earth. Mama would pull out every quilt, and we'd light a campfire. Stella would play the mandolin and sing songs like "From Jerusalem to Jericho" and "When the Roll Is Called Up Yonder, I'll Be There." We'd all join her on the chorus, then fall asleep together under the stars.

We went clear to western Kansas like that, to a little farm with an orchard and a red two-story house. Jack and I loved standing in the stairwell and yelling our names. We'd try to see who could be the loudest, our voices echoing back. Then we'd run every which way, our new home so big we thought it was a castle! We had beds to sleep on, and real cotton sheets. Mama sewed curtains out of old dresses. We scrubbed the walls and woodwork with rags, and soon the place looked good.

Most of the land was prairie. It rolled on forever, like the back of some huge animal that might get up and run. The wind would whip out of nowhere, and sometimes Jack and I would grab the thick cushions off the sofa, take them outside, and hold them against our bellies. When the wind blew, we'd let go. The cushions would hold to us like magic!

It was hard for Papa to get the new place going. But wealthy wheat farmers *did* live in Kansas, and one little rich boy liked me.

He invited me to his house for dinner one time, where there were
all these cantaloupes and watermelons, but I was too bashful to
taste any of them.

    We had a horse named Major, who wouldn't get started once
he'd stopped. One game was to pretend we were in the Big Top,
then walk under Major or sit on his back. All the time, he'd just
stand there, covered with the wild prairie flowers we'd decorated
him with, nothing able to make him budge.

One day I was upstairs looking out our window, and there was the funniest sight I'd ever seen—a big black cloud winding up. I ran downstairs to Papa, who'd just come in from the fields.

"Take a look at this, Papa!" I cried. "There's something in the sky!"

At first he thought I was seeing things, but then he hollered, "It's a tornado!" and rushed us all to the cellar. The air was thick as a stampede. We huddled in the dark together, underground,

our hands over our ears. Violet wouldn't stop crying.

A big river ran between our house and town. The tornado followed it, so we were saved.

We went barefoot through summer and fall and had to walk to school that way. Stella had always wanted a pair of white dress shoes, but Papa said no, we couldn't afford them. We sat with the other barefoot kids in the back of our one-room schoolhouse, the rich kids and their shoes up front.

omehow, a front-row girl and I became friends. She had red hair and could really jump rope. She wore beautiful shiny black shoes, but I got to where I barely noticed them. We'd sing "Every Time I Go to Town Boys Start Kicking My Dog Around" and run through the playground, laughing.

Christmas Eve Papa went out and chopped down a small tree with bare branches. Mama had cut pictures out of the Sears-and-Roebuck catalog, and we hung them all over till the tree looked alive. She'd made rag dolls with button eyes and long yarn braids for us girls, and Papa had carved Kenneth a toy horse and made Jack a wagon. After all our popcorn was popped and eaten, all our cranberries strung, we sang "Away in a Manger" with Stella.

Then Christmas day, Opal had her baby! We tiptoed upstairs to peek at our first nephew, as big as a hand, healthy and screaming. Arthur was so happy about being a father he asked Stella to play her mandolin in the kitchen, then he danced.

321

Papa raised wheat, hay, and corn, but the second year in Kansas came a drought. Fields turned to dust. Plants wouldn't grow. Our horses went hungry, and the river ran dry. Jack and I could walk across it from mud bank to mud bank, seeing the dead fish and rounded river rocks. We'd pick those rocks up and hurl them just as far as we could, asking ourselves what happened.

Papa lost all his money, and we had to sell the farm. I said

good-bye to my ducks. Our hound dogs, Papa gave to some neighbors. We auctioned off our horses, cows, and furniture, keeping only what would fit into the wagon, then we loaded it up and were gone.

Stella played "Diamonds in the Rough" as we bumped down the dusty road. There was just the sound of her fingers plucking strings and the sight of our own farm floating away.

We headed south, down to Oklahoma. Mama's folks lived near Oologah in a log cabin that reminded us of our home in Missouri. They were part Indian, Grandpa with his coal-black hair and mustache. He wore a felt hat with a big brim and played the fiddle, always wanting us kids to stay put and be his audience.

"You sit there," he'd say, "I want you to listen to this fiddle." But all *we* wanted was to go to the creek and swim.

Grandma'd tell us animal stories every night, smoking a clay pipe that we loved to light. Grandpa'd give us a stick to put in the coals, then we'd get the tip of it on fire and touch it to the

tobacco while Grandma puffed.

There was a big garden behind their cabin, and a kitchen that wasn't fastened on, and always plenty to eat. We camped at their place all summer and never wanted to leave.

But Papa heard about the oil fields in Big Heart, Oklahoma, and once more we loaded up the wagon. I tried to give Grandma the doll Mama'd made me. "I want Mary to have a real home like yours," I said, but Grandma thought Mary might need me, that I should take her.

Grandma and Grandpa waved to us from their porch as we left. Grandpa held his fiddle in one hand and Grandma cried.

ig Heart was a boom town. I'd never seen so many people or heard so much noise. The land was flat as a pancake, but the oil derricks that rose up every fifty feet made it look like a metal forest. Buildings were being put up left and right—banks, restaurants, saloons—and the streets were mud. There weren't any houses to live in. Papa set a tent up in a shantytown where other oil workers' families lived, and we parked the covered wagon. We sold our mules. Papa, Kenneth, and Arthur got jobs in the oil fields and were gone sunup to sundown, and always came home exhausted.

Stella began working for the Salvation Army to help raise money for the orphanage. As she played her mandolin and sang, oilmen would drop big silver dollars onto the drum. She sang in the streets all winter, then fell in love with the Salvation Army captain and planned to get married. But one day she took sick: just started coughing and couldn't stop. The doctor said she'd gotten ill from "exposure," being outside too long in the cold.

We prayed for her. We told her stories. We held her hand. Nothing would make her better.

One cold day in March, Stella died. Papa walked downtown and bought her a pair of white dress shoes, like she'd always wanted, to be buried in. But he wouldn't go to the funeral. He sat in the tent by himself while Mama and the rest of us went out past the oil derricks to the cemetery. The preacher said a few words, then we sang. And for a moment we all swore we heard Stella singing with us.

329

Mama thought I could get a job waiting tables, to help the family out. I was scared to try, but one day I walked into the Black Gold Restaurant and asked if they needed any help.

"How old are you?" this big woman asked.

"Fourteen," I lied.

"Well, let's see if you can work," she said, and soon I was carrying trays of food with my hands shaking the whole time and bringing home tips.

After a year in Big Heart we had saved enough to go. We bought two new mules and loaded the covered wagon for the last time. "We're heading back to Missouri," Papa said, and we moved to Seneca, on the Missouri-Oklahoma border. Opal and Arthur rented a house, and Papa bought a farm. It wasn't as nice as our place in Kansas, but we were so glad to have a home. Where the floors had cracks, Mama laid out rugs she'd made. She even wallpapered with newspapers to cover the spaces between the walls' wooden slats. And we went to bed nights feeling good.

There was a huge strawberry patch out back, so we went into business. When the berries ripened, we picked and boxed them, twenty-four to a crate, to be shipped out on the train. I made friends with a neighbor girl who worked for us, and sometimes before we started to fill a new quart we'd each write our name and address on the bottom. That way whoever bought the strawberries would know who we were.

One day Mama called me into the house. "A letter's come to you from New York City," she said. It was from a boy who'd gotten one of the strawberry quarts with my name inside. He said he wanted to marry me, but Mama wouldn't let me go.

Papa broke up the old covered wagon and sawed it to pieces. He made things from the wood—a table and chairs, a bookcase, a porch swing like the one we're sitting on.

I stayed in Seneca until I grew up and met your grandpa, an iron ore miner from Diamond. He was handsome. One day we went to Joplin and got married. Then we bought this house almost seventy years ago—here where I had my babies. My babies grew up, left home, and had their babies. But I never moved away.

AUTHOR'S NOTE

As far back as I can remember, I've been listening to Grandma Essie's stories. Every summer my parents would take us kids "back home" to Missouri to sit on her porch swing and hear about things far different from what we knew. Grandma's father had once boarded Frank and Jesse James. She knew Wyatt Earp's cousin. And then there was the wonderful story of the covered wagon.

The stories Grandma Essie told from her childhood had a huge effect on me as a young boy, and in the fall of 1988 when Grandma came to visit, at the age of eighty-seven, I talked to her about capturing one in a book. Grandma was excited by the idea. All the details of her early days traveling in the covered wagon flooded back, and over the course of a week we went over them, meticulously re-creating each of the scenes. Here, then, is her story, in mostly her words, that I've helped shape and arrange.

The above photograph is of the family's Kansas farm. Twelve-year-old Essie is standing barefoot at the far right. To her left are sister Opal and her baby; sister Violet; brothers Kenneth and Jack; sister Stella; an unknown hired hand; Grandma Essie's Mama; and finally Papa. Grandma remembers when the picture was taken—everyone was working in the fields when a traveling photographer happened by.

Grandma Essie has lived from the covered wagon days to the days when people fly to the moon. When you listen to her, I hope you can see the stern Midwestern landscape, feel the rowdy Kansas wind, and hear Grandma Essie's own voice as I hear it, wiser and stronger for having lived this life, but with an echo of the young girl who has never completely gone away.

Meet
DAVID WILLIAMS

David Williams loves music. He began singing when he was two. When he was 12, Williams started playing guitar. He also loves travel. Every summer his family drove from Illinois to Missouri to visit Grandma Essie. When he grew up, Williams traveled the country playing music for audiences.

Eventually, Williams became a teacher. One day he and some fourth graders decided to write a song about the environment. Williams went on to write more songs for children on his own. His album *Oh, the Animals* won an award from the American Library Association.

If you enjoyed *Grandma Essie's Covered Wagon*, you might also enjoy David Williams's music and his book *Walking to the Creek*.

WALKING TO THE CREEK

by David Williams
Illustrated by Thomas B. Allen

Story Questions & Activities

1 In which state does this story begin?

2 What steps does the family take to fulfill Papa's dreams?

3 How is Grandma Essie's family like other pioneer families? Explain.

4 What happens in this story?

5 Grandma Essie and her family left their home several times. Mi Fei in "The Paper Dragon" also left his home. Suppose that Grandma Essie and Mi Fei could meet. What might they say about their journeys?

Write a How-to Manual

Grandma Essie sees a tornado headed her way in Kansas, and Papa rushes the family to the cellar. What would you do today if you saw a tornado coming? Write a how-to manual to explain how to survive a tornado. Do some research, and include a diagram with step-by-step instructions.

Make a Poster

Grandma Essie's father thought he could become a successful wheat farmer. Create an information poster to show why wheat is such an important crop. Draw or cut out magazine pictures of food items, such as breads and pasta, that we get from wheat. Arrange these pictures in a poster and label each food.

Create a Brochure

What would happen if Grandma Essie and her family traveled to your state to try to make a better life? Where would you tell them to live and find work? Create a brochure of your community. Include a list of industries, schools, neighborhoods, libraries, parks, and other places of interest.

Find Out More

Grandma Essie's family worked at wheat farming. How is wheat made into flour? Start by checking in an encyclopedia or by using the Internet. Work with a small group of classmates to gather information and to prepare a report. Choose a member from your group to give the report to the class.

Use a Time Line

A **time line** is a diagram that shows important or related events in the order they take place. The time line below tells about a family named Phillips.

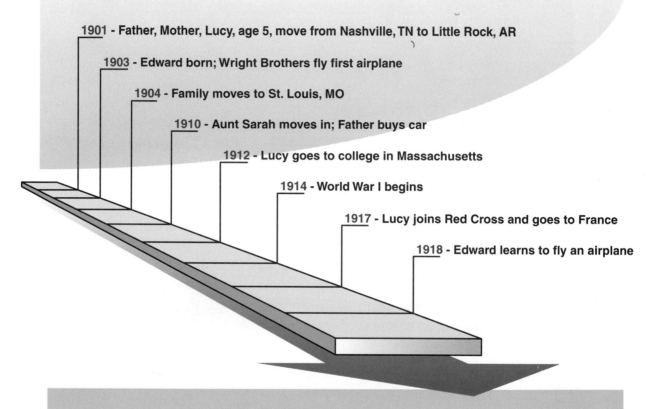

1901 - Father, Mother, Lucy, age 5, move from Nashville, TN to Little Rock, AR

1903 - Edward born; Wright Brothers fly first airplane

1904 - Family moves to St. Louis, MO

1910 - Aunt Sarah moves in; Father buys car

1912 - Lucy goes to college in Massachusetts

1914 - World War I begins

1917 - Lucy joins Red Cross and goes to France

1918 - Edward learns to fly an airplane

Use the time line to answer these questions.

1 How many years does this time line cover?

2 Where was Edward born?

3 How old was Lucy when her father bought a car?

4 Why do you think the time line mentions the Wright Brothers?

5 Why might a time line be good to include in a biography?

338

TEST POWER

DIRECTIONS

Read the sample story. Then read each question about the story.

SAMPLE

Trouble in Space

Star trooper Justin Le Croix had just settled back for a game of computer chess when the alert siren began screaming in the recreation room. Red neon lights began flashing everywhere. A recorded voice from the ship's main computer said: "Warning! All hands: Warning! Entering uncharted asteroid belt! Alert status: Alpha."

Justin turned off the chess game and pulled up a status report from the starship's navigation control panel.

The news didn't look good. The ship had apparently run into a group of asteroids that drifted off Orion's moon. Some of the rocks in the asteroid belt were twice the size of the ship.

Justin grabbed the microphone and shouted into it. "Who's on duty up there?" he cried. "Is anyone there? I need assistance. Is there anybody out there?"

1 At the end of the story, Justin might best be described as —

A calm

B frightened

C brave

D foolish

2 Why did Justin decide to stop his chess game?

F He needed to get some sleep.

G He lost the game.

H He didn't have an opponent.

J He heard the warning message.

Did you skim the story to find clues to the answers? Tell how and why.

339

Stories in Art

When you look at this painting, you almost feel as if you are sitting in the storyteller's circle. That's because the artist painted this picture from a certain point of view.

∼∼∼∼∽

Look at the painting. Why does the artist focus on the storyteller? Who is the boy who is standing? What is the artist's purpose in painting the scene in this way?

∼∼∼∼∽

Imagine that you are listening to the storyteller. Do you think he is telling an old story? Why? What story could you tell about your family or ancestors? Why is it important to tell stories about the past?

Story Teller
by Velino Shije Herrera, c. 1925–1935
National Museum of American Art,
Washington, DC

Author's Purpose and Point of View

Develop a strategy for determining the author's purpose and point of view.

1 **Decide why the author wrote the selection.** What is the article about?

2 **Look for clues** to the author's purpose. Are there facts?

3 **Figure out if the author** has more than one purpose. Does the writing inform? entertain? persuade?

4 **Identify the author's point of view.** How does the author feel about the subject?

5 **Explain the author's purpose.** Does the author want people to learn more about Lawrence?

Jacob Lawrence:
Art as History

Jacob Lawrence was born in Atlantic City, New Jersey, in 1917, during the time of a large African-American migration to northern cities from the south. Seeking better jobs and living conditions in the north, his parents and countless others had already made the journey.

Lawrence's family had settled first in Philadelphia. They moved to New York City in 1930, when Lawrence was 13 years old. Since his mother worked, he attended an after-school arts-and-crafts program. It was there that he decided to become an artist. He later studied at the Harlem Workshop and the American Artists School.

Lawrence painted vivid scenes from African-American life and history. During 1940 and 1941, Lawrence created his most famous work. He was 23 when he began this series of sixty paintings, which present images of the Great Migration. Remarkably, he painted all sixty panels together, one color at a time, in order to have a consistent use of color. The sequence is called *The Migration of the Negro.*

These paintings show the hardships, struggles, and dangers faced by the people who uprooted their lives in search of a better world.

Jacob Lawrence died in 2000, but he left behind a powerful vision of one aspect of America's past.

The Migration Series, Panel No. 10: "They were very poor"
(1940-41) by Jacob Lawrence. Tempera on gesso on composition board. 12 x 18 inches. The Museum of Modern Art, New York. Gift of Mrs. David M. Levy

MEET MICHELE WOOD

You could say that Michele Wood is an explorer. She is an African American artist in search of her family's past. Wood was born in Indiana. Yet she lives in the South because her family was originally from there. She has visited Africa, too, to learn about the culture of her ancestors. The paintings in *Going Back Home* are the result of Wood's search for her family's history. Creating paintings and making art are her way of looking back at her family's past and of expressing who she is now.

MEET TOYOMI IGUS

Like Michele Wood, Toyomi Igus is also interested in her family history. Igus was born in Iowa, but her ancestors are Japanese and African American. To Igus, learning about different cultures is a way of life. When the opportunity came to work with Michele Wood on *Going Back Home*, Igus was delighted. This book was unusual because Wood had already created the illustrations. Yet no words had been written. Igus's job would be to create a story based on her ideas about Wood's pictures. The project was a success, and the two women plan to work together on another book in the future.

GOING BACK HOME

An Artist
Returns to
the South

Pictures by
Michele Wood

Story Interpreted
and Written by
Toyomi Igus

When I was a little girl, I heard many stories about my family—where they came from, what life was like before I was born. This is a picture of me sitting at my aunt's knee, listening to her tales as she did my hair.

Of course, I didn't grow up in a house like this. I grew up in a big city in Indiana. But I tried to imagine what kind of house my ancestors lived in when they were enslaved on a plantation in the South. I thought it might look something like this.

I was fascinated by my family's stories. I was the curious one who would listen to the grownups' tales. As I grew older, I tried to piece together my family's history from the scraps of memories they would share with me. When you look at my art, you will see that I often create quilt-like backgrounds. This is my way of showing how pieces of life can fit together.

Because I am an artist, I express my thoughts and feelings visually, through pictures. This picture, "The Family Way," represents family love and togetherness. When I set out to trace my family tree, my family supported me in every way.

I call this picture "Inheritors of Slavery" to represent the many generations of my people who were enslaved. The woman is holding a black pot, which she used in Africa and here in her new homeland. It symbolizes family and the continuation of our heritage. Behind the couple, you can see symbols of their life in America: the well, from which they drew their water; the wash tub and scrub board, which they used to clean their clothes; the hen, which provided food for people here and in Africa; and the little house they were given by their masters to live in. The hen and the house are powerful symbols for me. I use them a lot in my artwork.

When I got older, I had a strong desire to go back home to the South to actually see and feel the land where my ancestors lived. So I left Indiana, moved to Atlanta, Georgia, and started exploring the southern United States. I visited plantations and read a lot about the history of African Americans.

I once saw a picture of a doll that a little slave girl named Emmaline made for her white master's daughter. I felt sad when I thought about the doll that Emmaline could not own, so I painted this picture. I dressed the doll in red, white, and blue to represent America. Behind her you can see an African American soldier who fought for this country even though our people were not allowed to be free here.

oth my mother's and father's families were from the Mississippi Delta. After the Civil War, my family, like many former slaves, did not leave the South right away. Instead they stayed and sharecropped. Sharecropping was a method of farming where poor farmers had to borrow land to farm—and also tools and seed. The crop they grew went to pay off their debts.

This picture of my great-grandparents is similar to "Inheritors of Slavery," two scenes ago. But I painted the couple standing *inside* their house to show the wonderful possibility they now had of making their own home. The pinwheels on the woman's skirt are ancient symbols that stand for good luck and the changing cycles of life. The mule in the man's hands represents the "forty acres and a mule" that were promised—but never delivered—to the freed slaves.

348

My family grew cotton. From dawn to dusk, everyone on the farm had to work. The women looked after the children, picked the cotton during harvest time, tended the livestock, and planted the family vegetable garden. The men plowed and weeded the fields day after day and hunted 'possums, 'coons, and deer for food.

In this picture you can see how the women would pick cotton and put it in their aprons. As their aprons filled up, the women—and children too—would drag their load behind them as they picked the bits of fluff. Slaves had picked cotton the very same way one hundred years before. It was a very hard life. If you look closely, you can see that I even made the hens work!

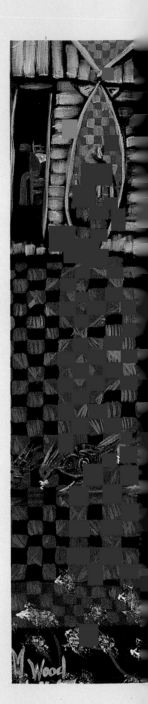

In those days, families depended a lot more on each other. Survival, demanded that people work together in harmony—like the man and the woman in this picture.

Water was important too. It was the source of life—for my family, for their livestock, for the crops. This is why I made the well the central image in this painting. The wheel on the well is there to bring good fortune. Behind the couple I painted bottle trees. People believed that bottle trees brought rain.

I wanted this picture to say that with hard work, a little luck, and a strong community, my family was able to thrive even under the harshest of conditions.

Music has always been an important part of African American culture. Slaves sang work songs to make their hard work easier and used field hollers—long, drawn out notes—to express emotion and warn each other of danger. From these songs and religious spirituals came the blues.

American music has been greatly influenced by the blues. Important blues songs and singers came from the Mississippi Delta where my family lived. As I traveled around the South, I would often see scenes like this—men sitting on the front stoop playing the guitar or harmonica and singing the blues. It was easy for me to imagine my own great-grandfather easing out of his tiresome day by making some music.

Despite the hard work, or maybe because of it, families took every opportunity to celebrate life. Births, weddings, harvest time, baptisms—then, as now, families rejoiced in the good times. The women would prepare for days, cooking and baking, using the precious white sugar and white flour to create the confections reserved for such occasions.

Whenever I think of my foremothers cooking for special days, I see this picture of my grandmother Kathryn and remember how she used to bake a treat for each family member on every holiday.

Do you see the snails on her dress? I copied the pattern from one of my favorite Nigerian outfits. My grandmother didn't really have a dress like this, but I liked it, so I gave the dress to her in this picture.

I call this painting "The Wedding Dance to Happiness." The women in my family didn't have fancy wedding dresses, just their usual cotton frocks. But even though the fabric was simple, they would make the dresses beautiful by using colorful dyes. On a wedding day, the men would get all cleaned up and put on their Sunday best. The preacher might ride out to the farm from a neighboring town to say the wedding vows. Maybe the couple would "jump the broom," which was an old wedding ritual from the slave days that marked the beginning of a couple's new life together. On that special day, all work would stop and the music would flow.

359

As a child I remember going to churches that were converted old houses, like the one I painted here. After church, folks would always stand outside for a while and talk— about the preacher, about his sermon, about the neighbors, about their kids.

My ancestors probably did the very same thing. Every Sunday after a hard week of farming, they would go to a church like this to socialize and renew their faith. In the South during the early 1900s, the church was often the only safe and welcoming place for African Americans to congregate.

This picture is called "Sunday Morning." I hope it shows how much I respect my elders and their faith in God and in each other.

After many years of struggle, it became just too difficult to make a living sharecropping. You never could tell about the cotton crop. If the boll weevils attacked the plants, the harvest would be very poor. If big rains came, the water would flood out the fields. Sharecroppers had to borrow more and more to live, so their debts would grow and grow. Over time many black people, like my family, moved North, where there were now other jobs on the railroads and in the steel mills.

I call this picture "The Wagon to Freedom." I tried to imagine what it was like for my family to leave the land where they had lived for so long and to look—for the last time—at the houses that were the only homes they had ever known.

Of course not everyone went North seeking new opportunities. Many African Americans moved West. Although it's not very well known, black men worked all over the West as cowboys. I didn't realize this until I saw a picture of Nat Love, a famous black cowboy. So I painted him. Doesn't he look proud? Nat Love became an expert roper and shooter and was one of the best cowboys of his time.

If you look very closely, in the background you will see that I have painted little pictures of a storefront and of a soldier. This is to show that African Americans were—and are—very self-sufficient. We owned businesses, fought in all of the American wars, and contributed greatly to the building of this country.

365

My grandmother Kathryn's branch of the family left
Mississippi and moved north to Kentucky, where she was born
and raised. For a long time Kathryn never went to fancy
restaurants or hotels because black people were not allowed
inside. After segregation ended, my grandmother was able to
eat in one of these restaurants for the very first time. It must
have taken a great deal of courage. I imagine that she looked
like this—dignified, with her head held high, but clutching her
purse close beside her. Even though she looked proud and
courageous, deep down inside she was a little bit scared!

As I learned about my family's history and all that they
endured, I realized that I come from a very strong people. I
never tried to create a self-portrait before, but after going back
home, an image of myself started to form in my mind.

Here it is. I laughed when I painted the square on my forehead. When I was little, I tried to take a picture of myself, and I put the camera too close in front of my face. The flash-bulb made a square-shaped burn on my forehead. The mark is gone now, but I remembered it in this picture.

The house and fence represent the foundations of my past. The boards are my life's lessons—the crooked ones are the tragedies and hardships. I am holding a hen, which is the link to my rural southern heritage.

And the woman in the window? She's the person I have yet to become. After going back home, I know more about who I am and I can picture the person I want to be—a seeker of knowledge, a creator of visions, and a keeper of my family's history.

Story Questions & Activities

1 Who is telling this story?

2 Why is the artist trying to piece together her family's history?

3 How is this story like a family album?

4 What is the main idea of this selection?

5 How do the paintings in this selection compare with the picture on page 340? Which artist do you prefer? Why?

MUFFINS

Write a Recipe

In this story, the narrator remembers that her grandmother used to bake treats for the family on holidays. Which recipes are special in your family? Choose one recipe, and write it on an index card. List all the ingredients and the steps in the right order. Draw the finished product.

Make a Patchwork Quilt

The artist sees her family's stories as something like a patchwork quilt. As she grew older, she tried to piece together her family's history from her scraps of memories. Make a patchwork quilt of your own family's history. Draw pictures of important events on large squares of light-colored art paper. Arrange the squares in time order, and write a caption for each patch. Display your "quilt" in class. Then show it to family members.

Record a Song

The author explains that "Music has always been an important part of African American culture." Think of a song that is important to your family, culture, or country. Find the lyrics and write them down. Record the song on audiocassette. Play it for classmates.

Find Out More

The author describes several ways in which freed slaves made new lives for themselves. Many sharecropped, built railroads, worked in steel mills, and became cowboys. Find out more about what life was like for slaves after they were freed. Start by looking in your social studies textbook or in an encyclopedia. Share your findings with classmates.

Read a Family Tree

The artist's paintings are like a family album. They also tell a story like a family tree. A **family tree** is a type of diagram. The boxes contain the names of people and the years in which they lived. Lines connect the boxes, showing the reader how the family members are related.

Look at this family tree. Notice how it organizes a family's history.

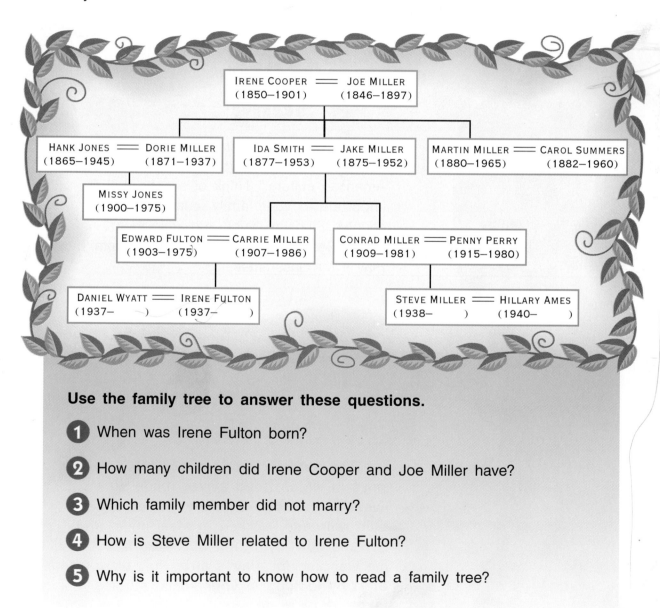

Use the family tree to answer these questions.

1 When was Irene Fulton born?

2 How many children did Irene Cooper and Joe Miller have?

3 Which family member did not marry?

4 How is Steve Miller related to Irene Fulton?

5 Why is it important to know how to read a family tree?

TEST POWER

Test Tip

Ruling out wrong answers will make it easier to find the best answer.

DIRECTIONS

Read the sample story. Then read each question about the story.

SAMPLE

Bacteria

Bacteria are so small that 25 thousand of them fit in a one-square-inch space. By weight, one ounce contains 30 trillion bacteria—that is six times the number of people on Earth!

Bacteria can be found in the air as well as six miles below the surface of the ocean. They can be found in frozen soil and in volcanic cracks. They can also be found in plants, in animals, and in people.

Some bacteria are good for humans. For example, some foods would not exist without bacteria. Cheese and yogurt are both made with bacteria. Also, many animals rely on bacteria. Cows, for instance, have a certain kind of bacterium in their stomachs that helps them digest the grass that they eat.

Although you might think all bacteria are harmful, it is safe to say that some of the bacteria around us are good for us.

1 Which is a FACT in this passage?

   A Bacteria are as large as a cow.

   B It's easy to see bacteria deep in the ocean.

   C Cows have bacteria in their stomachs.

   D All bacteria are harmful.

2 You can tell from the passage that bacteria are —

   F found only in the air

   G easily seen with the naked eye

   H in many of the foods we eat

   J always extremely dangerous

Stories in Art

If you look at this photograph quickly, you might realize that you are seeing one of the greatest stone monuments ever made. Built 4,500 years ago in Egypt, the Great Sphinx still stands today, though part of its stone has been worn away.

Study the photograph. What is the Sphinx? What has happened to it through the years? How have sand, wind, and sun damaged it? What else may have happened to it over time?

Look at the Sphinx again. How do you think this monument was made? In whose honor do you think it was built?

The Great Sphinx and Pyramids,
Third Millennium B.C.
Giza, Egypt

372

Sequence of Events

Develop a strategy for determining the sequence of events.

1 **Look for clue words.** Dates and words such as *during* and *first* will help you to understand the order of events.

2 **Ask yourself** what happened first, next, and so on, to follow events that are told out of time order.

3 **Check your under-standing** as you read. If the order of events is confusing, reread the selection.

4 **Retell the order** of events in your own words.

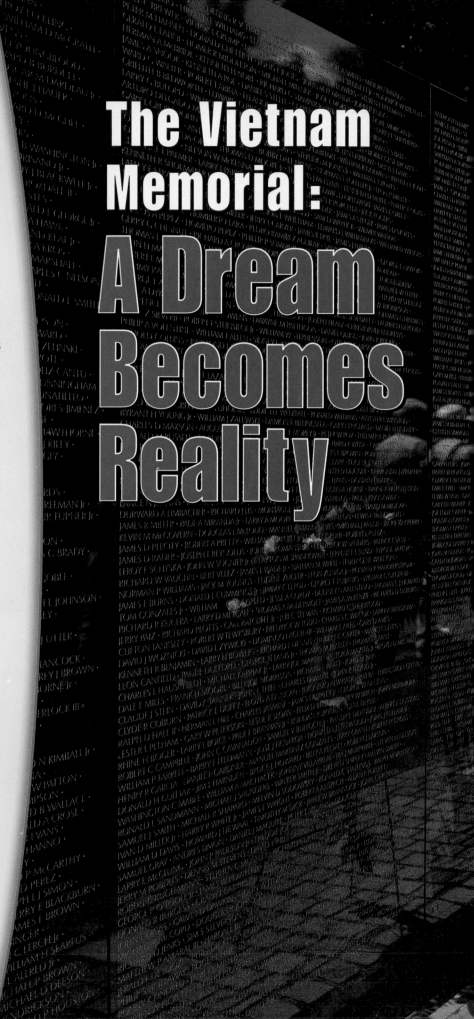

The Vietnam Memorial: A Dream Becomes Reality

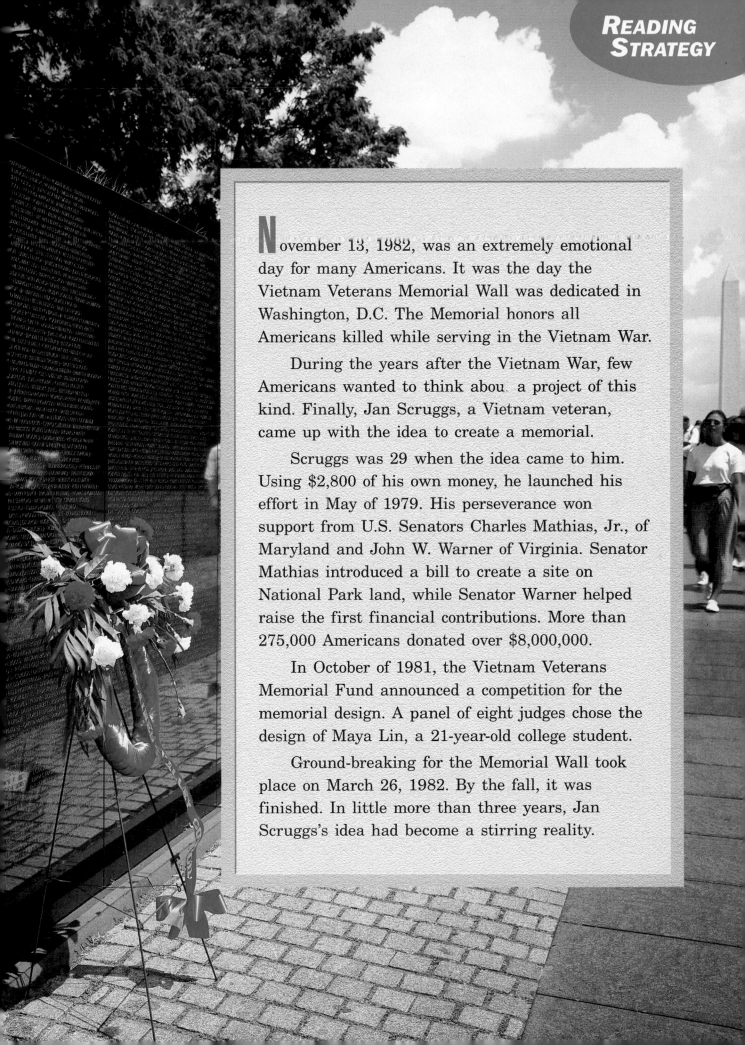

November 13, 1982, was an extremely emotional day for many Americans. It was the day the Vietnam Veterans Memorial Wall was dedicated in Washington, D.C. The Memorial honors all Americans killed while serving in the Vietnam War.

During the years after the Vietnam War, few Americans wanted to think abou_ a project of this kind. Finally, Jan Scruggs, a Vietnam veteran, came up with the idea to create a memorial.

Scruggs was 29 when the idea came to him. Using $2,800 of his own money, he launched his effort in May of 1979. His perseverance won support from U.S. Senators Charles Mathias, Jr., of Maryland and John W. Warner of Virginia. Senator Mathias introduced a bill to create a site on National Park land, while Senator Warner helped raise the first financial contributions. More than 275,000 Americans donated over $8,000,000.

In October of 1981, the Vietnam Veterans Memorial Fund announced a competition for the memorial design. A panel of eight judges chose the design of Maya Lin, a 21-year-old college student.

Ground-breaking for the Memorial Wall took place on March 26, 1982. By the fall, it was finished. In little more than three years, Jan Scruggs's idea had become a stirring reality.

TIME

FOR KIDS
SPECIAL REPORT

A Mountain of a Monument

Visitors to the Crazy Horse
Memorial in South Dakota

Hail to a Chief

The world's biggest statue is being carved out of mountain rock

Crazy Horse was a brave Native American chief who believed that after he died, his bones would turn into rocks. He was just about right! For over 50 years, a stunning statue has been slowly taking shape in the rocky Black Hills of South Dakota. It is a memorial to Chief Crazy Horse and stands as a symbol for Native Americans everywhere. When it is finished, it will be by far the largest sculpture in the world.

After Crazy Horse died in 1877, Native Americans searched for a way to honor their hero. In 1939, the Sioux chief Standing Bear asked Korczak Ziolkowski, a Polish American artist, to design a huge statue. Standing Bear wrote, "My fellow chiefs and I would like the white man to know the red man had great heroes, too." The two men got together and chose a site on Thunderhead Mountain, not far from Mt. Rushmore—home to the faces of four U.S. Presidents.

Ziolkowski and Standing Bear dedicate the statue after the first blast, in 1948.

ALL PHOTOS: ROBB DEWALL

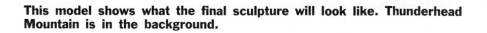

This model shows what the final sculpture will look like. Thunderhead Mountain is in the background.

375

Carving the statue may take another 50 years.

Ziolkowski painted a giant outline of the fearless leader riding his horse, with Crazy Horse's arm pointing across the lands he loved. Then Ziolkowski set off explosives to blast away the rock.

Ziolkowski died suddenly in 1982. His family and others continue to carve his dream. During the summer, 13 people work full-time on the carving. If the weather isn't too cold in winter, carving takes place then, too.

How big will the statue be? All four faces of the Presidents on nearby Mount Rushmore could fit inside Crazy Horse's head, which is $87\frac{1}{2}$ feet high. One nostril of the big horse will be wide and deep enough to hold a five-room house. So far, more than 9 million tons of rock have been blasted away in the process of carving the memorial. (Blasting takes place on only two nights a year.)

The statue may not be finished until the year 2040 or beyond. But the awesome sight already attracts visitors.

Twice a year, night blasts light up the South Dakota sky. Here 70 fireballs help carve Crazy Horse's arm and 88-foot-high head.

376

Who Was Crazy Horse?

Crazy Horse was a Native American warrior and chief who belonged to the Oglala Sioux nation of South Dakota. He tried to protect the Sioux people from white settlers who wanted to take over Sioux land in the 1870s. Until then, the Native Americans had lived in a huge area that today makes up the states of Minnesota, North and South Dakota, Nebraska, and Wyoming. When the U.S. sent soldiers to force the Native Americans to live on reservations, Crazy Horse fought back. He was fighting for the rights and freedom of his people.

The great and proud chief was killed by a U.S. soldier in 1877. He was only about 30 years old.

CORBIS-BETTMANN

Once a year, people can hike to the top of the mountain to view the face of Crazy Horse up close and see how the work is coming along. On that day, as many as 13,000 people have climbed the 600-foot peak to view the statue.

There's more to do than just look at the Crazy Horse Memorial, however. Visitors can also tour the Indian Museum of North America at the base of Thunderhead Mountain. They can learn about the history of Native Americans and see how they lived. Displays include clothing, arts and crafts, pottery, and hunting weapons. So the next time you are in the Black Hills of South Dakota, pay a visit to the Crazy Horse Memorial. It's definitely worth the trip!

FIND OUT MORE
Visit our website:
www.mhschool.com/reading

*inter*NET
CONNECTION

Based on an article in *TIME FOR KIDS*.

Story Questions & Activities

1. Why did Chief Standing Bear want to have a huge statue designed of Chief Crazy Horse?

2. Why does Crazy Horse's arm point across the South Dakota landscape?

3. Why do you think the sculptor and Standing Bear chose a site near Mount Rushmore for the statue of Chief Crazy Horse?

4. What is the sequence of events in this selection?

5. Suppose that the sculptor of the statue of Chief Crazy Horse had a chance to meet Michele Wood, the artist in "Going Back Home." Do you think they would agree that saving the past through art is important? Why or why not?

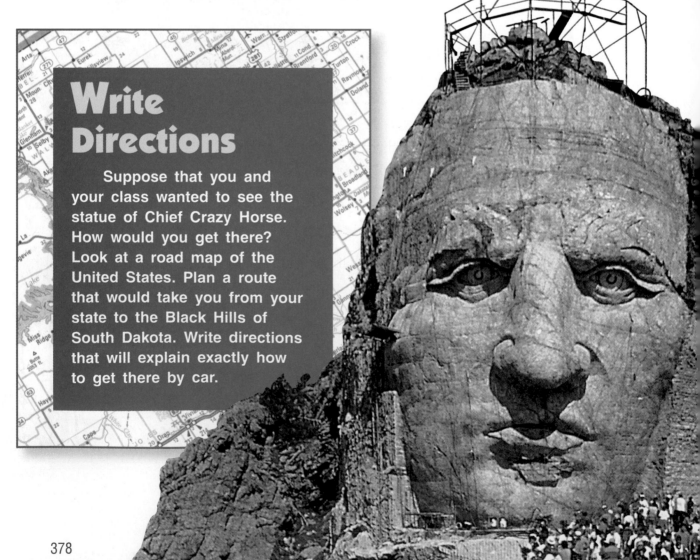

Write Directions

Suppose that you and your class wanted to see the statue of Chief Crazy Horse. How would you get there? Look at a road map of the United States. Plan a route that would take you from your state to the Black Hills of South Dakota. Write directions that will explain exactly how to get there by car.

Create a Picture Postcard

The Black Hills of South Dakota are home to Mount Rushmore and the statue of Chief Crazy Horse. They are also a range of beautiful mountains. Create a Black Hills picture postcard. Use a collage of scenic photos and drawings on one side of an index card. On the other side, write several sentences about the scene as if you were there.

Design a Community Statue

Is there someone in your community who deserves a statue? Brainstorm with your classmates to create a list of possible candidates. Then vote for one. Draw a statue of that person. Write a plaque for the statue to explain who the person is. What has the person done to earn this honor?

Find Out More

Chief Crazy Horse was an important Native American leader, but so was Chief Powhatan in Virginia, Chief Tomochichi in Georgia, and many others. Start by checking in an encyclopedia or in a book about Native Americans. Choose a Native American leader and write a short biography. Include a description of his or her achievements. Share your work in a class book of Native Americans.

Use Scale Drawings

"A Mountain of a Monument" shows that before a sculptor can start to carve a statue, he or she must make drawings of it. The drawings show the statue from different angles. In addition, the sculptor must include the scale of the statue. The scale shows how many inches in the drawings equal a foot in the finished work. These drawings are a guide for the sculptor when the carving of the statue begins.

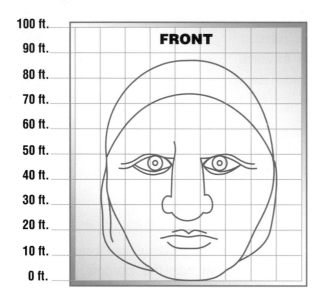
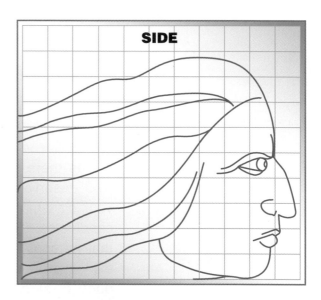

1/4 inch = 10 feet

Use the drawings to answer these questions.

1 What do the drawings show?

2 How large is Chief Crazy Horse's head in the finished statue?

3 How do you know that Chief Crazy Horse is in motion?

4 Why is it taking so long to carve the statue of Chief Crazy Horse?

5 Why is it necessary for a sculptor to make drawings before carving a statue?

TEST POWER

DIRECTIONS

Read the sample story. Then read each question about the story.

SAMPLE

Good Music

Floyd hunted through the music store, but he couldn't find anything to get for his grandfather's birthday. He wanted to buy his grandfather a compact disk for his new compact disk player.

The salesclerk asked Floyd if she could help.

"Yes, I hope so," Floyd said. "I'm trying to find a compact disk for my grandfather, but there is so much to choose from that I don't know where to begin. What's your recommendation?"

"Well, we carry several different types of music," the salesclerk replied. "What type of music does he usually listen to?"

"He generally likes classical," Floyd responded.

"Then let's get you to the classical section of the store. It's <u>adjacent</u> to the 'musicals' section, and I'm sure you'll find what you're looking for there!"

1 In this passage the word <u>adjacent</u> means —

A next

B far

C matched

D underneath

2 Floyd asked the salesclerk for help because he —

F thought she looked friendly

G didn't know where to look

H wanted to buy some country music

J had no idea what his grandfather would like

381

To Dark Eyes Dreaming

Dreams go fast and far
 these days.
They go by rocket thrust.
They go arrayed
 in lights
  or in the dust of stars.
Dreams, these days,
 go fast and far.
Dreams are young, these days,
 or very old,
They can be black
 or blue or gold.
They need no special charts,
 nor any fuel.
It seems, only one rule applies,
 to all our dreams—
They will not fly except in open sky.
 A fenced-in dream
  will die.

by Zilpha Keatley Snyder

383

Investigate!

FIRST FLIGHT

Said Wilbur Wright, "Oh, this is grand,

But, Orville, you must understand.

We've discovered all right

The secret of flight—

The question is, how do we land?"

by Frank Richards

Stories in Art

Artists learn to use their imagination. Look at this work of art. What do you see? The artist has combined two very different ideas. These ideas make one imaginary scene that you can see in two different ways.

Look at the painting. What shapes do you see? Look again to see the painting in a different way. Do you notice the painting on the easel? What would happen if you removed the white edge from the canvas? Why do you think the artist painted the picture in this way?

Study the painting. Can you imagine another way to show where the ocean stops and the painting begins? What is the artist saying about the way art imitates life? About the way life imitates art? Do you like this painting? Give reasons.

The Human Condition, II
by René Magritte, 1935
Private Collection, Belgium

386

The Pest

Make Judgments and Decisions

Develop a strategy for making judgments and decisions.

1 **Think about the actions** of the main character.

2 **Decide on the reasons** for those actions.

3 **Think about what** you would do in a similar situation. How would you feel?

4 **Compare what you** would do with what Tom did.

5 **Make a judgment** based on evidence from the selection and your own beliefs and opinions.

Tom's younger brother Brian followed him everywhere. He begged to go with Tom to the park and to the community pool. Brian played with Tom's favorite toys and even read his favorite books. Brian was a pest!

One afternoon, Tom's best friend Mike came over for a game of checkers. Tom and Mike had been playing checkers for years. As they began to set up the game on the edge of Tom's bed, Brian came wandering into the room.

"May I play?" Brian asked.

"You don't know how to play checkers. Besides, you're much too young," said Tom.

"Please! Just let me watch. I bet if I watch long enough, I'll learn how to play," said Brian.

"Fine. You can watch, but just for a few minutes," said Tom.

Brian sat so quietly that Tom and Mike played for almost two hours before they realized he was still in the bedroom.

Just after dinner, Brian pleaded with his brother to play a game of checkers. Tom finally agreed and thought to himself, "This will be an easy win."

Tom and Brian played three games of checkers, and to Tom's surprise, Brian won all three games. Brian was a great player! "Maybe I'll even ask him to go to the park with me next week," Tom thought.

Jan Romero Stevens was born in Las Vegas, New Mexico. *Carlos and the Skunk* is her third book in the "Carlos" series. The first two books were *Carlos and the Squash Plant* and *Carlos and the Cornfield*. When Stevens is writing her books, she reads them to her two sons, and they give her suggestions and ideas. They are my "best and most helpful critics," she says.

Stevens enjoys sharing her Mexican heritage and the culture of the Southwest with the readers of her books. Today, the writer lives in Flagstaff, Arizona, with her husband and sons. In addition to writing the "Carlos" books, she writes articles for newspapers and magazines. She also finds time to play the flute in a local orchestra.

Meet Jeanne Arnold

Jeanne Arnold is an illustrator and a painter. Her work includes all three books in the "Carlos" series, as well as *When You Were Just a Little Girl* by B.G. Hennessy. Arnold has spent time backpacking in the Southwest. This helps her capture the regional flavor of the "Carlos" books.

Carlos and the Skunk

Written by Jan Romero Stevens Illustrated by Jeanne Arnold

Carlos could not remember how long he and Gloria had been best friends.

When they were little, Gloria's mother would prop them up on old catalogs at the kitchen table while she strung red chiles together or rolled the dough for tortillas. If they were at Carlos's house, his mother would let them play in the garden while she sorted through the shiny green chiles, ripe red tomatoes, and sweet corn.

It seemed as if Carlos and Gloria were always together, but as they grew older, Carlos's feelings toward his friend started to change. He began gazing at himself in the mirror, combing his hair this way and that to see which looked better. He started showing off for Gloria, wanting her to notice how brave and smart he was becoming.

Carlos and Gloria lived in the fertile Española Valley nestled in the mountains of northern New Mexico. Their thick-walled adobe homes, with high tin roofs and matching gardens, were within walking distance from one another.

392

After school each day, Gloria and Carlos did their chores—weeding the garden, feeding the chickens, and doing their homework. After dinner, they were allowed to play.

One fall evening, when they were running through the cornfield playing hide and seek, they caught a glimpse of a striped skunk slinking through the shadows of the garden. The children had seen the skunk many times before. It had only two toes on its right front paw, and they had nicknamed it Dos Dedos (Two Toes).

Gloria feared the chance of arousing the skunk's anger and kept far away from it. But one afternoon, Carlos, wanting to impress Gloria, moved closer and closer until he could clearly see the narrow, single white stripe running from its head onto its tail.

"Carlos, you'd better be careful," whispered Gloria as Carlos inched along on his stomach toward the skunk.

"Gloria, don't worry. I know just how to catch a skunk," Carlos boasted. "You know what I heard? If you pick a skunk up by its tail, it can't spray you."

Gloria covered her mouth and giggled.

"Oh, Carlos," she said. *"No puedes creer todo lo que te dicen—*you can't believe everything you hear."

"But it's true," Carlos insisted to his doubting friend, and he became more determined than ever to prove himself right. He went to sleep that night still pondering over how to catch the skunk.

The next day, Carlos had planned to take Gloria fishing so he awoke early and got dressed. His mother prepared warm flour tortillas, fried eggs, and fresh salsa for breakfast. Salsa was a family tradition in Carlos's home. Made from tomatoes and green chiles grown in the garden, the salsa was spicy and tasty. Carlos spooned it on just about everything—from breakfast to dinner.

After breakfast, Carlos rushed outside to get his fishing pole and a can for worms. Rounding the corner of his house, he saw Gloria waiting for him by the gate. As they began walking down the road together, they saw Dos Dedos in the garden.

Qué suerte! (What luck!) thought Carlos. "I will catch Dos Dedos this time!"

Carlos gave no thought to what he might do with the skunk if he did catch it, but instead began creeping up behind it. He got closer and closer until he was inches away. For just a moment, Carlos hesitated, then winked at Gloria before he reached out and grabbed the tail. In an instant, the skunk's tail arched, and Carlos was sprayed from head to toe.

With a gasp, Carlos fell backward onto the ground. He was so stunned he hardly realized what had happened. He had never smelled such a strong odor. His eyes itched. He coughed and snorted and blew his nose. He did his best not to cry in front of Gloria.

Quite unconcerned, Dos Dedos disappeared down the side of an arroyo. And Carlos ran off to the river—leaving both Gloria and his fishing pole far behind.

Carlos chose a secluded spot and pulled off all his clothes as fast as he could. The smell of them was unbearable. He jumped into the stream and washed out his clothing, laying it out on a branch to dry in the sun. By afternoon his shirt and pants were dry, but the strong odor still lingered, especially on his shoes. He dressed and walked the long way home, climbing up and down the sides of the arroyos and stopping to gather piñon nuts. When he finally reached his house, he carefully took off his shoes and left them by the back door.

When his mother came into the kitchen, she noticed a strange smell, but before she could question Carlos, he slipped out the door and into the garden.

Carlos had heard that tomato juice helped to get rid of the smell of skunk, so he picked every ripe tomato he could find and sneaked into the bathroom. He squeezed the tomatoes into the bathtub and all over his hair, scrubbing himself as hard as he could with a washrag.

Beginning to think he smelled better, he crawled into bed and fell asleep quickly after his very unpleasant day.

The next morning was Sunday, and Mamá was up early, patting and shaping the dough for tortillas.

Dressed in his best shirt and pants, Carlos sat down at the table.

"Carlos, you look very nice for church this morning," said Mamá as she untied her flowered apron. "Where are your shoes?"

"They're outside, Mamá. I will get them when we leave," said Carlos, feeling uneasy.

Carlos's family walked to the church near their home. When they arrived, they squeezed into a bench near the back. Carlos was pleased that he was able to sit next to Gloria.

But a most peculiar thing happened in church that day.

As the choir began a hymn, some of the singers began to make strange faces and cover their noses with handkerchiefs. The priest, as he walked to the altar, sneezed loudly and cleared his throat.

The people in the first few rows of the congregation turned to each other with puzzled looks. The women began vigorously fanning their faces with their church programs. The children started squirming and pinched their noses. Little by little the strange behavior began working its way toward the back of the church.

Carlos couldn't figure out what was going on until he looked down at his feet. He was sitting next to an air vent for the church's heating system. The smell from his shoes, which he had forgotten to clean after being sprayed by Dos Dedos, was spreading through the heating ducts to the entire church.

"Papá I think we better go home," whispered Carlos, hoping no one would realize he was the source of the terrible smell.

Several families began heading for the door. The priest dismissed the service early.

Embarrassed, Carlos pushed his way out of the church. He heard Gloria calling to him, but he bolted through the door, and ran all the way home. He untied his shoes, pulled them off, and left them on the back doorstep. Then he hurried to his room and shut the door.

Troubled over how he might rid himself of the strong-smelling shoes, Carlos stayed in his bedroom until his mother called him for dinner. While they were eating, his parents noticed he was unusually quiet but said nothing to him.

Finally, when dinner was over, Papá turned to Carlos.

"Carlos, I've noticed your shoes are looking a little small," said Papá, with a glance toward Mamá. "Isn't it time for a new pair?"

Carlos nodded, breathing a sigh of relief.

"Oh, *sí, sí,* Papá," he stammered. "My feet are getting too big for those shoes now."

The next day, Carlos and Papá drove to town. After trying on several pairs of shoes, Carlos chose a pair of heeled cowboy boots that made him appear much taller.

A few weeks passed and Carlos forgot about his encounter with the skunk. One evening, after a big dinner of pinto beans, rice, tortillas, and his favorite salsa, he decided to visit Gloria. He put on his new boots and took a good look at his hair in the mirror. As he was getting ready to leave, his father called him outside.

"I need your help," said Papá, and he pointed beneath the bushes alongside the house.

Carlos could just make out the shape of a small, black-and-white animal with three little ones that had made their home under the leaves.

"Dios mío!" ("Oh my goodness!") said Carlos. "What will we do?"

"It's no problem, Carlos," said Papá. "You know what I hear? You can catch a skunk if you pick it up by its tail. You go first."

Carlos's nose and eyes began to water just with the thought of it.

"Oh, Papá, *no puedes creer todo lo que te dicen*—you know you can't believe everything you hear," Carlos said, and he drew himself up a little taller, smoothed back his hair, and headed for Gloria's house.

FRESH TOMATO SALSA

3 tomatoes, diced

1/4 white or yellow onion, diced

2–3 scallions with green tops, chopped

1 medium clove garlic, minced

2 teaspoons vinegar

1 teaspoon vegetable or olive oil

3–4 sprigs of cilantro, chopped

1 roasted green chile or 2 serrano chiles, diced
   (or 2 tablespoons canned green chile)

1 teaspoon salt

1/4 teaspoon pepper

Mix all ingredients in a food processor, leaving salsa chunky, or stir by hand. Chill. Spoon over anything—eggs, beans, tacos—or use as a dip for tortilla chips.

403

Story Questions & Activities

1 Where does the story take place?

2 Why does Carlos pick up the skunk?

3 Who is the main character in this story? How do you know?

4 What lesson does this story teach?

5 Does Carlos remind you of any other character you have read about or anyone you know in real life? Why or why not?

Write a TV News Story

Imagine you are a television news reporter. You have about 90 seconds on camera to describe what happened when Carlos went to church on Sunday. Make sure you cover all the facts: Who was involved? What happened? When and where did the incident take place? If you can, videotape your report and play it for your classmates.

Find a Recipe

Carlos loves fresh tomato salsa. He puts it on almost everything. Do you have a favorite Mexican food? Find a recipe for a Mexican or a Southwestern treat, such as tortillas or *chile con carne,* and write it down. Share the recipe with your friends. You might want to try the recipe and tell how it tasted!

Make a Poster

What kind of skunk does Carlos catch in the story? Choose one kind of skunk—striped, hog-nosed, or spotted. Create a "skunk" poster. Draw a picture of your skunk, and tell where it lives. Include at least three other facts, such as what a skunk's spray—musk—is used for.

Find Out More

This story takes place in the Southwest, in New Mexico. What do you know about this area? What people lived there 1,000 years ago? Start by checking in your social studies textbook or an encyclopedia. Find out about the Anasazi. Who were these early American people? How and where did they build their unusual houses? What were their villages like? Share what you learn with your classmates.

Read a Diagram

Carlos and Gloria's families both keep gardens. Before planting a garden, you may want to make a plan. A **diagram** is a plan in the form of a picture.

Use the diagram to answer these questions.

1 How many different types of fruits and vegetables are in the garden?

2 What should you look out for near the tomatoes?

3 Which plant gets the largest part of the garden?

4 Which plants are Mamá's responsibility?

5 Why do you think they want to build a tool shed?

Test Tip

Always remember to look for the best answer to the question.

DIRECTIONS
Read the sample story. Then read each question about the story.

SAMPLE

Jackie's Dilemma

Jackie's parakeet, Tatters, wouldn't calm down. Jackie knew that Tatters could be <u>clamorous</u>, but today the tiny bird was making an unbearable amount of noise. Everyone who came near the bird became extremely annoyed.

"What's disturbing your bird?" growled Jackie's father.

Jackie's mother covered her ears and said, "Jackie, will you please ask your feathered friend to keep it down?"

Jackie didn't know what to do. Tatters had been loud on a few occasions before, but it had only been when his water dish had been empty.

"That's it!" Jackie exclaimed. She slipped a tiny dish of water inside the cage. "Last time he was this noisy, he just needed some water," she said.

Sure enough, the little parakeet became silent as he hopped over to the water dish.

1 How did Jackie realize that Tatters was thirsty?

   A She saw his water dish was empty.

   B She remembered that Tatters had done this before.

   C She could tell that he had a sore throat.

   D She realized that she, too, was thirsty for some water.

2 When something is <u>clamorous</u>, it is very —

   F foolish

   G hungry

   H ugly

   J loud

Stories in Art

This photograph shows a scene from a movie about the great English detective Sherlock Holmes. Think about the job of a detective. How do detectives sift through clues to solve mysteries?

Look at the photograph. Notice what Holmes is doing. Why is he looking through a magnifying glass? How is a magnifying glass like a scientist's microscope? How is a detective like a scientist? Explain.

Imagine that you are Sherlock Holmes. Besides a magnifying glass, what methods could you use to discover information? How would you separate the unimportant clues from the important ones? How would this help you solve a mystery?

Basil Rathbone as Sherlock Holmes, c. 1940

Important and Unimportant Information

Develop a strategy to identify important and unimportant information.

1 **Find the main idea.** What is the main point of the article?

2 **Identify details** that are needed to understand the main idea. This is the important information.

3 **Decide which details** are unimportant. They add interest to the story but aren't necessary for you to understand it.

4 **Review the important information** and restate it in your own words.

Woolly Mammoth Found

Mammoths were huge, elephant-like creatures that once roamed most of the Earth's continents. About 10,000 years ago, these creatures died out.

In October of 1999, on the frozen tundra of central Siberia, an amazing event took place. An expedition led by French explorer Bernard Buigues dug out from the permafrost (a layer of soil and water that is permanently frozen) the carcass of a 20,000-year-old woolly mammoth. It was so well preserved that it still had some of its hair, skin, muscle, and other tissue.

The chunk of permafrost containing the mammoth was lifted by helicopter and flown 150 miles to an ice cave. Scientists there began defrosting the huge beast with hair dryers, one small section at a time, over a period of months. They called it the "Jarkov Mammoth" for the Siberian family who first discovered it.

Dutch scientist Dick Mol has been working on mammoths for more than 25 years. He is supervising the analysis of the mammoth. "This is a dream for me—to find the parts and touch them," said Mol. "It's very exciting."

Mol believes that this creature can help scientists learn why mammoths became extinct. Were they killed off by disease? The frozen mammoth may give scientists real answers to this question and to many others.

HOW to THiNK

ANSWERING QUESTIONS BY

LiKe a ScIENtiST

THE SCIENTIFIC METHOD

by Stephen P. Kramer

illustrated by Kim Behm

"Whump, whump" went the tires of Pete's bike. The sounds were so close together they seemed like one noise.

"Hey!" screamed Pete. He pointed to the side of the road. "Look out! Get over!"

Jim could barely see the outline of Pete's arm in the darkness, but he swerved to the left. He coasted along the shoulder of the road until he caught up with Pete. Pete had stopped and was looking back.

"What's wrong?" asked Jim.

Pete shook his head. "A snake! A huge snake . . . I rode over it! On the side of the road! I didn't see it until too late . . . I couldn't even turn."

"Probably just an old inner tube," said Jim. "Come on, let's go."

"Was not," replied Pete, shaking his head again. "Want to go back and see?"

Jim hesitated for a moment. "All right," he answered. "I'm not scared."

Pete unhooked the flashlight from the frame of his bike. The boys laid their bicycles in the weeds beside the road and slowly walked back. The flashlight made a faint yellow spot on the pavement.

Pete shone the flashlight far ahead. "Up there," he said. "That's where I rode over it."

Jim looked around. "I don't see anything."

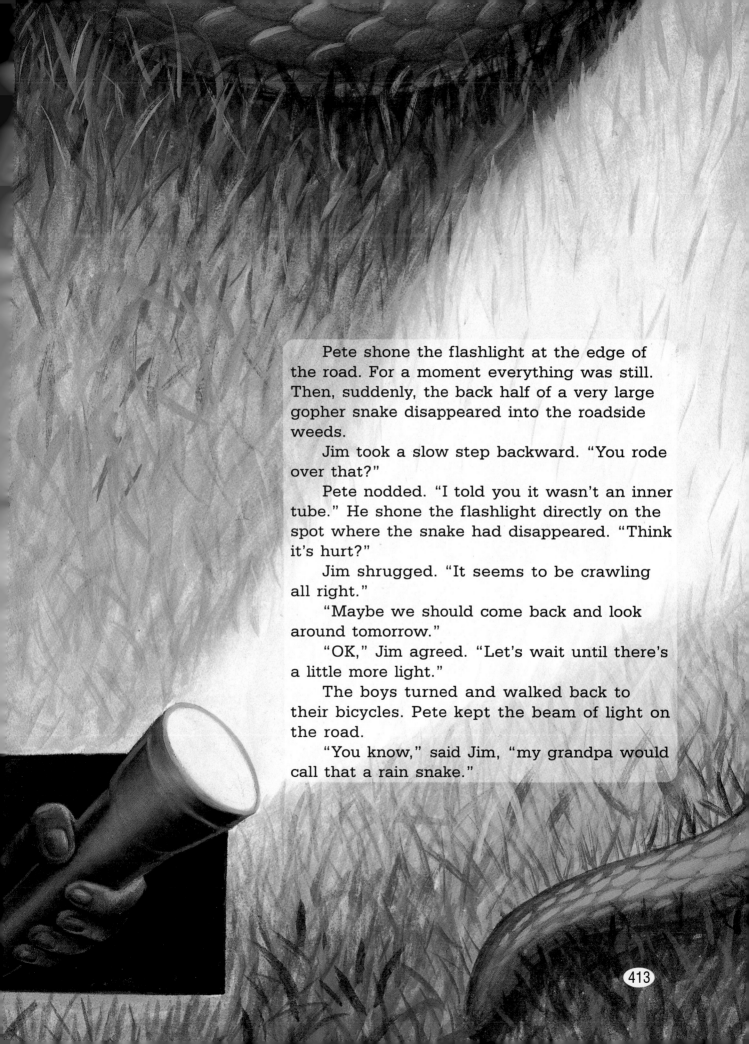

Pete shone the flashlight at the edge of the road. For a moment everything was still. Then, suddenly, the back half of a very large gopher snake disappeared into the roadside weeds.

Jim took a slow step backward. "You rode over that?"

Pete nodded. "I told you it wasn't an inner tube." He shone the flashlight directly on the spot where the snake had disappeared. "Think it's hurt?"

Jim shrugged. "It seems to be crawling all right."

"Maybe we should come back and look around tomorrow."

"OK," Jim agreed. "Let's wait until there's a little more light."

The boys turned and walked back to their bicycles. Pete kept the beam of light on the road.

"You know," said Jim, "my grandpa would call that a rain snake."

413

"What?" asked Pete.

"A rain snake. He'd say you could make it rain for sure with a snake like that."

"How?"

"Well," said Jim, "my grandpa grew up way back in the hills. When he was a boy, the farmers would sometimes use a dead snake to make it rain. They'd find a large tree with a strong low branch and throw the snake over the branch. A big snake like that would bring rain for sure."

Pete leaned over and picked up his bike. "You believe that?"

"Naw," answered Jim quickly. Then he scratched his head and looked back down the road. "But, well, I never tried it. I don't know. My grandpa says they did it a lot. Maybe it'd work for some people, sometimes. . . ."

What do *you* think? Can throwing a dead snake over a tree branch bring rain?

Every day you answer questions—dozens or even hundreds of them. What should I wear today? What assignments do I need for school? Can I eat an extra piece of toast and still get to the bus on time? What should I do tonight?

Some questions you answer correctly. Others you don't. Some questions are important. You spend lots of time thinking about them. Other questions aren't important. You guess at the answer or just choose an answer automatically.

How Do You Answer Questions?

You think about many things when you try to answer a question. You try to remember things you know that might help you. You look for new information about the question. Sometimes you try to guess how someone else would answer the question. Other times you might pick an answer because of what you would *like* the answer to be.

Sometimes these things help you find a correct answer. Other times they lead you to a wrong answer.

Here are three stories. Each story has a question. Each story tells about something that could happen to you, and each story will show a different way of answering a question.

INFORMATION

You're sitting on your bed one afternoon reading a book about a mountain climber. Things are getting very exciting (an avalanche has just started) when your little brother Ralphie walks into the room. He strolls past your bed and looks out the window.

"Hey," he says, "someone's in Mr. Murphy's backyard."

Your teeth start to grind. You've lost your place but you try not to show it. A long time ago you learned that sometimes the best way to get along with Ralphie is to ignore him.

"Hey," says Ralphie, "they're going into the Murphys' house."

You frown and roll over, wondering when Ralphie is going to go away.

"Hey," says Ralphie, "they're coming out of the Murphys' house. They're carrying something that's all covered up. They're stealing something from the Murphys!"

You sit up straight. The Murphys? Someone is stealing something from the Murphys?

AVALANCHE!

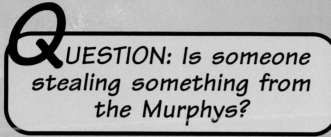

QUESTION: Is someone stealing something from the Murphys?

Then, out the window you see a truck. It is parked in front of the Murphys' house. Painted in large blue letters on the side of the truck are the words "Jake's TV Repair."

You shake your head.

"Go on," you tell Ralphie. "Take off."

"They're stealing something from the Murphys' house," says Ralphie. "The bad man just went back inside."

"It's not a bad man," you explain. "Someone's just picking up the TV. Can't you see that truck out there?"

"They're not taking the TV," Ralphie insists.

"Get out!" you shout.

"No!" says Ralphie.

"I said get out!" you scream, throwing a pillow at Ralphie.

So Ralphie finally leaves, walking out of the room very slowly.

417

RRRING!

That night at dinner the telephone rings. Your father answers it. When he returns to the table, he says, "The Murphys just got home. While they were gone this afternoon, someone broke into their house and stole some money. The burglars also took some silverware and Mr. Murphy's violin.

"Most of our neighbors were gone this afternoon. The Johnsons didn't see anything because they were watching a repairman fix their TV all afternoon. Did any of you see anything?"

Ralphie sits up straight and begins nodding.

What happened? The question was: Is someone stealing something from the Murphys? You and Ralphie both made observations. Ralphie's observations told him the answer was yes. Your observations told you the answer was no. Why did you and Ralphie end up with different answers to the same question?

You answered the question incorrectly because of the way you used an observation. You saw a TV repair truck through the front window. Your observation was a good one. You noticed what kind of truck was on your street and where it was parked. The problem was how you used your observation. You thought the truck was giving you information about who was in the Murphys' house. Actually, Ralphie was giving you better information.

Information must be used carefully. Having information does not always mean you will answer a question correctly. If the information is not true or is not used in the right way, it can lead to a wrong answer.

It's Wednesday morning, just before lunch. Your teacher arranged for someone from the zoo to come and show your class some animals. You have seen an iguana, a mongoose, and a large snake. Now the zookeeper reaches into a wooden box and pulls out a fishbowl. He sets the bowl on a low table at the front of the room. Three small gray fish swim back and forth.

"Who knows the name of these fish?" asks the zookeeper.

Everyone is quiet. You stare at the fish for a moment. Of course you know what they are. They're guppies! They look just like the fish in your sister's aquarium. You've spent hours watching guppies.

Quickly, you raise your hand, but you're sitting in the last row and the zookeeper doesn't see you.

You wave your hand back and forth. The girl next to you ducks.

"These are gastromorphs," says the zookeeper. "They live in slow, muddy streams in Africa. They are very dangerous. They will eat almost anything that moves."

Quickly, you pull your hand down and look around. "Whew," you think. "That could have been embarrassing." Then you lean forward and squint at those fish again.

"We always keep a strong screen over this fishbowl when we visit schools. If anyone were to stick a hand in the water, well, these little fish would immediately attack and begin taking bites out of it."

GASTRO

QUESTION: What kind of fish is in the bowl?

This time the question seems easy. The fish look a lot like guppies. They swim like guppies. They're even the size and color of guppies. But would you stick your hand in the bowl? Of course not! The zookeeper just told you they are gastromorphs. Zookeepers know their animals, right? So the fish must be gastromorphs. Maybe.

Here's what really happened. The zookeeper who was supposed to visit your class got sick. The zoo sent over the person who normally takes care of birds. The zookeeper who came to your class knew a lot about birds, but not much about fish.

His first stop that morning was at the mammal house to pick up the mongoose. Then he went to the reptile house to get the iguana and the snake. He took all three animals with him into the fish house.

It was dark in the fish house. All the fish were arranged alphabetically in separate aquariums. The guppies were in the aquarium next to the gastromorphs. The zookeeper picked up a net, walked over to the gastromorphs, and leaned over the aquarium to dip some out. Just then the snake began to crawl out of its bag, so the zookeeper reached down to push it back in. When he stood up straight again he had three fish in his net. He dumped them into the fishbowl and hurried to your school. What he didn't know was that he had accidentally dipped the net into the wrong tank. He had netted three guppies instead of three gastromorphs.

422

MORPHS?

You really were right! The fish were guppies, but you changed your mind because of what the zookeeper said.

Sometimes other people are wrong. Usually zookeepers know much more about animals than you do, but maybe not every time. If you answer questions by depending too much on other people's answers, you probably will make mistakes.

Because We Want To

Sometimes we know how we would like a question to be answered. We choose an answer to a question because it's the answer we like. Let's look at another story.

It's Friday afternoon, and the last bell of the day has just rung. You gather up your books and start toward the door of your classroom. As you step into the hallway your teacher calls out, "Don't forget to finish your math assignment. It's due Monday morning." You look down and check to be sure you have your math book.

The weekend passes quickly. On Friday night you go to a basketball game. On Saturday your family goes to the beach. Finally, on Sunday evening you clear a spot on the kitchen table and start to work on your assignment.

Just then the telephone rings. You hurry to answer it.

"Hi," says Pat. "What are you doing?"

"Math," you answer.

"Hey," says Pat, "I've got a better idea. There's a good movie downtown. My dad gave me some money. Let's go."

"I can't," you answer. "I haven't even started this assignment yet."

"It's a great movie," says Pat. "Everyone says so."

"Look, report cards are coming out next week. I need a good grade on this paper."

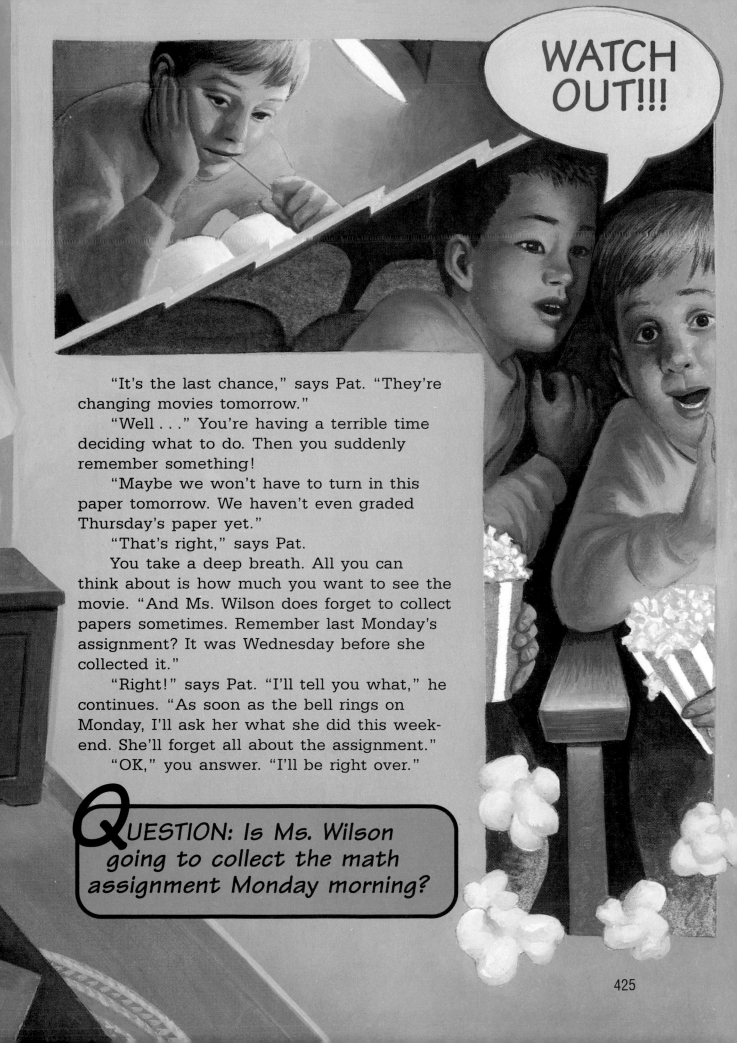

WATCH OUT!!!

"It's the last chance," says Pat. "They're changing movies tomorrow."

"Well . . ." You're having a terrible time deciding what to do. Then you suddenly remember something!

"Maybe we won't have to turn in this paper tomorrow. We haven't even graded Thursday's paper yet."

"That's right," says Pat.

You take a deep breath. All you can think about is how much you want to see the movie. "And Ms. Wilson does forget to collect papers sometimes. Remember last Monday's assignment? It was Wednesday before she collected it."

"Right!" says Pat. "I'll tell you what," he continues. "As soon as the bell rings on Monday, I'll ask her what she did this weekend. She'll forget all about the assignment."

"OK," you answer. "I'll be right over."

QUESTION: Is Ms. Wilson going to collect the math assignment Monday morning?

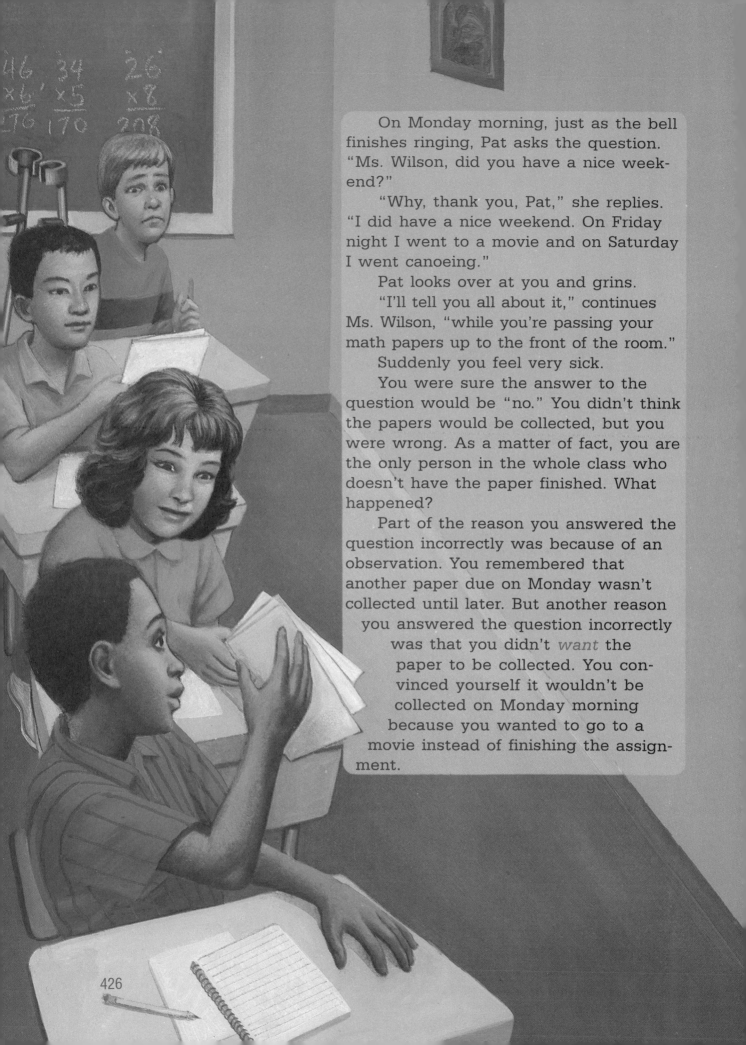

On Monday morning, just as the bell finishes ringing, Pat asks the question. "Ms. Wilson, did you have a nice weekend?"

"Why, thank you, Pat," she replies. "I did have a nice weekend. On Friday night I went to a movie and on Saturday I went canoeing."

Pat looks over at you and grins.

"I'll tell you all about it," continues Ms. Wilson, "while you're passing your math papers up to the front of the room."

Suddenly you feel very sick.

You were sure the answer to the question would be "no." You didn't think the papers would be collected, but you were wrong. As a matter of fact, you are the only person in the whole class who doesn't have the paper finished. What happened?

Part of the reason you answered the question incorrectly was because of an observation. You remembered that another paper due on Monday wasn't collected until later. But another reason you answered the question incorrectly was that you didn't *want* the paper to be collected. You convinced yourself it wouldn't be collected on Monday morning because you wanted to go to a movie instead of finishing the assignment.

426

Sometimes we really want the answer to a question to turn out in a certain way. Such a question can be difficult to answer correctly or fairly. Often it is easier to find an answer we like than an answer that is correct.

Carelessly used information, what others think, what we want to happen—none of these are very reliable ways of answering questions. Too many times they lead to wrong answers. Is there a better way? How can you find out whether throwing a dead snake over a tree branch really will bring rain?

There *is* a better way to find answers. Scientists use a series of steps called *the scientific method* to find accurate and reliable answers to their questions.

Good scientists are skeptical, but they keep an open mind. They know that experiments sometimes show that the correct answer to a question is not *always* the one you think it will be!

MEET STEPHEN P. KRAMER

Science has always fascinated Stephen P. Kramer. In college, he studied biology, the science of living things. After graduation, he taught science for four years on a Navajo reservation. Today, Kramer lives in Vancouver, Washington, where he writes and helps care for his two sons. His books combine his training as a biologist and his experience as a teacher. His first book, **Getting Oxygen: What Do You Do If You're Cell Twenty-Two?,** explains how the body gets and uses oxygen. **How to Think Like a Scientist** describes the scientific method, the step-by-step process that scientists use to learn about our world.

Story Questions & Activities

1. Did Ralphie or his sister have the correct answer to the question, "Is someone stealing something from the Murphys"? Explain.

2. Why didn't the girl in the zookeeper story give the answer "guppies" when she knew she was right?

3. Why do scientists need to use information correctly when answering a question?

4. What is the main idea of this selection?

5. Imagine that a famous scientist had a chance to meet the detective in the picture on page 408. Do you think they would see similarities in their jobs? What would the differences be?

Write a Scientific Report

How does your cat let you know when it wants to come inside? How does a person eat an ice-cream cone? Choose an action to observe closely. Write a scientific report that presents clear and accurate facts. State the purpose of your report in the introduction. Supply the facts in the body of your report. End by summarizing your findings. Tell why they are important.

Draw a Scene

In the theft story, Ralphie saw people robbing the Murphys' house, while his sister saw a TV repairman simply taking the Murphys' TV set to the fix-it shop. Draw a scene like the one Ralphie and his sister witnessed. Include details that could be interpreted differently by two different people. Ask your partner to observe the scene. Under your drawing, write what you and your partner observed from looking at the same picture.

Create Two Comic Strips

Create two comic strips that both start with the same beginning but have two different endings. Show how one scene or situation can have a different ending depending on who is telling the story. Show what is happening in each picture with clear drawings and thought or speech balloons.

Find Out More

In the story you learned that many discoveries are made by answering questions in the right way. Choose a scientist, such as Albert Einstein or Marie Curie. What was the scientist's major discovery? How did the scientist become interested in his or her research project? Start by checking an encyclopedia, a book about science, a video, or a true story about the scientist. Take notes. Use your notes to prepare an oral report.

Use an Outline

An **outline** is a summary that shows how the information in a report, chapter, or story is or will be organized. When you have to write a report, making an outline first can help you group facts and ideas.

This outline is for a report about the inventor Thomas Edison. Roman numerals indicate the main topics. Capital letters indicate facts or details that support or explain the main topics.

I. Edison's Early Life
  A. Born in Ohio, 1847; spent childhood in Michigan
  B. Worked as newspaper boy on railroad; lost hearing in accident
  C. Became a telegraph operator

II. Menlo Park
  A. Sold first invention; used money to open research lab in Menlo Park, NJ
  B. Improved Alexander Graham Bell's telephone design
  C. Invented phonograph, many other things

III. The Light Bulb
  A. 1879: Made first practical light bulb
  B. 1880: Set up factory to manufacture light bulbs
  C. 1882: Built power plant that provided electricity to New York City

Use the outline to answer these questions.

1. What are the three main topics of the report?

2. Did Edison open the lab in Menlo Park before or after he invented the light bulb?

3. Where would you put information about Edison's school years?

4. Where would you add details about the design of the light bulb?

5. If you wanted to remember the key points of a magazine article, would making an outline be helpful? Explain.

TEST POWER

Test Tip

Restate the questions to make sure you understand them.

DIRECTIONS

Read the sample story. Then read each question about the story.

SAMPLE

Erica's Drawings

Erica wasn't a very good speller or a great mathematician. But she loved to draw. Whenever her teacher gave her the chance, Erica turned to the back of her notebook and drew a picture.

The other students in her class liked Erica's pictures so much that they often passed their notebooks to her. They, too, wanted to have wonderful pictures in the backs of their notebooks.

One day, Erica's teacher collected everyone's notebooks. "I see that there are a lot of drawings in all of your notebooks. Where did they come from?" the teacher asked.

Nobody said a word.

"I'm asking because I'd like to hang some of these beautiful pictures on the walls," the teacher continued.

The class cheered. Soon Erica's drawings covered the walls of the classroom.

1 Information in the passage shows that Erica is very —

  A playful

  B talented

  C organized

  D gloomy

2 In the future, Erica will probably NOT —

  F draw at lunchtime

  G study her spelling words

  H refuse to share her drawings

  J hang her drawings on the wall

Artists play tricks on your imagination. Playing tricks on your imagination is part of why art is so interesting.

Look at the picture. What can you tell about it? Do you know that you are looking at a tabletop? Do you think that the seashells, pearls, and coral are real? They're not. In fact, they are actually small pieces of marble placed within a blue marble tabletop. Even the shadows are not really shadows. Can you guess how they were made?

Study the picture. Why do you think the artist worked so hard to trick your eye? Why didn't he just use real seashells, pearls, and coral? What would they do to a tabletop? How is this picture like and unlike a real "undersea garden"?

432

Marble inlay tabletop of the seabed, c.1760
Hermitage Museum, St. Petersburg, Russia

Komodo

Fact and Nonfact

Develop a strategy for distinguishing fact from nonfact.

1 **Look for statements** that can be scientifically proved. They are facts.

2 **Ask: Can this statement be proved** through observation? If the answer is yes, it is a fact.

3 **Identify statements that cannot be proved** to be true. These are not facts.

4 **Restate the facts in your own words** to help you remember them.

Fire-breathing dragons exist only in fairy tales, right? Not true. On the island of Komodo, in Indonesia, lives a creature that the locals call an *ora*.

This remarkable animal is also known as the Komodo dragon. Though it looks like a dinosaur, the ora is actually a giant lizard.

How big is an ora? The largest ones measure over 10 feet in length and weigh more than 300 pounds.

Oras are the most common predators in the few Indonesian islands where they live. They hunt wild pigs, goats, monkeys, rodents, and deer.

Typically, oras sit motionless in the bushes for hours, waiting for prey to pass by. Then, with sudden speed, they strike. Imagine a lightning-fast 300-pound reptile coming right at you!

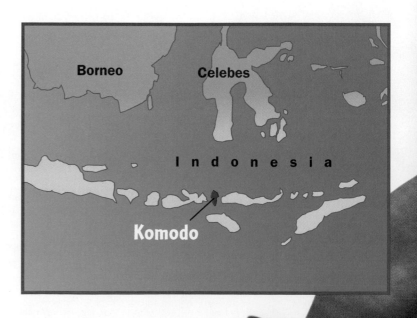

Dragons

The bite of an ora is deadly. If the bite itself doesn't kill, bacteria that live in the ora's mouth will transmit a lethal infection. These bacteria also have a terrible smell that many say is as strong as fire. Thus, the huge size and "fiery" breath of this amazing creature may be the true origin of the tales of "fire-breathing dragons."

Meet Virginia Wright-Frierson

The author and illustrator of *An Island Scrapbook*, Virginia Wright-Frierson, remembers that she loved to draw and paint from the time she was two years old. In school, instead of paying attention to math or geography, she says she was "constantly writing little stories and drawing pictures to go with them." These little stories and pictures eventually paved the way for *An Island Scrapbook,* a special book about her island discoveries.

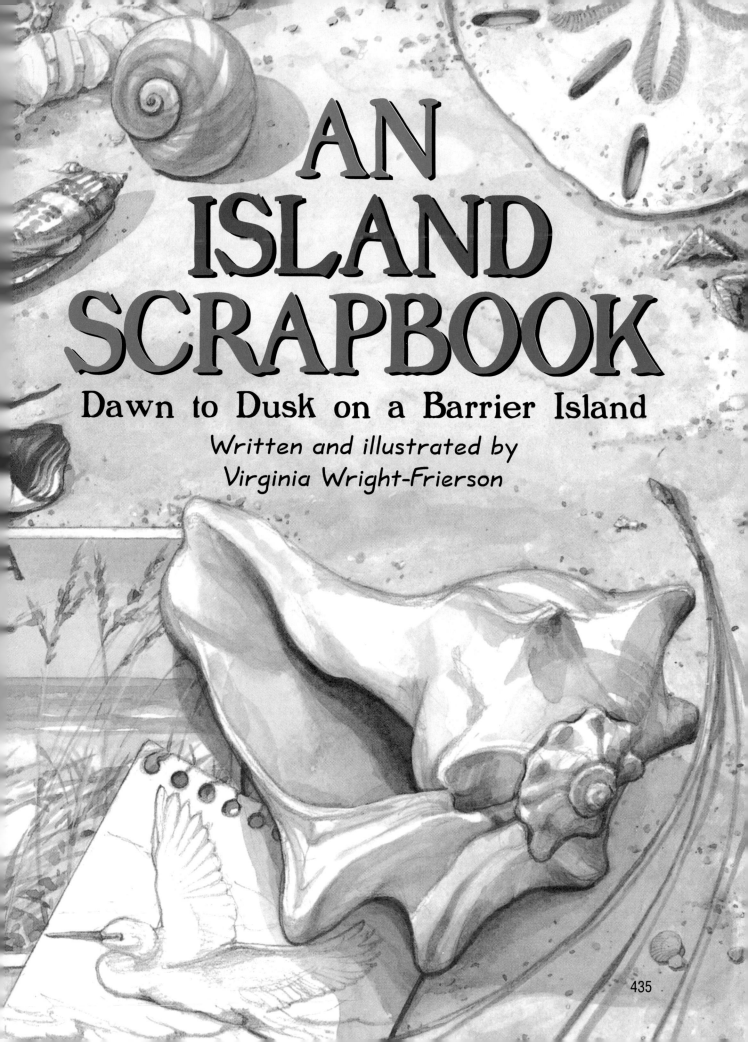

AN ISLAND SCRAPBOOK

Dawn to Dusk on a Barrier Island

Written and illustrated by
Virginia Wright-Frierson

Amy and I are awake before dawn on this September morning. It is the last week at our island house until next summer, and we don't want to waste a minute of it. We dress quietly, grab our packs, and slip outside into the cool darkness of the salt marsh.

437

"The sun!" calls Amy. It is a
fingernail sliver, glowing above the distant trees. We unpack
our watercolors, brushes, and sketch pads as fast as we can. I
paint a tiny study of the sunrise every few minutes until the
soft orange light becomes a fireball.

438

clapper rail – often heard
but rarely seen

Amy

Amy paints one sunrise study with more
detail of the fiery sky and choppy water. As we
work, we listen to the whisper of the rustling
cordgrass, the lapping of the tide, the call of a
clapper rail, and the skittering and claw-clicking
of fiddler crabs. The warming breezes bring us
the rich muddy smell of the salt marsh.

The Tides

There are two high tides and two low tides every day, caused by the gravitational pull of the sun and moon on the oceans.

Life in the salt marsh is wonderfully adapted to the changing depth and salinity of the water.

Marsh creatures

The salt marsh is a mixture of
- swimming
- flying
- crawling
- burrowing
- filtering
- wriggling
- growing

creatures and the decaying dead plants, animals, and algae that provide food for them.

All the microscopic life makes the marsh water and the ocean around our island a rich green and brown color.

Sand fence and shadows

If a male fiddler loses his big claw, the other will grow large. He will grow a new small claw in place of the lost one!

The male fights with the large claw and also waves it to attract a female. He eats by scooping up mud with the small claw, sucking out the nutrients, then discarding the rest in piles of tiny mudballs.

The female can shovel in food with both of her claws.

female

When our paintings are finished, we walk under the old dock to look at the mudflats teeming with fiddler crabs and patterned with the tracks of night-prowling raccoons.

One fiddler threatens us with his huge violin-shaped claw while the others vanish into their burrows. In a few hours, the water will reach the high tide mark on the dock piling. The fiddlers will plug up their tunnels with a mud-ball and wait for low tide to return.

441

wax
myrtle

lo blo
pin

A pine tree knocked over during the storm.

442

Insects in the maritime forest

mosquito

no-see-ums

deer fly

ticks

horse fly

chigger

(red bug)

ladybird beetle

carpenter ant

cricket

honey bee

cicada

red cedar

laurel oak

Our island is the northernmost range of this Sabal or cabbage

dogwood

Yaupon

muscadine vine

smilax vine

dwarf palmetto

We decide to walk through the maritime forest to the ocean. The springy, sandy floor is covered with acorns, palm fronds, pine cones and needles, grasses, and poison ivy. This ground cover provides food and shelter for deer, birds, and other forest animals.

443

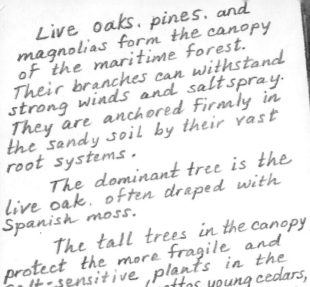

Live oaks, pines, and magnolias form the canopy of the maritime forest. Their branches can withstand strong winds and salt spray. They are anchored firmly in the sandy soil by their vast root systems.

The dominant tree is the live oak, often draped with Spanish moss.

The tall trees in the canopy protect the more fragile and salt-sensitive plants in the understory: palmettos, young cedars, dogwoods, bays, hollies, and the toothache tree (Hercules' Club). Chewing its leaves or bark numbs the mouth.

Amy climbs up into her lookout tree for a bird's-eye view of the rainwater pond where the egrets roost at night.

She counts eight yellow-bellied turtles before they slip underwater. There are deer tracks and more raccoon prints (they look like tiny human handprints). Amy spots a great blue heron, almost as tall as she is, standing as still as a tree on the far bank, waiting to dart after a fish or frog.

444

We emerge from the forest shade to a beautiful view of the windswept grasses on the dunes, and the sparkling ocean stretching on forever. Pelicans fly low over the waves in a dotted line. We make our way carefully around the patches of sandspurs and prickly pear cactus to the clean, hard-packed sand of the ocean beach. Only shrimpers, fishermen, and shorebirds are out this early.

445

shark fin shapes

Almost all of the fins seen in our waters are bottle-nosed dolphins or manta rays.

Amy being held up by the wind.

We walk along, filling our hats with shells, a sand dollar, interesting pieces of driftwood, sea glass, and smoothed, round rocks. There are rows of small fish visible in the cresting waves. We munch on peanut butter crackers and stop often to watch the birds.

I make some quick pencil sketches of a snowy egret that has flown up right in front of us. Amy watches two bottlenose dolphins arching in and out of the clear water as they swim past.

Gulls trying to fly in ⬚⬚⬚⬚⬚ gale.

Amy pulling her sweatshirt over her face to shield it from the blowing sand.

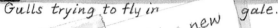

Hurricanes are nothing new round here, and we are very watchful and ready to leave in a hurry!

This is a barrier island, one of a chain of almost 300 on the Atlantic coast from Maine to Texas.

Barrier islands protect the mainland coast from the worst winds during hurricane season from June 1st to November 30th. They are long, thin islands that lie parallel to the coast and have ocean beaches, dunes, maritime forests with freshwater ponds, salt marshes, and tidal flats.

Debris still washing up a week after the hurricane. The ocean around our island is still dark brown from all the flooding of the rivers that feed into it.

A few weeks ago a small hurricane passed over the island. It was not expected to be very strong, so we were not asked to evacuate.

Amy and I were alone in our house. Luckily we live on the marsh side of the island, which is protected by the forest. But we still spent a nearly sleepless night as the winds roared, the house leaked, and the windows were slammed open. Trees cracked and crashed around us and lightning lit up the marsh. The next morning we went outside to explore and take these photos.

447

Every shell you find on the beach once had a living creature in it. Here are a few:

moon snail

scallop

coquina

angel wing

great heart cockle

sand dollar

oysters

pen shell

great heart cockle

razor clam

slipper shell

baby's ear

coquinas

angel wing

coral

jingle shells (sailor's toenails)

disk shell

moon snail sand collar

scallops

Some beautiful shells were washed up from the ocean floor during the hurricane. Amy made a collection in an old crate she found.

Oyster drills - and moon snails can drill holes into shells to eat the creatures inside.
Shipworms - burrow into driftwood (and boats, piers, and pilings).

Now we head back to our house to sort out our treasures on the front porch. Amy has gathered a pile of shiny jingle shells, and also a hat full of ark shells with holes in them for a wind chime.

She has been busy all summer making picture frames and flower pots with glued-on shells, sea glass windows, and a grapevine wreath for our door.

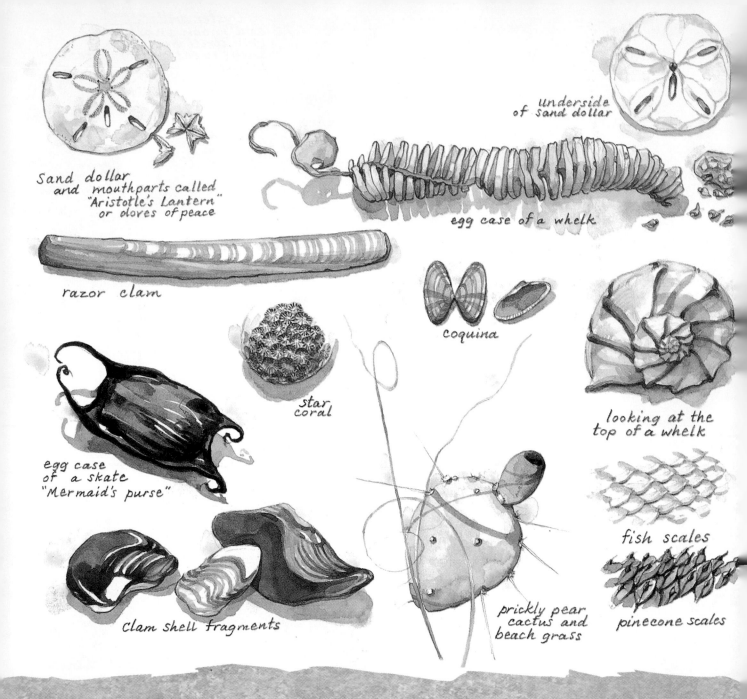

Sand dollar
and mouthparts called
"Aristotle's Lantern"
or doves of peace

underside
of sand dollar

egg case of a whelk

razor clam

coquina

looking at the
top of a whelk

star
coral

egg case
of a skate
"Mermaid's purse"

fish scales

pinecone scales

Clam shell fragments

prickly pear
cactus and
beach grass

I draw and paint some of the shells we have collected and some patterns I remember from our beach walk.

While I finish drawing, Amy packs a surprise lunch. We walk out to the dock to eat, sharing our crusts with some gulls. Amy sees a large black bird diving into the marsh water and looks it up in the bird book: a double-crested cormorant.

When I first came to the island, I used to walk along with my painting bag until I found a beautiful natural

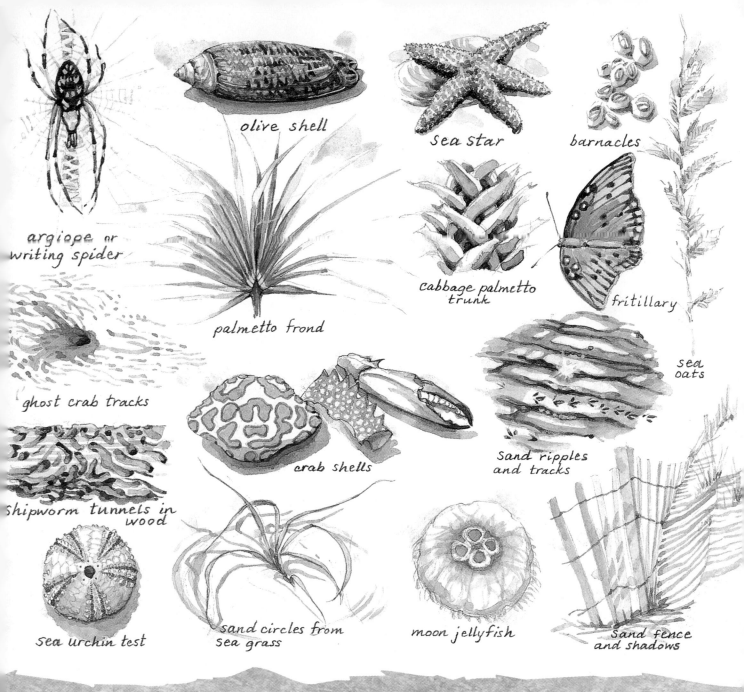

argiope or
writing spider

olive shell

sea star

barnacles

palmetto frond

cabbage palmetto
trunk

fritillary

ghost crab tracks

sea
oats

shipworm tunnels in
wood

crab shells

sand ripples
and tracks

sea urchin test

sand circles from
sea grass

moon jellyfish

sand fence
and shadows

arrangement of shells and shadows, maybe a feather or a sand dollar. I would plop down and paint it, my only rule being I couldn't touch a thing. I called these paintings "found still lifes" and sometimes I painted large oils on canvas from them, back in my studio.

Amy stays on the dock to read and I walk along the marsh to the river. I always feel like I will find something just ahead, and often I do.

One day I was painting with a class near the egret pond. One of the students pointed out a huge alligator crawling out of the pond behind me (as if I had asked it to show up to model for us!)

A second later:
We cleared out so fast, I think we scared the poor alligator as much as it had scared us!
We decided to paint at the beach instead of the pond that day.

Once I found a fossil shark's tooth on the ocean beach.

Once I found some false teeth sticking up out of the sand! I have heard of people losing them overboard when they get seasick.

I see a black skimmer burst from her nest, faking a broken wing to distract me from her three small, speckled eggs. She flops and falls and limps, leading me away, then flies back, just fine, to sit on her nest again after I hurry past.

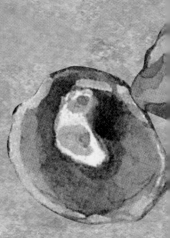

A month ago I came upon a dead baby whale washed up on the beach. When I called my naturalist friend to report it, she told me it was a baby sperm whale. Scientists had already studied it to learn why it had died. Its stomach had contained a marine oil bottle, nylon rope, a black plastic trash bag, a plastic buoy, and some rubber and Styrofoam. The whale had starved because there was no room for food.

Things that wreck the beach

Natural
- erosion
- hurricanes
- flooding
- tsunamis
- animals (overpopulation of one species)
- red tide

Un
- dogs - bark, dig up dunes
- people - walk on dunes, build houses, cut down trees, step on plants & crabs & eggs
- oil spills
- pollution - trash dumped into water, toxic waste/sewage
- motor boats - leak gas, scare animals, run over sea turtles & whales
- cars - drive on dunes, smush turtles

When I come back to our dock, I find some very mysterious footprints in the sand. Each print has toenails of jingle shells. The prints lead right to the house, where I find Amy inside writing some kind of list. We both stretch out to read during the hot Indian summer afternoon.

At sunset, we walk back through the forest to the pond. Egrets are flying soundlessly down to roost in the live oaks, squawking only if one lands too close to another's sleeping spot. Soon there are so many it looks like snow has fallen on the trees. Amy counts 150 egrets, and one alligator in the middle of the pond leaving an S-shaped trail behind its powerful tail as it slowly circles in the dark water.

Two months ago:

We saw the tracks of the huge mother loggerhead the morning after she came ashore to lay her eggs. Naturalists then fenced off the nest site and covered it with wire mesh to protect the eggs from raccoons, foxes, crabs, and people. Sea turtles are now a threatened species.

We race each other down the forest path to the beach. Reaching the dunes, we see a small group of people working to clear a path to the water…the baby loggerhead sea turtles are hatching!

Sea turtle hatchlings always move toward light. If there are bright lights from motels, parking lots, and homes behind them, they will head away from the ocean and soon die on the dunes or roads. On the darkest nights, if there is no light, the babies still go toward the water. Do they hear the waves or smell the ocean? Do they follow the slope of the beach to the water? Are they guided by the Earth's magnetic field?

456

Dangers to Sea Turtles

lights

Birds

Fishing line + nets

Trash: (plastic bags and balloons look like their favorite food... jellyfish)

sharks

ghost crabs

cats

foxes + raccoons

motor boats

cars

people

A Sea Turtle's Diet

Portuguese man-of-war

jellyfish

fish

squid

crab

shrimp

sea grass

mollusks

horseshoe crab

Three days after a hatching, naturalists come back to excavate the nest. They count the empty egg shells and rescue any weak hatchlings that may not have made it to the surface. Only a licensed naturalist is allowed to touch a sea turtle or an egg or a nesting site.

Amy and I watch as the last of these little loggerheads push their way to the ocean, are tumbled back to shore by the waves, then finally swim out to deeper waters.

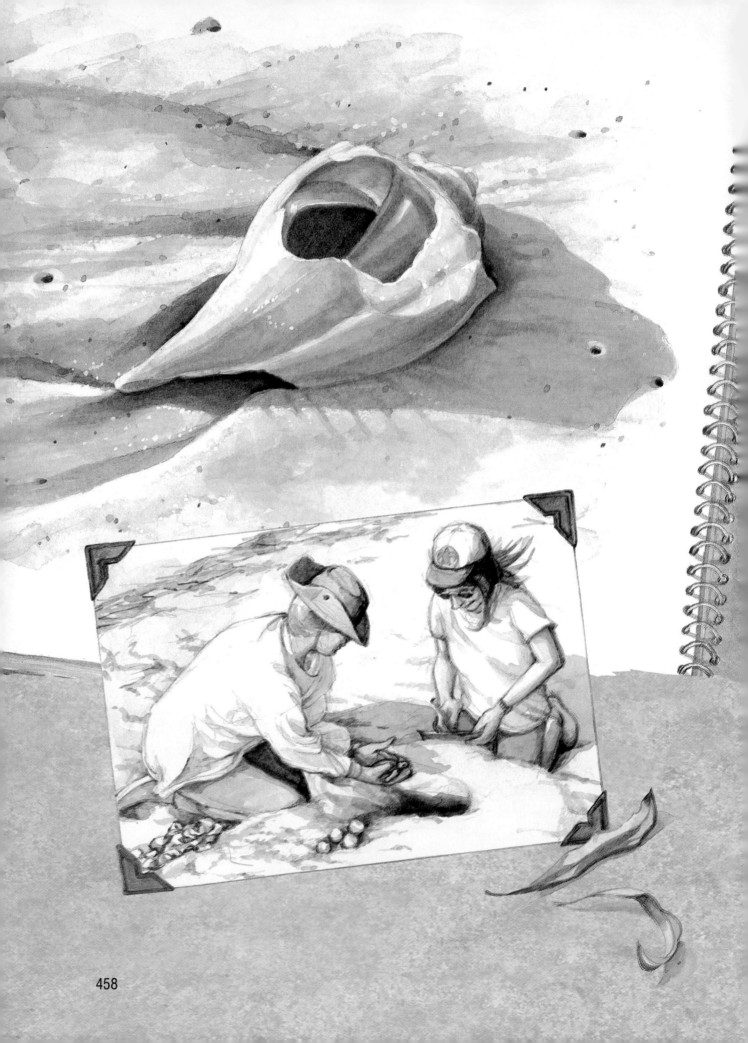

We head quietly back to our cottage.

Tomorrow when we walk out to the ocean, the tide will have swept clean the shells and tracks from today. We will look at the ocean surface, broken by a fin from below or a boat or diving bird from above. Only traces of the hidden undersea world will wash up on the beach again: shells, bones and teeth, a jellyfish, a skate egg case.... We want to look deeper below the shining surface, to walk farther along the shoreline, to stay longer at our island home.

Story Questions & Activities

1 Who is telling the story?

2 Why is it important for Amy and her mother to draw exactly what they see?

3 How does the scrapbook support the facts in the rest of the selection?

4 What is the main idea of this selection?

5 Amy and her mother draw as they learn about the island. How do their drawings compare with the picture on page 432? What is one major difference?

Write an Observation Report

"An Island Scrapbook" carefully observes and records the actions of some island creatures. Write your own observation report describing an animal you enjoy watching. Make a chart with two columns, labeled *Actions* and *Reasons*. List the animal's actions and the reasons it responds in this way. Use this chart to write an observation report of your animal.

Draw an Island Mural

Amy has been busy all summer drawing and making picture frames and flower pots with seashells. Now it's your turn. Use "An Island Scrapbook" for inspiration to draw an island mural. Work with a group of classmates to paint an ocean, trees, rocks, coastline, marshes, and beach on a long sheet of paper. Include some of the animals and plants from the selection. Give your mural a title and have your group sign it.

Keep a Record of Facts

What's the difference between a fact and an observation? Choose three situations or actions, such as a dog rolling over, a friend laughing, and a tree rustling in the wind. After observing each action, write three facts about it in your journal.

Find Out More

Amy and her mother create a scrapbook of the island. Pick one of the shells, fish, plants, or island creatures from the selection. Learn more about it by looking in an encyclopedia or on the Internet. Create your own scrapbook page of words and illustrations that describe your "island treasure."

461

Read an Observation Chart

As Amy and her mother discover, you can find out a great deal about an animal by observing how it eats, sleeps, reacts to danger, and interacts with other animals. An animal's behavior depends on its physical body, training, and skills. Its habitat—the place in which it lives—also influences its behavior.

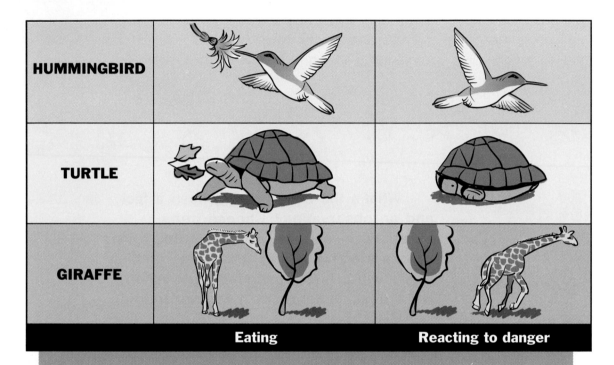

	Eating	Reacting to danger
HUMMINGBIRD		
TURTLE		
GIRAFFE		

Use the observation chart to answer these questions.

1 Which animals eat standing up?

2 Compare and contrast how turtles and giraffes respond to threatening animals.

3 Which two animals do you think use the most energy? Give two examples for each animal you choose.

4 For each animal on the chart, choose one characteristic and explain how it helps that animal survive or adapt to its habitat.

5 How does an observation chart help you gather facts and information?

TEST POWER

DIRECTIONS

Read the sample story. Then read each question about the story.

SAMPLE

The Talent Show

During the activities club meeting on March 15, Mr. Gomez, the club advisor, announced that the Washington Elementary School would hold its first annual talent show. It would be held on May 15 in the school auditorium.

TALENT SHOW RULES

- **Each group may enter only one act in the talent show.**

- **Each act must have at least two people but no more than 4 people.**

- **Performances longer than 10 minutes will be disqualified.**

- **Groups must provide their own stage props.**

- **All groups will be judged on the following: originality, preparation, and teamwork.**

- **No entry form will be accepted after April 15.**

1 Which is a FACT stated in the Talent Show rules?

  A Groups may enter as many acts as they want.

  B Entry forms will be accepted on the night of the performance.

  C Groups must perform a song.

  D Entrants must provide their own stage props.

2 About how much time do students have to prepare for their acts?

  F Two weeks

  G Two months

  H Six weeks

  J Three months

Stories in Art

Everything you see or imagine can give you ideas for artwork.

~

Look at this satellite photograph of Hurricane Andrew. How do meteorologists use satellite images to judge the path of storms? Notice the "eye" of the storm? Why do you think it is that color and shape?

~

Close your eyes. If you knew a hurricane was headed your way, what would you do? What could you draw to show that a hurricane was coming?

Satellite image of Hurricane Andrew, 1992

A Perfect

Judgments and Decisions

Develop a strategy for making judgments and decisions.

1 **Think about a person's actions** in a particular situation.

2 **Examine the reasons** for those actions. Why did the captain decide to head east?

3 **Think what you would have done** in the same situation.

4 **Consider the results** of the person's actions. What happened to the men on the *Andrea Gail*?

5 **Make a judgment** about the person's actions based on facts and your own beliefs. Did it matter that the captain didn't know about the storm?

In the last few days of October, 1991, the crew of the fishing boat *Andrea Gail* had a decision to make. Should they head for home or make one last run to the east in the hopes of finding plentiful swordfish? The captain chose to head east, unaware that he and his crew were heading toward one of the most powerful storms of the century.

The "October Nor'easter of 1991" developed rapidly and unexpectedly off the coast of Massachusetts. A harmless low-pressure air mass moved east into the Atlantic. There, it collided with a cold high-pressure air mass heading south. Such a combination often means bad weather. When a third storm system charged onto the scene, however, the results were extraordinary—what many have called "the perfect storm."

STORM

The third storm system was actually a worn-down hurricane named Grace. Between October 26 and 31, Grace wandered north and picked up more energy from the other two systems. The reborn hurricane produced 100-mph winds and waves up to 100 feet tall.

Nine people died in the fierce weather, including all of the men on board the *Andrea Gail*. The storm took everyone by surprise, including local weathermen. Since then, scientists have tried to be more careful predicting the weather. But they also know that, as always, you have to expect the unexpected.

March 31

April 1

April 2

N

Pacific
Ocean

Sierra Nevada
Snow

Great Basin

Blizzards

Rocky Mountains

Great Plains
Tornadoes

MEET
BRUCE
HISCOCK

Bruce Hiscock began work on *The Big Storm* by calling up weather reporters from the radio. "I had them suggest storms to write about. I wanted a spring storm because they are the most violent and active." Hiscock then studied weather for six months. He felt he had to learn all he could about weather to understand this storm fully. For details, Hiscock read newspaper accounts from towns hit by the storm. He also visited places pictured in his book.

From his cabin in the Adirondack Mountains, Hiscock stays in touch with nature. "I spend time every day in the woods with the birds and the animals. At night I watch the stars with a telescope. . . ." A billion-year-old boulder near his home is the subject of another Hiscock book, *The Big Rock*.

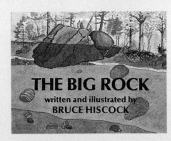

THE BIG ROCK
written and illustrated by
BRUCE HISCOCK

April 3 April 4 April 5 April 6

Mississippi River

Tornadoes

Rain Appalachian Mountains

Hail Blizzards Atlantic Ocean

E

THE BIG STORM

written and illustrated by Bruce Hiscock

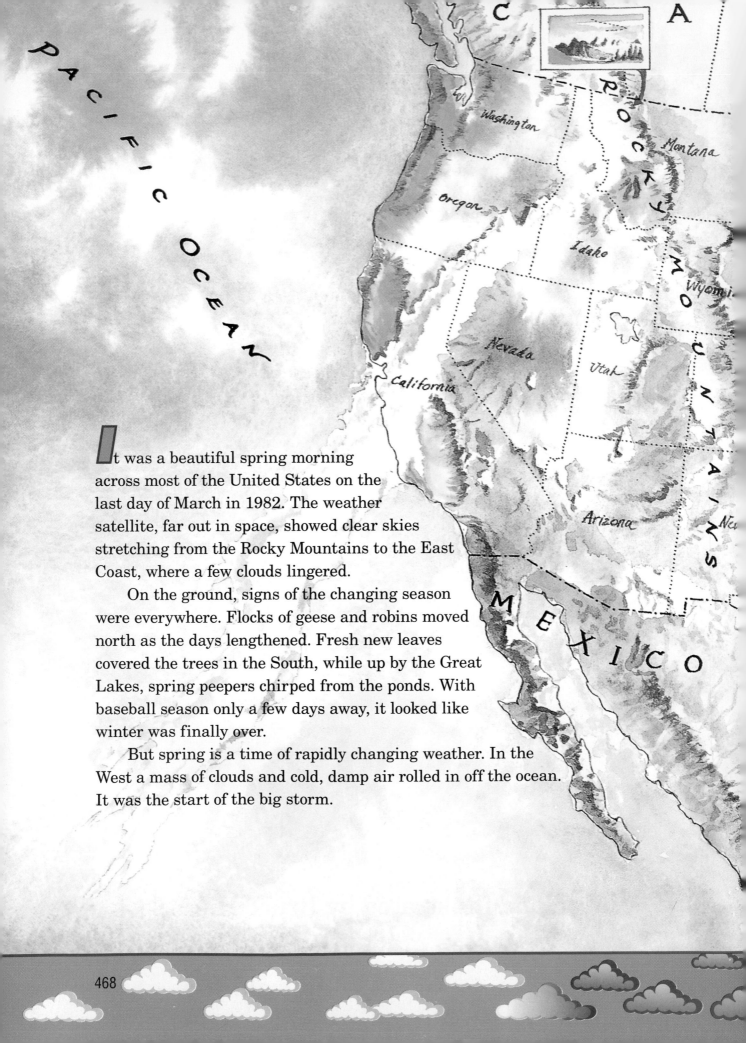

It was a beautiful spring morning across most of the United States on the last day of March in 1982. The weather satellite, far out in space, showed clear skies stretching from the Rocky Mountains to the East Coast, where a few clouds lingered.

On the ground, signs of the changing season were everywhere. Flocks of geese and robins moved north as the days lengthened. Fresh new leaves covered the trees in the South, while up by the Great Lakes, spring peepers chirped from the ponds. With baseball season only a few days away, it looked like winter was finally over.

But spring is a time of rapidly changing weather. In the West a mass of clouds and cold, damp air rolled in off the ocean. It was the start of the big storm.

N   A   D   A

North Dakota

Minnesota

South Dakota

GREAT

Nebraska

rado

Kansas

Iowa

Illinois

Indiana

Ohio

Wisconsin

G R E AT   L A K E S   New York

Michigan

PLAINS

Oklahoma

Missouri

Kentucky

Tennessee

Arkansas

Mississippi   Alabama   Georgia

Texas

Louisiana

Florida

Pennsylvania

Maryland

West Virginia

Virginia

North Carolina

South Carolina

Maine

Vermont

New Hampshire

Massachusetts

Connecticut

New Jersey

Del.

Ohio

ATLANTIC OCEAN

CUBA

The clouds brought heavy rain to the Pacific Coast as the gathering storm moved inland. Like most weather systems in North America, it was carried along by the westerlies, the winds that nearly always blow from west to east across the continent.

When the storm ran up against the mountains of the Sierra Nevada range in California, the wind pushed the clouds up the steep slopes. In the cold mountain air the rain changed to snow.

W

E

CALIFORNIA

SIERRA NEVADA
SPANISH FOR
SNOWY MOUNTAINS

It snowed hard all day in the Sierras. The flakes clung to the tall pines, coating them in heavy layers of white. But near the mountaintops, where no trees grow, the wind piled the snow into great drifts. Soon the drifts became so deep that the slopes would hold no more.

The snow began to slide from the high places, gently at first, then faster and faster, until the slides became huge avalanches. The avalanches roared down the mountains and slammed into buildings. Several people were killed.

Any storm can be dangerous as well as beautiful, but this one was a real powerhouse. And it was just getting started.

The storm moved swiftly over the Rocky Mountains, spreading blizzards from Montana to Arizona. In Colorado fierce winds gusted to 141 miles per hour, overturning vans and campers. In Nebraska the wind blew hard enough to move cow chips around.

The strongest winds came right at the leading edge of the storm. There a cold front marked the boundary between the warm springlike air covering most of the country and the cold, stormy air rushing in. Big masses of warm and cold air do not mix when they meet but instead push each other around. The line where the air masses bump is called a front.

This front was a cold front because the cold air was pushing the warm air away. Strong cold fronts usually bring high winds and sometimes violent weather.

The tremendous power of weather comes from the sun. Our planet is surrounded by a thin layer of air called the atmosphere, which is a mixture of gases, clouds, and dust. Heat from the sun causes the atmosphere to flow and swirl around the earth.

For instance, imagine that your city or county is covered by a blanket of cool, cloudy air. No wind stirs the leaves, and temperatures are the same everywhere.

Now let the clouds open slightly so that sunlight falls on a plowed field or a parking lot at the mall. The sun warms the earth or the pavement, which in turn heats the air right above it. Hot air rises, and soon a huge bubble of warm air is going up like an invisible balloon.

As the warm air rises, cool air flows in along the ground to take its place, causing a breeze. Temperatures begin to change. The sun has made the atmosphere move.

The same sort of uneven heating keeps the atmosphere moving worldwide. Warm air rises from the tropics while cold air flows down from the poles. This heating pattern and others create the vast wind and weather systems of the planet. Of course, these weather systems change with the seasons. The long summer days provide much more sunlight to warm and lift the air than the short, cold days of winter.

The sun moves the weather, but the land and sea affect it too. Ocean currents cool or warm the air. Hills and mountains block the wind. Even the spinning of the earth changes the wind's direction.

In fact, so many things affect the weather that when a storm comes up, it is not easy to predict exactly what it will do.

The big storm grew worse as it swept out over the Great Plains. Flocks of robins huddled on the ground, unable to fly in the blowing snow. Across the Dakotas and Minnesota, weather forecasters watched their barometers as the readings fell to record low levels. A deep low-pressure center was forming.

Barometers measure the pressure of the air directly overhead. Air, like water, has weight, and tons of air press down on the earth. This force, called barometric or atmospheric pressure, changes constantly as the air moves.

Forecasters pay close attention to these changes, for they help predict the weather to come. High pressure usually brings fair skies. Low pressure means storms, and the lower the pressure, the stronger the storm.

As the blizzard raged on, the weather stations in the storm reported the low pressure, the freezing temperatures, and the gusty wind and snow conditions to the National Meteorological Center near Washington, D.C. The data went directly into their huge computers along with data from hundreds of other weather stations, satellites, and instrument-carrying balloons.

The computer gave an overall picture of the weather to the forecasters at the National Center. Then, using more computers, they predicted what the storm would do next. These predictions were sent back to each weather station. There, a detailed forecast was made for the local area.

This work goes on every day, but with a killer storm on the loose, the forecasts were especially important.

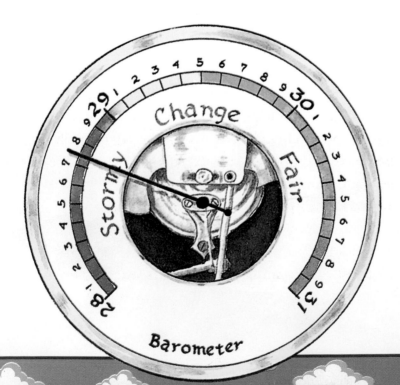

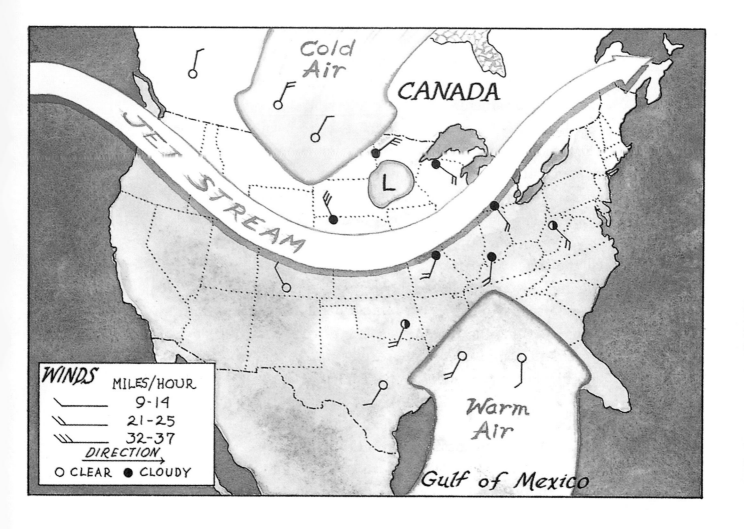

On the morning of Friday, April 2, the weather map showed strong surface winds blowing in toward the low-pressure center. Areas of low pressure push enormous amounts of air upward, causing air near the ground to rush in from all sides, like air rushing into a vacuum cleaner. Far above the surface, the jet stream, a narrow band of high-speed wind that snakes across the continent, formed a giant curve around the low.

All this was creating a huge counterclockwise swirl in the atmosphere typical of big storms. On one side of the swirl warm, moist air from the Gulf of Mexico was being drawn north. On the backside, frigid air was coming down out of Canada.

The National Severe Storm Forecast Center in Kansas City, Missouri, began plotting where these two air masses would meet. Chances were good that the collision would result in a powerful cold front, producing violent thunderstorms and tornadoes.

Local weather stations from Texas to Iowa and east were alerted. A Severe Weather Watch was announced on radio and television to warn that bad weather was possible. Forecasters checked their radar screens constantly, looking for signs of the front. Everyone waited.

The afternoon was warm and humid when a line of towering clouds appeared across the Texas plains. Lightning flashed in the distance. Soon the rumble of thunder was heard. Airports closed. Dogs whined and hid under beds. The clouds came on, churning and billowing. An eerie darkness fell. Then slashing winds hit. Rain and hail poured down. The cold front raced through. Temperatures dropped sharply.

All along the front, police and other spotters watched for tornadoes. Tornadoes are violent whirlwinds, funnel-shaped clouds that may spiral down from thunderstorms. They are extremely dangerous. The spotters watched anxiously, for they knew that weather radar can pinpoint thunderstorms but usually cannot "see" tornadoes. Eyes are better for that.

Suddenly a tornado was sighted heading for Paris, Texas. Sirens blew. A Tornado Warning was broadcast. Families rushed for the nearest bathroom, closet, or basement shelter.

The tornado hit with the roar of a freight train. Houses and churches were torn apart. Trees shattered. Cars were tossed around.

The funnel cloud stayed down for twenty minutes, ripping a path through the city two blocks wide and five miles long. Most of the people in the path survived, though many were injured. Ten people were killed.

Tornado Areas April 2-3

More than eighty tornadoes touched down that afternoon and night in Texas, Oklahoma, Arkansas, Missouri, and other states as far east as Ohio. Even with the warning broadcasts, over thirty people died, and the damage was horrendous. The United States has more tornadoes than anyplace else in the world, but this was the worst outbreak since 1974.

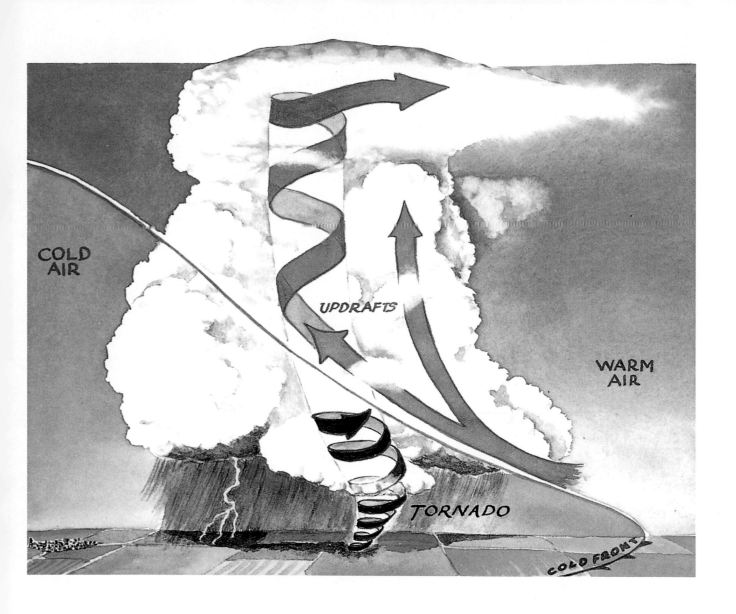

Tornadoes usually form just behind a cold front as the wedge of cold, dense air pushes in, forcing the warm, moist air to rise very quickly. This produces strong updraft winds and huge thunderclouds.

If an updraft begins to spin, it may set off a tornado. Exactly what causes the spinning is not completely understood, but once the twister is formed, it sucks in air, dirt, and anything else it touches with winds of over two hundred miles an hour. Boards, bricks, and glass become deadly flying missiles. Huge funnel clouds can even lift railroad cars.

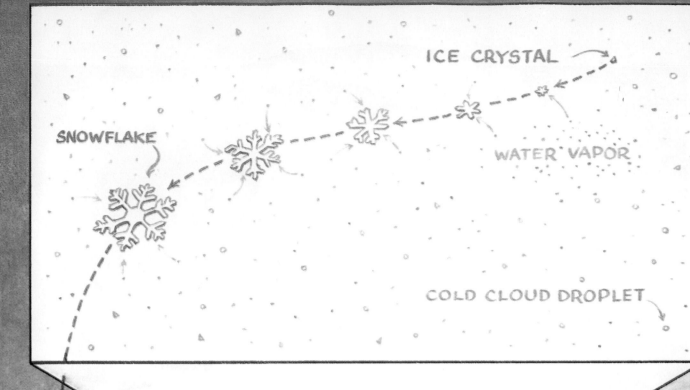

ICE CRYSTAL

SNOWFLAKE

WATER VAPOR

COLD CLOUD DROPLET

RAINDROP

When the front passed, the tornadoes stopped, but thunderstorms continued throughout the South. Heavy rain drenched Alabama and Georgia. Hail the size of golf balls dented cars and broke windows in Kentucky.

Rain and hail are formed from the moisture in clouds, but they are not simply falling bits of mist and ice. The water droplets and tiny ice crystals that make up clouds are far too small to fall by themselves, and so they remain suspended in air like fog.

Surprisingly, most raindrops start out as snowflakes. High in the cloud where the air is very cold, ice crystals gradually grow into snowflakes that are heavy enough to fall. The snowflakes then melt, if it is warm near the ground, and become raindrops. A raindrop is about a million times larger than a cloud droplet.

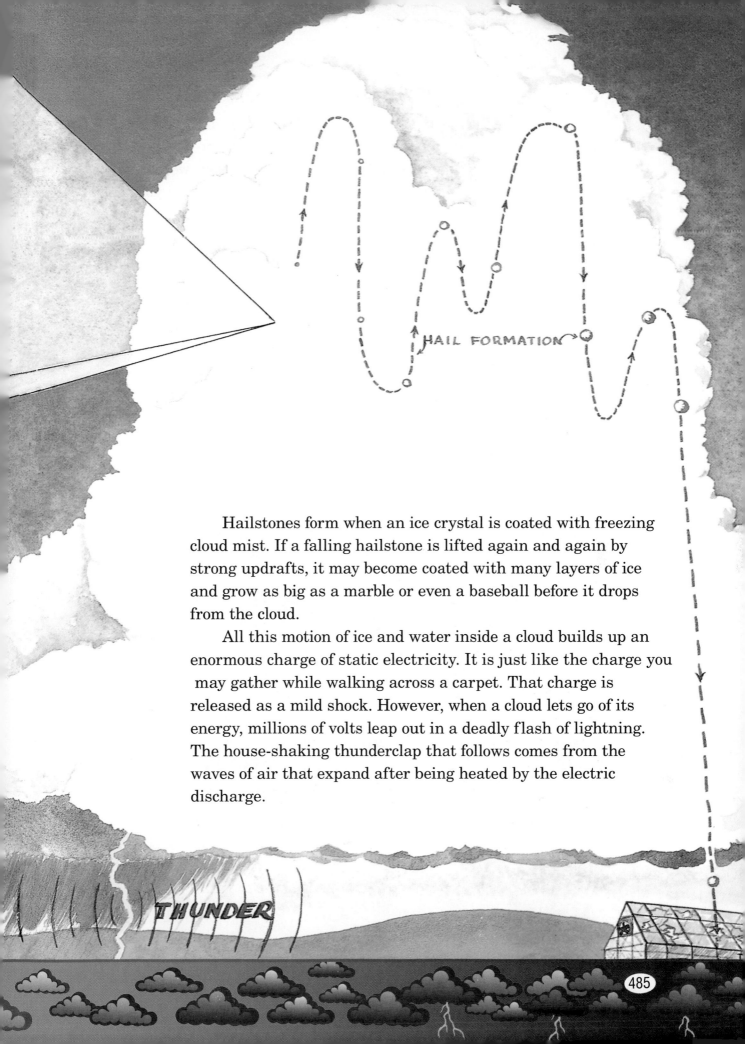

HAIL FORMATION

Hailstones form when an ice crystal is coated with freezing cloud mist. If a falling hailstone is lifted again and again by strong updrafts, it may become coated with many layers of ice and grow as big as a marble or even a baseball before it drops from the cloud.

All this motion of ice and water inside a cloud builds up an enormous charge of static electricity. It is just like the charge you may gather while walking across a carpet. That charge is released as a mild shock. However, when a cloud lets go of its energy, millions of volts leap out in a deadly flash of lightning. The house-shaking thunderclap that follows comes from the waves of air that expand after being heated by the electric discharge.

THUNDER

For the next three days the huge mass of Arctic air behind the cold front brought more snow and high winds to the Midwest. Driving became very dangerous. Five hundred travelers were stranded in Michigan and had to spend the night in school gyms. Rush-hour traffic in Chicago was a tangle of accidents.

The great swirl of clouds around the low was clearly visible from space, and as the swirl drifted east, clear skies and intense cold followed it. With no blanket of clouds at night, the earth rapidly lost heat to outer space. Low temperature records were set from Idaho to the Appalachians. And still the storm was not through!

Tuesday, April 6, was opening day for the baseball season, and the New York Yankees were scheduled to play at home. The main storm center was now out at sea, but still the forecast was not good. Cold air continued to pour in, forming new lows over Pennsylvania and the New Jersey coast.

Around three in the morning, snow began to fall softly on New York City. In the Northeast the great snowstorms often begin very quietly. Soon the wind picked up. By noon it was a howling blizzard. Traffic snarled. Trains were delayed. The pace of the great city slowed to a sloppy walk.

Over a foot of snow fell in New York before the storm moved on to Boston. It was the first blizzard ever to hit New York City in April. The Yankee game was delayed for four days. Many adults said bad things about the weather, but few kids complained. They all had a day off from school.

The big storm finally ended. Snow turned to slush and melted away. People cleaned up their towns. Spring returned. Birds began traveling north again, and the evenings lost their chill.

The storm is just a memory now, but every spring the cycle repeats itself. Warm air from the south meets with cold Arctic air, triggering storms of all sizes and giving the United States one of the most varied and exciting climates on earth.

1 What was the weather like in most of the United States on the morning of the storm?

2 What makes it so difficult to predict what a storm will do?

3 Why do you think that "spring is a time of rapidly changing weather"? Explain.

4 How would you summarize Bruce Hiscock's findings in this selection?

5 In what way is the tornado in "The Big Storm" like the hurricane in "An Island Scrapbook"? What are the differences between the two storms?

Write a Report

Choose a type of precipitation—rain, snow, sleet, or hail—and write a report that explains it. Start your report with a main-idea statement. Find out *how, why, when,* and *where* the precipitation might start. Write the answers as details or facts in the body of your report. End with a conclusion that summarizes your information.

Create a Diorama

In an empty shoebox, create a model of a town in the middle of a bad storm. Use construction paper, cotton, sticks, stones, soil, sand, paints, and other art supplies. Build houses, streets, cars, people, and trees in the midst of a storm, such as a blizzard or a tornado. In your diorama, show the power of weather to destroy property, crops, and trees.

Explain the Tools of the Trade

Meteorologists use instruments, computers, radar, and satellite cameras to predict the weather. Explain how these tools work together to produce a weather forecast. For example, what can the computer tell the meteorologist if changing ground temperatures, changing barometer readings, and moving clouds are studied?

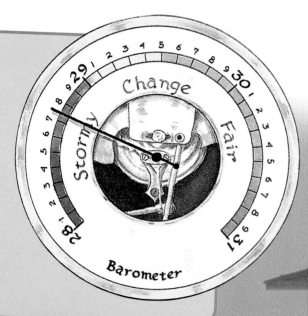

Find Out More

Choose a place you have never been to but would like to visit. What kind of weather would you find there? Start by checking in an encyclopedia, a travel brochure, or a book about the area. Write a few sentences that describe the weather. Include the average temperature, the amount of rain- or snowfall, and the kinds of storms the area has. Show your findings on a chart or a graph.

489

STUDY SKILLS

Read a Weather Map

The weather maps that you see on television during the weather report show many facts about weather patterns. Some weather maps show the different temperature readings for the day in several different areas. Other weather maps show wind and cloud movements, and possible rain- or snowfall.

H = High Pressure System   L = Low Pressure System

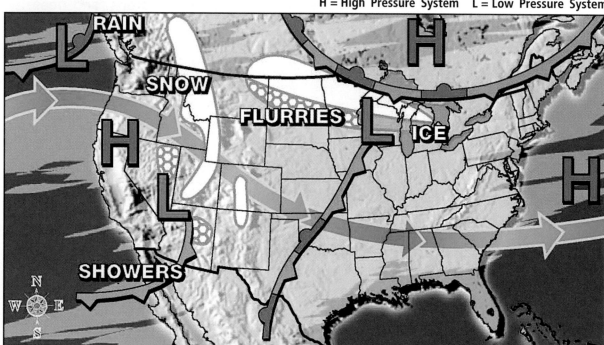

Use the weather map to answer these questions.

1. In what region is there a state where it looks as if there is not a cloud in the sky? Do you know what state it is?

2. Which parts of the country look as if they have rain showers?

3. If the wind is moving from west to east, do you think the Middle West is going to have snow tomorrow? Explain.

4. Can meteorologists guarantee their weather forecasts a day in advance? Why or why not?

5. Why do you think it is important to know how to read a weather map?

TEST POWER

DIRECTIONS

Read the sample story. Then read each question about the story.

SAMPLE

Hilary Wants to Play the Drum

Hilary went down to the park every day after school to hear the drummers perform. Hilary enjoyed listening to the marches that the drum corps were practicing for the upcoming parade.

When she tried to play the same music on her drum, however, it didn't sound like the music she had heard. She couldn't get the rhythm even and smooth. Every time that she tried to repeat what she had heard at the park, she was disappointed.

One day, as the drummers were leaving, she noticed that one of them had forgotten the velvet drum cover that protected the drum when it wasn't being used.

Hilary grabbed the cover and ran after the drummers. When she caught up to one of the drummers, she gave her the cover. In return, the drummer offered Hilary a seat in the bandstand at the next parade.

1 Which of these is the best summary of the passage?

   A No one plays the drum better than Hilary does.

   B The drummers in the park liked the marches for the parade.

   C Hilary listened to the drummers and wanted to be like them.

   D Hilary spent every day in the park after her drum lesson.

2 This story mostly takes place —

   F in the park

   G at Hilary's house

   H at school

   J in a music store

Stories in Art

Space exploration is turning fantasy into fact. Today, the make-believe world of the science-fiction writer now seems very real.

Look at this painting of space stations and space-craft. What parts of it are already fact? What parts are not yet fact? Do you think they will become real? When? Why? How? What will life be like aboard one of these space stations? What makes you think so?

Look at the painting again. What do you think it would be like to explore new worlds? Would you like to go on such a journey? Explain.

Ships of the Long Range Pioneer Fleet
by Julian Balm

Fact and Nonfact

Develop a strategy for distinguishing fact from nonfact.

1 **Read the text.** What is the article about?

2 **Identify facts.** Look for statements that can be proved.

3 **Find details** that can be used to support each statement.

4 **Identify statements** that cannot be proved true or untrue.

5 **Determine whether** a statement is or is not a fact. Is it a fact that Sacajawea hoped to return to her family?

Sacajawea

Sacajawea, a Shoshone woman born in 1788 in what is now Idaho, is famous for playing a major part in the expedition of Lewis and Clark.

At age twelve, Sacajawea was kidnapped by warriors of the Hidatsa people and taken far from her home. She later became the wife of a Canadian trapper named Toussaint Charbonneau. In 1804, Lewis and Clark hired Sacajawea and Charbonneau to accompany their expedition as interpreters. Sacajawea brought along her newborn son.

In his journal, Clark tells how important Sacajawea soon became to the expedition. She was an excellent guide. She was also able to obtain supplies from people they met. As a Native American woman with a baby, she showed people that the explorers came in peace.

What did Sacajawea think of the explorers? She is said to have enjoyed observing their European ways. Perhaps she hoped they would return her to her Shoshone family.

When the expedition reached Shoshone territory, Sacajawea was able to find her family, but the reunion was short-lived. Sacajawea was now too important for Lewis and Clark to leave behind. She continued with the explorers all the way to the Pacific coast and back.

LEWIS ♥ CLARK EXPEDITION ♥ 1804

SACAJAWEA

Statue of Sacajawea

TIME FOR KIDS

SPECIAL REPORT

Artist N.C. Wyeth used his imagination to paint this picture of Sacajawea, Lewis, and Clark.

Catching Up with Lewis and Clark

Hot on Lewis and Clark's Trail

Historians and scientists follow in the footsteps of two of America's brave explorers

COVER: THE GRANGER COLLECTION. BELOW: ILLUSTRATION FOR TIME FOR KIDS BY MERLE NACHT

Nobody likes a litterbug, but historians wish that Meriwether Lewis and William Clark had left more behind as they bravely traveled across the North American continent nearly 200 years ago. They cleaned up so well after themselves that it's hard to tell exactly where they stopped on their journey from St. Louis, Missouri, to the Pacific Ocean.

But researchers hope to answer age-old questions about these great trailblazers of the West, whose work made it possible for the U.S. government to claim the Oregon territory. This led to pioneers settling the West in the mid-1800s.

In 1803, President Thomas Jefferson asked Lewis to explore the Louisiana Purchase, a huge area of land that the United States was about to buy from France. He hoped to learn of a water route between the Mississippi River and the Pacific Ocean that would help U.S. trade.

BRUCE SELYEM/MUSEUM OF THE ROCKIES

Ken Karsmizki has been busy digging up the facts about Lewis and Clark.

The red dashes show the explorers' route. They wintered at Fort Mandan and Fort Clatsop and split up on the way back.

Sifting dirt through a giant strainer can reveal important finds at Great Falls, Montana.

Lewis and his best friend, Clark, left St. Louis in May 1804 with a party of 42 men. They never found the water route, but they became the first U.S. citizens to see many of America's wonders—the endless Great Plains, the jagged Rocky Mountains, and the glistening Pacific. They faced many hardships and dangers, including bear attacks and bitter cold. In Great Falls, Montana, they carried heavy canoes for weeks around waterfalls under the hot sun. At times they had little food to eat and almost starved.

More than 500 days and 4,000 miles after they had set out, Lewis and Clark reached the Pacific. "Ocian in view! O! the joy!" wrote Clark in his journal. (Clark was smart and brave, but not a very good speller.)

The explorers kept superb maps and diaries. They were the first to describe 122 kinds of animals and 178 plants, and to meet many native tribes. But they left barely a trace behind at their campsites. That makes it hard for historians to say "Lewis and Clark were here!"

PINNING DOWN LEWIS AND CLARK

Montana scientist Ken Karsmizki and others have been trying to pin down such facts. They have been digging in the soil at Great Falls and at Fort Clatsop, Oregon, where the pair rested before making their way home. Recently, a campsite was found

FIND OUT MORE
Visit our website:
www.mhschool.com/reading

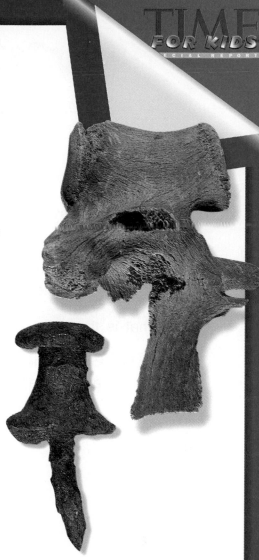

near Great Falls. Scientists think it may be one of Lewis and Clark's camps, but they are not sure. Beads and ammunition were found at Fort Clatsop. Scientists think the remains belonged to the explorers.

In fact, scientists will be digging around Fort Clatsop for years to come. "Lewis and Clark wintered here for 106 days," explains Cindy Orlando, head of the Fort Clatsop National Memorial. Scientists have found the remains of what may have been a wooden wall from the original campsite. "What we're finding could prove to be from Lewis and Clark's trip," says Orlando.

JOIN THE CELEBRATION!

As the 200th anniversary of their journey approaches, Americans are getting plenty of chances to learn about the brave pioneers. Visitors to Great Falls can visit the Lewis and Clark Interpretive Center. And special events to mark the anniversary. will take place along the route from 2003 to 2006.

"When Lewis and Clark left, we were a seaboard collection of former colonies," says Ken Burns, who made a movie about the two explorers. "What they saw transformed us from a small country into a great one."

Scientists say the bison bone (top) and the iron pushpin are both from the time of Lewis and Clark.

Sacajawea

When Lewis and Clark needed a guide to help them talk with Indians they met on their trip, they turned to Sacajawea. (Her name means Bird Woman.) Sacajawea was an English-speaking Shoshone Indian who traveled with the explorers in 1805 and 1806. During her travels, she visited what are now the states of Montana, Idaho, Washington, and Oregon.

When the group arrived in the Rocky Mountains, the explorers met a band of Shoshone Indians whose chief was Sacajawea's brother. She helped the explorers communicate with him and with his band. Sacajawea also helped Lewis and Clark get horses and food from the Shoshone. Her work made it possible for the group to continue on to the Pacific. A number of monuments have been built in Western states to honor her.

Story Questions & Activities

1. Who were Lewis and Clark?

2. What facts have researchers discovered about the journey of Lewis and Clark? Why are they important?

3. How did the work of Lewis and Clark make it possible for pioneers to settle the West?

4. What is the main idea of this selection?

5. In "Digging Up the Past" archaeologists and historians have created an accurate picture of how early colonists lived. Why are such people having a difficult time piecing together a picture of the Lewis and Clark expedition?

Write a Magazine Article

Write a short magazine article about the Lewis and Clark expedition. Focus on a question such as "What route did they take?" or "What did they find?" Start by looking in your social studies textbook or in a book about Lewis and Clark. Check your facts in two sources to make sure they are correct. Then include your facts in the middle of your article. Summarize your findings at the end.

Draw a Cartoon

Imagine that you are either Lewis or Clark. The time is 1804. You have been traveling west for months. Draw a cartoon describing your journey. Remember that Lewis and Clark are human beings just like you. Perhaps Lewis is tired of hearing Clark complain about his sore feet or tired back. Label your cartoon with a thought balloon or a clever caption.

Create a Research Journal

Recently, a Montana scientist has found a campsite that may be one of Lewis and Clark's. Create an archaeologist's journal of drawings of objects found along the Lewis and Clark trail. These could include beads, ammunition, a carved bison bone, a pushpin, or a wooden wall from the original campsite. Write a sentence or two under each object. Identify it, and explain why it was important to the explorers.

Find Out More

Sacajawea joined Lewis and Clark on their journey. Who was she? Why did the explorers ask her to join them? How did she learn English? Why were they lucky to have her along? Find out more about Sacajawea in an encyclopedia or a book about her life. List five facts about her and share them with your classmates.

Use a Map

From 1804 to 1806, Lewis and Clark mapped more than 3,000 miles. The maps that Lewis and Clark drew on their trip and the detailed diaries they kept made it easier for the pioneers to follow the way west.

Look at this map of the Louisiana Purchase and of the route of Lewis and Clark.

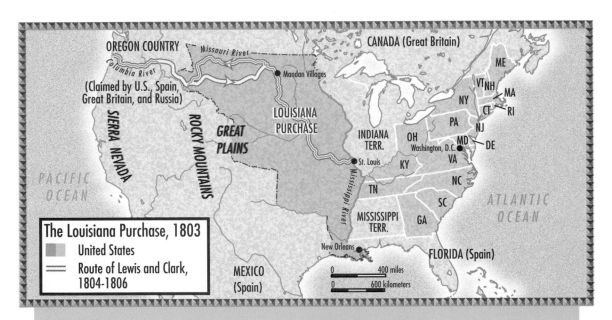

Use the map to answer these questions.

1 What were the years of the Lewis and Clark expedition?

2 What rivers did Lewis and Clark travel?

3 Which countries in Europe claimed areas that later became the United States?

4 The United States bought the land in the Louisiana Purchase from France in 1803. Why do you think Jefferson wanted Lewis and Clark to explore the Louisiana Purchase and all the land to the Pacific Ocean?

5 How can this map help you understand the journey of Lewis and Clark?

TEST POWER

Test Tip

Take your time as you do your work.

DIRECTIONS

Read the sample story. Then read each question about the story.

SAMPLE

Darlene's Adventure

Darlene and her mother had planned the canoe trip for weeks. The trip was now only days away.

Darlene looked again through the pictures and at the <u>brochures</u> they had gotten about their trip. This is one of the pamphlets she studied:

PALMER LAKE CANOE VENTURES

- You can rent a canoe on Palmer Lake anytime between May 1st and October 31st.

- No experience is required to rent a canoe. Trained instructors are always available to help you understand the basics of proper canoeing.

- Canoe rentals are $20 for the day. Paddles are included.

- A canoe can hold three adults and some light supplies.

- During the summer months, you may reserve a canoe up to three days in advance.

1 In this passage, <u>brochures</u> means—

  A postage stamps

  B experiences

  C calendar

  D booklets

2 Which is the best summary of this passage?

  F Darlene and her mother plan their vacation.

  G Darlene reviews information about a place she will visit.

  H Darlene and her mother decide between biking and canoeing.

  J Palmer Lake rents canoes during the summer.

Early Spring

In the early spring, the snowfall is light
upon the mesa.
It does not stick to the ground very long.
I walk through this patchwork of snow and earth,
watching the ground for early signs.
Signs of growth. Signs of rebirth.

Larkspur and wild onions are still
within the warmth of the earth.
I hear cries of crows off in the distance.
A rabbit bounds off into the sagebrush flat.
A shadow of a hawk disturbs the landscape momentarily.
It sees food and life abundant below that I cannot see.
The cycle of life continues.

Even as I stand here shivering in the afternoon chill,
just below me, young seedlings start
their upward journey.
Insects begin to stir.
Rodents and snakes are comfortable in their burrows.
Maybe to them we also disappear with the cold.
Not to be seen until spring.

For this generation, and many more to come,
this land is beautiful and filled with mysteries.
They reveal themselves and their stories—
if you look very carefully, and listen....

by *Shonto Begay*

502

503

UNIT
5

Bright Ideas

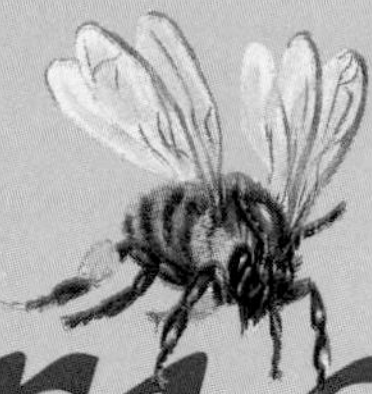

To Make a Prairie

To make a prairie it takes a clover
    and one bee,
One clover, and a bee.
And revery.
The revery alone will do,
If bees are few.

by Emily Dickinson

Stories in Art

Some paintings have a message. By looking at the clues the artist gives, you can discover what the artist is trying to say.

~

Look at the garden in the picture. How is it like a garden you have seen? Did your garden have trees and bushes? What were the differences?

~

Look at the painting again. Compare two of the shapes. Then compare one of the shapes to the bird standing on it. What might the artist be saying about some kinds of gardens and gardeners? Could her message be to leave nature alone? If so, why?

Gardeners
by Judy Byford, 1995
The Grand Design,
Leeds, England

THE RIDDLE

Compare and Contrast

Develop a strategy for comparing and contrasting.

1 **Identify characters and** events that can be compared or contrasted.

2 **Look for clue** words, such as *also, but,* and *however* that signal comparisons.

3 **Look for specific** details about the characters and the events.

4 **Identify the ways** in which the characters and events are alike.

5 **Identify differences.** What differences are there between Haemon and Oedipus?

In ancient Greece, only one road led into the city of Thebes. One day, a horrible creature appeared on that road and would not let people pass unless they answered a riddle.

The creature, called the Sphinx, had a woman's head, a lion's body, an eagle's wings, and a snake's tail. The riddle was this: "What creature moves on four feet in the morning, two feet in the afternoon, and three feet in the evening?" The wrong answer meant death.

Among the first few people to see the Sphinx was the king's nephew, Haemon.

"Stand your ground and answer my riddle!" shouted the Sphinx.

Haemon was fearless, but not too smart. "Is it a frog? A goat? I give up."

The next moment the Sphinx pounced on him and tore him apart.

On another day, a young man named Oedipus approached the city.

"Stand your ground and answer my riddle!" shouted the Sphinx.

OF THE SPHINX

Oedipus was also courageous. However, he was much smarter than Haemon. "Why, the creature must be man," he answered. "Man crawls on four legs in the morning of his life, walks on two in the afternoon, and, in the evening of his life, walks with the help of a stick."

Upon hearing the answer, the Sphinx flew into a rage and exploded. Oedipus then freed the city of Thebes.

Meet Adele Vernon

The Riddle is a favorite fairy tale of writer Adele Vernon. Vernon, who lives in New Zealand with her husband and two children, was delighted to have the chance to retell this old Catalan story. Originally called *The King and the Charcoal Maker*, *The Riddle* is Vernon's first book for young people.

Meet Robert Rayevsky

Robert Rayevsky was born in Moscow. As a child he loved reading books. "When I read them," he says, "I saw them in pictures that formed in my mind." When Rayevsky moved to the United States, he went to school to become an illustrator. Like the work of Vladimir Radunsky, Rayevsky's illustrations are magical.

Meet Vladimir Radunsky

Like Robert Rayevsky, Vladimir Radunsky grew up in Russia. There, he studied architecture and graphic design before moving to the United States. A prize-winning artist, Radunsky's books include *Pup Grew Up!*, *Hail to Mail*, and *Square, Triangle, Round, Skinny*. Today, Radunsky lives in New York City.

The RIDDLE

RETOLD BY
Adele Vernon

ILLUSTRATED BY
Robert Rayevsky
&
Vladimir
Radunsky

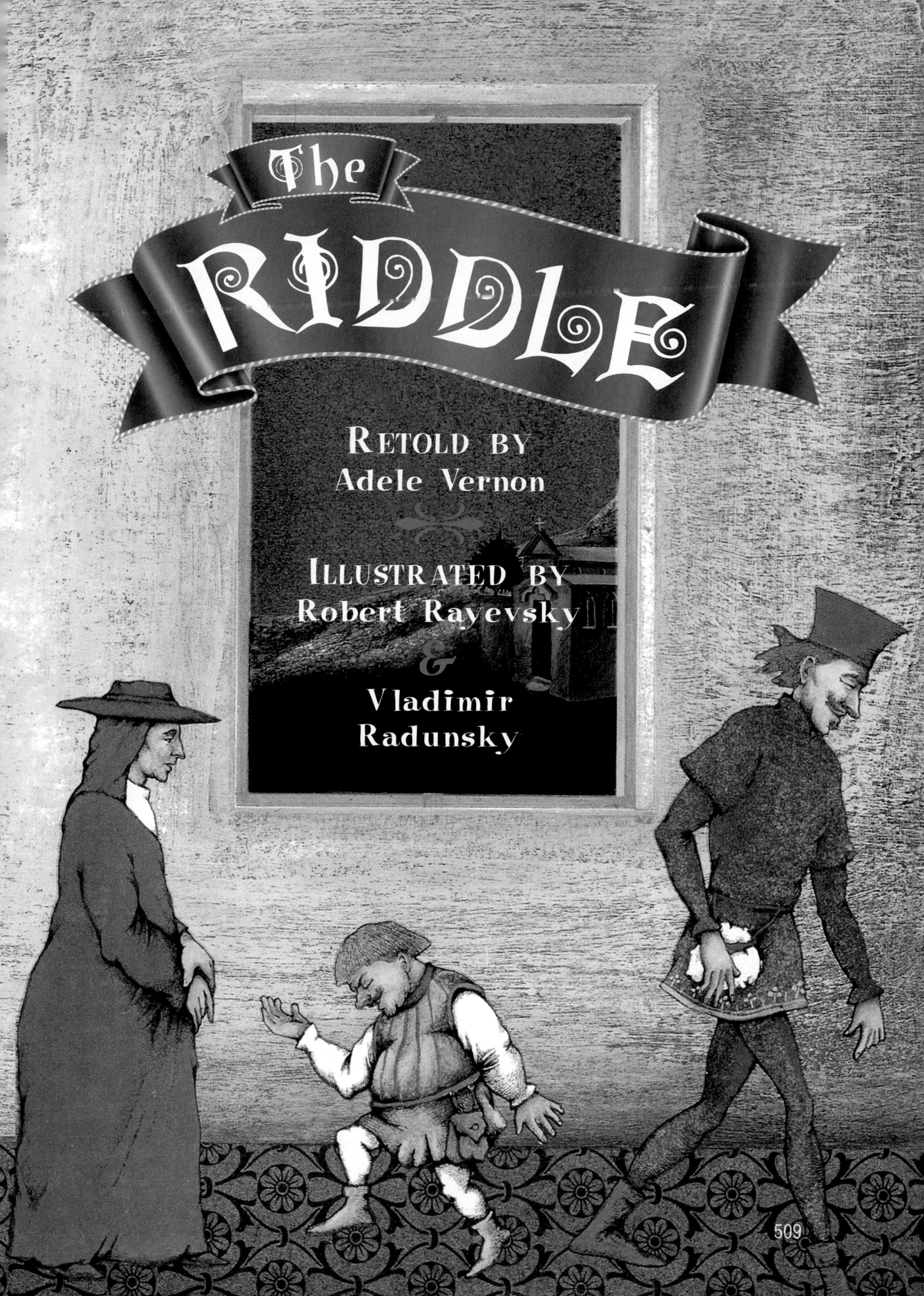

nce upon a time, long, long ago a king lost his way while hunting in a great forest. The king was cold, tired, and hungry, but there was no one around to help him.

"Oh, where are all my companions?" the king lamented. When suddenly, not far off, he noticed thin spires of smoke drifting up through the tall trees. Guided by the smoke, the king soon came to a clearing in the forest where there lived a poor charcoal maker and his family.

The charcoal maker was busily stacking wood into a mound and didn't hear the king approaching.

"Good day!" greeted the king in a booming voice.

This so startled the charcoal maker that he spun around, sending

510

sticks of wood flying in all directions. His face and hands were covered with soot, and he stepped forward and peered at the king from beneath a mat of reddish hair.

"Ah, my good man," continued the weary king, "could you spare me a drink of water and some food? I have had no refreshment all day."

The charcoal maker, who had been looking intently at this finely dressed stranger, suddenly realized that it was THE KING who stood before him.

"Y . . . Your Majesty? Oh, dear! C . . . can it really be you?" stammered the charcoal maker, not quite believing his own eyes. "Yes, of course, Your Majesty. Please, sit down. Here, by the fire."

After making a hasty bow he called excitedly to his wife.

"Anna, Anna! Some water! Some food! Quickly! It is His Majesty, THE KING!"

In the space of a wink, a plump, ruddy-faced woman came scurrying out of the hut, balancing a plate of steaming roasted onions and carrying a jug of cold water.

"Pardon us, Your Majesty. We have so little to offer you," apologized Anna as she set the food down near the king. And with a flustered curtsey, she hurried back to the hut.

The king ate and drank with great gusto.

"Mmmmm, delicious! How hungry and thirsty I was. This fresh cold water is better than wine. You see, I was hunting with my

companions when we got separated and I lost my way. They must
have returned to the castle thinking that I had gone home."

After his meal, the king looked around at the smoking mounds
and wondered about the hard life of a charcoal maker.

"And you, charcoal maker," inquired the king, motioning for him
to sit down, "living here in the middle of the forest, far from village or
castle, working long hours to make charcoal for others to burn and
receiving little thanks for your labor, how much do you earn a day for
your work?"

The charcoal maker answered the king cheerfully as he put more
wood on the fire, "No more than ten cents a day, Your Majesty. And a
great plenty it is too!"

"What!?" exclaimed the king, unable to hide his surprise. "You can't mean it! How can you live on so little?"

"Not only do I make enough to live on," explained the charcoal maker briskly, "but I also pay back a debt, save for my old age, and still have something left over to throw out the window!"

Amazed, the king leaned forward to look more closely at the sturdy little man sitting before him.

"But it is not possible! How can you do so much with such meagre earnings?"

"It is very simple, Your Majesty," said the charcoal maker with a twinkle in his eye.

"With my earnings I support my family which includes my mother, who took care of me when I was young. Now I am taking care of her. Thus, I am paying back a debt. I also provide for my son, whom I hope will do the same for me when I am old.

So, I am saving for my old age. Finally, I must provide a dowry for my daughter who will marry some day. And as you know, Your Majesty, money spent on a dowry is as good as throwing it out the window."

The king laughed long and hard at the charcoal maker's riddle. He was delighted with the story but now he was curious to see if such an ingenious man was also honest and trustworthy. So he made a bargain with him.

"Well, charcoal maker, I see that you are both clever and resourceful. I admire you greatly. But I ask you to keep this talk of ours a secret. Do not reveal the answer to this riddle to anyone until you have looked upon my face one hundred times. Agreed?"

The charcoal maker stood up quickly and made a deep bow. "Yes, of course, Your Majesty. You have my word of honor." Pleased with his bargain, the king made ready to go.

"Thank you for the delicious meal. Now I must go. Please be good enough to show me the way back to the main road."

"It has been an honor, Your Majesty," answered the charcoal maker, bowing again. "Please come this way."

The next day in the great dining hall of the castle, the king feasted and jested with the members of his court. After the huge meal, he challenged them with the charcoal maker's riddle.

"Now tell me, can any of you solve this riddle? How can a poor charcoal maker, who earns only ten cents a day, make enough to live on, pay back a debt, save for his old age, and even have something left over to throw out the window? Whoever is the first with the answer shall be made First Counsellor of the Kingdom."

Immediately the hall was filled with a great hum-buzz as wisemen, courtiers, and scholars talked about the riddle. Many attempted to solve it, but the king, his eyes shining with delight, shook his head—No!—again and again. No one in the whole court could find the answer.

Only one courtier did not participate in the debate. He quietly got up from the table, tied a bag to his belt, and with a cunning smile, slipped out of the palace unnoticed.

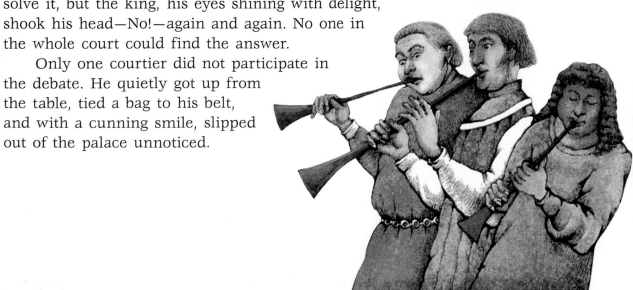

After a long ride, he approached the charcoal maker's home.

"I say, you there, charcoal maker," called out the courtier, "I have come a very long way to ask you to solve a simple riddle for me. How can a charcoal maker, such as yourself, who earns only ten cents a day, make enough to live on, pay back a debt, save for his old age, and still have something left over to throw out the window?"

Glancing up from his work at the eager courtier, the charcoal maker slowly shook his head, "Please pardon me, Sir. I am sorry you have made such a long journey, but I can't tell you the answer to the riddle for I have promised not to."

"Hmmm. Yes, of course," smiled the courtier slyly. "But what do you say to these ten gold pieces?" And he pressed them, one by one, in the charcoal maker's hand.

The charcoal maker looked thoughtfully at the coins but shook his head again, "No, Sir. I really cannot break my promise."

"Well, then, how about this?" demanded the courtier impatiently as he counted out more and more shiny coins.

The charcoal maker picked up each coin and studied it carefully. But still he shook his head, no.

Soon there were one hundred coins in front of him.

"Well, have you anything to say to one hundred?" demanded the courtier.

"Hrrhhumm. Well, you see, Sir," said the charcoal maker as he cleared his throat. "It is very simple. With my earnings I support my family which includes my mother, who took care of me when I was young. Now I am taking care of her. Thus, I am paying back a debt. I also provide for my son, whom I hope will do the same for me when I am old. So, I am saving for my old age. Finally, I must provide a dowry for my daughter, and *that* is as good as throwing money out the window!"

The courtier laughed heartily at the charcoal maker's reply.

"Ah, ha. How very clever. Thank you, my good man, thank you, indeed."

522

Hastily, he mounted his horse and rode off in the direction of the castle, already picturing himself as First Counsellor of the Kingdom.

That evening when the courtier returned to the castle, the king was seated on his throne by a roaring fire. The courtier boldly approached the king and whispered something in his ear. The king's face suddenly turned bright red with angry surprise.

"So you see, Your Majesty," boasted the courtier in a loud voice, I have guessed the answer to the riddle and *I* should be made First Counsellor of the Kingdom, as you have promised."

"Yes, yes. I must keep my word, if you did indeed guess the answer to the riddle," replied the disappointed king. "But first I must have a word with the charcoal maker. Have him brought to me at once!"

Before the king had finished his dinner, swift riders brought the charcoal maker to him. Dazzled by the splendor of the castle, the charcoal maker approached the king hesitatingly and bowed.

"Your Majesty, you sent for me?"

"You have broken your promise to me and have told the answer to the riddle!" said the king angrily to the poor charcoal maker. "I thought you were as honest as you were clever. I see now, that this is not so. You deserve to be punished, for dishonesty is the very worst of crimes!"

The charcoal maker stood silently for a few moments and then he spoke out bravely.

"Your Majesty, your anger at me is unjust, for I did exactly as you requested. I did not tell the answer to the riddle until I had seen your Majesty's face one hundred times."

"But that is absolutely impossible!" exploded the king. "You couldn't have!"

"But I did," grinned the charcoal maker, "on each and every one of the hundred coins that the courtier gave to me."

The king looked at the charcoal maker in astonishment, and then burst out laughing, as did everyone in the court.

"Yes, yes you are right. I see that you are even more clever than I thought. And still you kept your promise. I praise you, and curse the courtier in front of the whole court. And I give you three bags of gold. One for your debt, one for your old age, and one to throw out the window."

Story Questions & Activities

1 Why does the king go to the charcoal maker's hut?

2 How are the king and the charcoal maker alike? How are they different?

3 Do you think the charcoal maker is clever? Explain.

4 How would you summarize this story? Be sure to include the charcoal maker's riddle.

5 Compare this story with another fairy tale or folk tale you have read. How are the setting, characters, and storyline similar? What are the differences?

Write Paired Diary Entries

Could the king and the charcoal maker ever become friends? Write a diary entry for each of these two characters, describing their first meeting. Begin with "Dear Diary" and a date that makes sense for the story. As you write from each character's point of view, include your feelings about the other man.

Create a Charcoal Sketch

Artists often draw with small sticks of charcoal. Sometimes they use charcoal to make a rough sketch of something before they make a detailed painting. Make a rough charcoal sketch of a character or a scene from the story. Then use the sketch to create a detailed painting.

Solve Riddles

Can you solve this famous Irish riddle?

From house to house he goes;
So sure and yet so slight.
And, whether it rains or snows,
He sleeps outside all night.

Make up riddles, and ask classmates to solve them. Talk about the kind of thinking you used to solve each riddle.

(Answer: A country lane)

Find Out More

In "The Riddle," the charcoal maker produces charcoal for others to burn. What is charcoal? Where does it come from? Can it be used for things other than burning? Start by checking in an encyclopedia. Use what you find to make a chart showing charcoal and its uses.

Follow Directions

In the story, the king loses his way while hunting and rests a while at the charcoal maker's home. He then asks the charcoal maker to show him the way back to the main road. Imagine that you are the king. Follow these directions to get to your castle from the charcoal maker's hut.

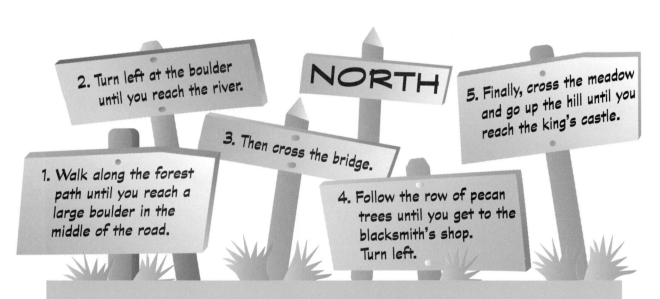

2. Turn left at the boulder until you reach the river.

NORTH

5. Finally, cross the meadow and go up the hill until you reach the king's castle.

3. Then cross the bridge.

1. Walk along the forest path until you reach a large boulder in the middle of the road.

4. Follow the row of pecan trees until you get to the blacksmith's shop. Turn left.

Follow the directions to answer these questions.

1 Do you turn right or left when you reach the boulder?

2 Is the blacksmith's shop higher or lower than the castle?

3 Which way do you turn after you reach the blacksmith's shop?

4 What do you cross first, the meadow or the bridge?

5 Why do you think it is important to know how to follow directions?

TEST POWER

Test Tip

A FACT must be stated in the passage.

DIRECTIONS
Read the sample story. Then read each question about the story.

SAMPLE

The Shortwave Radio

Walter had been saving his money for months. His parents gave him a small allowance each week. Walter was careful with it. He saved it until he had enough to buy the things he really wanted.

Recently, Walter spent thirty dollars on a shortwave radio set. He and his father read the instruction booklet that came with the radio. They checked all the dials and switches and knobs on the radio. Finally, Walter and his father determined that they had set up the radio so that it would work perfectly.

All week, Walter talked with other radio operators in faraway cities and towns. He was really developing a skill with the short-wave set.

"So how is it going, Walter?" his father asked.

"This is fun," exclaimed Walter as he <u>beamed</u> at his father.

1 In this passage, the word <u>beamed</u> means —

  A spoke quietly

  B smiled joyfully

  C shouted angrily

  D said sadly

2 Which of the following is a FACT in this passage?

  F Walter's father bought him the shortwave radio as a gift.

  G Walter had no skills.

  H Walter read the instruction booklet.

  J Walter's father talked with radio operators.

When you first look at this painting, you might just see a rooster and a dove. If you look again, you might begin to realize that the figures stand for something more than themselves.

What can you tell about this painting by Pablo Picasso? Could knowing something about the artist help you understand it? How? What do you know about a rooster? What does the white dove represent? What might the artist be saying about peace and freedom? Explain.

Look at the painting again. What colors does the artist use? What shapes? How do the colors affect what the artist is saying?

The Cock of Liberation
by Pablo Picasso, 1944
Milwaukee Art Museum, Milwaukee, Wisconsin

Author's Purpose, Point of View

Develop a strategy for recognizing author's purpose and point of view.

1 **Decide what the story** is about.

2 **Look for clues** to the purpose. Are there facts and information or narration and dialogue?

3 **Tell about the characters.** Are they likable? How would you describe them?

4 **Consider point of view.** How do you think the author feels about math?

5 **Identify author's purpose.** Does the story *entertain*, *inform*, or *persuade*?

The Oak Island Treasure

"Everybody has heard about the Oak Island Treasure," Janine's dad told her on the first day of their vacation on the island. "But nobody knows where it is. It was supposedly buried here long ago. We can look for it if you like."

"How will we know where to look?" asked Janine.

"The only clue is a poem carved on a rock," said her dad. "But no one knows what it means." He recited the poem:

Everyday paces: they are the measure

You need to follow to find the treasure.

Start at Big Oak with its leaves of dark green.

Go 30 north, 20 east, then north by 13.

You can find what you want: Just go east by the mean.

"The part I don't get," said Janine's dad, "is 'go east by the mean.' The mean what?"

Janine thought for a moment. "Dad," she said excitedly, "I know! The mean is the average. The average of three numbers is the sum of those numbers divided by 3. So you add 30 plus 20 plus 13 to get 63. Then divide by 3 to get 21, which is the *mean*. The last line of the poem is telling us to go east 21 paces to find the treasure!"

"That's pretty smart!" said Janine's dad. "Now we just have to find Big Oak!"

Meet A. Square

It is no wonder that Edwin Abbott, the author of *Life in Flatland,* gave School Teachers at least six-sided shapes. Abbott, also known by his pen name in this selection, A. Square, was a well-respected teacher in the 1800s. Born in England in 1838, Abbott served as the headmaster of the City of London School. He was also an expert on the works of William Shakespeare. In his lifetime, Abbott wrote more than 45 books. Yet only one of these books is still remembered, although it was written more than 100 years ago.

Meet Wallace Keller

Wallace Keller, the illustrator of *Life in Flatland,* was born in Madisonville, Louisiana. As a child, he spent many hours filling his notebooks with sketches of trucks. His family recognized his talent as an artist and encouraged him. After attending art school in California, Keller worked as an animator for several Saturday morning cartoon programs on television. Yet Keller wanted to illustrate books for young people. When he couldn't find the right book to illustrate, he wrote his own! This book was called *The Wrong Side of the Bed,* and it was an instant success. Today, besides illustrating books, Keller spends his time cycling and flying airplanes.

Life in FLATLAND

Written by
A. Square
&
Illustrated by
Wallace Keller

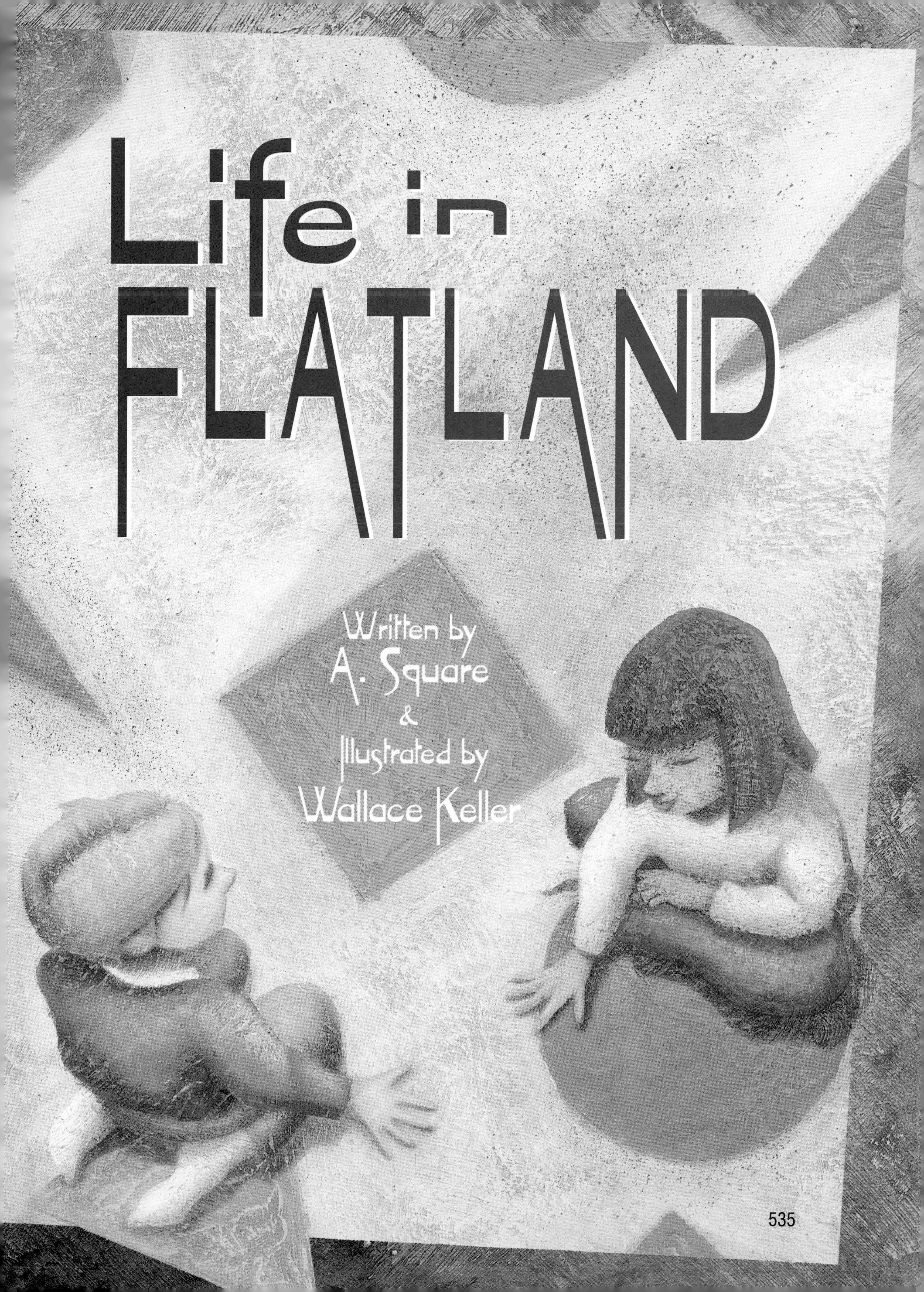

We live in a world of three dimensions—length, height, and width. What would it be like if the world had only two dimensions?

The book *Flatland* was written nearly one hundred years ago. The author, A. Square (his real name was Edwin Abbott), had a unique viewpoint. In his imaginary world, all the people are Triangles, Squares, Circles, and other flat shapes.

I call our world Flatland—not because this is what we call it, but so that you will know what it is like. You must understand at once that in my country there is nothing of the kind you call a solid shape. As you know, a solid, or three-dimensional shape, has length, width, and thickness. But in Flatland, *everything* is flat. That is, there are only two dimensions—length and width.

Imagine a huge sheet of paper on which Straight Lines, Triangles, Squares, Pentagons, Hexagons, and other shapes move freely about, very much like shadows. You will then have a pretty correct idea of what my country and countrymen look like. You might think that we can tell Triangles, Squares, and other flat shapes by sight. But this is not so. We cannot tell one shape from another. We can see only Straight Lines. Let me show you why this is so.

537

Place a penny in the middle of a table. Now, lean over the table and look straight down upon the penny. It will appear to be a Circle.

But, move back to the edge of the table and lower your head. When your eyes are exactly level with the edge of the table (so that you are, as it were, a Flatlander) the penny will no longer look like a Circle. It will seem to have become, so far as you can see, a Straight Line.

The very same thing will happen if you take a piece of cardboard and cut out a Triangle, or Square, or any other shape. Put the shape on a table and look at it from the edge of the table. You will find that you see only a Straight Line.

Well, that is exactly what we see in Flatland when we meet a friend. As our friend comes ever closer to us, the line becomes larger and brighter. When our friend goes away from us, the line becomes smaller and dimmer. Our friend may be a Triangle, Square, Pentagon, Hexagon, or any other shape, but all we see is a Straight Line.

You may wonder how we can tell one friend from another. I will explain in a moment. But first, let me now tell you about the kinds of people there are in Flatland.

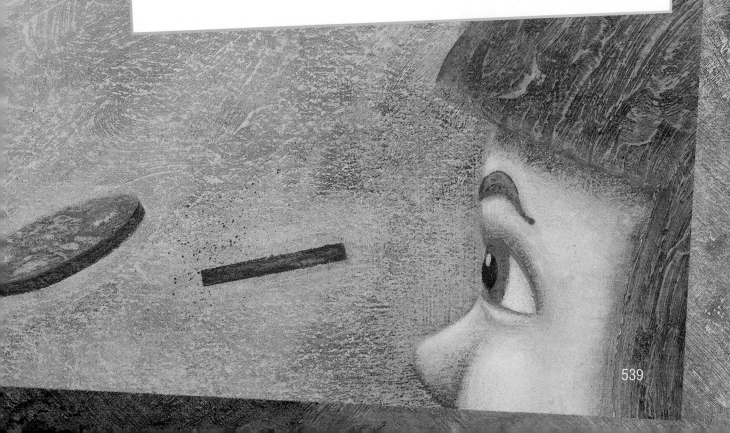

539

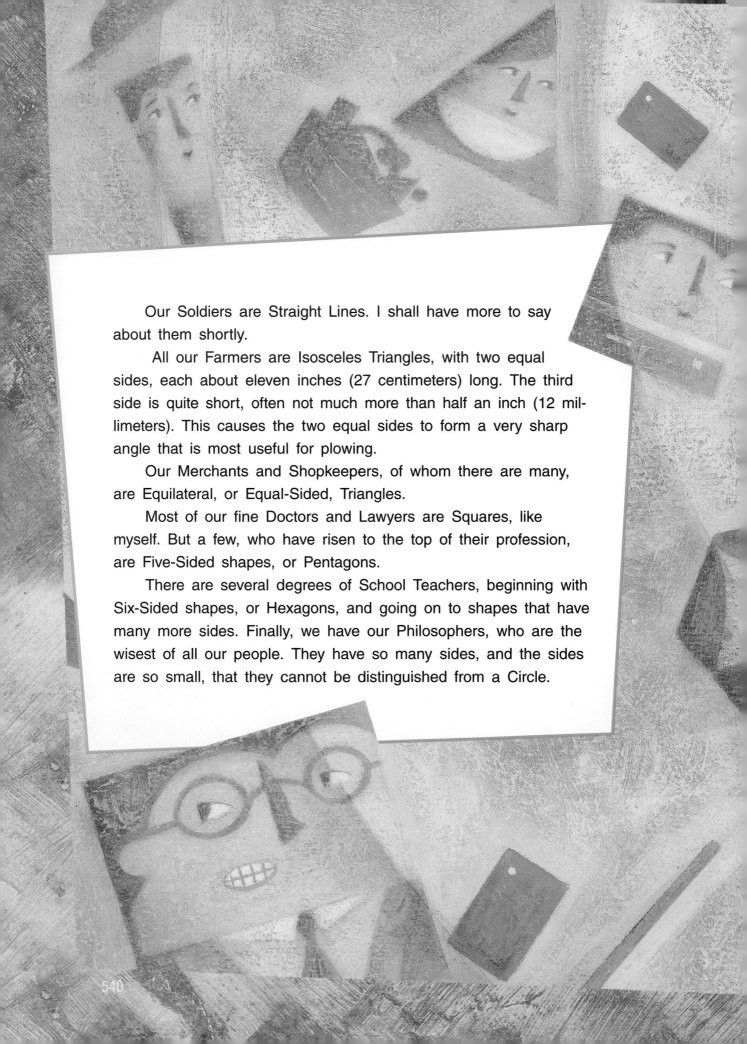

Our Soldiers are Straight Lines. I shall have more to say about them shortly.

All our Farmers are Isosceles Triangles, with two equal sides, each about eleven inches (27 centimeters) long. The third side is quite short, often not much more than half an inch (12 millimeters). This causes the two equal sides to form a very sharp angle that is most useful for plowing.

Our Merchants and Shopkeepers, of whom there are many, are Equilateral, or Equal-Sided, Triangles.

Most of our fine Doctors and Lawyers are Squares, like myself. But a few, who have risen to the top of their profession, are Five-Sided shapes, or Pentagons.

There are several degrees of School Teachers, beginning with Six-Sided shapes, or Hexagons, and going on to shapes that have many more sides. Finally, we have our Philosophers, who are the wisest of all our people. They have so many sides, and the sides are so small, that they cannot be distinguished from a Circle.

There are many dangers in Flatland, just as there are in your world. The greatest of these dangers is our shapes. We have to be careful not to bump into one another. A Flatlander who has a sharp shape can easily hurt another person. For this reason, our sharply pointed Farmer Triangles are quite dangerous.

This being so, you can see that our Soldiers are far more dangerous. If a Farmer is like an arrowhead, a Soldier is like a needle, inasmuch as a Soldier is all point (for a line, as you know, is made up entirely of points). Add to this the power Soldiers have of making themselves almost invisible and you can easily see that a Soldier of Flatland is not a person to trifle with!

Perhaps you are wondering how our Soldiers can make themselves invisible. Let me explain.

Place a needle on a table. Then, with your eye at the edge of the table, look at the needle sideways. You will see the whole length of it. But look at it end-ways and you see nothing but a point. It has become practically invisible. This is how it is with all of our Soldiers. When a Soldier's side is turned toward us, we see a Straight Line. When the end containing the Soldier's eye faces us, we see nothing but a rather gleaming point. But when a Soldier's back is to us, it is a dim point that is almost impossible to see.

You can understand, then, how dangerous our Soldiers are. You can get a gash by running into a Merchant Triangle. And you can be quite badly wounded in a collision with a Farmer Triangle. But it is nothing less than absolute death to bump into a Soldier! And when a Soldier is seen only as a dim point, it is difficult, even for the most cautious, to avoid a collision!

For this reason, our Soldiers must be careful. When any Soldiers are out in the street, either standing or walking about, they must move their backs constantly from side to side so that anyone behind them will be able to see them.

You lucky people who live in a world of three dimensions are blessed with shade as well as light. You enjoy many colors. You can see an angle and the complete shape of a Circle. But in Flatland, we do not have these blessings. How, then, can I make you understand the difficulty we have recognizing one another?

The first means of recognition is the sense of hearing. Our hearing is keener and more highly developed than is yours. It enables us not only to tell the voices of our friends, but even to tell the difference between shapes, at least for the Triangle, the Square, and the Pentagon.

But feeling is the best way of recognizing another Flatlander. What an "introduction" is to you, feeling is with us. However, you must not think that feeling is as slow and difficult for us as it might be for you. Long practice and training, which begins in school and goes on throughout life, make it possible for us to quickly tell the difference between the angles of an Equal-Sided Triangle, a Square, or a Pentagon.

It is not necessary, as a rule, to do more than feel a single angle to tell a person's shape, unless he or she belongs to the higher class of shapes. That makes it much more difficult. Even the professors in our University of Wentbridge have been known to confuse a Ten-Sided Polygon with a Twelve-Sided one. And there is hardly a Doctor of Science anywhere in Flatland who would know at once, just by feeling a single angle, the difference between a Twenty-Sided and a Twenty-Four-Sided shape.

Many of us prefer still a third method, which is recognition by the sense of sight.

That this power exists anywhere, and for any class, is the result of Fog. For Fog is present everywhere during most of the year, except in the very hot parts of Flatland. For you, Fog is a bad thing that hides the landscape, makes you feel poorly, and damages your health. But for us, Fog is a blessing, nearly as important as the air itself!

If there were no Fog, all our friends would look like exactly the same kind of Straight Line. But wherever there is a rich supply of Fog, an object only slightly farther away than another is a bit dimmer than the nearer object. So, by carefully examining the dimness and brightness of things, we are able to tell the exact shape of an object.

For example, suppose I were to see two people coming toward me. Let us say that one is a Merchant (an Equilateral Triangle) and the other is a Doctor (a Pentagon). Both appear to be Straight Lines, so how am I to tell one from the other?

In the case of the Merchant, I see a Straight Line, of course. The center of this line, which is the part nearest to me, is very bright. But on either side, the line fades away rapidly into the Fog. I can tell at once, then, that the line slants back quite sharply from the center.

On the other hand, the Doctor has a slightly different appearance. As with the Merchant, I see only a Straight Line with a very bright center. On either side, the Doctor's line also fades into the Fog, but not as rapidly as the Merchant's line. Thus I can tell at once that the Doctor's line does not slant back as sharply. Because of the slight difference in brightness, I know that one shape is an Equilateral Triangle and that the other is a Pentagon.

But enough about how we recognize one another. Let me now say a word or two about our climate and our houses.

Just as you do, we have four points of the compass: North, South, East, and West. But because there is no sun—or, indeed, any other heavenly body—in Flatland, it is impossible for us to tell North in the way you do. However, we have a method of our own.

By a Law of Nature in Flatland, there is a constant pull from the South. This pull is quite enough to serve as a compass in most parts of Flatland. Moreover, the rain, which falls at regular times each day, comes always from the North, so this is an additional help. And in the towns we have the help of the houses, for every house is built with the roof pointing North, to keep off the rain.

However, in our more northern regions, the pull of the South is hardly felt. Sometimes, when walking across an open plain where there have been no houses to guide me, I have had to stand and wait for hours until the rain came. Only then could I be sure of the direction in which I was going.

Our houses are quite comfortable and very well-suited to our climate and way of life. The most common form of house construction in Flatland is Five-Sided, or Pentagon-Shaped.

The two northern sides make up the roof, and usually have no doors. On the east, there is the door by which we go in. On the west side, there is another door by which we go out. In this way, we are able to go in and out without bumping into and hurting one another. The south side, or floor, is usually doorless.

Square and Triangular houses are not allowed. There is a good reason for this. The angles of a Square (and still more of a Triangle) are much more pointed than the angles of a Pentagon. The lines of houses and almost all other objects are dimmer than the lines of Men and Women. Therefore, there is a danger that the points of a Square or Triangular house might do serious injury to an absent-minded traveler suddenly running against them.

As early as the eleventh-century of our era, Triangular houses were forbidden by law. The only exceptions were forts and similar kinds of buildings, where the sharp points might serve a useful purpose. At this period, Square houses were still permitted. But about three centuries later, the Law decided (for reasons of public safety) that in all towns with a population above ten thousand, the angle of the Pentagon was the smallest house angle that could be allowed. It is only now and then, in some very romoto and backward farming district, that one may still discover a Square house.

We have no windows in our houses. This is because light comes to us both inside and outside, by day and by night, equally at all times and in all places. But where light comes from, we do not know. In the old days, our wise men liked to try to discover the cause of light, but this filled our hospitals with those who went mad trying to solve the problem.

I—alas, I alone in Flatland—know the true solution to this mysterious problem. But I cannot make my knowledge understandable to a single one of my countrymen. I am mocked at—I, the only one who knows the truth: that light comes from your strange world of three dimensions!

Story Questions & Activities

1 Why does the author call the setting of his story "Flatland"?

2 What do you think a person in Flatland would rather be: a doctor, a lawyer, or a teacher? Why?

3 What is the author's purpose in writing this selection? Is it to entertain or to give information about different kinds of shapes? Explain.

4 What would you say about this story in a summary?

5 Imagine that a Flatlander became part of the picture on page 532. What effect would he or she have on the painting?

Write a Description

Flatlanders have many different shapes. If you lived in Flatland, what shape would you be? Write a funny description of what your shape and your life would be like in Flatland. Use *like*, *as*, or *than* to describe yourself and show comparisons.

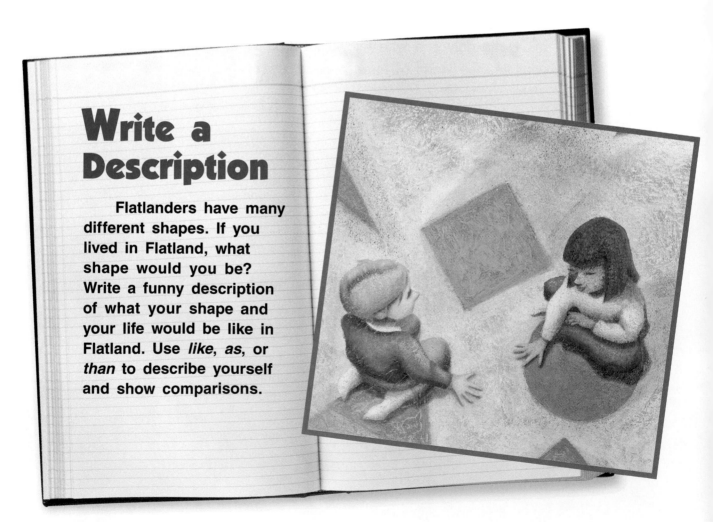

Draw a Flatland House

The most common houses in Flatland are five-sided. The two northern sides make up the roof. There are doors on the east and west sides of the house, but no windows. Draw a Flatland house. Label the drawing with the four points of the compass: North, South, East, and West.

Find the Area

A square has four equal straight sides. To find the area of a square, multiply two sides. A square with sides 2 inches long would have an area of 4 square inches because 2 x 2 = 4. Draw a square family from Flatland. The four squares should have sides 4 inches, 3 inches, 2 inches, and I inch long. Then find the area of each square in the family.

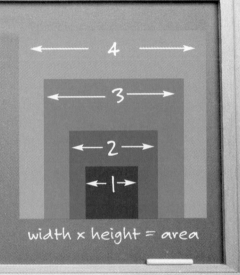

width x height = area

Find Out More

All the farmers in Flatland are isosceles triangles. This means they have two equal sides. How many other kinds of triangles are there? How are scalene, obtuse, acute, and right triangles different from isosceles triangles? Look in a math book or an encyclopedia. Compare and contrast the different kinds of triangles.

Read Signs

Signs may be useless in Flatland, where they'd be impossible to read. But in our three-dimensional world, signs provide us with many kinds of information. Some signs warn about danger, or tell when it is safe to cross the street. Other signs give directions. Still others give information about rules you must follow.

RULES AND REGULATIONS FOR FLATLAND PARK

- **OPEN** 7 AM – 5 PM
- **NO** Swimming, Loud Music, Glass Containers
- **WATCH OUT FOR** Soldiers, Farmers, and Merchant Triangles
- **CLOSED** Days When It's Not Foggy
- Rule Breakers Subject To $50 Fine

EMERGENCIES/ WHERE TO CALL

ALL EMERGENCIES - 911

- FIRE - 222
- POLICE - 333
- AMBULANCE - 444
- POISON CONTROL - 555

Use the signs to answer these questions.

1. What hours is the park open?

2. What would happen if the police caught someone in the park on a day when it was not foggy?

3. What number would you call to report a fire?

4. A small child has accidentally swallowed some detergent. What two numbers could you call?

5. Why is it important to read signs and understand the information on them?

552

TEST POWER

Test Tip

If you see a word in the passage you do not know, try to figure out what it means by looking for clues in the passage.

DIRECTIONS

Read the sample story. Then read each question about the story.

SAMPLE

Bats

Bats are not like most mammals. Unlike most warmblooded creatures, bats are nocturnal; they sleep during the day and are active at night. There are so many different kinds of bats that one quarter of all the mammal species on earth are bats.

Bats are one of the most diverse species of mammals. Bats range in size from <u>minuscule</u> to quite large. The smallest of the bat species, the bumblebee bat, weighs less than a penny, while the largest bat, the flying fox, has a wingspan of nearly six feet. In addition, while some bats can see very well, others must rely completely on their hearing. Some bats can hear a beetle walking on sand from six feet away.

Bats are very important to our environment. However, because many people are afraid of bats, they often don't give the bats the space they require for survival.

1 The word <u>minuscule</u> in this passage means —

   A hard to hear

   B very small

   C huge

   D ancient

2 You can tell from the passage that bats —

   F are not warmblooded

   G are the size of a quarter

   H vary in size

   J cannot fly at night

Stories in Art

Fall of Icarus
by Pieter Brueghel the Elder, c.1555–1558
Musées Royaux des Beaux-Arts, Brussels

If you look quickly at this painting of the myth of Icarus, you might see a calm scene of sheep grazing and a farmer plowing his field. But if you take in the details, you will notice a problem.

～

Look carefully at the painting. What do you see in the lower right-hand corner? Is the boy drowning? How do you think he fell into the water? Will the boy solve his problem? How do you think the boy's story will end?

～

Look at the painting again. Why would it help to know the myth of Icarus? What happened to Icarus's wings when he flew too close to the sun? How might it feel to be able to fly?

Problem and Solution

Develop a strategy for recognizing a problem and its solution.

1 **Identify the character** that has a problem.

2 **Look for details** that explain the problem. State the problem in your own words.

3 **Look for the actions** taken by the character to solve the problem.

4 **Determine if the problem is solved.** What is the solution?

5 **Evaluate the solution.** Was the boy's solution a good one? Why?

THE LEOPARD

One day Leopard sat crying beside a pool of water. A boy collecting water for his nearby village saw Leopard and asked, "Why are you crying? You are one of the mightiest beasts of the plains."

"I am hungry," said Leopard. "I have hunted for days now and have not caught a thing. The animals always see me coming."

The boy, feeling sorry for the young Leopard, promised to meet him the next day. "I will help you!" exclaimed the boy.

The next day Leopard waited by the pool of water. The boy came bounding toward him carrying a small bucket and brush.

AND HIS SPOTS

"How will a bucket and brush help me?" asked Leopard.

"You will see. Now sit still while I paint you," said the boy.

The boy sat beside Leopard and painted small spots all over his skin. He motioned Leopard to the pool of water. Leopard looked at his reflection and gasped. "But what good will spots do me?" he cried.

"Now you can creep and hide in the tall grasses. You will blend into the shadows. The animals will no longer see you coming," said the boy.

Just before dusk, Leopard sat patiently at the edge of a small patch of grass. A herd of zebra were making their way across the plains. Leopard leapt and, to his surprise, he caught one. The spots had worked! Leopard would no longer be hungry!

MEET ROSEBUD YELLOW ROBE

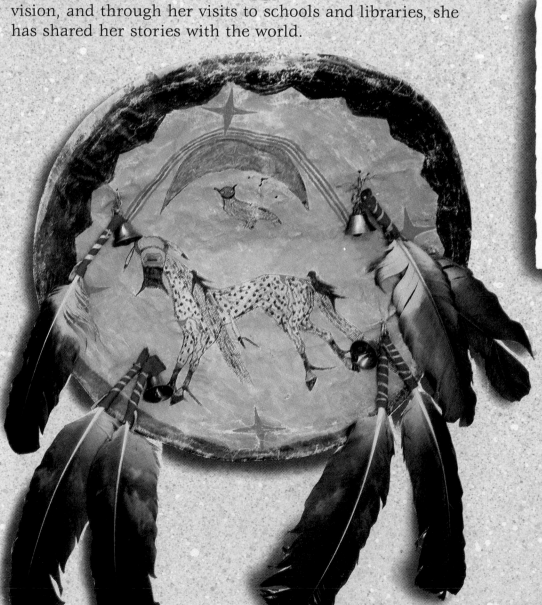

When Rosebud Yellow Robe was young, her parents told her the stories of her people, the Lakota-oyate. Children were expected to memorize the stories and pass them on to their own children.

Yellow Robe, however, has passed these tales on to a much wider audience. Through her books *Tonweya and the Eagles and Other Lakota Indian Tales* and *The Album of the American Indian,* through her appearances on radio and television, and through her visits to schools and libraries, she has shared her stories with the world.

TONWEYA AND THE EAGLES

RETOLD BY
ROSEBUD YELLOW ROBE
ILLUSTRATIONS BY
RICHARD RED OWL

FOREWORD

This story was told to me by my father, Canowicakte. Canowicakte was the boy Chano. Chano was a shortened name used for him. The *c* is pronounced like a *ch,* and the *a* as in *ah.*

My father was born in the southern part of what is now Montana. He lived with his people, the Lakota-oyate, or Sioux nation, roaming the Plains of what are now South Dakota, North Dakota, Nebraska, Wyoming, and Montana. My grandfather was named Tasinagi, or Yellow Robe. He was the son of a hereditary chief. He had won his title to chieftainship as a fearless warrior and great hunter. He too

Native Americans crafted many items of both beauty and utility. At far left, an Oglala Sioux love flute shaped like the bird whose song it echoes. Next to it, a Sioux painted shield. On this page, the teepee of Old Bull is covered with a winter count, and below is shown a scene from High Hawk's Winter Count. A winter count shows a pictorial history of the Sioux.

557

was a leader of his people. My grandmother was named Tahcawin, meaning fawn or female deer. My father was her favorite child because he was her firstborn.

When my father was an infant, my grandfather Tasinagi and my grandmother Tahcawin gave a huge feast for the great men of the tribe in his honor. At that time he was named Canowicakte, meaning kill-in-the-woods. The lobes of both his ears were pierced so that he might wear earrings. Tasinagi gave away two of his best ponies.

Canowicakte spent many hours in the tipi of his grandfather and grandmother. They were his tutors in legends and history of the tribe. He was expected to memorize all these stories so that he in turn would be able to relate them to his children. He was taught respect and reverence for Wakan-tanka, the Great Mystery. He learned of the great and inspiring deeds of the famous chiefs, warriors, and medicine men. He was trained in the old customs of how to make bows and arrows for hunting and for wars. He learned to ride ponies bareback. He learned how to hunt deer and buffalo. He enjoyed

wrestling, swimming, and foot-racing with his companions.

Often Canowicakte followed his father on his hunting trips and learned how to kill a deer or elk and drag it back to camp over the prairie.

Living so close to nature he became familiar with the characteristics and habits of the animals and birds. He knew that his people did not kill buffalo or other game for pleasure. They killed only for use.

He saw his first white man when his parents made camp near one of the trading posts along the Missouri River. He was playing near the camp with his brother when he saw a creature coming toward them. It had long fair hair and a beard and was wearing a large hat and a fringed buckskin suit. It carried a musket on its shoulder. Chano couldn't decide if it was a man or an animal of some kind. As the creature came near the boys, Chano decided it was an evil spirit. For the first time in his life his bravery failed him. He screamed, and leaving his brother behind, he ran to his father in the tipi. His father laughed when he heard the story of the evil spirit. He told Chano he had seen a white man. He told the boys not to go

▲▼ *Standing proudly is the father of Chano, Chief Yellow Robe. Above left is the buffalo, a much revered creature of the Sioux. Below it is a Sioux painted buffalo robe featuring a standard sunburst design.*

very far away or the white man would kidnap them.

Chano remembered warriors coming back and telling exciting tales of their battles with the white men who promised to stay away from the Lakota-oyate lands but who were always forgetting their promises.

When Chano was about fifteen years old, his dreams of glory in an Indian world vanished. General R. H. Pratt came to the headmen of the tribe and asked them to send one of their children east to a school called Carlisle. He told them that life would change rapidly for them. The buffalo were being killed off and reservations were being formed. He explained that the leaders should know about the new world so different from the Indian way of living.

Against his will my father was given to General Pratt to go away to Carlisle. I have pictures of my father taken when he first arrived at the school with skin clothing, moccasins, and long hair. Then pictures when his clothing had been taken away and he was given the uniform of the school to wear. His hair was cut short. For a long time he thought his mother had died. He had been

the first taken to the barber to have his hair cut. Among the Sioux it is a sign of mourning to do so. He thought the other boys were mourning her too, as they had their hair cut.

The children were not allowed to speak their own language, only English, and many weeks had passed by before my father learned that his mother was still alive.

The teachers were very kind to him, but until he learned the language and understood them, he did not trust them. He was a good student. He took part in all the athletics and played on the football team. During the summers he worked on the farms. He also attended the Moody Institute summer school at Northfield, Massachusetts.

Before he left Carlisle, Chauncey Yellow Robe, which was now Canowicakte's name, was chosen to represent the North American Indians at the Congress of Nations at the opening of the World's Columbian Exposition in Chicago.

Canowicakte graduated with honors with the class of 1895. Shortly thereafter he entered government service and spent the greater part of his life at various Indian schools. He was for many

▲▼ *Chauncey Yellow Robe shown before and after his entrance to the Carlisle Indian School. Below are a Sioux rawhide painting and a painted wooden horse.*

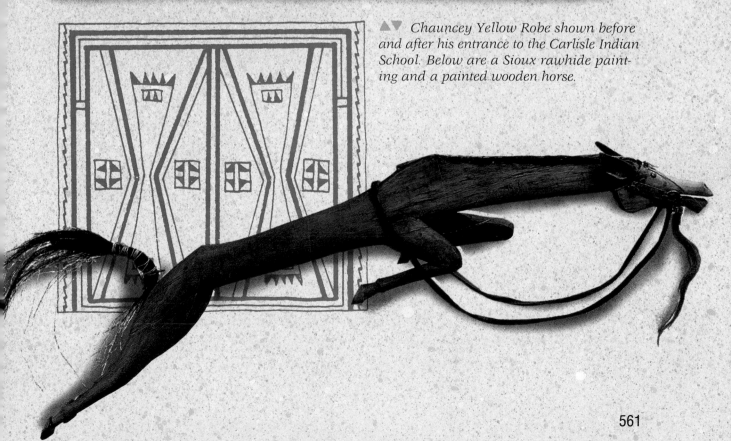

years at the large nonreservation boarding school at Rapid City, South Dakota.

At Rapid City my father met my mother. They fell in love and were married and continued living and working there. My father was disappointed that he did not have a son but soon reconciled himself to his three daughters.

We were very lucky to have parents who taught us about our cultural background and who tried as the Lakotas had for generations to tell us the stories they had heard in their youth. After they were dead, I found several of the stories written out in my mother's and father's handwriting.

My father became very well known for his activities, first with The Society of American Indians. He was much sought after by many organizations as a speaker and soon became known as a "bridge between two cultures."

He spoke out many times critically, and in such a way that he was considered a spokesman for the Sioux.

My father presided at the ceremonies at Deadwood, South Dakota, when the Sioux inducted President Calvin Coolidge into the tribe.

Despite his distaste for the way in which the American Indian was depicted in movies he was persuaded to play a leading role in *The Silent Enemy,* written and produced by Douglas Burden, a trustee of the American Museum of Natural History. This was the first movie produced with an all-Indian cast and no professional actors. It was the story of the Ojibways' struggle against their silent enemy, hunger.

During this time he was also running for Congress in his home state of South Dakota.

He did the talking prologue for the picture *The Silent Enemy;* since the prologue was made in New York City studios, it was last to be filmed. During that time he caught a cold that became pneumonia. He died at the Rockefeller Institute Hospital after a brief illness.

Shortly after my father's death President Coolidge, usually a man of few words, wrote a wonderful tribute to him. In part he said, "He represented a trained and intelligent contact between two different races. He was a born leader who realized that the destiny of the Indian is indissolubly bound up with the destiny of our country. His loyalty to his tribe and his people made him a most patriotic American."

TONWEYA
AND THE
EAGLES

Everyone was excited. It was the Month of Grass Appearing, and the whole camp was busy getting ready to move over the plains to a new home. They would be close to more game and they looked forward to the move. Everyone that is except Chano. He loved this camping spot and already felt lonely for the distant hills.

Tahcawin had packed the parfleche cases with clothing and food and strapped them to a travois made of two trailing poles with a skin net stretched between them. Another travois lay on the ground ready for the new tipi.

Chano was very happy when Tasinagi suggested the three of them ride up to their favorite hills for the last time.

As the three of them rode along, Tasinagi called Chano's attention to the two large birds circling overhead. They were Waŋbli, the eagle. Chano knew they were sacred to his people and that they must never be killed.

He looked at the eagle feather in his father's hair, a sign of bravery, and wondered why it was that the Lakotas as well as many other Indians held Waŋbli, the eagle, in

565

such great respect. Someday he would ask his father about this.

The two eagles they were watching did not seem afraid of the three travelers. They flew nearer and nearer, swooping down in ever narrowing circles. They seemed to be trying to attract the attention of the travelers.

Suddenly Chano called out, "Look, Ate! The feathers on their wings are tipped with red. I never knew that Waŋbli had red feathers!"

"Are you sure of this, my son?" Tasinagi asked.

"Yes, Father. Both birds had tips of bright red on their wings."

"Tahcawin," said Tasinagi, "our son has been favored by the sight of the sacred birds of Tonweya. Few have seen them and it is a sign of good for him."

"What do you mean, Ate?" asked Chano. "What are the sacred birds of Tonweya?"

"They are the eagles who saved Tonweya's life many, many snows ago. Tonweya was a great chief and a great medicine man."

Chano immediately begged his father to tell him the story. Tasinagi motioned for Chano to ride by his side and began:

"It was the summer when the big ball of fire fell from the sky. A band of Lakotas were camping just about where we are now. Among them was a young man whose name was Tonweya. He was not only good to look upon, but he was a great runner and hunter. He was very brave in the face of danger. Everyone said that someday he would be a chief. Brave and good chiefs are always needed in every tribe.

"One day Tonweya went out hunting. He found a small herd of buffalo grazing near the hills and picking out a young fat cow sent an arrow straight into her heart. While he was skinning the buffalo, he noticed a large eagle circling above him. Watching her flight he saw that she settled on a ledge

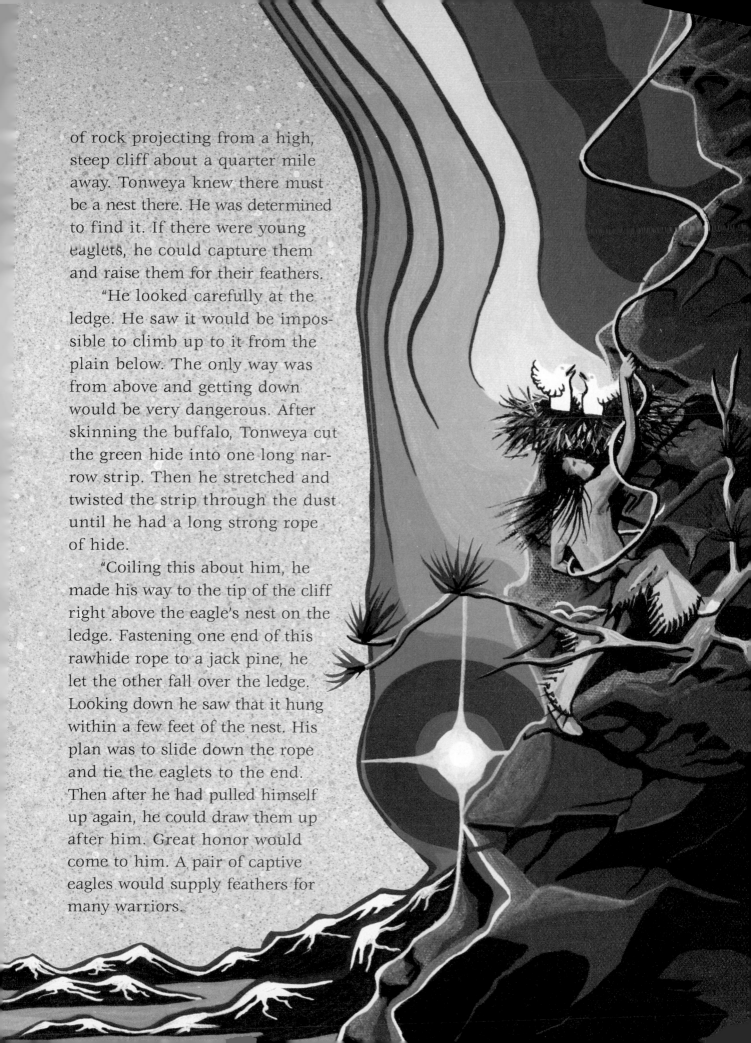

of rock projecting from a high, steep cliff about a quarter mile away. Tonweya knew there must be a nest there. He was determined to find it. If there were young eaglets, he could capture them and raise them for their feathers.

"He looked carefully at the ledge. He saw it would be impossible to climb up to it from the plain below. The only way was from above and getting down would be very dangerous. After skinning the buffalo, Tonweya cut the green hide into one long narrow strip. Then he stretched and twisted the strip through the dust until he had a long strong rope of hide.

"Coiling this about him, he made his way to the tip of the cliff right above the eagle's nest on the ledge. Fastening one end of this rawhide rope to a jack pine, he let the other fall over the ledge. Looking down he saw that it hung within a few feet of the nest. His plan was to slide down the rope and tie the eaglets to the end. Then after he had pulled himself up again, he could draw them up after him. Great honor would come to him. A pair of captive eagles would supply feathers for many warriors.

"Tonweya carefully lowered himself over the edge of the cliff and soon stood on the ledge. There were two beautiful young eaglets in the nest, full feathered, though not yet able to fly. He tied them to his rope and prepared to climb up. But just as he placed his weight on the rope, to his great surprise it fell down beside him. The green hide had been slipping at the knot where he had tied it to the tree; when he pulled on it to go up again, the knot came loose and down came the rope.

"Tonweya realized immediately that he was trapped. Only Wakantanka, the Great Mystery, could save him from a slow death by starvation and thirst. He looked below him. There was a sheer drop of many hundreds of feet with not even the slightest projection by which he might climb down. When he tried to climb up, he could find neither handhold nor foothold. Waŋbli had chosen well the place for a nest.

"Despite his brave heart terror gripped Tonweya. He stood looking off in the direction he knew his people to be. He cried out, '*Ma hiyopo! Ma hiyopo!* Help me!' but only the echo of his own voice answered.

"As the sun was setting, the mother eagle returned to her nest. She screamed in rage when she saw a man with her eaglets. Round and round she flew. Now and then she would charge with lightning speed toward Tonweya and the young birds. The two eaglets flapped their wings wildly and called out to her. Finally in despair the mother eagle made one more swoop toward her nest, and then screaming defiantly, flew off and disappeared. Night fell and the stars came out. Tonweya was alone on the ledge with the two little birds.

"When the sun came up, Tonweya was very tired. He had not slept during the night. The ledge was so narrow, he was afraid he might roll off if he fell asleep. The sun rose high in the heavens and then started its descent into the west. Soon it would be night. Tonweya looked forward with dread to the lonely vigil he must again keep. He was very hungry and so terribly thirsty.

"The second day Tonweya noticed a small spruce growing in a cleft of the rocks some four feet above him. He tied a piece of his rope to this tree and he fastened the other end around his waist. That way even if he stumbled, he would not fall off the ledge. More important still, he could chance some sleep, which he needed badly.

"The third day passed as the others had; heat, hunger, unquenchable thirst. The hope that some of his people might come in search of him was gone. Even if they came, they would never think of looking for him on the cliffs. The mother of the eaglets did not return. Tonweya's presence had frightened her away.

"By this time the two eaglets, seeing that Tonweya had no intention of hurting them, had made friends with him. They allowed Tonweya to touch them at will. Tonweya could see that they were as hungry as he was, so taking out his knife he cut small pieces from the rawhide rope and fed them. This act of kindness removed the last vestige of fear they might have had. They played all about him. They allowed him to hold them aloft. They flapped their wings bravely as he lifted them toward the sun. As he felt the upward pull of their wings, there came to him an idea. Since he had no wings of his own, why could he not make use of the wings of his eagle brothers? He raised his arms toward the sky and called upon Wakan-tanka for wisdom.

"The night of the third day, the one on which he had fed the eaglets for the first time, was raw and chill. When Tonweya stretched out for what little sleep he could get, he shivered with the cold. As if understanding his need, the two little eaglets left their nest and coming over to where he lay nestled their warm, fluffy bodies close beside him. In a few moments Tonweya was asleep.

"While he was asleep, he dreamed. In his dream Wakan-tanka spoke to him. He told him to be brave, the two eaglets would save him. Tonweya awoke suddenly. The eagles were still beside him. As they felt him move, they nestled even closer to him. He placed his arms around them. He knew that his time to die had not yet come. He would once more see his people. He was no longer afraid.

"For days thereafter Tonweya fed the rawhide rope to his eagle friends. Luckily it was a long rope, for it was, of course, almost a whole buffalo hide. But while the eaglets thrived on it and grew larger and stronger each day, Tonweya grew thinner and weaker. It rained one day and water gathered in the hollows of the rocks on the ledge. Still he was very hungry and thirsty. He tried to think only of caring for the eaglets.

"Each day Tonweya would hold them up by their legs and let them try their wings. Each day the pull on his arms grew stronger. Soon it was so powerful it almost lifted him from his feet. He knew the time was coming for him to put his idea into action. He decided he must do it quickly, for weak as he was he would be unable to do it after a few more days.

"The last of the rawhide was gone, the last bit of water on the ledge was drunk. Tonweya was so weak, he could hardly stand. With an effort he dragged himself upright and called his eagle brothers to him. Standing on the edge of the ledge he called to Wakan-tanka for help. He grasped the eaglets' legs in each hand and closing his eyes he jumped.

"For a moment he felt himself falling, falling. Then he felt the pull on his arms. Opening his eyes he saw that the two eagles were flying easily. They seemed to be supporting his weight with little effort. In a moment they had reached the ground. Tonweya lay there too exhausted, too weak to move. The eagles remained by his side guarding him.

"After resting awhile Tonweya slowly made his way to a little stream nearby. He drank deeply of its cool water. A few berries were growing on the bushes there. He ate them ravenously. Strengthened by even this little food and water, he started off in the direction of the camp. His progress was slow, for he was compelled to rest many times. Always the eaglets remained by his side guarding him.

"On the way he passed the spot where he had killed the buf-falo. The coyotes and vultures had left nothing but bones. However

his bow and arrows were just where he had left them. He managed to kill a rabbit upon which he and his eagle friends feasted. Late in the afternoon he reached the camp, only to find that his people had moved on. It was late. He was very tired so he decided to stay there that night. He soon fell asleep, the two eagles pressing close beside him all night.

"The sun was high in the sky when Tonweya awoke. The long sleep had given him back much strength. After once more giving thanks to Wakan-tanka for his safety he set out after his people. For two days he followed their trail. He lived on the roots and berries he found along the way and what little game he could shoot. He shared everything with his eagle brothers, who followed him. Sometimes they flew overhead, sometimes they walked behind him, and now and then they rested on his shoulders.

"Well along in the afternoon of the second day he caught up with the band. At first they were frightened when they saw him. Then they welcomed him with joy.

"They were astonished at his story. The two eagles who never left Tonweya amazed them. They were glad that they had always been kind to Waŋbli and had never killed them.

"The time came when the eagles were able to hunt food for themselves and though everyone expected them to fly away, they did not. True, they would leave with the dawn on hunting forays, but when the evening drew near, they would fly back fearlessly and enter Tonweya's tipi, where they passed the night. Everyone marveled at the sight.

"But eagles, like men, should be free. Tonweya, who by now understood their language, told them they could go. They were to enjoy the life the Great Mystery, Wakan-tanka, had planned for them. At first they refused. But when Tonweya said if he ever needed their help he would call for them, they consented.

"The tribe gave a great feast in their honor. In gratitude for all they had done Tonweya painted the tips of their wings a bright red to denote courage and bravery. He took them up on a high mountain. He held them once more toward the sky and bidding them good-bye released them. Spreading their wings they soared away. Tonweya watched them until they disappeared in the eye of the sun.

"Many snows have passed and Tonweya has long been dead. But now and then the eagles with the red-tipped wings are still seen. There are always two of them and they never show any fear of people. Some say they are the original sacred eagles of Tonweya, for the Waŋbli lives for many snows. Some think they are the children of the sacred ones. It is said whoever sees the red-tipped wings of the eagles is sure of their protection as long as he is fearless and brave. And only the fearless and brave may wear the eagle feather tipped with red."

When Tasinagi finished the story, he looked to see if the red-winged eagles were still following them. They were there. He knew then that his son Chano was one of those to be blessed by great good in his life.

Story Questions & Activities

1. Why does Tonweya want to find the eagle's nest?

2. Why are eagles sacred to the Lakota people?

3. Why do you think Tonweya would make a good chief for his people? Explain.

4. What problem does Tonweya face in this story? How does he solve it?

5. How is Tonweya's problem different from the problems that the people of Flatland face every day?

Write a Folk Tale

Tonweya and the eagles show great strength and courage in this Native American folk tale. Write your own folk tale to show how Tonweya and another hero could accomplish a great deed together. What problem could the two heroes face? How could they solve it? Use dialogue and description to show how your heroes are similar, yet different.

Make a Winter Count

The Lakota kept track of events with calendars called winter counts. Each winter they chose an important event of the past year. An artist then recorded this event by drawing a picture of it on a buffalo hide. With a group of classmates, create a list of important events from the school year. Choose one and draw the event. Then share your winter count with other groups. How are your winter counts alike? How do they differ?

Draw a Territory Map

Tonweya's tribe, the Lakota Sioux, roamed the plains of what are now the states of North Dakota, South Dakota, Nebraska, Wyoming, and Montana. Trace a map of the present-day United States. Shade the area where the Lakota Sioux lived more than two hundred years ago.

Find Out More

In the story, Tonweya spotted a beautiful eagle when he was hunting buffalo. What kind of eagle was it? How many different kinds of eagles are found in North America? Start by checking in an encyclopedia or in a book about North American birds. Use what you learn to prepare a chart that compares two different types of North American eagles.

577

STUDY SKILLS

Read a News Article

The events in "Tonweya and the Eagles" would make a good news article in a newspaper. A **news article** tells about an important current event. It begins with a **headline**, a word, phrase, or sentence printed in large type at the top. Usually, a news article also has a **dateline.** This tells where and when the story was written. Look at the news article below. How does the first paragraph catch your interest? How does it also answer the questions *Who? What? Where?* and *When?* Notice that the rest of the article gives more facts. News articles usually do not express the writer's opinions.

 # THE CHICAGO NEWS

Bald Eagle Stops for Dinner

by Diane Follett

Chicago, Friday, Feb. 2, 1999

It is a well-known fact that the bald eagle is the national bird of the United States. But until today, no bald eagle had ever stopped in for a "state dinner." High atop downtown Chicago, in the city's most scenic restaurant, Governor Tilson, Mayor Dean, and several state representatives shared their dinner with the bird.

At about 7:00 P.M. the bald eagle landed atop the balcony railing outside the politicians' table. The bird then moved to the window ledge, as if to get a stronger whiff of the roast duck and glazed trout, the politicians' main course. While affairs of state were being discussed, the conversation quickly changed to protecting the nation's bird. Today, the U.S. government has banned certain pollutants like pesticides, helping the bald eagle make a comeback, No one expected, however, that a comeback meant candlelight dinner at

Use the news article to answer these questions.

1 What is the headline of this news article?

2 When and where was the news article written?

3 What is the main idea of the article?

4 Why do newspaper writers answer these questions in the first paragraph: *Who? What? When?* and *Where?*

5 Why is it important to know how to read a news article?

TEST POWER

Test Tip

Try answering the question in your own words before looking at the answer choices.

DIRECTIONS

Read the sample story. Then read each question about the story.

SAMPLE

Alcatraz

In the cold waters of San Francisco Bay is one of the city's most popular tourist spots. Each year, thousands of people visit Alcatraz Island. But before 1963, Alcatraz was one of the nation's most famous and perilous prisons.

Surrounded by the strong currents of the bay, Alcatraz was known as "The Rock." Alcatraz was built on a huge rock in the middle of the bay in order to make an escape from the prison impossible.

In 1963, the prison was closed, and the National Park Service opened Alcatraz to the public ten years later. Visitors can now hear stories, see the old prison cells, and learn about what life was like for prisoners on "The Rock."

1 Most likely, an escape from Alcatraz was impossible because —

   A it was too high to jump

   B it was too far to swim

   C there were too many visitors

   D the prison cells were old

2 Why is Alcatraz also called "The Rock"?

   F It is made out of extra strong cement.

   G Prisoners hauled rocks when they misbehaved.

   H It is a steady place.

   J It was built on a rock in San Francisco Bay.

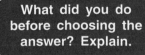

What did you do before choosing the answer? Explain.

Stories in Art

This Native American cliff dwelling in Mesa Verde was built hundreds of years ago. Why do you think the Anasazi built their houses in this way?

Look at the photograph. What can you tell about these houses? How are they like the apartment houses of today? What are the differences?

Study the photograph. Why are the houses deserted? What do you think drove the people away? Were the houses well built? What makes you think so? Would you like to live in these houses? Explain why.

Cliff Palace
Mesa Verde National Park, Colorado

580

Compare and Contrast

Develop a strategy for comparing and contrasting.

1 **Identify who or what** can be compared or contrasted.

2 **Look for clue** words such as *all, everyone, but,* and *instead* that signal comparisons and contrasts.

3 **Look for details** that explain the likenesses and differences.

4 **Tell the ways** in which the characters are alike. What is the same about the three brothers?

5 **Identify the** differences. How are the king and his brother different? How are the bridges different?

581

Once upon a time there was a king named Toll who lived on an island. There was no bridge to the island, but King Toll didn't mind. He loved the slow, peaceful boat ride to the castle. The king's brother, Prince Ralph, however, hated boats.

"The boats are too crowded. I get sea-sick," he said to the king. "Why can't you have a bridge to the castle?"

Tired of his brother's complaints, the king decided to have a bridge built. "I will hold a contest for the best bridge design," he proclaimed. "The winner will get a castle and a sack of gold."

News of the contest reached three brothers who were bridge builders. Tempted by the prize, all three brothers went to work. Ed drew ten enormous logs resting on

boulders. Ted drew a suspension bridge. Instead of drawing, Ned built a model of a bridge that could be drawn up to the castle entrance.

Finally, it was time for the king to choose a winner. Ed and Ted both displayed their designs. Ned opened a small box.

King Toll looked at the bridges and said, "These bridges are excellent. I'll build them all! They'll be called *Toll bridges*!"

So the brothers got their castle. Prince Ralph no longer got seasick. And King Toll liked the bridges so much that he hired the brothers to build them all over the kingdom. The tolls came later on!

BREAKER'S BRIDGE

by Laurence Yep

illustrated by David Wisniewski

There was once a boy who was always breaking things. He didn't do it on purpose. He just had very clumsy hands. No matter how careful he tried to be, he always dropped whatever he picked up. His family soon learned not to let him set the table or send him for eggs. Everyone in the village called him Breaker.

But Breaker was as clever as he was clumsy. When he grew up, he managed to outlive his nickname. He could design a bridge to cross any obstacle. No canyon was too wide. No river was too deep. Somehow the clever man always found a way to bridge them all.

Eventually the emperor heard about this clever builder and sent for him.

"There is a river in the hills," the emperor said to him. "Everyone tells me it is too swift and deep to span. So I have to go a long way around it to get to my hunting palace. But you're famous for doing the impossible."

The kneeling man bowed his head to the floor. "So far I have been lucky. But there is always a first time when you can't do something."

The emperor frowned. "I didn't think you were lazy like my other bridge builders. You can have all the workers and all the materials you need. Build

the bridge and you'll have
your weight in gold. Fail
and I'll have your head."

There was nothing
for Breaker to do but thank
the emperor and leave.
He went right away to see
the river. He had to take
a steep road that wound
upward through the hills
toward the emperor's hunting palace.

It was really more than a
palace, for it included a park
the size of a district, and only
the emperor could hunt the
wildlife. The road to it had to
snake through high, steep
mountains. Although the
road was well kept, the land
became wilder and wilder.
Pointed boulders thrust up
like fangs, and the trees grew
in twisted, writhing clumps.

Breaker became uneasy. "This is a place that doesn't like people very much."

The road twisted suddenly to the left when it came to a deep river gorge. On the other side of the gorge, the many trees of the palace looked like a dark-green sea. The yellow-tiled roofs looked like golden rafts floating on its top. Dark mountains, their tops capped with snow all year round, loomed behind the palace like monstrous guards.

Breaker carefully sidled to the edge of the gorge and looked down. Far below, he saw the river. When the snow melted in the distant mountains, the water flowed together to form this river. It raced faster than a tiger and stronger than a thousand buffalo. When it splashed against a rock, it threw up sheets of white spray like an ocean wave.

Breaker shook his head in dismay. "The emperor might as well have commanded me to bridge the sea."

But his failure would mean the loss of his head, so the next day Breaker set to work. The river was too wide to span with a simple bridge. Breaker would have to construct two piers in the middle of the river. The piers would support the bridge like miniature stone islands.

From the forests of the south came huge logs that were as tough and heavy as iron. From the quarries of the west came large, heavy stones of granite. The workers braved the cold water to sink the logs in the muddy riverbed. Breaker had to change the teams of workers often. The cold numbed anyone who stayed too long in the river.

Once the logs had been pounded into the mud, he tried to set the stones on top of the logs. But the river did not want to be tamed. It bucked and fought like a herd of wild stallions. It crushed the piles of stones into pebbles. It dug up the logs and smashed them against the rocky sides until they were mounds of soggy toothpicks.

Over the next month, Breaker tried every trick he knew; and each time the river defeated him. With each new failure, Breaker suspected more and more that he had met his match. The river flowed hard and strong and fast like the lifeblood of the earth itself. Breaker might as well have tried to tame the mountains.

In desperation, he finally tried to build a dam to hold back the river while he constructed the biggest and strongest piers yet. As he was supervising the construction, an official came by from the emperor.

"This bridge has already cost a lot of money," he announced to the workers. "What do you have to show for it?"

Breaker pointed to the two piers. They rose like twin towers toward the top of the gorge. "With a little luck, the emperor will have his bridge."

Suddenly, they heard a distant roar. The official looked up at the sky. "It sounds like thunder, but I don't see a cloud in the sky."

Breaker cupped his hands around his mouth to amplify his voice. "Get out," he shouted to his men. "Get out. The river must have broken our dam."

His men slipped and slid on the muddy river-bed, but they all managed to scramble out just as a wall of water rolled down the gorge. The river swept around the two piers, pulling and tugging at the stones.

Everyone held their breath. Slowly the two piers began to rock back and forth on their foundations until they toppled over with a crash into the river. Water splashed in huge sheets over everyone, and when the spray finally fell back into the river, not one sign of the piers remained.

"All this time and all this money, and you have nothing to show for it." The official took a soggy yellow envelope from his sleeve.

Breaker and the other workers recognized the imperial color of the emperor. They instantly dropped to their knees and bowed their heads.

Then, with difficulty, Breaker opened the damp envelope and unfolded the letter. "In one month," it said, "I will have a bridge or I will have your head." It was sealed in red ink with the official seal of the emperor.

Breaker returned the letter and bowed again. "I'll try," he promised.

"You will do more than try," the official snapped. "You will build that bridge for the emperor. Or the executioner will be sharpening his sword." And the official left.

Wet and cold and tired, Breaker made his way along a path toward the room he had taken in an inn. It was getting late, so the surrounding forest was black with shadows. As he walked, Breaker tried to come up with some kind of new scheme, but the dam had been his last resort. In a

month's time, he would feel the "kiss" of the executioner's sword.

"Hee, hee, hee," an old man laughed in a creaky voice that sounded like feet on old, worn steps. "You never liked hats anyway. Now you'll have an excuse not to wear them."

Breaker turned and saw a crooked old man sitting by

the side of the road. He was
dressed in rags, and a gourd
hung from a strap against
his hip. One leg was shorter
than the other.

"How did you know that,
old man?" Breaker wondered.

"Hee, hee, hee. I know a
lot of things: the softness of
clouds underneath my feet,
the sound of souls inside
bodies." And he shook his

gourd so that it rattled as if
there were beans inside. "It
is the law of the universe
that all things must change;
and yet Nature hates change
the most of all."

"The river certainly fits
that description." Although
he was exhausted and wor-
ried, Breaker squatted down
beside the funny old man.
"But you better get inside,

old man. Night's coming on and it gets cold up in these mountains."

"Can't." The old man nodded to his broken crutch.

Breaker looked all around. It was growing dark, and his stomach was aching with hunger. But he couldn't leave the old man stranded in the mountains, so Breaker took out his knife. "If I make you a new crutch, can you reach your home?"

"If you make me a crutch, we'll all have what we want." It was getting so dim that Breaker could not be sure if the old man smiled.

Although it was hard to see, Breaker found a tall, straight sapling and tried to trim the branches from its sides; but being Breaker, he dropped his knife several times and lost it twice among the old leaves on the forest floor. He also cut each of his fingers. By the time he was ready to cut down the sapling, he couldn't even see it. Of course, he cut his fingers even more. And just as he was trimming

591

the last branch from the sapling, he cut the sapling right in two.

He tried to carve another sapling and broke that one. It was so dark by now that he could not see at all. He had to find the next sapling by feel. This time he managed to cut it down and began to trim it. But halfway through he dropped his knife and broke it. "He'll just have to take it as it is," Breaker said.

When he finally emerged from the forest, the moon had come out. Sucking on his cut fingers, Breaker presented the new crutch to the funny old man.

The old man looked at the branches that grew from the sides of his new crutch. "A little splintery."

Breaker angrily took his cut finger from his mouth. "Don't insult someone who's doing you a favor."

The crooked old man lifted his right arm with difficulty and managed to bring it behind his neck. "Keep that in mind yourself." He began to rub the back of his neck.

Breaker thrust the crutch at the old man. "Here, old man. This is what you wanted."

But the old man kept rubbing the back of his neck. "Rivers are like people: Every now and then, they have to be reminded that change is the law that binds us all."

"It's late. I'm tired and hungry and I have to come up with a new plan. Here's your crutch." And Breaker laid the crutch down beside the old man.

But before Breaker could straighten, the old man's left hand shot out and caught hold of Breaker's wrist. The old man's grip was as strong as iron. "Even the least word from me will remind that river of the law."

Breaker tried to pull away, but as strong as he was, he could not break the old man's hold. "Let me go."

But the crooked old man lowered his right hand so that Breaker could see that he had rubbed some of the dirt and sweat from his skin.

"We are all bound together," the old man murmured, "and by the same laws." He murmured that over and over until he was almost humming like a bee. At the same time, his fingers quickly rolled the dirt and sweat into two round little pellets.

Frightened, Breaker could only stare at the old man. "Ar-ar-are you some mountain spirit?" he stammered.

The old man turned Breaker's palm upward and deposited the two little pellets on it. Then he closed Breaker's fingers over them. "Leave one of these at each spot where you want a pier. Be sure not to lose them."

"Yes, all right, of course," Breaker promised quickly.

The old man picked up the crutch and thrust himself up from the ground. "Then you'll have what you want too." And he hobbled away quickly.

Breaker kept hold of the pellets until he reached the inn. Once he was among the inn's bright lights and could smell a hot meal, he began to laugh at himself. "You've let the emperor's letter upset you so much that you let a harmless old man scare you."

Even so, Breaker didn't throw away the pellets but put them in a little pouch. And the next morning when he returned to the gorge, he took along the pouch.

The canyon widened at one point so that there was a small beach. Breaker kept his supplies of stone and logs there. Figuring that he had nothing to lose, Breaker walked down the steep path. Then he took the boat and rowed out onto the river.

As he sat in the bobbing boat, he thought of the funny old man again. "You and I," he said to the river, "are both part of the same scheme of things. And it's time you faced up to it."

Although it was difficult to row at the same time, he got out the pouch with the two pellets. "I must be even crazier than that old man." He opened the pouch and shook one of the pellets into his hand.

When he was by the spot where the first pier should be, Breaker threw the pellet in. For a moment, nothing happened. There was only the sound of his oars slapping at the water.

And suddenly the surface began to boil. Frantically, he tried to row away, but the water began to whirl and whirl around in circles. Onshore, the workers shouted and ran to higher ground as waves splashed over the logs and stones.

From beneath the river came loud thumps and thuds and the grinding of stone on stone. A rock appeared above the surface. The water rose in another

As the waters calmed, Breaker eagerly rowed the boat over to the second spot. At the same time that he tried to row enough to keep himself in the right place, Breaker reached for the pouch and opened it.

But in his hurry, his clumsy fingers crushed part of the pellet. He threw the remainder of the pellet into the water and then shook out the contents of the pouch. But this time, the river only swirled and rippled.

Breaker leaned over the side and peered below. He could just make out the pale, murky shape of a mound, but that was all. Even so, Breaker wasn't upset. His workers could easily build a second pier and meet the emperor's deadline.

So Breaker finished the bridge, and that summer the emperor reached his hunting palace with ease. When the emperor finished hunting and returned to his capital, he showered Breaker with gold and

wave. On top of the wave another stone floated as if it were a block of wood. The river laid the first stone by the second.

Open-mouthed, Breaker watched the river lay stone after stone. The watery arms reached higher and higher until the first pier rose to the top of the gorge.

promised him all the work he could ever want.

However, winter brought deep snows once again to the mountains. That spring, when the snow thawed, the river grew strong and wild again. It roared down the gorge and smashed against the first pier. But the first pier was solid as a mountain.

However, the second pier had not been built with magic. The river swept away the second pier as if it were nothing but twigs.

The bridge was repaired before the summer hunting, but the emperor angrily summoned Breaker to his hunting palace. "You were supposed to build a bridge for me," the emperor declared.

"Hee, hee, hee," laughed a creaky old voice. "He did, but you didn't say how long it was supposed to stay up."

Breaker turned around and saw it was the crooked old man. He was leaning on the crutch that Breaker had made for him. "How did you get here?" he asked the old

man. But from the corner of his eye, he could see all the court officials kneeling down. And when Breaker looked back at the throne, he saw even the emperor kneeling.

"How can we serve you and the other eight immortals?" the emperor asked the crooked old man.

Meet
LAURENCE YEP

"We are all bound by the same laws," the old man croaked again, and then vanished.

And then Breaker knew the old man for what he truly was—a saint and a powerful magician.

So the emperor spared Breaker and sent him to build other projects all over China. And the emperor never regretted that he had let Breaker keep his head. But every year, the river washed away part of the bridge and every year it was rebuilt. And so things change and yet do not change.

Laurence Yep's first published story was about a nonhuman, written from that character's viewpoint. This probably wasn't difficult for someone who felt "different" for most of his childhood. Yep, who is Chinese American, grew up in an African-American neighborhood in San Francisco. He went to school in Chinatown, but he felt like an outsider there, too, because he could not speak Chinese.

Even the books Yep could find to read were not about Chinese Americans like himself. So he turned to science fiction and fantasy. "In those books, children were taken to other lands and other worlds where they had to learn strange customs and languages," says Yep, "and that was something I did every time I got on and off the bus."

Years later, Yep began to write the stories for which he has won so many awards. The first, *Dragonwings,* described the United States in the early 1900s through the eyes of a newly arrived Chinese boy. "Breaker's Bridge" is from *The Rainbow People,* a book of Chinese tales. Yep still writes science fiction as well.

Story Questions & Activities

1. How did Breaker get his nickname?

2. How does Breaker try to solve the problem of building the bridge over the river?

3. How are Breaker, the old man, and the river bound by the same laws of change? Explain.

4. What is this story really about?

5. Compare the way Breaker and Tonweya solve problems. How is their approach alike?

Write an Essay

"We are all bound by the same laws," says the old man in the story. In a brief essay, show what binds Breaker and the old man together. Compare the two characters. How do their personalities help them succeed? How are they both part of the same scheme of things?

Design a Bridge

Breaker built a bridge over a raging river, with piers in the water to hold up the bridge. Design your own bridge. What will it cross—a river, or maybe a deep canyon? What will it look like? Use drawing paper and markers, paints, pencils, crayons, or charcoals to create your design. Give your bridge a name when you have finished "building" it.

Test Bridge-building Materials

How do builders test different materials before they use them to build a bridge? Start with a strip of styrofoam. Test for tension by holding each end and by pulling it apart. Press down gently on top to test for compression. Work with a partner to find materials that are strong in tension, weak in compression, and vice versa.

Find Out More

In the story, Breaker supports his bridge with two piers. How many different kinds of bridges are there? Why would you build one type of bridge instead of another? Start by checking in an encyclopedia to find the differences among arch, span, and suspension bridges. Compare these bridges with the bridge Breaker builds.

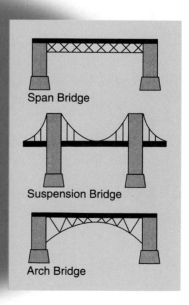

Span Bridge

Suspension Bridge

Arch Bridge

Read a Help-wanted Ad

Suppose that Breaker wanted to find another job as a bridge builder. Where would he look? The help-wanted section of the newspaper would be a good place to start.

A **help-wanted ad** contains the information a person needs to apply for a job. It may also include a description of the job's responsibilities, the hours, the salary, and the experience needed to do the work.

HELP WANTED

BRIDGE BUILDERS NEEDED
Excellent opportunities available for people with experience building bridges across rivers and canyons. Should be familiar with piers, dams, and have knowledge to overcome any obstacle. Long hours with high pay. Must be willing to travel. Apply at Office of Emperor's Affairs, China.

SALES REP
A leader in the
industry is seel
Minimum 1 yea
in related indus
Must be experi
please forward

Use the help-wanted ad to answer these questions.

1 What kind of job is being advertised in this help-wanted ad?

2 Who placed this help-wanted ad? How do you know?

3 Why do you think that people applying for this job must be willing to travel?

4 Should a person who has built only one or two bridges apply for this job? Explain.

5 How can a help-wanted ad help someone find a job?

TEST POWER

Test Tip

Clues to the meaning of the underlined word are usually near the underlined word.

DIRECTIONS

Read the sample story. Then read each question about the story.

SAMPLE

Ilse's Move

Ilse was so excited. She had graduated from college and was moving to Cincinnati. Her younger sister Olga was helping her pack. Olga was going to miss her sister.

"Are you taking this, or will you sell it in the garage sale?" Olga asked, holding a tattered violin case. The smaller violin inside had been perfect when both girls were young. Now that they were accomplished violinists, they each had full-size instruments.

Ilse planned to <u>audition</u> for the Cincinnati Symphony as soon as she arrived in the city. She already had an appointment with the conductor for the following week. She was hopeful that she would be hired.

1 The word <u>audition</u> in this passage means —

A try out

B get paid

C teach someone

D practice

2 Ilse was excited because —

F Olga was helping her get ready for the move

G she was going to be the conductor of the symphony

H she was moving to Cincinnati

J she had a new car

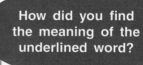

How did you find the meaning of the underlined word?

601

Stories in Art

This mural was created by a group of students who wanted to make their community aware of some of Earth's problems and of ways to solve them.

Look at this mural. What are some problems that our environment is facing? What are some of the solutions that these students suggest?

Look at this mural again. What are some choices that the Earth gives us? What can we do to protect the environment? What problem and solution would you add to this mural?

The Earth Gives Us Lifelong Choices,
a mural by seventeen sixth grade students at Gilbert Elementary School
Gilbert, Arizona

Problem and Solution

Develop a strategy for identifying a problem and its solution.

1 **Identify the problem** described in the article.

2 **Look for details** that explain the problem. Try to restate the problem in your own words.

3 **Identify the actions** taken to solve the problem.

4 **Read the chart.** Does the information in the chart help you to understand the problem or its solution? How?

5 **Explain the problem** and how it might be solved. How would you solve the problem if it were up to you?

Save Our Air!

The atmosphere is like a bubble of gases enclosing our planet. It extends almost 200 miles upward from Earth's surface and has many layers. These layers form a protective shield, an "air blanket" that protects Earth and its inhabitants from the harmful effects of the sun's rays.

The atmosphere seems so vast that people once thought anything we put into it just disappeared. We have learned that this is not true. Particles of many substances released from cars and factories stay in the atmosphere. These particles create air pollution. Air pollution harms life on Earth.

Another problem comes from smog, a combination of smoke and fog. Smog contains sulfur compounds that combine with water vapor to create acid rain. When acid rain falls into rivers and streams, it kills fish and animals. It can destroy entire forests. This creates bigger problems, because trees help to keep the air clean.

Scientists believe that some damage to the atmosphere can be repaired. Governments are putting pollution controls on cars and factories. The use of aerosol cans is decreasing. People are recycling paper and planting new forests.

Everyone can help to clean our air. Find out what you can do. Our planet is depending on you!

Problem	How You Can Help
AIR POLLUTION	walk or ride a bike take public transportation save power, turn off unnecessary lights don't use aerosol cans
ENDANGERED RESOURCES	use recycled products recycle paper reuse grocery bags and other packaging plant trees

TIME

FOR KIDS
SPECIAL REPORT

CLEANING UP AMERICA'S AIR

604

Wiping Out Smog and Soot

Stricter rules for air pollution will help Americans breathe a little easier

Yuck! As you wait to cross the street, a huge truck rumbles by and blasts a smelly black cloud of smoke in your face. But the truck's fumes don't just stink up the neighborhood. Dirty chemicals from factories and engines foul the nation's skies and threaten everyone's health.

The Environmental Protection Agency (EPA) has done something about this threat. This government agency created tough new limits on two big parts of air pollution: ground-level ozone gas and dusty

stuff called particulate matter. The EPA says the new regulations will help protect people's health *and* the environment.

TARGETING SOOT AND SMOG

Ground-level ozone, or smog, is the haze that often hangs over cities. (You may have heard of the ozone layer above Earth. This faraway ozone is protective, not harmful.) Particulates, or soot, are tiny flecks of dust, as small as one-seventh the width of a human hair. Both smog and

Cars, buses, and trucks help to create air pollution.

605

soot come from cars, trucks, factories, and construction sites.

Smog and soot can cause serious illness, including asthma and other breathing problems. Breathing the smog and soot for just one hour a day can lead to lung problems in some people, especially children. The American Lung Association and other health groups have been especially worried about dust particles, which irritate lungs. Air pollution plays a role in the deaths of thousands of Americans each year.

With the new law, even the tiniest amounts of soot will be controlled.

The rules on ozone have been tightened even more. Regions that fail to meet the limits will lose federal highway funds and other money.

These rules, which were approved by Congress in 1997, are all part of a move to toughen the Clean Air Act of 1970. That act sets limits on six kinds of pollution (*see chart below*). Every few years the EPA reviews some of these limits, as it has done with the new soot and smog rules.

Carol Browner, head of the EPA, says that the old rules didn't provide enough health protection, especially to children.

Danger in the Air: Ingredients of Pollution

POLLUTANT	SOURCE	DANGER
Ozone (Smog)	Cars, factories, landfills. Ozone gas is formed when the sun's heat causes oxygen to react with other chemicals.	Causes breathing problems, possible lung infections, eye irritation, serious damage to plants.
Carbon Monoxide	Cars, buses, trucks, factories	Causes headaches, dizziness, heart damage.
Nitrogen Oxides	Factories, cars, trucks, coal-burning stoves	Harms plants, causes breathing problems for humans, and reacts in the atmosphere to cause acid rain.
Particulate Matter (Soot)	Factories, cars, smoke from burning wood, and dust from construction	Causes breathing problems, eye irritation; also makes air dirty and harms plants.
Sulfur Dioxide	Factories and furnaces	Causes breathing problems, harms plants and waterways.
Lead	Cars, trucks, and buses that have lead in their fuel; factories	Harms the brain, kidneys, and blood.

Bike routes like this one along the Mississippi River in Illinois encourage pollution-free transportation.

ARE THE STANDARDS TOO STRICT?

Before the limits were put into law, the EPA listened to public reaction. Some politicians and businesspeople complained about the new standards. Industry leaders said they couldn't afford to spend billions of dollars to change the way their factories work. They said that the old standards were strict enough.

But in 1997, Congress agreed to the EPA's new standards. Because businesses need time to make changes, the tougher laws won't take effect until 2004 or beyond. And the EPA won't issue fines to businesses that are not following the law until 2010.

Factories aren't the only places that will have to make changes over the next few years. Hundreds of cities and towns are too polluted to meet the new standards. These communities are working with the EPA to create more car pools, improve public transportation, and increase smog checks on cars.

CLEARER SKIES AHEAD

Cleaning up the air has never been cheap or easy. The EPA thinks it will cost at least $7 billion to make the changes. Is it worth it? The new standards will save about 20,000 lives a year, according to the EPA. They will prevent a lot of illness. And for the 133 million Americans who now live in polluted areas, they will bring a much-needed breath of fresh air.

FIND OUT MORE
Visit our website:
www.mhschool.com/reading

*inter*NET
CONNECTION

Based on an article in *TIME FOR KIDS*.

Story Questions & Activities

1 What is the problem with today's air?

2 How does air pollution play a role in the death of thousands of Americans each year?

3 How does the Environmental Protection Agency (EPA) try to clean up America's air?

4 What are the main problem and solution presented in this article?

5 Look at the students' mural on page 602. What do you think these students would say to the polluters in this article? What advice might they give to people who want to clean up America's air?

Write an E-mail

Write an E-mail to a friend or relative in which you tell about an environmental group in your town. Describe some work that the group has done and compare the situation before the work to what it was like after the work. Use the comparison to persuade the friend or relative to join an environmental group.

Make a Poster

How are communities all across the country working with the EPA to help meet the new antipollution laws? Make a poster that describes what people can do to reduce air pollution. Be sure to include public transportation, bicycles, and ridesharing. Use a sheet of drawing paper and colored markers or paints to create your poster. Give it a clever title that will grab people's interest.

Solve a Math Problem

How much air pollution does a single car produce in one year?

For example, a gasoline-powered car traveling at 40 miles per hour gives off three pounds of carbon monoxide each hour. If it is driven two hours a day, how many pounds of carbon monoxide will the car put into the air in a year?

Find Out More

Gasoline-powered cars produce air pollution. Electric cars, however, do not run on gasoline. They are pollution-free. How does an electric car work? Does it need a battery? Use an encyclopedia or another source to find out more about electric cars. How can they solve our air pollution problems? Share your findings.

Read an Editorial

You know that newspapers contain more than just news articles. They have sports and entertainment pages, a help-wanted section, and an editorial page. An **editorial** is an article in which the editors or the people who run the newspaper give their opinions about important issues. These opinions are usually supported by facts.

THE NEW YORK NEWS

Morning Edition

EDITORIAL

Breathe Easier

Members of Congress voted yesterday to approve the new air pollution standards set forth by the Environmental Protection Agency (EPA). We applaud their decision. For years the American Lung Association and other groups have been worried about air pollution and public health. The new laws will strengthen the Clean Air Act of 1970 and save about 20,000 lives a year. The tougher laws won't take effect until 2004, which will give industry time to make needed changes. We had hoped the new laws would take effect immediately. Yet we understand that some time is needed to meet the new air pollution standards.

Use the editorial to answer these questions.

1 What is the subject of this editorial?

2 How does the headline help you predict the writer's opinion about the new Clean Air Act?

3 Why does the writer feel that Congress made the right decision in strengthening the Clean Air Act?

4 What facts does the writer use to support the newspaper's opinion?

5 Why is it important to know how to read an editorial?

TEST POWER

DIRECTIONS
Read the sample story. Then read each question about the story.

SAMPLE

How Frogs Protect Themselves

Frogs don't have fangs, protective shells, or claws. But they do have many ways to protect themselves.

The frog is covered by a soft, thin, moist skin. But a frog's skin can be poisonous. For example, the Golden Dart Frog's skin has enough poison on it to kill as many as 1000 people. Typically, brightly colored frogs are more poisonous than less colorful ones.

Many frogs are protected by changing their skin color. This change allows the frogs to blend into their surroundings and to be hidden from <u>predators</u> who might want to eat them. Other frogs become brightly colored when they are scared. This tricks their enemies into thinking that the frogs are poisonous.

1 The word <u>predators</u> in this passage means —

  A food

  B insects

  C enemies

  D fangs

2 You can tell that the author wrote this story to —

  F describe new places

  G explain how frogs survive

  H show how to have a pet frog

  J tell you about a new discovery

PHILBERT PHLURK

The major quirk of Philbert Phlurk
was tinkering all day,
inventing things that didn't work,
a scale that wouldn't weigh,
a pointless pen that couldn't write,
a score of silent whistles,
a bulbless lamp that wouldn't light,
a toothbrush with no bristles.

He built a chair without a seat,
a door that wouldn't shut,
a cooking stove that didn't heat,
a knife that couldn't cut.
He proudly crafted in his shop
a wheel that wouldn't spin,
a sweepless broom, a mopless mop,
a stringless violin.

He made a million useless things
like clocks with missing hands,
like toothless combs and springless springs
and stretchless rubber bands.
When Phlurk was through with something new,
he'd grin and say with glee,
"I know this does not work for you,
but ah! it works for me."

by Jack Prelutsky

612

CROSSROADS

Paper I

Paper is two kinds, to write on, to wrap with.

If you like to write, you write.

If you like to wrap, you wrap.

Some papers like writers, some like wrappers.

Are you a writer or a wrapper?

by Carl Sandburg

Stories in Art

Like writers and musicians, artists communicate through their art. Some express their ideas about culture. Others use their art to get their values and "message" across.

Look at the painting. What do you see? Notice the use of repeated colors, lines, and shapes. How does it balance the painting? Does it give you the feeling of harmony? How?

Look at the painting again. Which people are singing? Do they seem to be in harmony with nature? With each other? What might the artist be saying about the need to lift our voices together? Could that be his message? What do you think?

Village Voices
by Ashley Bryan, 1992

Judgments and Decisions

Develop a strategy for making judgments and decisions.

1 **Think about the story.** What main point is being made?

2 **Think about a character's actions.** What happens as a result of those actions?

3 **Decide what you would do** in a similar situation.

4 **Make a judgment** based on evidence from the selection and your own beliefs. What would Douglass have done if he had not been declared a free man?

Frederick Douglass Chooses Home

In the fall of 1846, respected African-American writer Frederick Douglass had been lecturing for two years in England on the evils of slavery. He began thinking about returning home to the United States. He weighed the pros and cons.

In England he was safe from the slave catchers who searched for runaway slaves. Douglass was a runaway, a former slave born in Maryland in 1817 and held captive until he escaped in 1838. In the United States, Douglass would always run the risk of being recaptured.

On the other hand, he thought, there was much work to be done in the United States. As a well-known writer and speaker against slavery, he could help his people in their struggle. He had also left all of his family back home in the United States.

As he considered what to do, several of Douglass's friends paid off his former owner. In December of 1846, Douglass was declared a free man. Now he could return home and continue the fight against slavery.

Meet Veronica Chambers

Veronica Chambers' interest in different cultures didn't just teach her valuable lessons, it helped her become a writer. Today, Chambers is a culture writer for *Newsweek* magazine. She is also a freelance writer for such national magazines as *Essence*, *Seventeen*, and *The New York Times Book Review*.

The story of Joseph Cinqué was of particular interest to Chambers. She says that she loved making discoveries about her African-American heritage and communicating the book's message about freedom.

Meet Paul Lee

Although *Amistad Rising* is Paul Lee's first book for young people, Lee is no stranger to the world of illustration. After having graduated with honors from Art Center College of Design in Pasadena, California, Lee has spent several years working as a freelance illustrator. Today, Lee lives in Connecticut, near New London, the place where the *Amistad* docked more than 150 years ago.

AMISTAD RISING

A STORY OF FREEDOM

Written by
Veronica Chambers

Illustrated by
Paul Lee

Stand here with me on the shores of New London, Connecticut. Feel the cool breeze of the Atlantic Ocean on your face. Feel the dirt beneath your feet; this land is far from ordinary. It was here, upon this very spot, that Joseph Cinqué set foot in America, bringing with him a group of renegade slaves and leaving his mark on history.

This is a story about the changing winds of fortune, about a man who was born free, was made a slave, and battled nations to be free again. It is a true story. And like so many stories, it begins not on land but at sea.

Have you ever wondered why the ocean is so wide? It's because it holds so much history. There's not a drop of seawater that doesn't have a secret; not a river or a lake that doesn't whisper someone's name. Ask the ocean about the legend of Joseph Cinqué, and this is what you might hear.

The year was 1839. Owning slaves was still legal, although the stealing of slaves from Africa was not. Slavery was a huge business. Many slave traders had grown rich from selling human beings, and they were reluctant to give it up.

It was nightfall when the slave ship *Teçora* set sail from Sierra Leone, a small country on the coast of West Africa. The water rippled like quicksilver in the moonlight as the ship voyaged toward Cuba. But in the ship's hold, more than five hundred Africans were held prisoner. There was no toilet, there was no bath, and the stench was unbearable. The Africans were chained together in pairs. Heavy iron shackles bound their hands and their feet. Movement was difficult. Escape was impossible. Disease and malnutrition claimed the lives of many; others perished under the murderous beatings of the slave traders. The dead were tossed overboard without a thought.

After two tempestuous months at sea, the *Teçora* arrived in Cuba. There, fifty-three of the prisoners—including four children—were sold to two Spanish slave traders and forced to board yet another ship to take them to a Cuban plantation.

This ship was called *Amistad*, the Spanish word for "friendship."

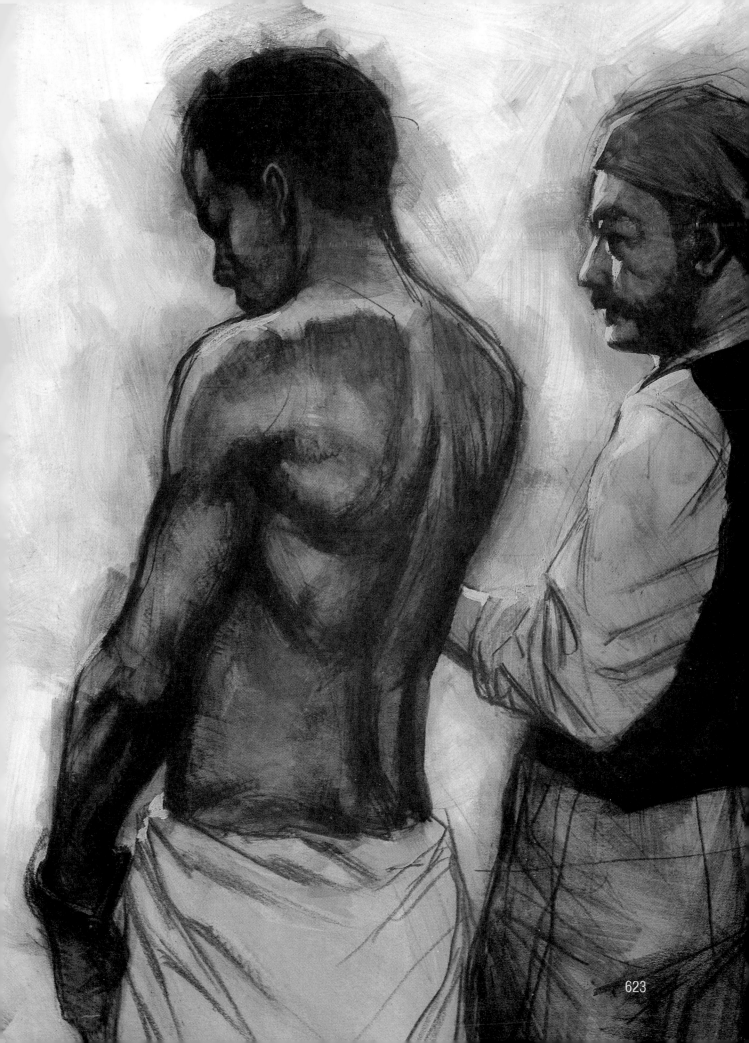

Three days into the journey, the *Amistad* sailed through an unexpected storm. The ship was battered by roaring rain and wind. The trip took longer than the crew expected and provisions were low. Each slave survived on a daily meal of two potatoes, a banana, and just a little water.

In the hold of the ship, a young man tried to quell his unsettled stomach. Fear gripped him as he watched his fellow Africans suffer and starve. He was young and afraid, but destiny had a plan for him. His name was Singbe, although the slavers had given him the Spanish name Joseph Cinqué, and he belonged to a group of people called Mende who lived near Sierra Leone. He had been working on a village road when he was seized and sold to the slavers of the *Teçora*.

During the first two months of his captivity, Cinqué was disturbed
to find that he had begun to forget little things about Africa—the
smell of freshly harvested rice, the color of the sunsets, the feel of
wet grass beneath his running feet. When he closed his eyes, he could
see these things only as distant and blurry as a dream. But he could
never forget the people he had left behind. His wife. His three
children. His mother and father.

Every day Cinqué grew more restless, wondering what the
Spaniards intended to do with him and the other Africans. Though
they were forbidden to speak, his companions whispered questions:
What lay ahead? What would slavery mean? Would they simply be
transported from ship to ship indefinitely?

Cinqué had to find out.

627

Occasionally, a few captives were allowed on deck for some air. Cinqué waited for his turn, and when he was finally ushered above, he attempted to coax some answers from Celestino, the cook. The two men communicated with hand gestures, for neither spoke the other's language.

Cinqué demanded to know what would happen to them.

Celestino smiled devilishly, intent on playing a cruel joke. He signaled to Cinqué that the slave traders planned to kill the Africans.

Fear and anger filled Cinqué. He would not be killed by the white men who held him captive. He would not.

He decided to strike that night. With a loose nail he had found earlier in a deck board, he picked the lock on his shackles, freeing himself and then the other prisoners. Once free, they quieted the four children and searched the cargo hold. A box of sugarcane knives was discovered—a boon!

Sneaking up to the deck, they took the crew by surprise. In the fight, Celestino, the captain, and one African were killed. Two of the crew jumped overboard. Three were taken prisoner. Cinqué needed them to navigate the ship back toward Africa, back toward home. When the sun rose again, Cinqué and his companions greeted the day as free people.

But they had claimed victory too soon.

Cinqué ordered the Spaniards to steer the ship toward the rising sun. They obeyed and sailed the ship east toward Africa during the day, but then at night turned the ship around and sailed northwest toward North America. For two months the ship pitched back and forth across the Atlantic Ocean. Nine more Africans died during that time—some from their battle wounds, some from food poisoning, and some from starvation.

Then, on August 27, 1839, the *Amistad* was escorted by an American ship into the harbor of New London, Connecticut. Weary, hungry, and hopelessly lost, Cinqué and the others were forced to come ashore.

An American naval lieutenant saw the possibility for quick profits in the Africans. But this was the North, and a group of whites and free blacks campaigning against the institution of slavery was gaining popularity. They called themselves abolitionists, and they took on Cinqué and the other Africans as their most important case.

The Africans were sent to prison in New Haven, Connecticut, until a decision could be made.

The abolitionists managed to find a translator, and Cinqué told his story in a U.S. court. He was only twenty-five years old, but his experience on the *Amistad* had given him the confidence of a much older man.

The courtroom was crowded, and many were moved by Cinqué's impassioned words.

"I am not here to argue the case against slavery," Cinqué said, "though I will say it is a sin against man and God. I am here to argue the facts. The indisputable, international law is that the stealing of slaves from Africa is now illegal."

"The men who kidnapped us, who beat and tortured us, were—and are—guilty of this crime," Cinqué continued.

"We are a peaceful people. We regret the loss of life caused by our mutiny. But we are not savages. We took over the ship to save our lives. We have done no wrong. Allow us to go home."

The weekend before the judge made his decision, Cinqué and his companions waited in the New Haven jail, their hearts filled with fear and hope. The judge held the power to make the Africans slaves or to set them free. On Monday morning, January 13, 1840, they worried no longer. He had decided they should be returned home.

They were free.

But as Cinqué was soon to learn, the passage to freedom was as winding as the *Amistad's* journey across the sea. President Martin Van Buren, concerned that freeing the Mende would enrage southern slave holders, ordered the district attorney to file an appeal so the case would be heard in the U.S. Supreme Court. And because of this, Cinqué gained his greatest American ally: former president John Quincy Adams.

Having heard about the mutineers, Adams came out of retirement to argue Cinqué's case. He was seventy-two years old. It had been more than thirty years since he had argued a case in a courtroom, and the thought of bearing the responsibility for this one worried the elderly statesman deeply.

But inspired by Cinqué, whom many of the abolitionists had begun to refer to as the Black Prince, Adams tirelessly prepared his defense. In court he spoke on behalf of the Mende for seven and a half hours. Sweat poured from his brow, and his voice filled the packed courtroom as he presented his case. There were many factors at play: Were the Africans the rightful property of the Spaniards? Were they brutal murderers? Or were they freedom fighters, no different than the men and women who had rebelled against England and founded the United States of America? There was also international pressure. Spain wanted the slaves and the *Amistad* returned to Cuba; could the United States risk provoking European ire over the lives of the thirty-five surviving Africans?

After Adams made his closing arguments, the Supreme Court retired to deliberate. For Cinqué and the others, the fearful process of waiting and praying began again.

A week later, on March 9, 1841, the Supreme Court announced that Adams had prevailed.

The Africans were truly free.

It took eight months for the abolitionists to raise the money for the Africans' long journey back to West Africa. But at last the ship sailed, and when the African coast was finally in sight, Cinqué gathered everyone together.

"Let us give praise and thanks," Cinqué called out, his voice booming across the deck. "By the strength of our spirit and with the assistance of our ancestors, we are not slaves today. Our children will not be slaves. And their children will not be slaves. We are exactly as God willed us to be. My brothers, my sisters, we are free." Savoring the word, he let it melt like sugar on his tongue. He paused and then tasted the word again. "Free," he said, more softly now.

Each person aboard the ship felt the word coming up from their hearts, tasted the sweetness of it in their mouths, then released it into the salty sea air. "Free," they said in unison. "We are free."

If you stand right here on the New London shore, you can hear the words of the great Joseph Cinqué. His voice is so powerful that it travels across both space and time. If you bend down to the Atlantic, you can hear it in the beating of the waves. The wind whispers it as it blows around your head. And when the rain falls, it's like tears of happiness.

You can hear his words almost anywhere you listen for them: "We are free. Free. Free. Free."

643

Story Questions & Activities

1 How were the Africans treated on the slave ship *Amistad?*

2 Why does Joseph Cinqué decide to take over the ship? Do you think his decision was a good one? Explain.

3 How did Joseph Cinqué leave his mark on American history?

4 What happens in this true story?

5 Imagine that Joseph Cinqué became part of the painting on page 616. What do you think he would say to the people who are singing in the picture?

Write the Next Chapter

What do you think happened after Cinqué went home to his village in West Africa? Choose events that could have happened, and write a follow-up chapter to the story. Include a beginning, a middle, and an end. Write character dialogue, and make sure there is a strong setting and plenty of action.

Freewrite

Choose one of the many beautiful illustrations from "Amistad Rising." Look carefully at the picture and visualize the setting, characters, and events. Freewrite for three minutes. Put down everything that you see and your feelings about the picture.

Charlestown, July 24th, 1769.

TO BE SOLD,

On THURSDAY the third Day of AUGUST next,

A CARGO

OF

NINETY-FOUR

PRIME, HEALTHY

NEGROES,

CONSISTING OF

Thirty-nine MEN, Fifteen Boys, Twenty-four WOMEN, and Sixteen GIRLS.

JUST ARRIVED,

In the Brigantine DEMBIA, Francis Bare, Mafter, from SIERRA-LEON, by

DAVID & JOHN DEAS.

Find a Primary Source

"Amistad Rising" is a secondary source. Secondary sources are written by people who were not there themselves when the events were taking place. Yet they are usually based on primary sources. Find a primary source that sheds light on "Amistad Rising." Letters, diaries, news articles, speeches, and court records are all primary sources. Paintings, portraits, and posters of the period are, too. Compare and share sources with classmates.

Find Out More

John Quincy Adams defended Joseph Cinqué in court. What do you know about Adams, the sixth President of the United States? What were some of his greatest achievements? Start by checking in an encyclopedia or in a book about Presidents. Use what you learn to write a brief biography. Place your work in your portfolio. Refer to it when reading about John Quincy Adams in your social studies textbook.

Use the Card Catalog

Each library book usually has three cards in the **card catalog**: the **author card**, the **title card**, and the **subject card**. All three cards give the same information about the book, but in a different order. You use the author card when you know the author of the book but not the title. You use the title card when you know the name of the book but not who wrote it. You use the subject card if you do not have any authors or titles in mind but are looking for a book on a particular topic. The **call number** tells you where to find the book on the library shelf.

387.16La

Larson, Stanley

    The Tall Ships and 19th Century Travel.
New York: Chelsea House, 1995, © 1992. 232 pp.;
ill. (some col.) 25 cm.
    Includes index. Details the rise and decline of the
tall ships, from why they were used to what replaced
them.
    1. Ships - 19th c.
    2. Transportation
    3. History - 19th c.

387.16La

    The Tall Ships and 19th Century Travel.

Larson, Stanley

    The Tall Ships and 19th Century Travel.
New York: Chelsea House, 1995, © 1992.
232 pp.; ill. (some col.) 25 cm.

387.16La

SHIPS - 19th C.

Larson, Stanley

    The Tall Ships and 19th Century Travel.
New York: Chelsea House, 1995, © 1992.
232 pp.; ill. (some col.) 25 cm.

Use the sample cards from the card catalog to answer these questions.

1 What is the title of the book?

2 Who is the author?

3 What is the subject?

4 How would you use the call number in the upper left-hand corner?

5 Why is it important to know how to use the card catalog when you are writing a research report?

TEST POWER

DIRECTIONS

Read the sample story. Then read each question about the story.

SAMPLE

The Krispies Contest

Trisha saw an advertisement for a contest on the back of her favorite box of cereal. Trisha decided to enter as soon as she could. This is what she saw:

Krispies!

Krispies cereal is having an essay contest!
Write a fifty-word essay that tells why you love to eat Krispies cereal. The deadline is November 1—so don't delay!

1st Place: A lifetime supply of Krispies cereal!
2nd Place: A Krispies cereal jean jacket.
3rd Place: A Krispies cereal T-shirt and a <u>coordinating</u> baseball cap—both with our logo on them!

1 In this story the word <u>coordinating</u> means —

A matching

B colorful

C important

D different

2 According to the contest advertisement, to enter the contest you need to —

F give your friends Krispies cereal

G write an essay

H order a jean jacket

J wear a Krispies cereal T-shirt

Did you rule out wrong answers? Tell how.

647

Stories in Art

Landscapes often create a peaceful scene. What does the artist want you to see in this painting? A quiet day along the Hudson River? A day long ago?

Look at this picture. Notice the details. What colors does the artist use? How do they help create a quiet mood? What is the effect of the setting on the painting? How do the setting and the mood affect you?

Suppose that you had a time machine. Would you want to go back to the time in the painting? How would you feel in that setting? What things would you want to know? Why?

648

View of the Hudson River from Fort Knyphansen
by Thomas Davies
Royal Ontario Museum, Toronto, Canada

Identify Cause and Effect

Develop a strategy for identifying causes and effects.

1 **Pay attention to** what happened and why it happened.

2 **Look for clue words,** such as *since* and *because,* that signal cause-and-effect relationships.

3 **Think: Does this text tell what happened?** If so, it usually describes an effect.

4 **Look for causes.** Does the text tell why something happened? This is a cause.

5 **Identify causes and effects** in the story. How do they create the events in the story?

REAL History Class

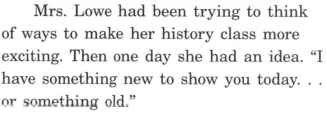

Mrs. Lowe had been trying to think of ways to make her history class more exciting. Then one day she had an idea. "I have something new to show you today. . . or something old."

Mrs. Lowe placed a strange metal box on her desk. "I just came across this old time machine in my attic," she explained. "And since we're studying the Declaration of Independence, I thought it might be fun if. . ." She flicked a switch, and in an instant the class was at the meeting of the Second Continental Congress in Philadelphia. The students saw a date flashing on the front of the time machine: July 4, 1776.

A man in a blue coat stood behind a chair. "That's Benjamin Franklin," Mrs. Lowe whispered to her class. "He helped write the Declaration of Independence."

Franklin began to speak, and the other men in the room listened quietly. A few minutes later, a student tugged on Mrs. Lowe's arm. "When are they going to sign the Declaration?" he asked.

"Not until August 2," Mrs. Lowe answered. "Would you like to see that?"

The whole class nodded eagerly.

"Then hang on!" Mrs. Lowe smiled because her machine was a success. She turned a few knobs. The date on the machine changed to August 2, 1776, and the class was off again!

Meet Washington Irving

Washington Irving was born in New York City in 1783. He came from a very large family and was the youngest of eleven children. His father, a veteran of the American Revolution, named his youngest child after his commander-in-chief, General George Washington.

As an adult, Irving worked as a lawyer for several years. He also considered becoming a painter. At the same time, he was writing essays and stories. Yet it wasn't until his mid-thirties that he published *The Sketch Book*. This book contains the two stories for which he is best known, "The Legend of Sleepy Hollow" and "Rip Van Winkle."

Meet Adele Thane

Adele Thane was born in 1904 and grew up in Massachusetts. At an early age she was bit by the acting bug. From 1953 to 1965, Thane directed and acted in a series of plays for young people. These plays were produced by a Boston television station. During this time, Thane began to publish her own plays for children and teenagers. She wrote many one-act plays and also adapted many literary classics such as "Rip Van Winkle."

RIP VAN WINKLE

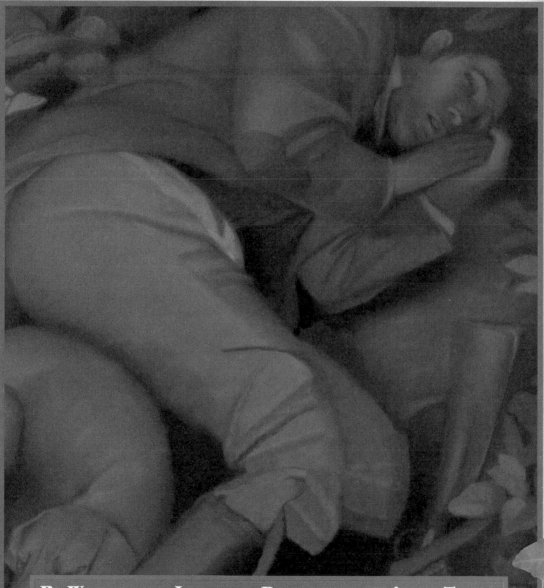

BY WASHINGTON IRVING   DRAMATIZED BY ADELE THANE
ILLUSTRATED BY GARY KELLEY

CHARACTERS

RIP VAN WINKLE

DAME VAN WINKLE, *HIS WIFE*

JUDY, *HIS DAUGHTER*

LUKE GARDENIER

KATCHEN

MEENIE, *A GIRL*

JACOB

JUDY'S PLAYMATES

NICHOLAS VEDDER,
LANDLORD OF THE KING GEORGE TAVERN

DERRICK VAN BUMMEL,
THE SCHOOLMASTER

PETER VANDERDONK

BROM DUTCHER

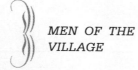

MEN OF THE VILLAGE

OFFSTAGE VOICE

HENDRIK HUDSON

SAILORS, *HUDSON'S CREW*

ORATOR

JONATHAN DOOLITTLE,
PROPRIETOR OF THE UNION HOTEL

JUDITH GARDENIER, *JUDY GROWN UP*

LITTLE RIP, *HER SON*

TOWNSPEOPLE

CHILDREN

SCENE 1

Time: *Early autumn, a few years before the Revolutionary War.*

Setting: *A village in the Catskill Mountains. At left, there is an inn with a sign,* KING GEORGE TAVERN, *and a picture of King George III. A British Union Jack hangs on the flagpole.*

At Rise: NICHOLAS VEDDER, DERRICK VAN BUMMEL, BROM DUTCHER *and* PETER VANDERDONK *are seated outside the tavern.* VEDDER *is sprawled back in his chair.* DUTCHER *and* VANDERDONK *are at the table, playing a game of checkers.* VAN BUMMEL *is reading aloud from a newspaper. From time to time, a rumble of thunder can be heard in the distance.*

Van Bummel *(reading):* ". . . and it has been learned that Massachusetts favors a Stamp Act Congress to be held in New York to protest English taxation in the Colonies."

Dutcher *(looking up from his game):* Good! It's high time we did something about this English taxation.

Vanderdonk: Taxes and more taxes! The English are a pack of rascals with their hands in our pockets.

Van Bummel: There's even a revenue stamp on our newspapers. One of these days the people here in the American Colonies will revolt, you mark my words.

653

VEDDER (*pointing off right as a merry whistle is heard*): Well, here comes one man who is not troubled by these problems—Rip Van Winkle. (RIP VAN WINKLE *enters, a wooden bucket in one hand, his gun in the other. He props his gun against the tree trunk, then crosses to the group of men.*)

RIP: Good afternoon, Nick Vedder—Brom—Peter. (*to* VAN BUMMEL) Good afternoon, Mr. Schoolmaster. (*They return his greeting. There is a loud rumble of thunder and* RIP *cocks his head.*) Just listen to that, will you!

DUTCHER: We're probably in for a storm after this heat all day.

VEDDER: Sit down, Rip. Derrick is reading us the news.

VANDERDONK: How about a game of checkers, Rip?

RIP (*hesitating*): I don't know. Dame Van Winkle sent me for a bucket of water, but—maybe *one* game. (*He sets down the bucket and draws a stool up to the table, as* VANDERDONK *rises.*)

DUTCHER: Your move, Rip. (*Suddenly* DAME VAN WINKLE'S *voice is heard from off right.*)

DAME VAN WINKLE (*calling from off right*): Rip! R-i-p! *Rip Van Winkle!*

RIP: Oh, my galligaskins! It's my wife! (*Before he can get to his feet,* DAME VAN WINKLE *enters with a broom. She looks at the men, then crosses directly to* RIP.)

DAME VAN WINKLE: So this is how you draw water from the well! Sitting around with a lot of lazy good-for-nothing loafers. (*She tries to hit* RIP *with the broom.*) Pick up that bucket, you dawdling Dutchman, and fill it with water!

RIP (*snatching up the bucket and dodging out of the way*): Hey there, Dame, I'm not an old rug to be beaten with a broomstick.

DAME VAN WINKLE: Well, you might better be. An old rug is more use than you. At least it would keep our feet warm in winter, which is more than you can do. Little you care that your family is starving and the cow is gone.

RIP: The cow gone?

DAME VAN WINKLE: Aye, the cow is gone and the cabbage trampled down. When are you going to mend the fence?

RIP: It rained yesterday—

DAME VAN WINKLE: If excuses were shillings, we'd be rich!

RIP: I'll mend the fence—tomorrow.

DAME VAN WINKLE: Tomorrow, tomorrow! All your work is going to be done tomorrow! (RIP *goes to the well as she starts off right, still talking.*) You show enough energy when there's a husking bee or an errand to run for the neighbors, but here at home . . . *(She exits.* RIP *lowers his bucket into the well. The other men rise to go into the tavern.)*

VEDDER: Poor Rip! His wife has the scoldingest tongue in the Hudson Valley.

VAN BUMMEL: A sharp tongue is the only tool that grows keener with use.

DUTCHER: What would you do, Derrick, if you had a wife like Van Winkle's?

VAN BUMMEL: War could be no worse. I would enlist. (*They all laugh and exit through the door of the tavern.* RIP *turns to leave, then stops and smiles, as children's voices are heard off left.* JUDY, LUKE, KATCHEN, MEENIE, *holding a kite, and* JACOB, *carrying a bow, run in, left, and shout with delight when they see* RIP.)

CHILDREN *(ad lib):* There he is! There's Rip Van Winkle! *(etc. They surround him, chattering excitedly.)*

JUDY: Hello, Father, I've brought some of my friends.

RIP: Glad to see you, children.

JACOB *(holding out bow):* Oh, Rip, there's something wrong with my bow. Every time I go to shoot, the cord slips. (RIP *takes the bow, draws his knife from his pocket and cuts the notch deeper for the cord.)*

RIP: There, Jacob, try that, and see if it doesn't work.

Jacob *(pretending to shoot):* Yes, it's all right now.

Meenie *(holding out kite):* My kite won't stay up, Rip.

Rip *(taking off part of the tail):* Now it will, Meenie—and this breeze is just right for it. *(He hands kite to* Meenie.*)*

Katchen: My mother wants you to plug up her rain barrel, so she'll be able to wash next week.

Rip: Tell her I'll fix it tonight, Katchen.

Luke: Rip, will you see what's the matter with my whistle? I made it just the way you showed me, but it isn't any good. *(He hands* Rip *a whistle.)*

Rip *(examining it):* You haven't whittled it right there, Luke. Here, I'll fix it for you. *(He sits on the bench under the tree and begins to whittle.)*

Judy: Tell us a story, Father!

Luke: Yes, you tell better stories than anybody in the Catskills. *(The children all gather around* Rip, *sitting on the ground.)*

Rip: What shall it be about?

Jacob: Indians!

Katchen: I like witches and goblins best. *(A long roll of thunder is heard.)*

Judy: Oh, Father, hear that! Hear the thunder!

Rip: Why, don't you know what that is, Judy? That's Hendrik Hudson and his famous crew, playing ninepins up in the mountains. *(More thunder is heard.)*

Meenie: Oh, what a noise they make!

Rip: Yes, they are jolly fellows. They sail the wide sea over in their ship, the *Half-Moon*, then every twenty years they come back to the Catskills.

Jacob: What do they do that for?

Rip: Oh, old Hendrik Hudson likes to revisit the country he discovered and keep a watchful eye over his river, the Hudson.

JACOB: I wish I could see Hendrik Hudson and his crew.

RIP: Peter Vanderdonk says his father saw them once in their funny breeches, playing at ninepins up in the hills. *(A loud peal of thunder is heard.)* Listen to the balls rolling! That must be Hendrik Hudson himself, the Flying Dutchman! *(DAME VAN WINKLE enters with broom as RIP is speaking.)*

DAME VAN WINKLE: So! Here you are, telling stories without a word of truth in 'em! Oh, *I* could tell a story or two myself—about a shiftless husband who does nothing but whittle and whistle. Whittle and whistle! What a job for a grown man! *(She snatches the whistle from RIP.)*

LUKE *(pleadingly)*: It's my whistle! Please don't break it, Dame Van Winkle.

DAME VAN WINKLE: Take it and begone! *(She gives LUKE the whistle and he runs off.)* Judy, you go and ask Dame Vedder for an armful of wood. Your father is too busy spinning yarns to split wood for *our* fire. *(JUDY goes off behind the tavern.)* As for the rest of you, go home if you have any homes, and don't keep hanging around here like stray dogs looking for bones. *(She sweeps the children off the stage with her broom.)* Get along! Begone, all of you! Go home now! *(With arms akimbo, she faces RIP.)* Well, what do you have to say for yourself? *(RIP shrugs, shakes his head and says nothing.)* Nothing as usual. *(RIP goes to the tree for his gun.)* What are you getting your gun for? Going off to the mountains, no doubt. Anything to keep you out of the house.

RIP *(good-naturedly):* Well, wife, you have often told me— *my* side of the house is the *outside.* Where's my dog? Where's Wolf?

DAME VAN WINKLE: Wolf is tied up in the cellar.

RIP: You didn't tie up Wolf?

DAME VAN WINKLE: I certainly did. That dog tracked up my kitchen floor right after I'd finished scrubbing it.

Well, if you're going hunting, go, and don't come back until you bring us something for supper. And if you can't bring any supper, don't bring yourself.

JUDY (*re-entering from up left, her arms full of logs*): But, Mother, it's going to rain.

DAME VAN WINKLE (*taking the wood*): Pooh! Your father won't get as wet as we will in the house, with the roof leaking and the windows broken. You hurry home now. And bring that bucket of water your father managed to get this far. (DAME VAN WINKLE *starts right, but* JUDY *stays behind with* RIP.)

RIP (*calling after his wife*): Wife, turn Wolf loose when you get home. (DAME VAN WINKLE *looks back at him angrily, tosses her head, and exits right.*)

JUDY (*starting to cry as she puts her hand in* RIP'S): Father, where will you go if it rains?

RIP: I'll find a place. Don't cry, Judy. Remember your little song? Come, we'll sing it together. (*They sing an appropriate folk song, such as "Rosa, Will We Go Dancing?"*)

JUDY (*hugging* RIP): Oh, Father, I hope you have wonderful luck. Then Mother won't be so cross.

RIP: I don't blame her for being cross with me sometimes. I guess I don't do much work around here. But I'm going to do better, Judy. I'm going to do all the jobs your mother has been after me about.

DAME VAN WINKLE (*calling from off*): Ju-*dee*! Ju-*dee*!

RIP: There's your mother. I'd better be off. Goodbye, Judy dear. (*He walks left, whistling for his dog*) Come, Wolf! Come, boy! (*A dog's bark is heard off left, as* RIP *turns, waves to* JUDY, *and exits.*)

JUDY (*waving*): Goodbye, Father. (LUKE *enters from right and joins* JUDY *as loud crash of thunder is heard. Startled,* JUDY *clings to* LUKE.) Oh, Luke, listen to that thunder!

LUKE: It's only Hendrik Hudson's men playing ninepins. Don't be scared, Judy.

JUDY: I'm not—that is, not very.

DAME VAN WINKLE *(calling from off):* Judy! Ju-dee!

LUKE: You'd better go in or you'll catch it. Your mother is getting awfully free with her broomstick lately. Here, I'll carry your bucket for you. *(He exits right with the bucket of water.* JUDY *lingers behind to look off in direction her father has taken as the thunder gets louder. Then humming softly to herself, she exits right.)*

CURTAIN

SCENE 2

TIME: *Later the same afternoon.*

SETTING: *A forest glade, high in the Catskill Mountains. There is a tree stump at right center, and a large bush at far left. This scene may be played before the curtain.*

AT RISE: RIP, *carrying his gun, enters left, dragging his feet wearily. He sinks down on the stump.*

RIP: Whew! That was a climb! All the way up the mountain. How peaceful it is up here. No one to scold me, no one to wave a broomstick. Ah, me! *(He gives a big sigh of contentment.)* I wonder where Wolf is. Wolf! Here, boy! *(He whistles and a dog barks off left.)* That's it, Wolf, sick 'em! I hope we get something this time. We can't go home until we do. *(A loud crash of thunder is heard.)* That thunder sounds much louder up here in the mountains than down in the valley. Maybe it's going to rain after all.

VOICE *(calling from off, high-pitched, like a bird-call):* Rip Van Winkle! *(RIP looks around wonderingly.)* Rip Van Winkle!

RIP *(rising):* That's my name. Somebody is calling me.

VOICE *(off):* Rip Van Winkle!

RIP: Is it Dame Van Winkle? No—she would never follow me up here. *(Sound of a ship's bell is heard from off right.)* What was that? *(Bell rings again.)* A ship's bell! But how can that be? A ship? Up here in the mountains? *(He gazes off right, in astonishment.)* It *is* a ship! Look at it! Sails all set—a Dutch flag at the masthead. *(Ship's bell is heard again, fainter.)* There, it's gone. I must have imagined it. *(1ST SAILOR with a keg on his back, enters from right and goes to center, as RIP watches him in amazement.)* By my galligaskins, what a funny little man! And how strangely he's dressed. Such old-fashioned clothes! *(1ST SAILOR stops at center. RIP goes to meet him.)* Hello, old Dutchman. That keg looks heavy. Let me carry it for you. *(He relieves 1ST SAILOR of the keg.)* By golly, it is heavy! Why did you bring this keg all the way up here to the top of the mountain? And who are you, anyhow?

1ST SAILOR *(gruffly)*: Don't ask questions. Set it down over there. *(He points left to a spot beside the bush.)*

RIP *(obeying cheerfully)*: Anything to oblige. *(There is a commotion off right, and HENDRIK HUDSON and his crew enter, capering and shouting. They carry bowling balls and ninepins and a drum. 2ND SAILOR has a burlap bag containing drinking mugs thrown over his shoulder. RIP turns to 1ST SAILOR.)* Why, bless my soul! Here are a lot of little fellows just like yourself. *(to SAILORS, as they gather at center)* Who are you?

SAILORS *(shouting)*: Hendrik Hudson and his merry crew!

HUDSON *(stepping forward)*: Set up the ninepins, men, and we'll have a game. *(Two or three sailors set up the ninepins at extreme right. HUDSON speaks to the 1ST SAILOR.)* You there, fill up the flagons! *(2ND SAILOR opens sack and passes out the mugs. HUDSON turns to RIP.)* Now then, Rip Van Winkle, will you drink with us?

RIP: Why, yes, thank you, Captain Hudson. I'm quite thirsty after my long climb up the mountain. *(The mugs are filled from keg.)*

2ND SAILOR *(raising his mug in toast)*: To Hendrik Hudson, the *Half-Moon*, and its merry crew!

ALL *(as they raise their mugs):* To Hendrik Hudson, the *Half-Moon*, and its merry crew!

RIP *(lifting his mug):* Well, gentlemen, here's to your good health. May you live long and prosper. (RIP *drinks and smacks his lips.)* Ah! This is the best drink I ever tasted, but it makes me feel very sleepy. (HUDSON *and his men begin to bowl. As they roll the balls, the thunder increases.* RIP *yawns.)* Ho, hum! I can't keep my eyes open. I guess I'll lie down—*(Carrying his gun, he goes behind bush at left, and lies down out of sight.* NOTE: *Unseen by audience,* RIP *may go offstage for necessary costume changes and return in time for his awakening.)*

HUDSON *(to* SAILORS*):* Now, men, let's stop our game of ninepins, and have a merry dance. Then we'll be off, to return again in twenty years. *(One of the men beats the drum, and* SAILORS *dance. At the end of the dance,* 1ST SAILOR *points to bush where* RIP *is sleeping.)*

1ST SAILOR: Look! Rip Van Winkle is asleep.

HUDSON: Peace be with the poor fellow. He needs to take a good long rest from his nagging wife. Sh-h-h-h! *(He places his finger to his lips and they all go about quietly gathering up the ninepins, balls, mugs, keg, etc., then they tiptoe off the stage, their voices dying away to a whisper. The lights may dim briefly to indicate the passage of twenty years, and recorded music may be played. When the lights come up,* RIP *is heard yawning behind the bush, then he stands up with great difficulty. He limps to center, carrying a rusty gun. His clothes are shabby, and he has a long white beard.)*

RIP *(groaning):* Ouch, my back! It's so stiff. And my legs—just like pokers. My, my, but I'm shaky! I feel as if I'd grown to be an old man overnight. It must be rheumatism coming on. Oh, won't I have a blessed time with Dame Van Winkle if I'm laid up with rheumatism. Well, I'd better get along home to Dame Van Winkle. *(He looks at the gun he is carrying.)* Why, this rusty old thing is not my gun! Somebody has

663

played a trick on me. *(suddenly recollecting)* It's that Hendrik Hudson and his men! They've stolen my gun, and left this rusty one for me! *(He puts his hand to his head.)* Another scolding in store from the Dame. *(He whistles.)* Wolf! Here, Wolf! Have those scamps stolen my dog, too? He'd never leave me. *(He whistles again.)* Come on, old boy! Maybe he found it too cold and went home to be warmed by his mistress' broomstick. Well, I will follow after and get my hot welcome, too. *(He shoulders the rusty gun and totters off.)*

CURTAIN

SCENE 3

TIME: *Twenty years after Scene 1.*

SETTING: *Same as Scene 1, except that the sign above the tavern door reads:* UNION HOTEL—PROPRIETOR, JONATHAN DOOLITTLE. *A picture of George Washington has replaced that of King George III. Washington's name is printed below the picture and an American flag flutters on a pole above it.*

AT RISE: *An* ORATOR *is standing on a bench, haranguing a crowd of* TOWNSPEOPLE.

ORATOR: Remember the Boston Tea Party! Remember Bunker Hill! Who saved this country? Who is the father of this country?

TOWNSPEOPLE: George Washington! Washington for President! *(etc. They sing "Yankee Doodle.")*

> Father and I went down to camp
> Along with Captain Good'in,
> There we saw the men and boys
> As thick as hasty puddin'.
>
> Yankee Doodle keep it up.
> Yankee Doodle Dandy.
> Mind the music and the step
> And with the girls be handy.

*(*RIP *enters with a troop of children, who laugh and jeer at him.)*

CHILDREN *(ad lib):* Look at him! He looks like a scarecrow! Where did you come from, Daddy Long-legs? Where did you get that gun? *(etc.* RIP *and* CHILDREN *go to center.* 1ST CHILD *stands in front of* RIP, *and crouches down, pulling on an imaginary beard.)*

1ST MAN: Billy goat, billy goat! *(*CHILDREN *begin stroking imaginary beards until* RIP *does the same. He is amazed to find he has a beard.)*

RIP: By my galligaskins, what's this?

2ND CHILD: It's a beard, old Father Time. Didn't you know you had a beard?

RIP: But I didn't have one last night. *(*CHILDREN *laugh and mock him.)*

ORATOR *(to* RIP*):* What do you mean by coming here at election time with a gun on your shoulder and a mob at your heels? Do you want to cause a riot?

RIP: Oh, no, sir! I am a quiet man and a loyal subject of King George!

CHILDREN AND TOWNSPEOPLE *(shouting, ad lib):* A spy! Away with him! Lock him up. *(etc.)*

JONATHAN DOOLITTLE *(stepping forward from crowd):* Hold on a minute! We must get to the bottom of this. *(to* RIP*)* Aren't you a supporter of Washington for President?

RIP *(puzzled):* Eh? Supporter of Washington? *(shaking his head, wholly bewildered)* I don't understand. I mean no harm. I only want to find my friends. They were here at the tavern yesterday.

DOOLITTLE: Who are these friends of yours? Name them.

RIP *(hesitantly):* Well, one is the landlord—

DOOLITTLE: *I* am the landlord of this hotel—Jonathan Doolittle.

RIP: Why, what happened to Nicholas Vedder?

1ST WOMAN *(pushing her way out of the crowd):* Nicholas Vedder? Why, he's dead and gone these eighteen years.

RIP: No, no, that's impossible! Where's Brom Dutcher? And the schoolmaster, Van Bummel—?

1ST MAN: Brom Dutcher was killed in the war at Stony Point.

2ND MAN: And Van Bummel went off to the war, too. He became a great general, and now he's in Congress.

RIP: War? What war?

2ND MAN: Why, the war we fought against England, and won, of course.

RIP: I don't understand. Am I dreaming? Congress? Generals? What's happened to me?

DOOLITTLE *(impatiently):* Now, we've had enough of this nonsense. Who are you, anyway? What is your name?

RIP *(utterly confused):* I don't know. I mean, I was Rip Van Winkle yesterday, but today—

DOOLITTLE: Don't try to make sport of us, my man!

RIP: Oh, indeed, I'm not, sir. I was myself last night, but I fell asleep on the mountain, and Hendrik Hudson and his crew changed my gun, and everything's changed, and I'm changed, and I can't tell what my name is, or who I am! *(*TOWNSPEOPLE *exchange significant glances, nod knowingly, and tap their foreheads.)*

2ND MAN *(shaking his head):* Hendrik Hudson, he says! Poor chap. He's mad. Let's leave him alone.

RIP *(in great distress):* Isn't there anybody here who knows who I am?

WOMAN *(soothingly):* Why, you're just yourself, old man. Who else do you think you could be? *(JUDITH GARDENIER enters from left, leading LITTLE RIP by the hand. He hangs back, whimpering.)*

JUDITH: Hush, Rip! The old man won't hurt you.

RIP *(turning in surprise):* Rip? Who said Rip?

JUDITH: Why, I did. I was just telling my little boy not to be frightened.

RIP *(scanning her face):* And what is your name, my good woman?

JUDITH: My name is Judith, sir.

RIP: Judith? Did you say Judith? *(in great excitement)* And your father—what was his name?

JUDITH: Ah, poor man, his name was Rip Van Winkle. It's twenty years since he went away from home. We never heard of him again.

RIP *(staggered):* Twenty years!

JUDITH: Yes, it must be all of that. His dog came back without him. I was a little girl then.

RIP: And your mother—where is she?

JUDITH: My mother is dead, sir.

RIP *(sighing):* Ah, but that woman had a tongue! Well, peace be with her soul. Did you love your father, Judith?

JUDITH: With all my heart. All the children in the village loved him, too.

RIP: Then look at me. Look closely, my dear Judy. I am your father.

JUDITH *(incredulously):* You? My father?

Rip: We used to sing a little song together, remember? *(He sings a few lines from the folk song sung in Scene 1.)*

Judith *(slowly):* Yes, my father used to sing that song with me, but many people know it.

Rip: Do you remember, Judy, that I told you the story of how Hendrik Hudson and his crew played ninepins in the mountains just before I went off hunting with Wolf?

Judith *(excitedly):* Yes! And Wolf *was* our dog's name! Oh, Father, it's really *you!*

Rip *(taking her in his arms):* Yes, my little Judy—young Rip Van Winkle once, old Rip Van Winkle now. *(*TOWNSPEOPLE *talk excitedly among themselves as they watch* RIP *and* JUDITH.*)*

Judith: Dearest Father, come home with me. Luke and I will take good care of you.

Rip: Luke?

Judith: Luke Gardenier, my old playmate. You used to make whistles for him and take him fishing. We were married when he came back from the war.

Rip: Ah, the war. There is so much I have to catch up with.

Judith: You will have plenty of time to do that—and you must tell us what happened to you.

Rip: Maybe you won't believe what happened to me, Judy—it was all so strange. *(*RIP *reaches out a hand to* LITTLE RIP, *who shyly takes it, and they start off left,* JUDITH *following. A loud clap of thunder stops them.* RIP *turns front and shakes his fist toward the mountains.)* Oh, no you don't, Hendrik Hudson! You don't get me back up there again. *(There is an answering roll of thunder that sounds like a deep rumble of laughter as the curtain falls.)*

THE END

669

Story Questions & Activities

1 When and where does the story take place?

2 What causes Rip to sleep for 20 years? What happens to him as a result?

3 Why is Rip a "dreamer" in more ways than one? Explain.

4 What is this famous story about?

5 Imagine that Rip Van Winkle awoke to find himself inside the painting on page 648. What might he ask the people in the picture? What might they ask him?

Write a Dialogue

As a play, Rip Van Winkle depends on dialogue to tell its story. Writing good dialogue is a skill that many writers work hard to achieve. Write a dialogue that might have been spoken between Rip and his wife if she had been alive when he returned. Make your dialogue sound as much like real life as possible.

670

Create a Time Line

Legend has it that Hendrik Hudson and his crew sailed up and down the Hudson River looking for a passage to the north. But they never found it. Who was the real Hendrik (or Henry) Hudson? What did he do or fail to do? What happened to him? Read about Henry Hudson in an encyclopedia, or in a social studies textbook. Draw a time line of his journeys. List the dates of his expeditions in order, and write a brief description of each.

1600   1610   1620   1630   1640

Draw a Costume

"By my galligaskins," says Rip, when he discovers that he has a long beard. Galligaskins are the loose trousers that Rip may have worn. Use an encyclopedia or a book about the history of fashion to find out how people in the 13 colonies dressed in the 1700s. Make a drawing and label the different articles of clothing.

Find Out More

The story of Rip Van Winkle takes place in the Catskill Mountains. Where are these mountains located? Who settled there? Find the Catskills on a map of New York State. Research five interesting facts about them and the surrounding area. Compare your information with a partner.

STUDY SKILLS

Use an Online Library Catalog

Searching on an **online library catalog** can help you find books quickly. You can search by author, title, or subject. When you search by subject, the online catalog lists books the library has on the topic, gives their call numbers, and tells if they are available.

SEARCH BY:

1. AUTHOR
2. TITLE
3. SUBJECT

SELECT A SEARCH: 3
ENTER KEY WORD(S):
Irving, Washington

Results of your search:
1. THE LIFE AND TIMES OF
   WASHINGTON IRVING
2. THE WORLD OF WASHINGTON
   IRVING
3. A BOY NAMED WASHINGTON
4. HE TOLD TALES OF
   TARRYTOWN
Press ENTER for more results.
Select number for more
information: 1

1. The Life and Times of
   Washington Irving, by
   An-mei Chen, 1991.
   Call no.: BIrvingC

STATUS: CHECKED IN

Press ENTER for more
information.

Use the online library catalog to answer these questions.

1. If you know the name of the book you want, what should you do at the first screen?

2. How would you search if you wanted to find all the books by your favorite writer?

3. Who wrote *The Life and Times of Washington Irving*?

4. Would you be able to take *The Life and Times of Washington Irving* out today?

5. Look at its call number. The *B* stands for "Biography." What do you think the *C* stands for?

TEST POWER

DIRECTIONS

Read the sample story. Then read each question about the story.

SAMPLE

Caterina Tries Something New

Caterina was frustrated with drawing. She could never seem to get her pen to draw what she saw in her mind. Whenever she completed a drawing on paper, it never looked the way that she wanted it to look.

One day, Caterina's art teacher invited her to try something new— computer art. Caterina sat down in front of the computer and held the special pen in her hand. As she moved the pen along the pad, lines simultaneously appeared on the computer screen.

Caterina carefully thought about what she wanted to draw. Slowly, she began to draw the lines on the screen. When she was finished, she looked at what she'd created. It was amazing! Her drawing was similar to what she had imagined before she started.

Caterina smiled at her new discovery.

1 Why did Caterina try computer art?

   A She was interested in computers.

   B Her teacher offered her the opportunity.

   C Caterina didn't enjoy her art class any more.

   D She was taking a computer art class.

2 You can tell that Caterina's computer art picture —

   F satisfied her

   G disappointed her

   H was crooked

   J was of a flower

Stories in Art

The Workplace, 19th Century Japanese
David David Gallery, Philadelphia

Like dialogue in a play, a picture can speak to you. It can tell you many things.

〜

Look at this Japanese woodcut. The artist printed it from a block of wood into which he carved many details. What details do you see? What events do they show you? Can you tell that the women are working with silkworms? How? What do you think they do in a workday? What might they do first? Next? Last?

〜

Look at the picture again. Notice the Japanese scroll at the top. Do you think it describes the events in the picture? Why or why not? Would you like to do this kind of work? Explain your reasons.

A LETTER HOME

Sequence of Events

Develop a strategy for recognizing the sequence of events.

1 **Picture the events** in the order that they happen.

2 **Think: What happens** first, next, and so on?

3 **Look for clue words,** such as *first, next, then, while,* and *finally* to help you know the order of events.

4 **Check your under-standing** as you read. Reread parts if the events are confusing.

5 **Retell the sequence of events.** Describe Marta's typical day. Then list in order the steps in her performance.

Berlin, April 14

Dear Family,

I have been with the Crown Circus for three months now. I have met many trapeze artists who are also from Mexico!

As you know, much of each day is taken up with rehearsals. I sightsee a little in the afternoon, but my favorite time is the evening performance with Miguel, Yolanda, and Luis.

How I wish you could see us perform! We first climb up to two tiny platforms high above the crowd. Luis and I stand on one platform, and Yolanda and Miguel wait on the other one across the tent. Next, Luis steadies the trapeze while I take hold. I push off and fly through the air. Then I switch positions and hang upside down by my knees.

While I swing freely, Miguel takes off from the other side and hangs by his knees. At the exact moment we meet in the middle, Miguel and I lock hands. I release my trapeze so that I am flying with him. After doing some spins, I return to my trapeze, which Luis has sent to me.

When I am finally back at the platform, Luis and I switch places. Then it's his turn to perform with Yolanda.

I truly love my work!

Love,
Marta

Meet
Lili Bell

Sports led Lili Bell to travel all over the world at an early age. She was a very good ski racer who later went on to become a top-ranked tennis player. One tennis competition in which she participated was held in Japan. It was on a Japanese beach filled with star sand that she was inspired to write *The Sea Maidens of Japan*. The story of young Kiyomi is Bell's first book for young people. Today, the writer lives in Colorado with her husband and two children.

Meet
Erin McGonigle Brammer

The Sea Maidens of Japan is Erin McGonigle Brammer's first book for young readers. Her stunning earth-tone illustrations capture the Asian style of the book and the traditions of the Japanese *ama*. Brammer is a freelance illustrator and graphic designer. About working on books for young people, Brammer says that she really enjoys the challenge.

The Sea Maidens of Japan

Written By
Lili Bell

Illustrated by
Erin McGonigle Brammer

We are called the *ama,* the sea maidens of Japan. My mother's mother and even her great-grandmother's mother were fisherwomen who dove to the ocean floor to harvest seafood for the great emperors of Japan.

When I'm older, I'll learn to hold my breath under water for over a minute and gather abalone and seaweed for my family and our village. Okaasan, that is what I call my mama, teaches me to dive and fish along the shallow reefs.

678

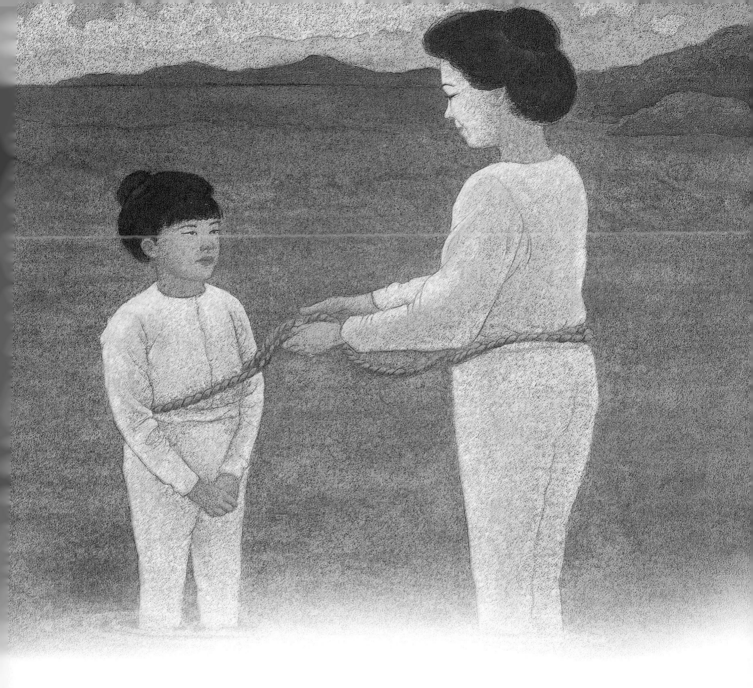

"Kiyomi, when you're older and follow our tradition," she tells me, "you will not have the rope attached to your waist. You must find your own way without me."

Hearing this, my stomach flutters. I must not disgrace Okaasan and fail because I am afraid of the deep waters. I long to be a brave ama diver, but I don't want to be swallowed up by the dark, deep waters.

My two older sisters chose the modern way of life and work in the city at the fish canneries. They will not become ama, like Okaasan and me.

While my mother dives, I wait alone for long hours on the shore of a special cove. On this coral beach, every grain of sand is shaped like a star. Sitting in a shallow pool, I pretend to host tea ceremonies for mermaids. I chase schools of fish away from my treasure chest. At the end of the day, I wait for Okaasan and count the stars on the beach and in the sky.

In the middle of the night, Okaasan wakes me. "Come, Kiyomi, the sea turtles will lay their eggs on the beach tonight," she whispers.

It is hard for me to open my eyes. Gently shaking my shoulder, she says, "Wake up, little one, the sea turtles come only once a year."

The moon is bright and the sky sparkles with stars. Gusts of wind sting my cheeks, leaving a strong, salty taste in my mouth. As each wave pounds at the shore, the ocean roars and foams like a terrible dragon. We wait a long time. I poke a stick at a pile of strong-smelling sea kelp circled with flies. I feel like a tiny fly next to the great power of the ocean.

Perhaps the ocean is too rough for the turtles to come. As we head home, rain clouds veil the starlight. The sky is so dark that I trip over pieces of driftwood. Okaasan waits for me and places her warm hand in mine.

Just then, with each incoming wave, the sea turtles begin to appear. They are graceful and smooth in the water. On land they struggle, slow and awkward, onto the beach to select a nesting spot. I cup my hand over my mouth to hush my giggling as they dig a hole with their hind flippers and spray sand in each other's faces.

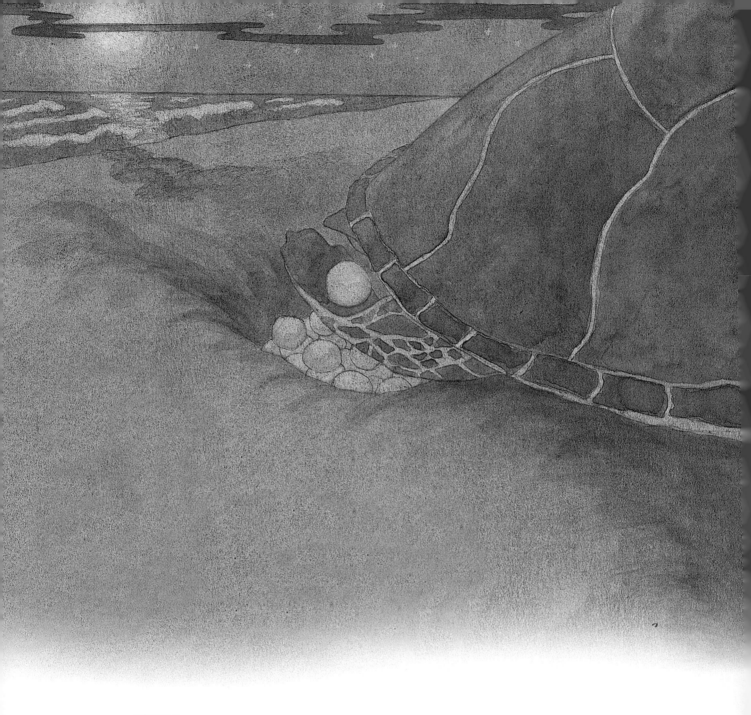

We hear one turtle moan and strain, tears running from her eyes, as she lays dozens of eggs that look like soft, shiny balls. She brushes sand over her nest and begins the slow trip back to the ocean, leaving her babies to find their own way. A wave sweeps her into the sea and she disappears.

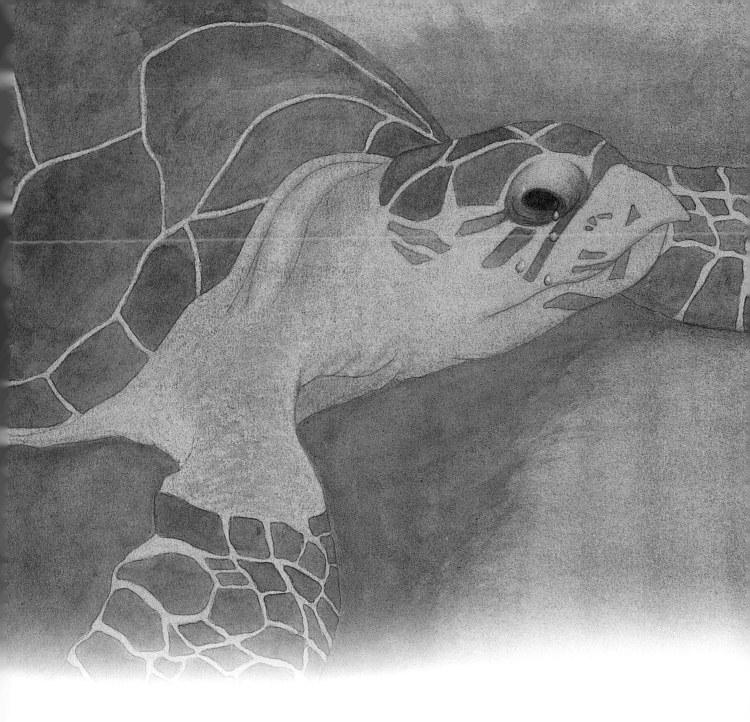

Every day I visit the beach to check the nests. The sun soaks the
sand with warmth for the eggs to grow. Some eggs are scooped up in
the fishermen's buckets. Others are eaten by hungry birds and crabs,
but I try to chase them away.

After two full moons pass, I see a nest hatch on the star cove. Out of the sand pops a tiny flipper, a head, and then an entire body. Ten, twelve, fifteen little turtles emerge from the depths of the star sand and scurry toward the ocean.

One confused baby turtle runs in the wrong direction—away from the water! He scrambles toward the soft orange light that glows from

the paper lanterns in the village. I run after the little turtle and pick him up. On his shell is the shape of a grain of star sand. He flails his neck and flippers. Gently, I guide the frightened turtle to the shoreline. A huge wave swallows him and carries him out to the deep sea.

I wonder if the star turtle is strong enough to survive. I wonder, too, if I am strong enough to be an ama diver.

687

Several fishing seasons come and go. The time arrives for me to make a deep water dive with the ama. I try, but I cannot peel my feet off the boat deck to jump into the dark, murky water. Okaasan sighs and looks down, away from me. To my despair, I hear muffled giggles.

At night I toss and turn in bed like a fish caught in a net. I get up, look out the window, and see the faint glow of the city lights. My mind is set. I will run to the city and find my sisters rather than embarrass Okaasan any further.

Okaasan is quiet as she serves our breakfast. Finally she says, "Kiyomi, you will come with me to the ama boats today."

Cupping my soup bowl in both hands, I take a sip but can barely taste or swallow.

"Kiyomi-chan, you must keep trying," she says.

At the dock, the ama prepare for a day of work. We put white cream on my face to protect it from the cold, salty water. Moments later, the boats creep through a thick fog, farther from the village than I've ever been. Almost ready to dive, I look at the black water and begin to shake.

Something moves in the water, but I cannot see what it is. A drum pounds in my chest. I look at Okaasan and she nods at me firmly. Again, I see something move in the water. This time, I see the outline of a turtle. My heart leaps. Could it be the star turtle?

I take a deep breath and blow through pursed lips, sounding like the distant cry of a gull on a wind-swept beach. I hold in another breath, force my feet off the deck, and dive.

Stroking the water furiously, I try to keep up with the sea turtle. As he swoops deeper to the ocean floor, I recognize the star on his shell. Grabbing his shell, we rise together to the surface for air. I turn loose, tread water, and watch the turtle gracefully swim away.

All morning I dive deep, hunt for abalone, and pry them off the
rocks with my knife. When I return to the boats, all the ama are pleased.

"Today, Kiyomi, you have become an ama," Okaasan says proudly.

On a small island beach we collect firewood and dry leaves.
Women, wrapped in thin, white clothing, huddle around the fire as
shellfish sizzle in the embers. I cannot tell if I tremble from the cold
or excitement. My skin is swollen and pale. An older ama places a
blanket on my shoulders. With chopsticks, we pick the flavorful fish
from the shells.

In the surf, I see the star turtle bobbing in the water, watching
me. I smile at my friend as a huge wave sweeps him into the deep
waters. On this island beach I sit for the first time among the brave
ama, the sea maidens of Japan.

Author's Note

The *ama* are Japanese sea divers who hunt for fish, shellfish, and seaweed without the aid of underwater breathing apparatus. Most of the ama are women, particularly in the fishing communities of central Japan. The *kachido,* "walking people," dive in shallow water from the shore and toss their catch into floating wooden tubs. The *funado,* "ship people," are older and more experienced and dive in deeper waters from an anchored boat. The ama hunt mostly for *awabi* (abalone), *sazae* (wreath shell snail), *tengusa* (agaragar), and *eganori* (a kind of edible seaweed). The ama's method of diving was first recorded by Chinese observers in Japan during the third century.

Pronunciation Guide

abalone	*ab-a-lo-nee*
ama	*a-ma*
awabi	*a-wa-bee*
eganori	*e-ga-no-ree*
funado	*fu-na-do*
kachido	*ka-chee-do*
Kiyomi	*Kee-yo-mee*
Okaasan	*O-ka-a-san*
sazae	*sa-za-e*
tengusa	*ten-gu-sa*

Story Questions & Activities

1 What does Kiyomi's mother do to prepare her to become an *ama?*

2 What happens the first time Kiyomi tries to dive alone? What does this tell you about her?

3 Why does Kiyomi want to be a brave *ama?*

4 What are the events in this story? List them in order.

5 How is Kiyomi's mother like the mother in "The Wise Old Woman"?

Write a Two-character Scene

Create a scene for a play based on "The Sea Maidens of Japan." Write a conversation between Kiyomi and her mother that could have taken place as Kiyomi prepares for her first deep-water dive. Begin by making a story map. Outline the setting, the characters, the problem, the events, and the solution. Then write your scene. Be sure to use the correct form for your dialogue.

Make a Shadow Box

What is abalone? Why do the *amas* have to dive for it? How is it used? Use an encyclopedia to learn more about this sea creature. Then bring to class a button or a piece of jewelry that is made from abalone shell. With a group, paste your abalone objects in a shadow box or a shoebox. Display your works.

Create a Japanese Cookbook

The people of the village eat the abalone and seaweed that the *ama* bring out of the sea. In fact, Japan relies on the sea for much of its food. In your library or at home, find a Japanese cookbook. Work with a group to choose some interesting Japanese seafood recipes. Copy these recipes, and place them in a Japanese cookbook of your own design.

Find Out More

One of the major uses for *amas* in modern times is as pearl divers. Use an encyclopedia or a book about gems to find out about pearls. If you can, invite a jeweler or a gemologist to speak to your class about this unusual gem.

Choose Reference Sources

When you want information, you can choose from a number of different reference sources.

Almanac: a book of information about important people, places, and events. An almanac is published each year so that it has up-to-date facts and figures.

Atlas: a book of maps that gives information about different places.

Dictionary: a book that lists words in alphabetical order, their meanings, pronunciations, parts of speech, and other information.

Encyclopedia: a set of books containing articles about people, places, things, events, and ideas. The articles are arranged in alphabetical order in volumes. When you use an encyclopedia to find facts about a topic, you need to have a **key word** in mind.

Thesaurus: a book of synonyms. **Synonyms** are words with the same or almost the same meaning. A thesaurus may be arranged like a dictionary, with the entry words shown in alphabetical order.

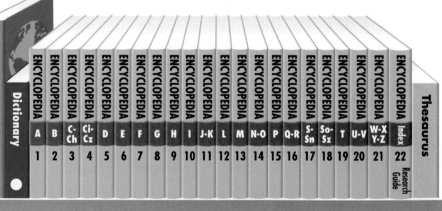

Use the information about different reference sources to answer these questions.

1. In which reference book would you look to find out how to pronounce *abalone*?

2. Where would you look to find out about deep-sea diving?

3. In which book would you find maps of Japan?

4. Where would you look to find synonyms of the word *strong*?

5. How can you save time if you know which reference book to use?

DIRECTIONS

Read the sample story. Then read each question about the story.

SAMPLE

Billy's Introduction to the News

Billy's father purchased a newspaper subscription for him for his eleventh birthday. Billy wasn't too sure about the gift, but he was polite when his father handed him the subscription notice.

"I think you'll enjoy the newspaper if you give it a chance. This will help you keep up with what's going on in town," his father said.

When Billy's first newspaper came the following week, he carefully spread it out and began to read it.

When his father got home that night, Billy asked, "Dad, did you see the front page of the newspaper today? The town is thinking about building a new high school. And the art guild is looking for more funding for the exhibit."

Billy's father chuckled and said, "It sounds to me as if the newspaper is a hit after all!"

1 At the beginning of the passage, how does Billy feel about reading the newspaper?

A Delighted

B Fortunate

C Excited

D Doubtful

2 When Billy gets the newspaper in the future, he will probably —

F give it to his father to read

G read it right away

H put it in the recycling bin

J send money to the art guild

697

Stories in Art

When Dr. Martin Luther King, Jr., looked at the United States, his judgment told him that something was wrong. He decided that the nation needed a new dream—a dream that included African Americans.

Look at the painting. How does the artist paint Dr. King? What do you notice about his hands? The window behind him looks like a church window. What does it say about the man and his career? How does it show what the artist thought about him?

Look at the painting again. Who are the people at the bottom? Why do you think they are marching? Why has the artist decided to show them with a picture of Dr. King?

Martin Luther King
by Thomas Blackshear
Smithsonian Institution,
Washington, DC

Judgments and Decisions

Develop a strategy for making judgments and decisions.

1 **Think about the story.** What main point is being made?

2 **Study the characters'** ideas and actions. Are the reasons for them clear?

3 **Think of how you feel** about the issue. How would you have felt in a similar situation?

4 **Make a judgment** about the topic, based on the selection and your own beliefs and opinions.

Lizzie Stanton Speaks Out

*E*lizabeth Cady Stanton rose to speak. It was a summer morning in 1848 at Seneca Falls, New York. Her listeners had assembled for the first Women's Rights Convention. As Stanton began to read the Declaration of Women's Sentiments, her voice grew stronger. Along with Lucretia Mott and others, she had worked hard to write the Declaration. They all felt strongly about the injustices women had to endure.

The list of grievances was a long one: Women could not vote or own property. Single women were subject to taxation without representation. Women were paid far less than men for the same work. They were denied the education and opportunities that men had.

By the time the two-day convention was over, sixty-eight women and thirty-two men had signed the Declaration. The meeting had been a success.

On her way home afterward, Elizabeth thought back to her first meeting with

Lucretia Mott. It had been in London, England, eight years earlier. They had talked about ways to improve the situation for women. It had taken them a long time, but with the Convention of 1848, the struggle for women's rights was at last officially under way.

Elizabeth Cady Stanton and Women's Rights

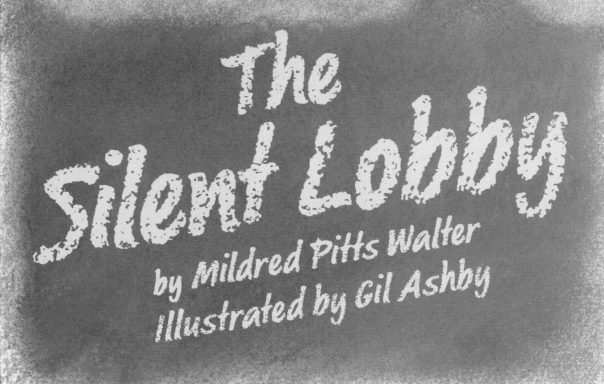

The Silent Lobby

by Mildred Pitts Walter
Illustrated by Gil Ashby

The old bus chugged along the Mississippi highway toward Washington, D.C. I shivered from icy winds and from excitement and fear. Excitement about going to Washington and fear that the old bus would stall again on the dark, lonely, icy road and we'd never make it.

Oh, just to sleep. The chug-chug-chugging of the old motor was not smooth enough to make soothing sounds, and I could not forget the words Mama and Papa had said just before me and Papa left to pick up twenty other people who filled the bus.

"It's too dangerous," Mama had said. "They just might bomb that bus."

"They could bomb this house for that matter," Papa said.

"I know," Mama went on. "That's why I don't want you to go. Why can't you just forget about this voting business and let us live in peace?"

"There can be no peace without freedom," Papa said.

"And you think someone is going to give you freedom?" Mama asked with heat in her voice. "Instead of going to Washington, you should be getting a gun to protect us."

"There are ways to win a struggle without bombs and guns. I'm going to Washington and Craig is going with me."

"Craig is too young."

"He's eleven. That's old enough to know what this is all about," Papa insisted.

knew. It had all started two years ago, in 1963. Papa was getting ready to go into town to register to vote. Just as he was leaving, Mr. Clem, Papa's boss, came and warned Papa that he should not try to register.

"I intend to register," Papa said.

"If you do, I'll have to fire you." Mr. Clem drove away in a cloud of dust.

"You ought not go," Mama said, alarmed. "You know that people have been arrested and beaten for going down there."

"I'm going," Papa insisted.

"Let me go with you, Papa." I was scared, too, and wanted to be with him if he needed help.

"No, you stay and look after your mama and the house till I get back."

Day turned to night, and Papa had not returned. Mama paced the floor. Was Papa in jail? Had he been beaten?

We waited, afraid. Finally, I said, "Mama, I'll go find him."

"Oh, no!" she cried. Her fear scared me more, and I felt angry because I couldn't do anything.

At last we heard Papa's footsteps. The look on his face let us know right away that something was mighty wrong.

"What happened, Sylvester?" Mama asked.

"I paid the poll tax, passed the literacy test, but I didn't interpret the state constitution the way they wanted. So they wouldn't register me."

Feeling a sense of sad relief, I said, "Now you won't lose your job."

"Oh, but I will. I tried to register."

Even losing his job didn't stop Papa from wanting to vote. One day he heard about Mrs. Fannie Lou Hamer and the Mississippi Freedom Democratic Party. The Freedom Party registered people without charging a poll tax, without a literacy test, and without people having to tell what the Mississippi Constitution was about.

On election day in 1964, Papa proudly voted for Mrs. Hamer, Mrs. Victoria Grey, and Mrs. Annie Devine to represent the people of the Second Congressional District of Mississippi. Eighty-three thousand other black men and women voted that day, too. Great victory celebrations were held in homes and churches. But the Governor of Mississippi, Paul B. Johnson, declared all of those eighty-three thousand votes of black people illegal. He gave certificates of election to three white men—William Colmer, John Williams, and a Mr. Whittier—to represent the mostly black Second Congressional District.

Members of the Freedom Party were like Papa—they didn't give up. They got busy when the governor threw out their votes. Lawyers from all over the country came to help. People signed affidavits saying that when they tried to register they lost their jobs, they were beaten, and their homes were burned and churches bombed. More than ten thousand people signed petitions to the governor asking him to count their votes. There was never a word from the governor.

y mind returned to the sound of the old bus slowly grinding along. Suddenly the bus stopped. Not again! We'd never make it now. Papa got out in the cold wind and icy drizzling rain and raised the hood. While he worked, we sang and clapped our hands to keep warm. I could hear Sister Phyllis praying with all her might for our safety. After a while we were moving along again.

I must have finally fallen asleep, for a policeman's voice woke me. "You can't stop here near the Capitol," he shouted.

"Our bus won't go," Papa said.

"If you made it from Mississippi all the way to D.C., you'll make it from here," the policeman barked.

At first the loud voice frightened me. Then, wide awake, sensing the policeman's impatience, I wondered why Papa didn't let him know that we would go as soon as the motor started. But Papa, knowing that old bus, said nothing. He stepped on the starter. The old motor growled and died. Again the policeman shouted, "I said get out of here."

"We'll have to push it," Papa said.

Everyone got off the bus and pushed. Passersby stopped and stared. Finally we were safe on a side street, away from the Capitol with a crowd gathered around us.

"You mean they came all the way from Mississippi in that?" someone in the crowd asked.

Suddenly the old bus looked shabby. I lowered my head and became aware of my clothes: my faded coat too small; my cotton pants too thin. With a feeling of shame, I wished those people would go away.

"What brings you all to the District?" a man called to us.

"We've come to see about seating the people we voted for and elected," Papa answered. "Down home they say our votes don't count, and up here they've gone ahead and seated men who don't represent us. We've come to talk about that."

"So you've come to lobby," a woman shouted. The crowd laughed.

Why were they laughing? I knew that to lobby meant to try to get someone to decide for or against something. Yes, that was

why we had come. I wished I could have said to those people who stood gawking at us that the suffering that brought us here was surely nothing to laugh about.

The laughter from the crowd quieted when another woman shouted, "You're too late to lobby. The House of Representatives will vote on that issue this morning."

Too late. That's what had worried me when the old bus kept breaking down. Had we come so far in this cold for nothing? Was it really too late to talk to members of the House of Representatives to persuade them to seat our representatives elected by the Freedom Party, *not* the ones chosen by the governor?

Just then rain began to fall. The crowd quickly left, and we climbed onto our bus. Papa and the others started to talk. What would we do now? Finally, Papa said, "We can't turn back now. We've done too much and come too far."

After more talk we all agreed that we must try to do what we had come to do. Icy rain pelted us as we rushed against cold wind back to the Capitol.

A doorman stopped us on the steps. "May I have your passes?"

"We don't have any," Papa replied.

"Sorry, you have to have passes for seats in the gallery." The doorman blocked the way.

"We're cold in this rain. Let us in," Sister Phyllis cried.

"Maybe we should just go on back home," someone suggested.

"Yes. We can't talk to the legislators now, anyway," another woman said impatiently.

"No," Papa said. "We must stay if we do no more than let them see that we have come all this way."

"But we're getting soaking wet. We can't stand out here much longer," another protested.

"Can't you just let us in out of this cold?" Papa pleaded with the doorman.

"Not without passes." The doorman still blocked the way. Then he said, "There's a tunnel underneath this building. You can go there to get out of the rain."

We crowded into the tunnel and lined up along the sides. My chilled body and hands came to life pressed against the warm walls. Then footsteps and voices echoed through the tunnel. Police. This tunnel . . . a trap! Would they do something to us for trying to get in without passes? I wanted to cry out to Papa, but I could not speak.

The footsteps came closer. Then many people began to walk by. When they came upon us, they suddenly stopped talking. Only the sound of their feet echoed in the tunnel. Where had they come from? What did they do? "Who are they, Papa?" I whispered.

"Congressmen and women." Papa spoke so softly, I hardly heard him, even in the silence.

They wore warm coats, some trimmed with fur. Their shoes gleamed. Some of them frowned at us. Others glared. Some sighed quickly as they walked by. Others looked at us, then turned their eyes to their shoes. I could tell by a sudden lift of the head and a certain look that some were surprised and scared. And there were a few whose friendly smiles seemed to say, Right on!

I glanced at Papa. How poor he and our friends looked beside those well-dressed people. Their clothes were damp, threadbare, and wrinkled; their shoes were worn and mud stained. But they all stood straight and tall.

My heart pounded. I wanted to call out to those men and women, "Count my papa's vote! Let my people help make laws, too." But I didn't dare speak in that silence.

Could they hear my heart beating? Did they know what was on my mind? "Lord," I prayed, "let them hear us in this silence."

Then two congressmen stopped in front of Papa. I was frightened until I saw smiles on their faces.

"I'm Congressman Ryan from New York," one of them said. Then he introduced a black man: "This is Congressman Hawkins from California."

"I'm Sylvester Saunders. We are here from Mississippi," Papa said.

"We expected you much earlier," Congressman Ryan said.

"Our old bus and bad weather delayed us," Papa explained.

"That's unfortunate. You could've helped us a lot. We worked late into the night lobbying to get votes on your side. But maybe I should say on *our* side." Mr. Ryan smiled.

"And we didn't do very well," Congressman Hawkins said.

"We'll be lucky if we get fifty votes on our side today," Congressman Ryan informed us. "Maybe you would like to come in and see us at work."

"We don't have passes," I said, surprised at my voice.

"We'll see about getting all of you in," Congressman Hawkins promised.

A little later, as we found seats in the gallery, Congressman Gerald Ford from the state of Michigan was speaking. He did not want Mrs. Hamer and other fairly elected members of the Freedom Party seated in the House. He asked his fellow congressmen to stick to the rule of letting only those with credentials from their states be seated in Congress. The new civil rights act would, in time, undo wrongs done to black Americans. But for now, Congress should let the men chosen by Governor Johnson keep their seats and get on with other business.

Then Congressman Ryan rose to speak. How could Congress stick to rules that denied blacks their right to vote in the state of Mississippi? The rule of letting only those with credentials from a segregated state have seats in the House could not *justly* apply here.

I looked down on those men and few women and wondered if they were listening. Did they know about the petitions? I remembered what Congressman Ryan had said: "We'll be lucky if we get fifty. . . ." Only 50 out of 435 elected to the House.

Finally the time came for Congress to vote. Those who wanted to seat Mrs. Hamer and members of the Freedom Democratic Party were to say, yes. Those who didn't want to seat Mrs. Hamer were to say, no.

709

At every yes vote I could hardly keep from clapping my hands and shouting, "Yea! Yea!" But I kept quiet, counting: thirty, then forty, forty-eight . . . only two more. We would lose badly.

Then something strange happened. Congressmen and congresswomen kept saying "Yes. Yes. Yes." On and on, "Yes." My heart pounded. Could we win? I sat on my hands to keep from clapping. I looked at Papa and the others who had come with us. They all sat on the edge of their seats. They looked as if they could hardly keep from shouting out, too, as more yes votes rang from the floor.

When the voting was over, 148 votes had been cast in our favor. What had happened? Why had so many changed their minds?

Later, Papa introduced me to Congressman Hawkins. The congressman asked me, "How did you all know that some of us walk through that tunnel from our offices?"

"We didn't know," I answered. "We were sent there out of the rain."

"That's strange," the congressman said. "Your standing there silently made a difference in the vote. Even though we lost this time, some of them now know that we'll keep on lobbying until we win."

I felt proud. Papa had been right when he said to Mama, "There are ways to win a struggle without bombs and guns." We had lobbied in silence and we had been *heard*.

President Lyndon B. Johnson shakes hands with Dr. Martin Luther King, Jr., after signing the Omnibus Civil Rights Act on June 29, 1964.

Note: *This story is a fictional account of one demonstration by African Americans during the decade of the 1960s. Many nonviolent demonstrations were held for voting rights, for jobs, and for freedom to use restaurants, libraries, schools, and public restrooms. This one took place on January 4, 1965.*

On June 29, 1964, President Lyndon Baines Johnson signed the Omnibus Civil Rights Act banning discrimination in voting, jobs, public facilities, and in housing. On August 6, 1965, President Johnson signed the Voting Rights Act, which guarantees the right to vote without penalties or poll taxes.

Meet Mildred Pitts Walter

Mildred Pitts Walter had never thought of writing books. Then she met a book salesperson. She told him that there were not enough stories about African American children. He suggested that Walter try writing one. She did, and his company published her first book, *Lillie of Watts*.

Writing "The Silent Lobby" was important to Walter. She herself was deeply involved in the civil rights movement. During the 1950s and 1960s, Walter worked hard for equal rights in Los Angeles, California, her home. She struggled to make sure that people of every color could live wherever they wanted.

Many of Mildred Pitts Walter's characters show the same courage she did. "My characters must make choices," Walter observed, "and once they have made those choices, they have to work them through. That's what life is—making a series of choices—and people who cannot choose for themselves don't grow."

Story Questions & Activities

1 Why are Craig and his father going to Washington, D.C.?

2 What do you think Craig's father means when he says, "There can be no peace without freedom"?

3 What makes the silent lobby so effective?

4 Do you think this selection has an important message? Explain.

5 Compare Craig's relationship with his father with Kyomi's attitude toward her mother in "The Sea Maidens of Japan." How are their relationships built on respect?

Write a Character Description

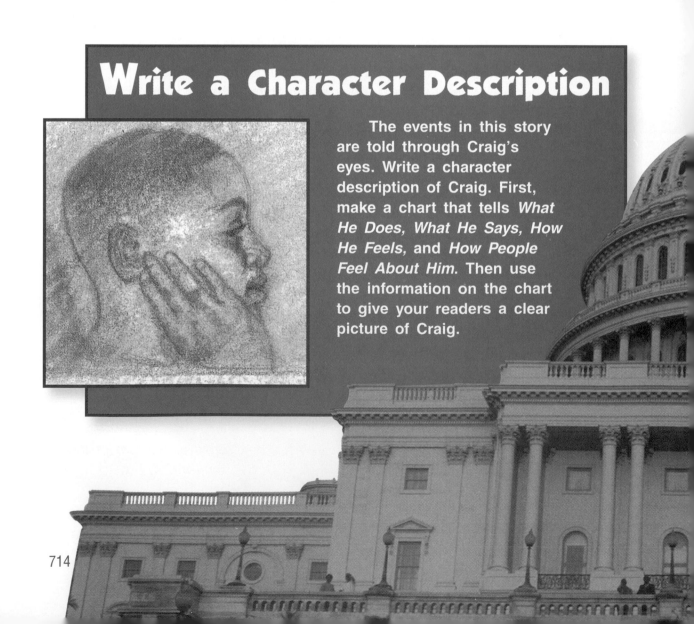

The events in this story are told through Craig's eyes. Write a character description of Craig. First, make a chart that tells *What He Does, What He Says, How He Feels,* and *How People Feel About Him.* Then use the information on the chart to give your readers a clear picture of Craig.

Make a Pamphlet

"The Silent Lobby" is about the struggle for civil rights in the United States in the 1950s and 1960s. Use your social studies textbook, an encyclopedia, or another book to learn about the civil rights movement. Focus on the leaders, the Civil Rights Act of 1964, and the Voting Rights Act of 1965. Share what you learn in a group pamphlet.

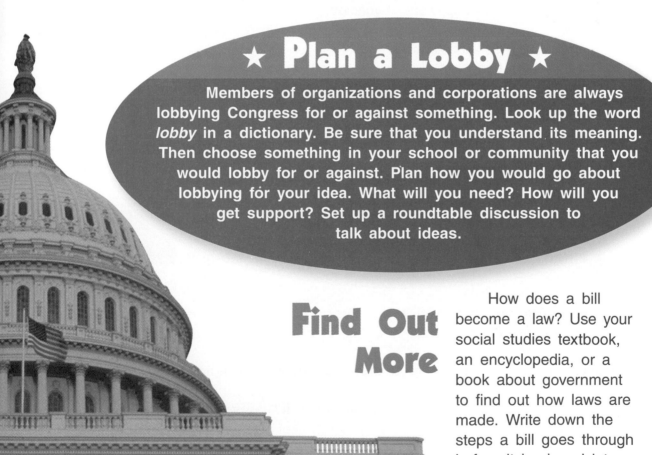

★ Plan a Lobby ★

Members of organizations and corporations are always lobbying Congress for or against something. Look up the word *lobby* in a dictionary. Be sure that you understand its meaning. Then choose something in your school or community that you would lobby for or against. Plan how you would go about lobbying for your idea. What will you need? How will you get support? Set up a roundtable discussion to talk about ideas.

Find Out More

How does a bill become a law? Use your social studies textbook, an encyclopedia, or a book about government to find out how laws are made. Write down the steps a bill goes through before it is signed into law. Use your notes to draw a diagram of the law-making process.

Use the Library

Most local libraries organize their books the same way. Fiction books are alphabetized by author, biographies by subject, and other nonfiction books are arranged according to the Dewey Decimal System. This system assigns groups of numbers to general subjects, which are then broken down to more specific categories and **call numbers**. This table gives an overview of the Dewey Decimal System.

Dewey Decimal System	
000–099	Generalities
100–199	Philosophy and Psychology
200–299	Religion
300–399	Social Sciences
400–499	Language
500–599	Natural Science and Mathematics
600–699	Technology (Applied Science)
700–799	The Arts/Fine and Decorative Arts
800–899	Literature and Rhetoric
900–999	Geography and History

Use the table to answer these questions.

1. Which numbers might contain information about the history of the Civil Rights Movement?

2. Where do you think you would find books to help you learn to speak Italian?

3. Where would you look for information about repairing a car?

4. Which numbers might cover books about the care and feeding of aardvarks?

5. How does the Dewey Decimal System help you find books at the library?

TEST POWER

Test Tip

If you are spending too much time on a question, see if there are any answer choices you can rule out.

DIRECTIONS

Read the sample story. Then read each question about the story.

SAMPLE

The Cactus

A cactus is a plant specially developed to live in a hot, dry area. There are thousands of different <u>species</u> of cacti on earth, and about 200 different kinds in the United States.

Cacti come in many different shapes and sizes. One kind is only a few inches across and grows very low to the ground. Another kind, the giant elephant cactus, can grow to be more than 60 feet tall and more than ten feet around. It would take you and two friends to encircle an elephant cactus with your arms. But you don't want to do it. With the sharp barbs on these plants, it's never worth hugging a cactus!

1 The word <u>species</u> in this story means —

   A types

   B weeds

   C deserts

   D animals

2 Which of these is a FACT presented in this story?

   F Cacti grow in warm, moist areas of the United States.

   G There are more than 2000 different kinds of cactus in the United States.

   H The elephant cactus can grow to be 60 feet tall.

   J Only one type of cactus has sharp barbs.

Which answer choices did you rule out right away? Tell why.

Stories in Art

This photograph of a flower growing on a rock shows two natural events—the making of a rock and the growth of a flower. How does each happen? Each involves a sequence of events.

❧

What can you tell about this photograph? What details do you notice? Why do you think the flower started growing? What might happen to the flower in this setting?

❧

Close your eyes. How is a flower different from a rock? This photograph is a study in contrasts. Explain why.

Rock and Flower,
by Kathleen Norris Cook
Potato Lake, Durango, Colorado

Sequence of Events

Develop a strategy for determining the sequence of events.

1 **Identify the events** being described. Use subheadings to help you.

2 **Pay attention to what happens** first, next, and so on.

3 **Look for clue words,** such as *after* and *eventually.* They help signal the order of events.

4 **Reread the story** if something does not make sense to you.

5 **Retell the order of events** in your own words. What is the life cycle of the giant sequoia?

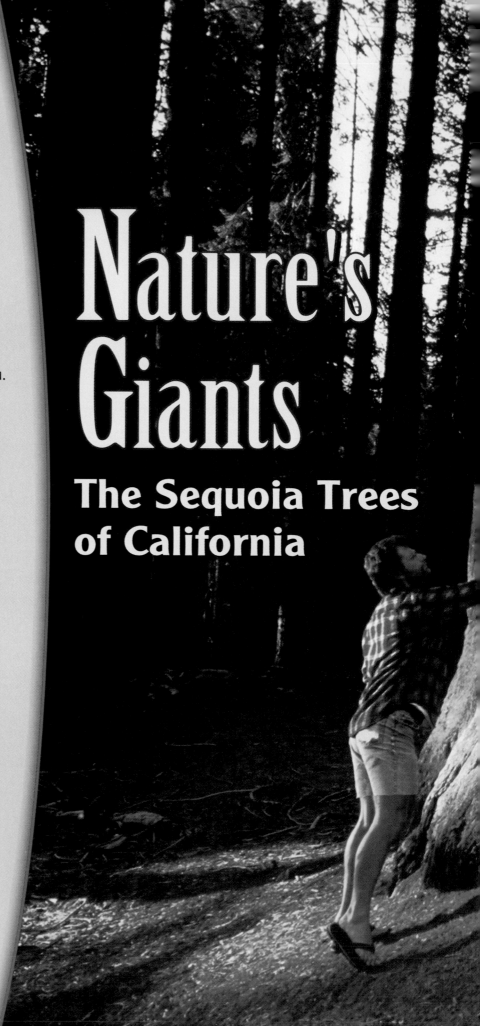

Nature's Giants

The Sequoia Trees of California

CONES

HIGH TEMPERATURE
CONES OPEN

Giant sequoias are enormous trees found in the Sierra Nevada Mountains of California. The largest known giant sequoia is 275 feet tall (and growing) and about 36 feet thick at its base. Some giant sequoias are over 2,000 years old and are thought to be the largest living things on Earth.

Life Cycle

Giant sequoias are a type of redwood tree with a unique life cycle. The seeds for new trees are found in cones, which may stay on a tree for twenty years. The cones open only when temperatures get extremely hot, which happens during a forest fire. After a fire, the seeds fall onto the newly burned earth. When it rains, they will germinate, or start to grow. Eventually, the cycle will be repeated with cones from the new trees.

SEEDS FALL
NEWLY BURNED GROUND

Fire helps in another way as well. It burns away undergrowth that keeps sunlight from reaching the young, newly growing trees.

Fire-Resistant Bark

You may wonder why the sequoias don't burn in a fire. The trees have thick, fire-resistant bark. The bark contains tannins, substances that are not only fire-resistant but also protect the trees from insects. This is one of the reasons why sequoias are not only the largest, but also one of the longest-living things on Earth.

RAIN HELPS THE NEW SEEDS TO GERMINATE

NEW TREES GROW IN THE SOIL

FOR KIDS

Amazon
ALERT!

People in Brazil burn down trees in the Amazon rain forest to make way for homes.

Brazil Acts to Save the Rain Forest

The lush Amazon rain forest stretches about 2.7 million square miles. Brightly colored parrots, swift jaguars, and fierce piranhas make their home in the tropical forest and its many rivers. Monkeys swing among high branches and vines. The Amazon holds one-fifth of the planet's fresh water supply and the world's widest variety of wildlife.

For decades, this wildlife wonderland has been shrinking as farmers and others clear the land. Brazil's government has confirmed what environmentalists have feared: the 1990s was a terrible decade for the rain forest. According to information from Brazil's government, the destruction of the forest there reached record levels in 1995. In that year alone, 11,200 square miles were burned or cleared. That's nearly twice what was lost in 1994. Overall, one-eighth of the giant rain forest has been destroyed.

The bad news from Brazil was followed by a ray of hope. Brazil has promised to do a better job enforcing laws that protect its natural treasure.

TIME FOR KIDS Map

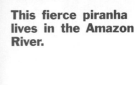

This fierce piranha lives in the Amazon River.

COVER: PAUL EDMONDSON/TONY STONE IMAGES; RIGHT: PAUL A. ZAHL/PHOTO RESEARCHERS

721

WHO'S KILLING THE FOREST?

Loggers, miners, and farmers from Brazil and nearby countries have been rapidly moving into the Amazon since the 1960s. Some cut down trees for wood and paper. The loss of trees is called deforestation. Others simply burn the forest to clear the land. Construction of roads and airplane runways has also damaged the region.

Space satellites regularly take pictures of the Amazon. The information that got Brazil to help save the rain forest was based on these pictures. Deforestation slowed down in 1996 and 1997. But that's not necessarily because people were protecting the forest. It's because heavy rainfall made it harder to burn trees.

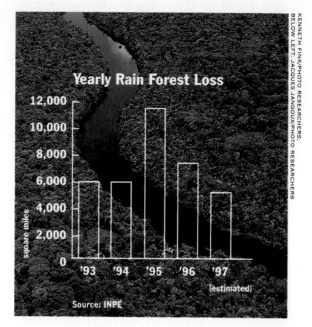

Yearly Rain Forest Loss

Source: INPE

Brazil's rain forest is filled with winding rivers like the one above.

Two macaws preen for the camera.

Stephan Schwartzman of the Environmental Defense Fund calls the pace of destruction "alarming." He and other scientists are worried that they will run out of time to study the plants and animals of the rich forest. "The great tragedy is how much isn't known," he says.

CRACKING DOWN ON CRIMINALS

To slow down deforestation, Brazil decided to get tougher on people who abuse the Amazon. In 1996 Brazil placed limits on clearing land in the region. But officials did not always enforce the laws. Now those who damage the rain forest will be punished with big fines and ordered to repair the damage. "This can make a big difference," says Schwartzman. "There is hope."

HELPING INDIANS

As the Amazon rain forest disappears, so may the way of life of native people who live there—that is, unless Sydney Possuelo has his way. Possuelo is the head of Brazil's Department of Isolated Indians, and an expert on the native tribes of the Amazon. He is helping to preserve not only the natives' ways of life but also their rain forest habitat.

Dozens of tribes make their home in unexplored areas of the Amazon. They hunt for food and make their own simple tools, clothing, and shelter. But this life is endangered by gold miners, farmers, and others pressing into new areas of the rain forest.

In the past, the Brazilian government responded by trying to prepare the tribes to live in modern society outside the forest.

Possuelo thought that the Indians and the rain forest deserved a better solution. Over time, he convinced the government that instead of trying to modernize isolated tribes, it should shield Indian land and traditions from the modern world. That way, says Possuelo, the Indians "can live their traditional life-style."

Today Possuelo has seven teams working full time to track down isolated tribes and protect them. The work is sometimes dangerous. Says Possuelo, "It involves months of being in the jungle." But finally the Indians are thankful they can again roam free through their lands. Environmentalists praise Possuelo for the protection he provides for the rich rain forest and all its species, human and nonhuman. But Possuelo insists that he is not a hero: "I like the jungle and Indians. It is not a sacrifice for me."

CLAUDIA ANDUJAR/PHOTO RESEARCHERS

This Indian woman is a member of the Yanomami tribe. Her way of life is in danger of disappearing.

FIND OUT MORE
Visit our website:
www.mhschool.com/reading

*inter*NET
CONNECTION

Based on an article in *TIME FOR KIDS*.

Story Questions & Activities

1 What is happening to the Amazon rain forest?

2 What is Brazil doing to save the rain forest?

3 What makes the Amazon rain forest important to everyone?

4 What is the main idea of this selection?

5 Imagine that one of the animals from the Amazon rain forest stepped into the painting on page 718. How could it use its own experience to describe the message of the picture?

Write a Story

Amazon Alert! is a nonfiction story. It contains real, factual information. Write an original fictional story that may or may not be based on real, or factual, information.

Make a Poster

You, too, can help save the Amazon rain forest by creating a colorful poster. What picture will you use to catch people's attention and show the problems of the rain forest? What slogan will you write to convince people that the rain forest is worth saving? It's up to you!

Draw a Map

How can you illustrate the Amazon rain forest? Find Brazil on a map of South America. Locate the Amazon River and the rain forest. Now draw your own map of the Amazon rain forest. Illustrate it with drawings of rain-forest plants and animals.

Find Out More

For decades, the "wildlife wonderland" in the Amazon rain forest has been shrinking. What are some of the wonderful plants and animals that are disappearing? Start by checking in an encyclopedia or in a book about the rain forest. Use what you learn to write a fact sheet about the Amazon rain forest's endangered wildlife.

Use an Encyclopedia

Suppose that you were asked to write a research report about the Amazon rain forest. How would you begin? You could start by looking in an encyclopedia. An **encyclopedia** is a set of books that has articles about people, places, things, events, and ideas. The articles are arranged in alphabetical order in volumes.

When you use an encyclopedia to find facts about a topic, you must have a **key word** in mind. For example, for a research paper on the Amazon rain forest, you would look under the key word *Amazon* or *rain forest*.

ENCYCLOPEDIA	ENCYCLOPEDIA	ENCYCLOPEDIA	ENCYCLOPEDIA	ENCYCLOPEDIA	ENCYCLOPEDIA	ENCYCLOPEDIA	ENCYCLOPEDIA	ENCYCLOPEDIA	ENCYCLOPEDIA	ENCYCLOPEDIA	ENCYCLOPEDIA	ENCYCLOPEDIA	ENCYCLOPEDIA	ENCYCLOPEDIA	ENCYCLOPEDIA	ENCYCLOPEDIA	ENCYCLOPEDIA	ENCYCLOPEDIA	ENCYCLOPEDIA	ENCYCLOPEDIA	ENCYCLOPEDIA
A	B	C-Ch	Ci-Cz	D	E	F	G	H	I	J-K	L	M	N-O	P	Q-R	S-Sn	So-Sz	T	U-V	W-X Y-Z	Index
1	2	3	4	5	6	7	8	9	10	11	12	13	14	15	16	17	18	19	20	21	22
																					Research Guide

Use the encyclopedia to answer these questions.

1 What kind of information does an encyclopedia have?

2 In which volume would you look for information on piranhas?

3 Do you think that you would find a separate article on jaguars? Why or why not?

4 What key word would you use to find information about Macaws in the rain forest?

5 How would you use an encyclopedia to write a research report?

TEST POWER

DIRECTIONS

Read the sample story. Then read each question about the story.

SAMPLE

Frida Kahlo

Many people consider Frida Kahlo to be one of the best Mexican artists of the twentieth century. Born in Mexico City in 1907, Frida was an active and beautiful child. At age 18, however, she was in a terrible bus accident. Afterward, she spent many months recovering in bed.

In order to pass the time, Frida began painting. What started as a hobby soon became her life's work.

Frida married artist Diego Rivera in 1929. Rivera encouraged Frida's painting. He also thought that she should wear traditional, colorful Mexican clothing and silver jewelry. Frida became known for always dressing in this style.

In 1953, a year before her death, Frida had her only art show. It was a great success. Today, Frida Kahlo's art is collected by art collectors around the world and is shown in many art museums.

1 In 1929, Frida —

  A was born in Mexico

  B married Diego Rivera

  C had her first art show

  D turned 18 years old

2 Which is a FACT stated in the story?

  F Kahlo's jewelry is in art museums.

  G Rivera was Kahlo's art instructor.

  H Kahlo was Mexico's best artist.

  J Kahlo's art is now in museums.

Frederick Douglass

1817-1895

Douglass was someone who,
Had he walked with wary foot
And frightened tread,
From very indecision
Might be dead,
Might have lost his soul,
But instead decided to be bold
And capture every street
On which he set his feet,
To route each path
Toward freedom's goal,
To make each highway
Choose *his* compass' choice,
To all the world he cried,
Hear my voice! . . .
Oh, to be a beast, a bird,
Anything but a slave! he said.

Who would be free
Themselves must strike
The first blow, he said.

He died in 1895.
He is not dead.

by Langston Hughes

Reading for

You get information from many sources such as television, newspapers, advertisements, and the Internet. In school, textbooks bring you information about different subjects. In this section, you will learn strategies to help you understand and use the many kinds of information that are a part of your everyday life.

Information

Contents

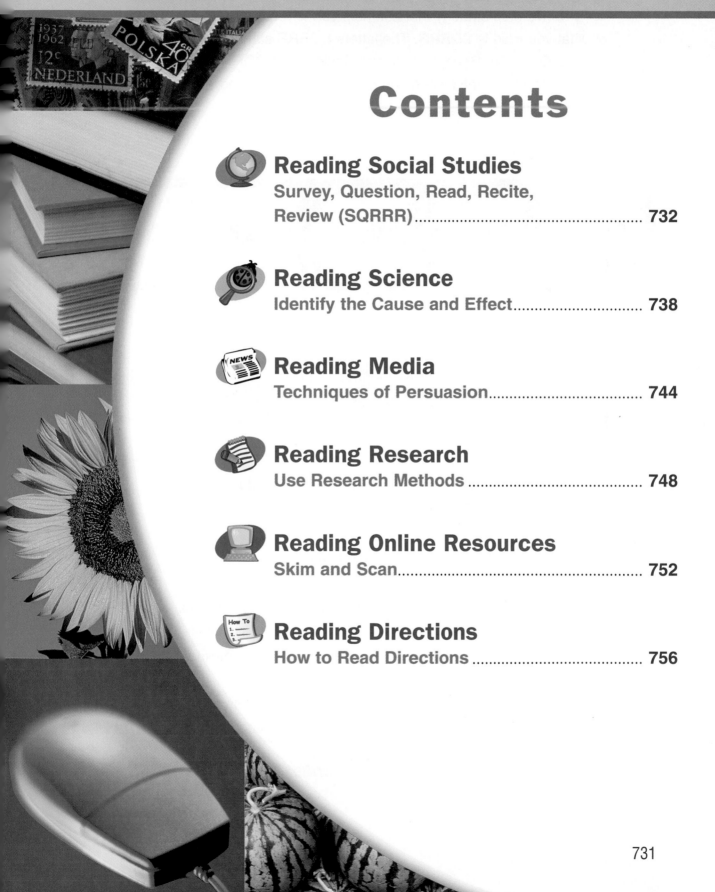

Reading Social Studies
Survey, Question, Read, Recite, Review (SQRRR) 732

Reading Science
Identify the Cause and Effect 738

Reading Media
Techniques of Persuasion 744

Reading Research
Use Research Methods 748

Reading Online Resources
Skim and Scan 752

Reading Directions
How to Read Directions 756

Reading Social Studies

A five-step strategy that can help you to remember more of what you read is **SQRRR**. The letters SQRRR stand for Survey, Question, Read, Recite, and Review. The SQRRR strategy can be helpful when you read social studies and science textbooks.

Survey 〉 Question 〉 Read 〉 Recite 〉 Review

Use SQRRR

1 **Survey**, or look over, the article. Read titles, headings, and captions. Notice words or phrases in darker type and look at photographs and illustrations.

2 **Ask yourself questions** as you read. For example, "What is the main idea of this paragraph? What is the author trying to tell me?"

3 **Read and reread**. Pay close attention to examples and details. Look up definitions of unfamiliar words.

4 **Recite**, or say aloud, what you have read. Explain to a partner what you have read.

5 **Review** by summarizing aloud or in writing. What are the important facts? What main point is the author making?

Native Americans of the Northwest Coast

VOCABULARY

salmon run

Main Idea Northwest Coast Native Americans used forest and sea resources.

How Did the Native Americans of the Northwest Coast Get Their Food?

For thousands of years, Native Americans of the Northwest Coast survived by using the resources of the forests and the sea. They gathered roots and berries from the forests that lined the shore. They also hunted deer, elk, and beaver. Nearly everything else they needed they got from the sea. One important food source was the **salmon run**, the yearly return of salmon to the coastal rivers to lay their eggs. During the salmon run a Native American family could catch over 1,000 pounds of fish.

Summarize

How did the Native Americans of the Northwest Coast make use of their environment?

Salmon provided food for Northwest Coast Native Americans.

Survey.
I'll look over this page. What can I learn from the title and headings?

Question.
I'll think about this question as I read.

Read and reread.
The main idea will help me focus my reading.

Recite.
I will explain what I've read to a partner.

Review.
If I can answer this question, then I know I have understood the passage.

Our Country's Natural Resources

Read Aloud

"When the well's dry, we know the worth of water," wrote Benjamin Franklin in the 1750s. His words are still true today. In the United States we have a great many valuable resources, including water. But we do not always appreciate their value until they become scarce.

Focus Activity

READ TO LEARN

What is a natural resource?

VOCABULARY

- natural resource
- nonrenewable resource
- renewable resource
- mineral
- fossil fuel
- environment
- economy
- pollution
- acid rain

The Big Picture

The United States is rich in **natural resources**. Natural resources are materials found in nature that people use to meet their needs and wants.

For a long time most Americans believed that we would always have enough natural resources. But our country's resources will not last forever. Some, such as coal, oil, and natural gas, cannot be replaced. These resources are called **nonrenewable resources.**

Our forests, on the other hand, are **renewable resources.** Renewable resources are resources that can be replaced. When we cut down trees, we can plant new ones. Yet both old and newly planted trees face many dangers. As you read about how Americans use our forests, you will also learn about some of these dangers.

RICH IN RESOURCES

As the chart on this page shows, all regions of the United States have natural resources. How many items in your classroom can you identify that came from natural resources?

Different Kinds of Resources

A good way to identify natural resources in the United States is to divide them into groups, as shown in the chart on this page.

You can see that in all regions people use forests, a plant resource, to provide wood for building and paper.

The United States has vast **mineral** resources. A mineral is a substance found in the earth that is neither a plant nor an animal. Minerals include metals such as iron, copper, and zinc.

Among the most widely used mineral resources are **fossil fuels**. These fuels were formed over millions of years from fossils, which are the remains of ancient plants or animals. Fossil fuels include the nonrenewable resources oil, coal, and natural gas.

OUR COUNTRY'S NATURAL RESOURCES

REGION	MINERALS	FORESTS PLANTS	FISH WILDLIFE	FOSSIL FUELS
West	Zinc Lead	Cedar Birch	Salmon Tuna Deer	Oil
Southwest	Iron Copper	Oak Cacti	Shrimp Deer Rabbit	Natural Gas Oil
Middle West	Iron Copper	Maple Sunflowers	Bass Deer	Oil Coal
Southeast	Iron	Pine Mangrove	Shrimp Bears	Coal Natural Gas
Northeast	Granite Copper	Fir Maple	Lobster Scallops Deer	Coal

FORESTS

Natural resources are all part of Earth's **environment**, which is made up of all the surroundings in which people, plants, and animals live. One of the most important parts of the environment is forests. Forests contribute in important ways to the health of the environment. As trees soak up sunlight, they keep the temperature of the air from getting too hot. A tree's roots hold the soil together. By producing oxygen and removing carbon dioxide from the air, the leaves of trees provide fresh air for us to breathe.

Using Forests

Most people may think of the forest as a place to enjoy our country's natural beauty. However, people use forests for other purposes besides recreation. Forests are an important part of our economy. A country's **economy** is the way its people use natural resources, money, and knowledge to produce goods and services. Can you think of some ways that forests are part of our economy?

We use trees to make a variety of goods. You are looking at one of the most important forest products right now: paper. The flow chart on these pages shows how a tree is turned into paper.

Dangers to Our Forests

One of the most serious threats to our forests comes from **pollution**. Pollution is something—such as harmful chemicals—that makes our air, soil, and water dirty. These chemicals mix with moisture in the air. When the polluted moisture falls to the ground, it is called **acid rain**.

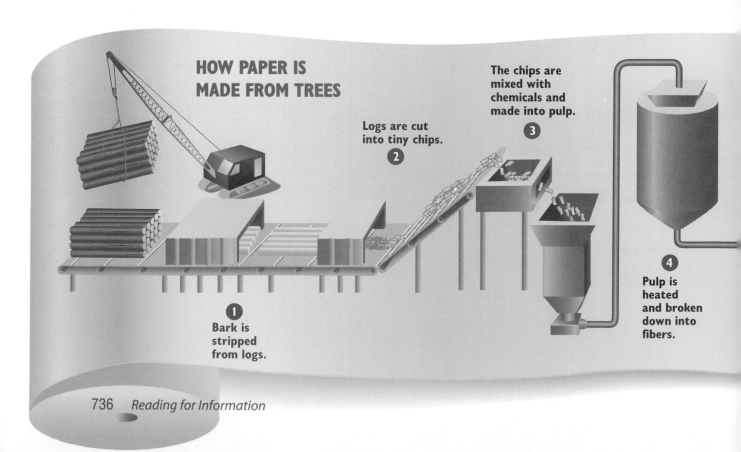

HOW PAPER IS MADE FROM TREES

1 Bark is stripped from logs.

2 Logs are cut into tiny chips.

3 The chips are mixed with chemicals and made into pulp.

4 Pulp is heated and broken down into fibers.

The lushness of this healthy green forest in North Carolina (left) seems remarkable when compared to the damage caused by acid rain (below).

In spite of its name, acid rain can take the form of snow, dew, or frost. Acid rain can destroy trees and pollute the soil so it cannot support new growth. When forests die, animals must find new shelter. Acid rain can also pollute rivers and lakes and kill the fish that live in them.

The making of paper from trees involves a number of complex steps. By which step has the wood been turned into something else?

How can we reduce the effects of acid rain? One thing that people can do is limit the amount of harmful chemicals that are released into the air. These chemicals often come from burning fossil fuels, such as gasoline in automobiles. Scientists are studying cleaner ways to burn fossil fuels.

Chemicals and unwanted materials are removed from the fibers.
5

Dried sheets of paper are pressed smooth on rollers.
7

The paper is rolled onto reels and stored.
8

Fibers are poured onto a wire mesh, dried, and shaped into sheets.
6

Review Questions

1. What is the difference between renewable and nonrenewable resources? Give one example of each type.

2. Why are forests one of our most important natural resources?

3. Did you follow each step in the SQRRR plan as you read? Are there any steps you would repeat in order to better understand the article?

Science books contain information about living and nonliving things. You will find many explanations that describe cause-and-effect relationships. To understand science, you will need to recognize these important relationships.

A cause is an event that makes something happen. An effect is what happens as a result. You can use clues in the text and what you already know yourself to identify cause-and-effect relationships that are not stated directly.

Cause → Effect

Identify the Cause and Effect

1. **Think about what happens** and why it happens.

2. **Look for clue words,** such as *because*, *since*, and *when*, that signal cause-and-effect relationships.

3. **Read:** Does the text tell about what happened? If so, I am probably reading about an effect. Does the text tell about why something happened? If so, I am probably reading about a cause.

4. **Check for more than one.** A cause may have more than one effect. An effect may have more than one cause. Sometimes a series of events can resemble a chain in which each effect becomes the cause of another effect.

Reading Science

Pollution

Vocabulary

pollution

How Can People Ruin Soil?

Think about what happens.
This heading tells me that people are a cause and ruined soil is an effect.

People depend on soil. Would you believe people ruin and waste soil? That might include you! It may be people in general or industries—such as factories or farms.

People often get rid of garbage and hazardous wastes by burying them in soil. Hazardous wastes are wastes that may be poisonous or cause diseases, such as cancer.

Look for clue words.
As I read, I'll look for clue words like *because* that signal causes or effects.

Spraying chemicals on soil to kill unwanted animals and plants also affects the soil, because these chemicals become a part of the soil. Tossing foam cups, plastic wrappers, and materials onto the ground, instead of using trash baskets, harms the soil. These materials do not decay. They remain as wastes in the soil. They may build up and make the soil unusable.

❸

Read.
I'll look for what happened (effects) and why (causes).

All these materials add up to **pollution**. *Pollution* means adding any harmful substances to Earth's land, water, or air. Pollution can make soil dangerous for crops, housing, people, and animals.

❹

Check for more than one.
I'll see if there is more than one cause or effect in the passage.

It takes people to make garbage. Each piece of garbage here was thrown away by somebody. What are some ways to prevent this kind of pollution?

Earth's Atmosphere

Get Ready

From space, Earth's atmosphere appears as a thin blue layer surrounding the planet. From the ground, the air may appear different from day to day.

The air may seem clear and clean on some days. If you live in or near a big city, you may have days when the air seems smoky, or "hazy." Why? What kinds of pollutants are in the air that can make it look that way?

Explore Activity

What Makes Air Dirty?

Procedure

1 Make square "frames" by taping together the corners of four cardboard strips. Make three frames, and label them A, B, and C. Tie a 30-cm string to a corner of each frame.

2 Stretch and attach three strips of tape across each frame, with all sticky sides facing the same way. Use a plastic knife to spread a thin coat of petroleum jelly across each sticky side.

3 **Use Variables** Hang the frames in different places to try to collect pollutants. Decide on places indoors or outdoors. Be sure to tell a parent or teacher where.

4 **Observe** Observe each frame over four days. Record the weather and air condition each day.

5 **Measure** Collect the frames. Observe the sticky sides with a hand lens and a metric ruler to compare particles.

Drawing Conclusions

Interpret Data How did the frames change over time? How did the hand lens and ruler help you describe any pollution?

Materials

12 cardboard strips

petroleum jelly

plastic knife

transparent tape

string

hand lens

metric ruler

marker

Read to Learn

Main Idea Earth's atmosphere supports life on Earth.

Why couldn't humans live on a planet that does not have an atmosphere as on Earth? Every minute of every day, you need air.

Air is a mixture of nitrogen, oxygen, and a few traces of other gases, including water vapor. This mixture is a vital resource. It supports and protects life on Earth in many ways.

Almost all organisms need air to live. Actually, they need oxygen, one of the gases that is in the air.

What is oxygen for? Living things take in oxygen for respiration. In this process, oxygen is used to break down food so that energy can be gotten from it. As a result of this process, living things give off wastes, including the gas carbon dioxide.

Why doesn't the atmosphere fill up with carbon dioxide? Plants and other producers take in carbon dioxide. They use it for making food. In the presence of light, these organisms carry on the process called photosynthesis. In this process they make food and give off oxygen.

How Earth's Atmosphere Supports Life

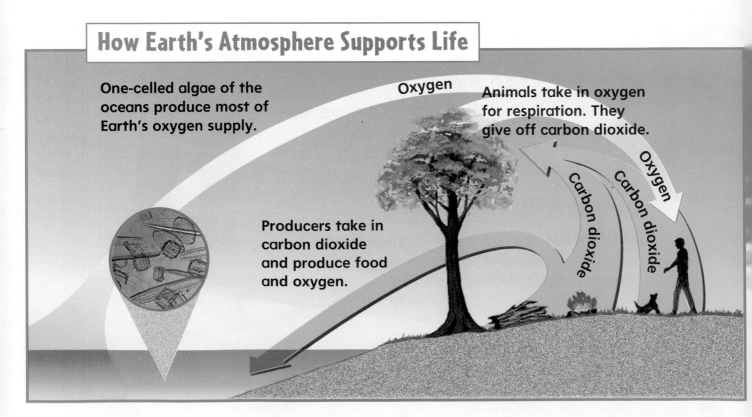

One-celled algae of the oceans produce most of Earth's oxygen supply.

Oxygen

Animals take in oxygen for respiration. They give off carbon dioxide.

Producers take in carbon dioxide and produce food and oxygen.

Carbon dioxide

Oxygen

Carbon dioxide

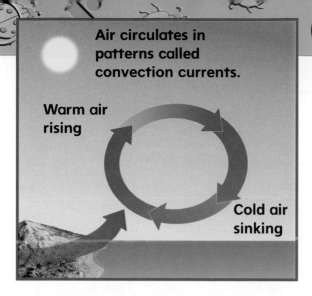

Air circulates in patterns called convection currents.

Warm air rising

Cold air sinking

Producers range in size from green plants to one-celled algae. They replace oxygen in the atmosphere. This makes oxygen a naturally **renewable resource**. A renewable resource is one that can be replaced. It can be replaced in a short enough period of time to support life on Earth.

Protection

The atmosphere also shields Earth's surface from harmful energy that comes from the Sun. The atmosphere helps screen out harmful ultraviolet rays (UV rays) from the Sun. About 30 km (18.6 mi) above your head is a layer of gas called ozone (OH·zohn). This **ozone layer** screens out 95 to 99 percent of the Sun's UV rays.

The atmosphere also shields Earth from rocks from space. The "shooting stars" you see on a clear night are not stars. They are rocks from space that burn up due to friction with the air as they speed through the atmosphere.

The atmosphere also protects life from extremes of temperature. Clouds block sunlight during the day. At night they keep much of the heat from escaping into space, so that the planet does not "cool off." Whenever one part of the atmosphere gets hotter than another, the air moves, or circulates, and spreads the heat around.

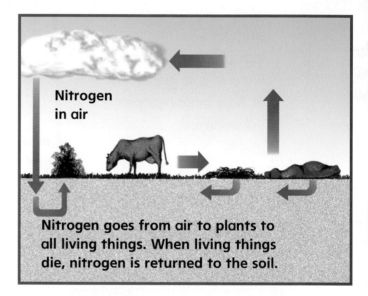

Nitrogen in air

Nitrogen goes from air to plants to all living things. When living things die, nitrogen is returned to the soil.

Review Questions

1. Why is air important to living things?
2. How does the atmosphere protect Earth?
3. How can recognizing cause-and-effect relationships help you to understand the causes of pollution?

Information is communicated through many different sources: radio, television, newspapers, magazines, and the Internet. We call these sources *media*.

One of the purposes of media is to persuade us to act or think in a certain way. Editorials, speeches, and advertisements are examples of media that persuade. It is important to be aware of how language can influence us.

Jack's Furniture

Number one furniture store in the area

Everyone loves Jack's beautiful, high quality funiture and low, low prices.

Tom Ross, a loyal Jack's customer since 1995, says:

"I just love my new sofa. Jack's low prices are impossible to beat."

BIG SALE TODAY!

Techniques of Persuasion

1. **Loaded Words:** Strong words, such as *beautiful* and *high quality,* are used to persuade us that we must have the product or service because it is the best.

2. **Information:** Ads often supply facts and statistics to support a claim that a product or service will perform well and meet our needs.

3. **Testimonials:** A testimonial shows someone praising a product or service. A famous person is often used.

4. **Bandwagon:** These ads try to persuade us to use a product or service because *everyone else* does.

Campaign Speech

Speeches are a necessary form of communication for people running for office. This speech uses several examples of persuasive techniques.

1 Loaded words
The word *outstanding* is a strong word that suggests quality.

2 Informational
Dina's experience as a project leader may persuade you that she would be a good president.

3 Testimonial
Dina notes that the principal, Ms. Pennington, supports her.

4 Bandwagon
The use of *Everyone* tries to persuade others to vote with the students who have school spirit.

Vote For Dina

★ ★ ★ ★ ★ ★ ★ ★ ★ ★ ★ ★ ★ ★ ★ ★ ★

**Fifth Grade President
Webster School**

Now that election day is here, I'd like to remind you of my outstanding qualifications for the office of Fifth Grade President.

I have excellent leadership experience. I organized the school recycling campaign, and I helped raise money for the library.

Ms. Pennington, our principal, says that I am dependable and a good student.

I'm really interested in increasing the kinds of activities we have at school. I promise that I will work hard for you.

Everyone with school spirit supports me!

So now that it's time to vote, vote for me — Dina Dempsey!

You'll be glad you did!

★ ★ ★ ★ ★ ★ ★ ★ ★ ★ ★ ★ ★ ★ ★ ★ ★

Magazine Advertisement

Stores and companies use art and brief, clever text to catch a reader's attention in magazine ads for their products. Note the persuasive techniques used in the ad below.

Radio Commercial

The Bubbly Bliss Company
100 Babbling Brook Road
Clearwater, Iowa 99999

Script

Brad B: This is Brad Bubbles at the Frothmans' house, interviewing yet another satisfied Bubbly Bliss laundry detergent customer.

Mrs. F: My family just loves Bubbly Bliss. Its bubbly action gets out even the toughest stains. Just yesterday, my son spilled grape juice on his favorite sweatshirt. I just reached for Bubbly Bliss and let the bubbles do the work.

Brad B: And how is the sweatshirt now, Mrs. Frothman?

Mrs. F: Like new!

Brad B: And there you have it, folks. The Frothmans are just one of the millions of families across America now enjoying Bubbly Bliss's stain removing power!

Review Questions

1. What persuasive techniques are used in the magazine ad?
2. What persuasive techniques did you find in the radio commercial?
3. How does learning about persuasive techniques help you better understand advertisements?

When you write a report, you must first do research on your topic. It is important that you read various sources to get enough information. Taking notes from multiple sources will help you gather different facts about your topic. As you research, select the best sources for your information, and check the accuracy of the facts you use.

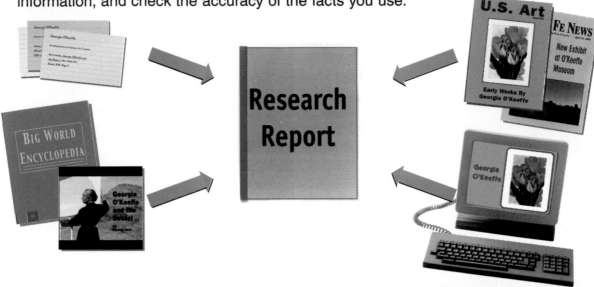

Use Research Methods

1. **Locate sources of information.** Use the library to find books and other sources. Cross-checking is also important—checking questionable or conflicting facts in a second or third source.

2. **Take notes on useful information.** Also record information about the source. You may need to list your sources in a bibliography.

3. **Organize your information.** Put your notes in categories based on the main ideas of your topic. Then use these categories to make a logical outline for your report.

4. **Write your report in your own words.** Be sure to write clear sentences that your readers will understand.

1

Locate several sources of information for your topic. This seems like a good source for my topic, Georgia O'Keeffe.

2

Take notes. This is an important fact for my report.

3

Organize. The early years of O'Keeffe will be a main part of my outline.

4

Write. I'll use my notes and outline to write my report.

Here is part of an article from a source that you will find listed on page 750.

Georgia O'Keeffe, American Artist

Georgia O'Keeffe was born in Wisconsin in 1887. By the age of ten, she knew she wanted to be a painter.

Her work was finally recognized when she was nearly thirty. She sent some drawings to a friend in New York. The friend gave them to the photographer Alfred Stieglitz, who ran an art gallery in New York. Stieglitz loved O'Keeffe's drawings and exhibited them immediately. From then on, people were eager to see her work.

Georgia O'Keeffe continued to develop her own unique style. Her paintings show natural forms such as flowers, shells, skulls, clouds, and hills. They also show skyscrapers and city streets. O'Keeffe's forms are drawn simply, and the colors are vivid.

See also Stieglitz, Alfred.

① Sources

You will find information for your report in reference books, magazines and newspapers, and the Internet. You may want to interview experts. You can even get information from different sections in the same source. When you see a *cross-reference*, turn to that section of the book. If different sources give you different information, it is important to evaluate each source. Is it up to date? Is the author knowledgeable? If sources disagree, check a third source.

② Notetaking

Take notes to help you remember and organize important details. Write notes in your own words, unless you plan to use exact quotes in your report. For each source, record the author or editor, title, place of publication, publisher, date, and page numbers. You may need this information to write a bibliography or to list your sources.

Georgia O'Keeffe

born Wisconsin, 1887

Wilsey, Yukiko. "Georgia O'Keeffe."
Big World Encyclopedia,
2003 edition. Volume 17, p. 202.

Georgia O'Keeffe

took private art lessons for 5 years

Arid, Wendy. Georgia O'Keeffe and
the Desert. New York: Art
Books, 1999. p. 7.

❸ Organize

Here is a sample outline for the first paragraph of a report.

I. O'Keeffe's early years

A. born in Wisconsin in 1887

B. by 10 knew she wanted to be a painter

C. had private art lessons for five years

❹ Write

The outline serves as a guide to write the opening paragraph.

Georgia O'Keeffe Report

The famous American painter Georgia O'Keeffe was born in Wisconsin in 1887. Even as a young girl, Georgia dreamed of becoming a painter. For five years she took private art lessons to help her realize that dream.

Review Questions

1. What other sources might you go to if you wanted to read more about Georgia O'Keeffe or Alfred Stieglitz?

2. How did the outline help in writing a first paragraph? How can you tell?

3. Why is it important to use more than one source of information when writing a research report?

Reading Online Resources

There are many ways to find information on the Internet. Search engines, online encyclopedias, dictionaries, and other reference sources all provide valuable information. By learning how to skim and scan, you will be able to sort through this information to find what you need quickly and easily. Skim to get a quick overview of the material on the page. Scan to find keywords that will help you find the information that you need.

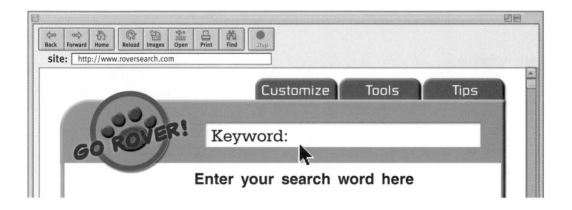

Skim and Scan

1 **Use keywords.** Choose a search engine. Think about your topic and type keywords that relate to it into the Keyword box.

2 **Skim the listings.** Once you get a listing of topics or Web pages, glance through them quickly to see if any match the topic you are looking for.

3 **Click on a listing.** Skimming can help you get an overview of what the page is about.

4 **Scan the page.** Look for keywords on the page that will help you find the information you need.

Search Engine

The keywords *Theodore Roosevelt* were typed to tell the search engine to find information about President Theodore Roosevelt.

① **Use keywords.** Make sure you use a keyword that relates to your topic.

② **Skim the listings.** There are three Web pages about Theodore Roosevelt. I am interested in the one about Theodore Roosevelt's childhood.

Back Forward Home Reload Images Open Print Find Stop

site: http://www.roversearch.com

Customize   Tools   Tips

GO ROVER!

Keyword: Theodore Roosevelt

3 Web Search Results
Society > History > United States> Presidents > Roosevelt, Theodore

1. Theodore Roosevelt: The Early Years–Sickly as a child, TR grew to be known as a "rough rider."

2. Theodore Roosevelt: Nobel Peace Prize winner

3. Theodore Roosevelt's letters to his children

---

③ **Click on a listing.** I'll click on the listing "Theodore Roosevelt: The Early Years." Then I'll skim the page to see if it has the information I need.

④ **Scan the Web page** that you have clicked on. You may discover other links that you want to explore.

Web Page

Here is the Web page that came up after clicking on the link "Theodore Roosevelt: The Early Years" shown on page 753. Skim the page to get an overview. Scan the page to find specific details. You may discover other links that you want to explore.

Theodore Roosevelt

THE EARLY YEARS

At age 10, Teddy Roosevelt went on a trip to Europe with his family. He hiked with his father in the mountains. From these hikes, Teddy learned that exercise helped his asthma.

Encouraged by his father, Theodore became a true believer in exercise and exercised every day. He became a powerful young man and went on to become the twenty-sixth president of the United States. He was also a writer, historian, explorer, and Nobel Peace Prize winner.

Theodore Roosevelt even had a toy named after him—the teddy bear.

Theodore Roosevelt Links:

U.S. Presidents Home Page
The Speeches of T. Roosevelt
The Story of the Teddy Bear

BACK   NEXT

100% Page : 1

Link Entry

After scanning the entry on Roosevelt's childhood, I want to find out why he had a toy named after him. Clicking on the link "The Story of the Teddy Bear" pulls up this Web page.

The story of the Teddy Bear

The Story of the Teddy Bear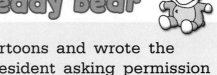

Did you ever wonder how that cuddly, soft creature known as the teddy bear got its name? In 1902, President Theodore Roosevelt went on a bear hunt. For three days the hunters hiked through the woods without finding any bears. When they finally did spot one, Roosevelt refused to shoot the bear.

Newspapers of the day carried cartoons of the event. A shopkeeper in Brooklyn, New York, had just made some stuffed toy bears for his shop. He had seen the cartoons and wrote the president asking permission to call his bears "Teddy's Bears." The president gave his permission, and the little stuffed bears became a huge success.

100% Page: 1

Review Questions

1. What information do you get from skimming the Theodore Roosevelt Web page?

2. How does scanning help you find the connection between Roosevelt and the teddy bear?

3. How can skimming and scanning help you find the information you need on the Internet?

Reading Directions

Learning how to read and follow directions is an important skill. Directions tell you how to do or make something. They take you through a process step by step. Most directions also include a list of materials you'll need and illustrations to show you what to do and how the finished product should look.

Directions have

a title

materials

steps to follow

diagrams

How to Read Directions

1 **Read through the steps before you begin.** That way you'll know how long the project will take and what you need to do to get ready.

2 **Look up unfamiliar words or terms.** Make sure you know what all the words mean so you know exactly what to do.

3 **Gather materials.** Before you begin, make sure you have everything you will need to complete the project.

4 **Do each step in order.** If you leave out a step, the project may not turn out the way it should.

Pita Pizzas

1 **Read through the steps before you begin.** I see that the first few steps should take only a few minutes each.

2 **Look up unfamiliar words.** What is pita bread? I will look it up.

3 **Gather materials.** Mushrooms are optional, so I don't need to use them.

4 **Do each step in order.** I need to preheat the oven before I begin.

What You Need

- 8 pieces of pita bread
- 1 jar of pizza sauce
- mozzarella cheese (shredded or whole)
- food grater
- Parmesan cheese (optional)
- 1/2 cup each of mushrooms or peppers (optional)
- cookie sheet

Steps

1. Preheat oven to 350°F. (Ask an adult to help you operate the oven.)
2. Shred mozzarella cheese into a bowl.
3. Place the pita bread on the cookie sheet.
4. Spread the pizza sauce onto the pitas.
5. Sprinkle mozzarella cheese on top of the sauce.
6. Add some grated Parmesan cheese. (optional)
7. Add peppers or mushrooms. (optional)
8. Bake in a 350°F oven for 10 minutes, or until cheese melts.
9. Serve and enjoy!

Transplanting a Houseplant

When your houseplants start looking cramped and unhappy in their pots, transplant them to new pots.

If you prepare the new pot properly and treat your plant gently, your plant will quickly adapt to its new home.

What You Need

 • houseplant to transplant

 • newspapers

 • potting soil

 • trowel

 • larger pot

 • gravel

 • watering can

What To Do

1. Spread newspapers where you will work.

2. Prepare the larger pot by placing two inches of gravel in the bottom. The gravel will help water to drain from the soil.

3. Fill a third of the pot with potting soil.

4. With the trowel, gently loosen the soil around the edges of the old pot. Then tip the pot over and tap it on the bottom so the plant falls into your hand.

5. Gently loosen the roots with your fingers. Be careful not to rip the roots. The plant depends on these to live.

6. Place the plant gently into the new pot. Hold the plant so that the roots are below the pot's rim and the stem is above. Fill in around the roots with soil.

7. Press gently on the soil around the plant to firm it.

8. Place the pot in a saucer to catch water draining out.

9. Water your plant and place it in a sunny spot.

Review Questions

1. What should you do before putting soil into the new pot?

2. Why is it important to treat the roots gently?

3. Why is it important to do the steps in order when following directions?

Glossary

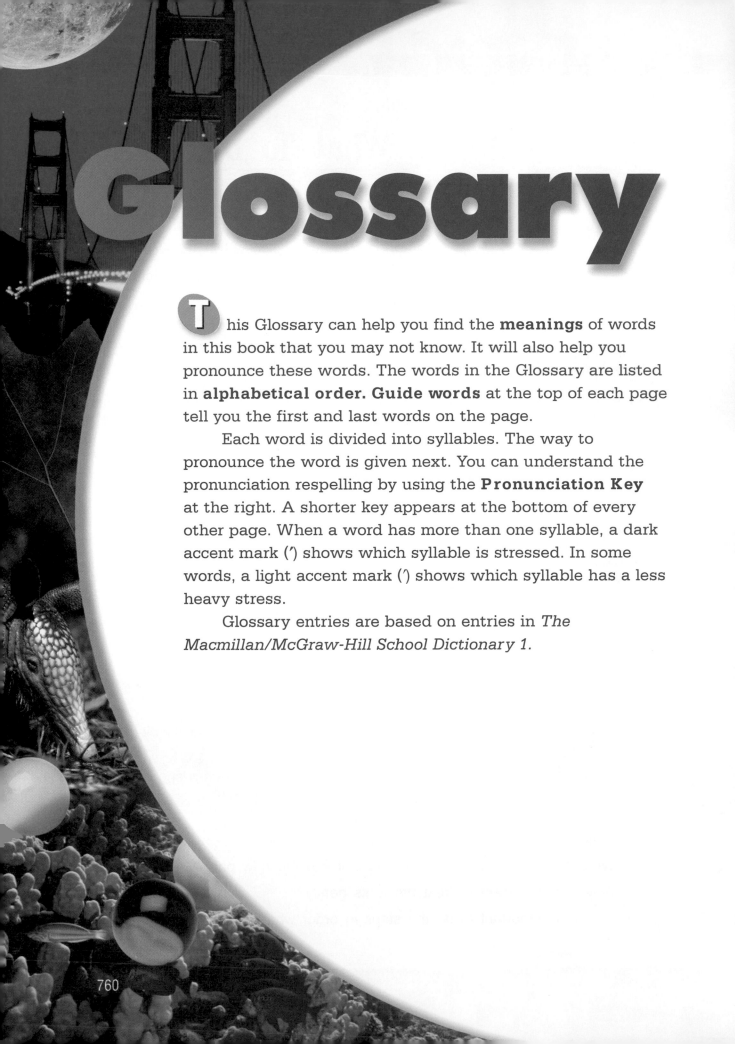

This Glossary can help you find the **meanings** of words in this book that you may not know. It will also help you pronounce these words. The words in the Glossary are listed in **alphabetical order. Guide words** at the top of each page tell you the first and last words on the page.

Each word is divided into syllables. The way to pronounce the word is given next. You can understand the pronunciation respelling by using the **Pronunciation Key** at the right. A shorter key appears at the bottom of every other page. When a word has more than one syllable, a dark accent mark (′) shows which syllable is stressed. In some words, a light accent mark (′) shows which syllable has a less heavy stress.

Glossary entries are based on entries in *The Macmillan/McGraw-Hill School Dictionary 1.*

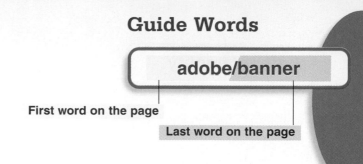
Sample Entry

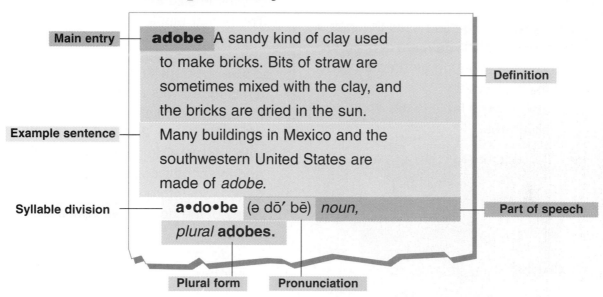

Main entry

adobe A sandy kind of clay used to make bricks. Bits of straw are sometimes mixed with the clay, and the bricks are dried in the sun.

Definition

Example sentence

Many buildings in Mexico and the southwestern United States are made of *adobe*.

Syllable division

a•do•be (ə dō′ bē) *noun,*

plural **adobes.**

Part of speech

Plural form

Pronunciation

a	at, bad	**d**	dear, soda, bad
ā	ape, pain, day, break	**f**	five, defend, leaf, off, cough, elephant.
ä	father, car, heart		
âr	care, pair, bear, their, where	**g**	game, ago, fog, egg
e	end, pet, said, heaven, friend	**h**	hat, ahead
ē	equal, me, feet, team, piece, key	**hw**	white, whether, which
i	it, big, English, hymn	**j**	joke, enjoy, gem, page, edge
ī	ice, fine, lie, my	**k**	kite, bakery, seek, tack, cat
îr	ear, deer, here, pierce	**l**	lid, sailor, feel, ball, allow
o	odd, hot, watch	**m**	man, family, dream
ō	old, oat, toe, low	**n**	not, final, pan, knife
ô	coffee, all, taught, law, fought	**ng**	long, singer, pink
ôr	order, fork, horse, story, pour	**p**	pail, repair, soap, happy
oi	oil, toy	**r**	ride, parent, wear, more, marry
ou	out, now	**s**	sit, aside, pets, cent, pass
u	up, mud, love, double	**sh**	shoe, washer, fish, mission, nation
ū	use, mule, cue, feud, few	**t**	tag, pretend, fat, button, dressed
ü	rule, true, food	**th**	thin, panther, both,
u̇	put, wood, should	<u>**th**</u>	this, mother, smooth
ûr	burn, hurry, term, bird, word, courage	**v**	very, favor, wave
		w	wet, weather, reward
ə	about, taken, pencil, lemon, circus	**y**	yes, onion
b	bat, above, job	**z**	zoo, lazy, jazz, rose, dogs, houses
ch	chin, such, match	**zh**	vision, treasure, seizure

Aa

abalone A large sea snail that has a flat, pearly shell; its meat is used for food. For dinner we ordered *abalone* at the restaurant.
    ab•a•lo•ne (ab′ə lō′nē) *noun, plural* **abalones.**

abolitionist A person who was in favor of ending slavery in the United States before the Civil War. The *abolitionists* wanted to set the slaves free.
    a•bo•li•tion•ist (ab′ə lish′ə nist) *noun, plural* **abolitionists.**

accurate Correct, exact, or precise. The newspaper stories about the accident were not *accurate*.
    ▲ **Synonym:** precise
    ac•cu•rate (ak′yər it) *adjective.*

Language Note

A **synonym** is a word that has the same meaning as another word. A synonym for *accurate* is *precise*.

---

acre A measure of land equal to 43,560 square feet. An acre is slightly smaller in size than a football field. The farmer planted one *acre* of corn.
    a•cre (ā′kər) *noun, plural* **acres.**

adobe **1.** A brick made of clay, sometimes mixed with straw, and dried in the sun. They built the house entirely of *adobe* bricks. **2.** A building made with adobe bricks, popular in Mexico and the southwestern United States. On our drive through New Mexico, many of the houses we saw were *adobes*.
    a•do•be (ə dō′bē) *noun, plural* **adobes.**

afford **1.** To have enough money to pay for. Can you *afford* a new car? **2.** To be able to give or do. They couldn't *afford* the time to help us.
    af•ford (ə fôrd′) *verb,* **afforded, affording.**

amplify **1.** To make louder or stronger. The microphone will *amplify* the speaker's voice so that everyone can hear. **2.** To give more details about; explain more. The teacher asked me to *amplify* my report by giving more details.
    am•pli•fy (am′plə fī′) *verb,* **amplified, amplifying.**

anchor A heavy metal device that is attached to a ship by a chain or cable. When an *anchor* is dropped overboard, it digs into the ground below the water and keeps the ship from drifting. *Noun.*—To hold something in place with an anchor. We will *anchor* the boat while we fish. *Verb.*
an•chor (ang′kər) *noun, plural* **anchors;** *verb,* **anchored, anchoring.**

Word History

Anchor comes from the Greek word *ankyra*. It was first used in the English language in the 12th century.

---

apologize To say one is sorry or embarrassed; make an apology. I *apologized* to my parents for being rude.
a•pol•o•gize (ə pol′ə jīz′) *verb,* **apologized, apologizing.**

approve **1.** To have or give a favorable opinion. My parents don't *approve* of my staying up very late. **2.** To consent or agree to officially; authorize. The town *approved* the construction of a public swimming pool.
ap•prove (ə prüv′) *verb,* **approved, approving.**

arrowhead The pointed tip or head of an arrow. The scientists found *arrowheads* on the site of ancient hunting grounds.
ar•row•head (ar′ō hed′) *noun, plural* **arrowheads.**

arrowhead

arroyo A ditch with steep sides that has been cut in the ground by the force of running water; gully. Arroyos are dry most of the year. During the rainy season, the rains cut *arroyos* into the ground.
ar•roy•o (ə roi′ō) *noun, plural* **arroyos.**

assignment **1.** Something that is assigned. My arithmetic *assignment* is to do ten multiplication problems. **2.** The act of assigning. The company's president is responsible for the *assignment* of tasks to employees.
as•sign•ment (ə sīn′mənt) *noun, plural* **assignments.**

astound To surprise very much; amaze; astonish. The first flight into outer space *astounded* the whole world.
▲ **Synonym:** surprise
as•tound (ə stound′) *verb,* **astounded, astounding.**

---

at; āpe; fär; câre; end; mē; it; īce; pîerce; hot; ōld; sông; fôrk; oil; out; up; ūse; rüle; pu̇ll; tûrn; chin; sing; shop; thin; <u>th</u>is; hw in white; zh in treasure. The symbol ə stands for the unstressed vowel sound in about, taken, pencil, lemon, and circus.

---

athletic 1. Of or having to do with an athlete or athletics. Our school has just bought new *athletic* equipment. **2.** Active and strong. My grandparents are very *athletic;* they love to swim and ice-skate.
> **ath•let•ic** (ath let′ik) *adjective.*

atmosphere 1. The layer of gases that surrounds the Earth. The atmosphere is made up of oxygen, nitrogen, carbon dioxide, and other gases. Outer space lies beyond the Earth's *atmosphere.* **2.** The layer of gases that surrounds any heavenly body. Scientists do not think people could live in the *atmosphere* of Mars.
> **at•mos•phere** (at′məs fîr′) *noun,* plural **atmospheres.**

auction A public sale at which things are sold to the person who offers the most money. My cousin bid five dollars for a rocking chair at the village *auction. Noun.*—To sell at an auction. We *auctioned* off our old furniture. *Verb.*
> **auc•tion** (ôk′shən) *noun, plural* **auctions;** *verb,* **auctioned, auctioning.**

automatically Done in a manner without a person's control. I breathe *automatically.*
> **au•to•mat•i•cal•ly** (ô′tə mat′i kəl lē) *adverb.*

avalanche The swift, sudden fall of a mass of snow, ice, earth, or rocks down a mountain slope. The *avalanche* completely covered the village with mud.
> **av•a•lanche** (av′ə lanch′) *noun, plural* **avalanches.**

awesome Causing wonder or fear. The huge whale was an *awesome* sight.
> **awe•some** (ô′səm) *adjective.*

banner A piece of cloth that has a design and sometimes writing on it. *Noun.* —Important; outstanding. With the hedges and roadsides full of raspberries, it was a *banner* season for raspberry pickers. *Adjective.*
> **ban•ner** (ban′ər) *noun, plural* **banners;** *adjective.*

Word History

The word *banner* appeared in the English language during the 13th century and is thought to have come from the language of the Goths. Their word *bandwo* meant "sign."

barrier Something that blocks the way. The fallen tree was a *barrier* to traffic on the road.
  bar•ri•er (bar′ē ər) *noun, plural* **barriers.**

bashful Shy around people. The *bashful* child hid behind the chair.
  bash•ful (bash′fəl) *adjective.*

billow To rise or swell in billows. The sail of the boat *billowed* in the wind. *Verb.*—A great swelling wave of something. *Billows* of smoke poured from the smokestack. *Noun.*
  bil•low (bil′ō) *verb,* **billowed, billowing;** *noun, plural* **billows.**

bison A large animal that has a big, shaggy head, short horns, and a hump on its back; buffalo. Bison are found in North America. Herds of *bison* once roamed the American prairies.
  bi•son (bī′sən) *noun, plural* **bison.**

board To provide lodging and meals for pay. I *boarded* a family from France last summer. *Verb.*—A long, flat piece of sawed wood, used in building houses and other things. The carpenters hammered nails into the *boards* on the floor. *Noun.*
  board (bôrd) *verb,* **boarded, boarding;** *noun, plural* **boards.**

boon A help; benefit. The rain was a *boon* to my vegetable garden after the dry weather.
  ▲ **Synonym:** favor
  boon (bün) *noun, plural* **boons.**

border To lie along the edge of. California *borders* Oregon. *Verb.*—A line where one country or other area ends and another begins; boundary. The tourists crossed the *border* into Mexico. *Noun.*
  bor•der (bôr′dər) *verb,* **bordered, bordering;** *noun, plural* **borders.**

boulder A large, usually rounded rock. We saw many huge *boulders* at the foot of the mountain.
  boul•der (bōl′dər) *noun, plural* **boulders.**

at; āpe; fär; câre; end; mē; it; īce; pîerce; hot; ōld; sông; fôrk; oil; out; up; ūse; rüle; půll; tûrn; chin; sing; shop; thin; this; hw in white; zh in treasure. The symbol ə stands for the unstressed vowel sound in about, taken, pencil, lemon, and circus.

bruise To cause a bruise on the skin of. The hard fall *bruised* my knee. *Verb.* —An injury that does not break the skin but discolors it. A *bruise* can be caused by a fall, blow, or bump. *Noun.*

> **bruise** (brüz) *verb,* **bruised, bruising;** *noun, plural* **bruises.**

bullet A small piece of rounded or pointed metal, made to be shot from a small firearm, such as a gun or rifle. Never play with a gun, even if it is not loaded with *bullets.*

> **bul•let** (bùl′it) *noun, plural* **bullets.**

burglar A person who breaks into a house, store, or other place to steal something. The *burglar* crawled in the open window and stole the silverware.

▲ **Synonym:** thief

> **bur•glar** (bûr′glər) *noun, plural* **burglars.**

bushel A measure for grain, fruit, vegetables, and other dry things. A *bushel* is equal to 4 pecks, or 32 quarts.

> **bush•el** (bùsh′əl) *noun, plural* **bushels.**

canvas A strong, heavy cloth. My sneakers are made of *canvas.*

> **can•vas** (kan′vəs) *noun, plural* **canvases.**

capture To succeed in expressing something. The story *captures* what it is like to be an only child. *Verb.* —The act of catching and holding a person, animal, or thing. The *capture* of the bank robber took place the day after the robbery. *Noun.*

> **cap•ture** (kap′chər) *verb,* **captured, capturing;** *noun, plural* **captures.**

carelessly 1. In a manner showing a lack of attention. I *carelessly* ran down the stairs, and I tripped and fell. **2.** Done without close attention or care. You will not get a good grade on your report if you *carelessly* make spelling mistakes.

> **care•less•ly** (kâr′lis lē) *adverb.*

cemetery A place where the dead are buried. While at the *cemetery*, I put flowers on my grandmother's grave.

▲ **Synonym:** graveyard

> **cem•e•ter•y** (sem′ə ter′ ē) *noun, plural* **cemeteries.**

Word History

Cemetery comes from the Greek word *koimeterion,* meaning "sleeping chamber."

---

characteristic A quality that belongs to and helps to identify a person or thing. Kindness and honesty are two good *characteristics* of my neighbor. *Noun.* Belonging to and helping to identify a person or thing; typical. The *characteristic* taste of a lemon is sour. *Adjective.*

    char•ac•ter•is•tic (kar′ik tə ris′tik) *noun, plural* **characteristics;** *adjective.*

charcoal A soft, black form of carbon, made by partially burning wood, used as a fuel and in pencils for drawing. The burning wood turned into *charcoal.*

    char•coal (chär′kōl) *noun.*

chase The act of running and trying to catch. The *chase* ended when the police caught the criminal. *Noun.* —To run after and try to catch. The dog *chased* the bouncing ball. *Verb.*

    chase (chās) *noun, plural* **chases;** *verb,* **chased, chasing.**

chemical A substance made by or used in chemistry. Ammonia is a *chemical* used in household cleaners. *Noun.* —Having to do with or made by chemistry. Rusting is a *chemical* process in which metal combines with oxygen. *Adjective.*

    chem•i•cal (kem′i kəl) *noun, plural* **chemicals;** *adjective.*

chile A hot pepper. Mama puts *chiles* in the salsa to make it spicy.

    chil•e (chil′ ē) *noun, plural* **chiles.**

cleft A space or opening made by splitting; crack. You can climb the cliff by holding on to the *clefts* in the rocks. *Noun.* —Divided by a crack or split. Two of my cousins have *cleft* chins. *Adjective.*

    cleft (kleft) *noun, plural* **clefts;** *adjective.*

coax To persuade or influence by mild urging. I *coaxed* my parents into letting me go to camp next summer.

    coax (kōks) *verb,* **coaxed, coaxing.**

cockpit The space in an airplane or a small boat where the pilot sits. The pilot showed us the airplane's control panel in the *cockpit.*

    cock•pit (kok′pit′) *noun, plural* **cockpits.**

---

at; āpe; fär; câre; **e**nd; mē; **i**t; īce; pîerce; hot; ōld; sông; fôrk; **oi**l; **ou**t; up; ūse; rüle; pu̇ll; tûrn; chin; sing; shop; thin; **th**is; hw in **wh**ite; zh in trea**s**ure. The symbol ə stands for the unstressed vowel sound in **a**bout, tak**e**n, penc**i**l, lem**o**n, and circ**u**s.

collision The act of colliding; a crash. The *collision* of the two cars made a great noise.
    col•li•sion (kə lizh′ən) *noun, plural* **collisions.**

commotion A noisy confusion; disorder. There was a *commotion* at the stadium as the crowd booed the referee's decision.
    com•mo•tion (kə mō′shən) *noun, plural* **commotions.**

concentrate 1. To focus one's mind on something. *Concentrate* on your homework. **2.** To bring together into one place. The population of our country is *concentrated* in the cities.
    con•cen•trate (kon′sən trāt′) *verb,* **concentrated, concentrating.**

confirm 1. To show to be true or correct. The newspaper *confirmed* the reports of a flood. **2.** To consent to; approve. The Senate *confirmed* the trade agreement.
    con•firm (kən fûrm′) *verb,* **confirmed, confirming.**

confront To meet or face. A difficult problem *confronted* us.
    ▲ **Synonym:** face
    con•front (kən frunt′) *verb,* **confronted, confronting.**

congratulate To give good wishes or praise for someone's success or for something nice that has happened. We *congratulated* them on doing such a good job.
    con•grat•u•late (kən grach′ə lāt′) *verb,* **congratulated, congratulating.**

conquer To overcome; defeat. We *conquered* our fears.
    con•quer (kong′kər) *verb,* **conquered, conquering.**

consent To give permission; agree. My parents *consented* to my going camping. *Verb.*—Permission. My parents gave me their *consent* to go camping. *Noun.*
    con•sent (kən sent′) *verb,* **consented, consenting;** *noun, plural* **consents.**

convenience 1. Ease; comfort. I like the *convenience* of canned foods. **2.** Something that gives ease or comfort. A washing machine is a modern *convenience.*
    con•ven•ience (kən vēn′yəns) *noun, plural* **conveniences.**

cove A small, sheltered bay or inlet. The pirates hid their ship in the *cove*. **cove** (kōv) *noun, plural* **coves.**

credentials Letters or documents that give the right to exercise authority. Without the proper *credentials* you cannot become president.
cre•den•tials (kri den′ shəlz) *plural noun.*

cripple 1. To injure badly. A car accident *crippled* him. **2.** To disable or incapacitate; keep from working properly. The power failure *crippled* the entire city.
crip•ple (krip′əl) *verb,* **crippled, crippling.**

Word History

Cripple appeared in the English language before the 12th century. It comes from the Old English word *creopan,* meaning "to creep."

cycle 1. A series of events that happen one after another in the same order, over and over again: the *cycle* of the four seasons of the year. *Noun.*—To ride a bicycle, tricycle, or motorcycle. I dream of *cycling* across America. *Verb.*
cy•cle (sī′kəl) *noun, plural* **cycles; verb,** **cycled, cycling.**

dangle 1. To hang or swing loosely. An old kite *dangled* from a tree. **2.** To tease by offering something as a treat. I *dangled* a bone in front of the dog.
dan•gle (dang′gəl) *verb,* **dangled, dangling.**

data 1. Individual facts, figures, and other items of information. These *data* from the computer don't seem to be accurate. **2.** Information as a whole. Adequate *data* on that subject is sometimes difficult to find.
▲ Used with either a singular or plural verb.
da•ta (dā′tə *or* dat′ə) *plural noun.*

at; āpe; fär; câre; end; mē; it; īce; pîerce; hot; ōld; sông; fôrk; oil; out; up; ūse; rüle; pull; tûrn; chin; sing; shop; thin; this; hw in white; zh in treasure. The symbol ə stands for the unstressed vowel sound in about, taken, pencil, lemon, and circus.

769

debt 1. Something that is owed to another. I paid my *debts* when I got my allowance. 2. The condition of owing. My parents are in *debt* because they borrowed money to buy our house.

debt (det) *noun, plural* **debts.**

dedicate To set apart for a special purpose or use. Their parents *dedicated* their weekends to playing with their children.

ded•i•cate (ded′i kāt′) *verb,* **dedicated, dedicating.**

defiantly Boldly refusing to obey or respect authority. The child *defiantly* slammed the door because he didn't want to go to bed.

de•fi•ant•ly (di fī′ənt lē) *adverb.*

delivery 1. The act of taking something to the proper place or person. We get a mail *delivery* every day except Sundays and holidays. 2. A way of doing something. The pitcher's *delivery* was low and outside.

de•liv•er•y (di liv′ə rē) *noun, plural* **deliveries.**

delta An area of land at the mouth of a river. A delta is formed by deposits of mud, sand, and pebbles. It is often shaped like a triangle. The Mississippi *Delta* is the area of land at the mouth of the Mississippi River.

del•ta (del′tə) *noun, plural* **deltas.**

delta

depict To show in pictures or words; describe. The artist tried to *depict* the movement of the ocean's waves. The story *depicted* a day in the life of a typical Chinese family.

de•pict (di pikt′) *verb,* **depicted, depicting.**

despair A complete loss of hope. The family was filled with *despair* when the fire destroyed their house. *Noun.*—To give up or lose hope; be without hope. I *despaired* of ever finding my lost watch in the pond. *Verb.*

de•spair (di spâr′) *noun; verb,* **despaired, despairing.**

desperation A willingness to try anything to change a hopeless situation. They gripped the log in *desperation* as they floated toward the waterfall.

des•per•a•tion (des′pə rā′shən) *noun.*

destruction 1. The act of destroying. The *destruction* of the old building became a media event. 2. Great damage or ruin. The earthquake caused widespread *destruction*.

> **de•struc•tion** (di struk′shən) *noun.*

detect To find out or notice; discover. I called the fire department after I *detected* smoke coming from the garage.

> **de•tect** (di tekt′) *verb,* **detected, detecting.**

devastation The act of destruction; ruin. The hurricane left *devastation* in its wake in the small towns along the coast.

> **dev•as•ta•tion** (dev′ə stā′ shən) *noun.*

devour 1. To eat greedily; consume. The hungry child *devoured* the sandwich. 2. To consume destructively. The flames *devoured* the house.

> **de•vour** (di vour′) *verb,* **devoured, devouring.**

diary A written record of the things that one has done or thought each day. I keep my *diary* hidden.

> **di•a•ry** (dī′ ə rē) *noun, plural* **diaries.**

Word History

The word *diary* appeared in its English form in the late 1500s. It comes from the Latin word *diarium,* derived from *dies,* meaning "day."

---

dimension 1. A measurement of length, width, or height. A cube has three *dimensions.* 2. Size or importance.

> **di•men•sion** (di men′shən) *noun, plural* **dimensions.**

discount An amount subtracted from the regular price. I bought a suit on sale at a 25 percent *discount.*

▲ **Synonym:** reduction

> **dis•count** (dis′ kount′) *noun, plural* **discounts.**

disgrace To bring shame to. Poor losers *disgrace* their teams. *Verb.* —The loss of honor or respect; shame. The president resigned in *disgrace* when the police learned about the stolen money. *Noun.*

> **dis•grace** (dis grās′) *verb,* **disgraced, disgracing;** *noun, plural* **disgraces.**

---

at; āpe; fär; câre; end; mē; it; īce; pîerce; hot; ōld; sông; fôrk; oil; out; up; ūse; rüle; pull; tûrn; chin; sing; shop; thin; this; hw in white; zh in treasure. The symbol ə stands for the unstressed vowel sound in about, taken, pencil, lemon, and circus.

771

dismay A feeling of fear or alarm. The family was filled with *dismay* when they saw the fire approaching their house. *Noun.*—To trouble or discourage. The rising flood *dismayed* the people of the town. *Verb.*
> **dis•may** (dis mā′) *noun; verb,* **dismayed, dismaying.**

disobey To refuse or fail to obey. The driver *disobeyed* the traffic laws by not stopping at the red light.
> **dis•o•bey** (dis′ə bā′) *verb,* **disobeyed, disobeying.**

distinguish 1. To know or show that there is a difference between certain things. The jeweler *distinguished* the real diamond from the fake one. 2. To make something special or different; set apart. The male cardinal's bright red feathers *distinguish* it from the female.
> **dis•tin•guish** (di sting′gwish) *verb,* **distinguished, distinguishing.**

distress Great pain or sorrow; misery. My grandfather's illness was a great *distress* to me. *Noun.*—To cause pain, sorrow, or misery. The bad news *distressed* us. *Verb.*
> **dis•tress** (di stres′) *noun; verb,* **distressed, distressing.**

division 1. One of the parts into which something is divided. Asian history is one of the *divisions* of our social studies course. 2. The act of dividing or the condition of being divided. The *division* of the house into apartments provided homes for five families.
> **di•vi•sion** (di vizh′ən) *noun, plural* **divisions.**

divorce To legally end a marriage. Our parents have been *divorced* for one year. *Verb.*—The legal ending of a marriage. The marriage ended with a *divorce. Noun.*
> **di•vorce** (di vôrs′) *verb,* **divorced, divorcing;** *noun, plural* **divorces.**

donate To give; contribute. The family *donated* their old clothes to people who needed them.
▲ **Synonyms:** present, bestow
> **do•nate** (dō′nāt) *verb,* **donated, donating.**

driftwood Wood that floats on water or is brought to the shore by water. We walked up the beach and collected the *driftwood* the waves washed in.
> **drift•wood** (drift′ wud′) *noun.*

772

drought A long period of time when there is little or no rainfall at all. Our garden suffered in the *drought*.
  drought (drout) *noun, plural* **droughts.**

dynamite A substance that explodes with great force. Dynamite is used to blow up old buildings and blast openings in rocks. Using *dynamite* is very dangerous. *Noun.*—To blow something up with dynamite. The builders *dynamited* the mountain so that they could put a road through. *Verb.*
  dy•na•mite (dī′nə mīt′) *noun; verb,* **dynamited, dynamiting.**

elementary Dealing with the simple basic parts or beginnings of something. We learned about addition and subtraction when we studied *elementary* arithmetic.
  el•e•men•ta•ry (el′ə men′tə rē *or* el′ə men′trē) *adjective.*

emerge 1. To come into view. The sun *emerged* from behind a cloud. **2.** To come out; become known. New facts about the case *emerged* during the trial.
  e•merge (i mûrj′) *verb,* **emerged, emerging.**

emerge

enlist 1. To join or persuade to join the armed forces. Many *enlisted* in the Navy as soon as the war broke out. **2.** To get the help or support of. The mayor *enlisted* the entire town in the drive to clean up the streets.
  en•list (en list′) *verb,* **enlisted, enlisting.**

erosion A wearing, washing, or eating away. *Erosion* usually happens gradually, over a long period of time.
  e•ro•sion (i rō′zhən) *noun.*

escort One or more ships or airplanes that travel with or protect another ship or airplane. The battleship's *escort* included three destroyers. *Noun.* —To act as an escort. The police *escorted* the mayor in the parade. *Verb.*
  es•cort (es′kôrt *for noun;* e skôrt′ *or* es′kôrt *for verb*) *noun, plural* **escorts;** *verb,* **escorted, escorting.**

at; āpe; fär; câre; end; mē; it; īce; pîerce; hot; ōld; sông; fôrk; oil; out; up; ūse; rüle; pull; tûrn; chin; sing; shop; thin; this; hw in white; zh in treasure. The symbol ə stands for the unstressed vowel sound in about, taken, pencil, lemon, and circus.

eventually At the end; finally. We waited and waited for our friends, but *eventually* we went to the movies without them.

 e•ven•tu•al•ly (i ven′chü ə lē) *adverb.*

explosive Something that can explode or cause an explosion. The bomb squad searched the building for *explosives. Noun.*—Likely to explode or cause an explosion. A bomb is an *explosive* device. *Adjective.*

 ex•plo•sive (ek splō′siv) *noun, plural* **explosives;** *adjective.*

fertile 1. Able to produce crops and plants easily and plentifully. *Fertile* soil is the best soil for growing vegetables. 2. Able to produce eggs, seeds, pollen, or young. An animal is *fertile* when it can give birth to young.

 fer•tile (fûr′təl) *adjective.*

fireball A ball of fire. The sun was a magnificent *fireball* in the evening sky.

 fire•ball (fīr′bôl′) *noun, plural* **fireballs.**

flabbergast To overcome with shock or surprise. I was *flabbergasted* when I saw my low grade on the test, because I had really studied for it.

 flab•ber•gast (fla′ bər gast′) *verb,* **flabbergasted, flabbergasting.**

flail To wave or move about wildly. The turtle *flailed* its legs when it was turned on its back.

 ▲ **Synonym:** thrash

 flail (flāl) *verb,* **flailed, flailing.**

former 1. Belonging to or happening in the past; earlier. In *former* times, people used fireplaces to heat their houses. 2. The first of two. Greenland and Madagascar are both islands; the *former* island is in the North Atlantic Ocean, and the latter island is in the Indian Ocean.

 for•mer (fôr′mər) *adjective.*

fraction 1. A part of a whole. Only a small *fraction* of the people watching the football game left before it was over. 2. A number that stands for one or more equal parts of a whole. A fraction shows the division of one number by a second number. 2/3, 3/4, and 1/16 are *fractions.*

 frac•tion (frak′shən) *noun, plural* **fractions.**

fume To be very angry or irritated. The driver *fumed* while stuck in traffic. *Verb.*—A smoke or gas that is harmful or has a bad smell. The *fumes* from the traffic made us sick. *Noun.*
    fume (fūm) *verb,* **fumed, fuming;** *noun, plural* **fumes.**

glisten To shine with reflected light. The spiderweb *glistened* in the sun.
    glis•ten (glis′ən) *verb,* **glistened, glistening.**

glory **1.** Great praise; honor; fame. They both did the work, but only one got the *glory.* **2.** Great beauty; splendor. The sun shone in all its *glory.*
    glo•ry (glôr′ē) *noun, plural* **glories.**

gorge A deep, narrow valley with steep, rocky walls. Over millions of years the river cut a *gorge* in the land. *Noun.*—To eat in a greedy way. Don't *gorge* your food. *Verb.*
    gorge (gôrj) *noun, plural* **gorges;** *verb,* **gorged, gorging.**

granite A hard kind of rock used to build monuments and buildings. The builders lifted the *granite* block to its place at the top of the monument.
    gran•ite (gran′it) *noun.*

gratitude A feeling of gratefulness. We are full of *gratitude* for your help.
    ▲ **Synonym:** thankfulness
    grat•i•tude (grat′i tüd′ *or* grat′i tūd′) *noun.*

grit Very small bits of sand or stone. The strong winds carried *grit* through the air. *Noun.* —To press together hard; grind. I *gritted* my teeth. *Verb.*
    grit (grit) *noun; verb,* **gritted, gritting.**

hail A motion or call used as a greeting or to attract attention. *Hails* from the crowd greeted the politician as he walked into the auditorium. *Noun.* —To greet or to attract the attention of by calling or shouting. We *hailed* a taxi by waving our arms. *Verb.*
    hail (hāl) *noun, plural* **hails;** *verb,* **hailed, hailing.**

at; āpe; fär; câre; end; mē; it; īce; pîerce; hot; ōld; sông; fôrk; oil; out; up; ūse; rüle; pu̇ll; tûrn; chin; sing; shop; thin; this; hw in white; zh in treasure. The symbol ə stands for the unstressed vowel sound in about, taken, pencil, lemon, and circus.

hasty 1. Quick; hurried. We barely had time for a *hasty* breakfast. **2.** Too quick; careless or reckless. Don't make a *hasty* decision that you'll be sorry for later.

>**hast•y** (hās′ tē) *adjective,* **hastier, hastiest;** *adverb,* **hastily;** *noun* **hastiness.**

herb 1. Any plant or plant part that is used for flavor in cooking, or in making medicines or perfumes and cosmetics. She used *herbs* in her cooking. **2.** Any flowering plant that does not form a woody stem, but instead dies down to the ground at the end of each growing season. Her garden of *herbs* supplies the whole neighborhood.

>**herb** (ûrb *or* hûrb) *noun, plural* **herbs.**

heritage Something handed down from earlier generations or from the past; tradition. The right to free speech is an important part of our American *heritage.*

>**her•i•tage** (her′i tij) *noun, plural* **heritages.**

heroic 1. Very brave; courageous. The firefighter's *heroic* rescue of the child from the burning house made all the newspapers. **2.** Describing the deeds of heroes. I wrote a *heroic* poem about Chief Crazy Horse.

>**he•ro•ic** (hi rō′ik) *adjective.*

hoist To lift or pull up. We *hoisted* the bags onto the table. *Verb.*—A device used to lift or pull up something heavy. The sailors used a *hoist* to raise the cargo. *Noun.*

>**hoist** (hoist) *verb,* **hoisted, hoisting;** *noun, plural* **hoists.**

host To serve as host for. I *hosted* a party for our friends. *Verb.*—A person who invites people to visit as guests. We thanked our *host* for a wonderful party. *Noun.*

>**host** (hōst) *verb,* **hosted, hosting;** *noun, plural* **hosts.**

hull The sides and bottom of a boat or ship. The waves crashed against the *hull* of the ship. *Noun.*—To remove the outer covering from a seed or fruit. Birds *hull* seeds before they eat them. *Verb.*

>**hull** (hul) *noun, plural* **hulls;** *verb,* **hulled, hulling.**

husk To take off the husk from. We cracked and *husked* the coconuts. *Verb.*—The dry outside covering of some vegetables and fruits. We took the green *husks* off the corn. *Noun.*
> **husk** (husk) *verb,* **husked, husking;** *noun, plural* **husks.**

Ii

immortal One who lives or is remembered forever. The ancient Greek gods were considered *immortals.*
> **im•mor•tal** (i môr′təl) *noun, plural* **immortals.**

incorrectly In a manner that is not right or correct. You must redo this problem because you answered it *incorrectly.*
> **in•cor•rect•ly** (in′kə rekt′ lē) *adverb.*

influence To have an effect on, especially by giving suggestions or by serving as an example. The older members of my family *influence* me in many ways. *Verb.*—The power of a person or thing to produce an effect on others without using force or a command. Use your *influence* to persuade your friend to study harder. *Noun.*
> **in•flu•ence** (in′flü əns) *verb,* **influenced, influencing;** *noun, plural* **influences.**

injure To cause harm to; damage or hurt. I *injured* myself when I fell off my bicycle.
> **in•jure** (in′jər) *verb,* **injured, injuring.**

inquire To ask for information. We stopped at a gas station to *inquire* about the way to the park.
> **in•quire** (in kwīr′) *verb,* **inquired, inquiring.**

insistent 1. Firm or persistent. Although we were having a good time, my cousin was *insistent* on going home. 2. Demanding attention. The *insistent* ringing of the doorbell woke us.
> **in•sis•tent** (in sis′ tənt) *adjective.*

---

at; āpe; fär; câre; end; mē; it; īce; pîerce; hot; ōld; sông; fôrk; oil; out; up; ūse; rüle; pull; tûrn; chin; sing; shop; thin; this; hw in white; zh in treasure. The symbol ə stands for the unstressed vowel sound in about, taken, pencil, lemon, and circus.

intense 1. Very great or strong; extreme. The heat from the iron was so *intense* that it burned a hole in the cloth. **2.** Having or showing strong feeling, purpose, or effort; concentrated. The worried parent had an *intense* look.

> **in•tense** (in tens′) *adjective.*

interpret 1. To explain the meaning of. The teacher *interpreted* what the author meant in the poem. **2.** To change from one language to another; translate. Since my friends couldn't speak Spanish, I *interpreted* what my cousin from Mexico was saying.

> **in•ter•pret** (in tûr′prit) *verb,* **interpreted, interpreting.**

isolate To place or set apart; separate from others. I was *isolated* from my sister and brother when I had the mumps so that they wouldn't get it.

> **i•so•late** (ī′sə lāt′) *verb,* **isolated, isolating.**

Jj

journal 1. A regular record or account; diary. Each student was told to keep a *journal* during the summer. The scientist entered the results of the experiments in a *journal.* **2.** A magazine or newspaper. The medical *journal* published a report on the doctor's most recent discoveries.

> **jour•nal** (jûr′nəl) *noun, plural* **journals.**

Kk

keg A small metal or wooden barrel. Beer is often put in *kegs.*

> **keg** (keg) *noun, plural* **kegs.**

Ll

lament To express sorrow, regret, or grief. The people sang a sad song to *lament* the loss of their leader.
 Synonym: mourn

> **la•ment** (lə ment′) *verb,* **lamented, lamenting.**

landlord A person or organization that owns houses, apartments, or rooms to be rented to other people. At the end of the month I have to send my *landlord* the rent for my apartment.

> **land•lord** (land′lôrd′) *noun, plural* **landlords.**

778

landscape A stretch of land that can be seen from a place; view. The train passengers watched the passing *landscape*. *Noun.*—To make an area of land more beautiful by planting trees, shrubs, and other plants, and by designing gardens. A gardener *landscaped* the grounds around these offices. *Verb.*

> **land•scape** (land′skāp′) *noun, plural* **landscapes;** *verb,* **landscaped, landscaping.**

lecture To give a talk to an audience. The scientist *lectures* on the history of aviation at the college. *Verb.*—A scolding. I got a *lecture* from my parents for breaking the window. *Noun.*

> **lec•ture** (lek′chər) *verb,* **lectured, lecturing;** *noun, plural* **lectures.**

legislator One who makes laws, especially for a political organization. The Senator knew all of the *legislators* in the state.

> **leg•is•la•tor** (lej′is lā′tər) *noun, plural* **legislators.**

livestock Animals raised on a farm or ranch for profit. Cows, horses, sheep, and pigs are livestock. We enjoy seeing the *livestock* when we go to the county fair.

> **live•stock** (līv′stok′) *noun.*

logger A person who cuts down trees for a living; lumberjack. The *loggers* cut down the trees.

> **log•ger** (lô′gər) *noun, plural* **loggers.**

lush Thick, rich, and abundant. That land is covered with *lush* forests.

> ▲ **Synonym:** luxuriant
> **lush** (lush) *adjective,* **lusher, lushest.**

luxury 1. Something that gives much comfort and pleasure but is not necessary. Eating dinner at the fancy restaurant was a *luxury* for our family. 2. A way of life that gives comfort and pleasure. The opera star is used to *luxury*.

> **lux•u•ry** (luk′shə rē *or* lug′zhə rē) *noun, plural* **luxuries.**

---

at; āpe; fär; câre; end; mē; it; īce; pîerce; hot; ōld; sông; fôrk; oil; out; up; ūse; rüle; pủll; tûrn; chin; sing; shop; thin; this; hw in white; zh in treasure. The symbol ə stands for the unstressed vowel sound in about, taken, pencil, lemon, and circus.

Mm

maiden A girl or young unmarried woman. The boy hoped one day to meet the *maiden* of his dreams. *Noun.*—First or earliest. The ship's *maiden* voyage was from England to New York. *Adjective.*
> **maid•en** (mā′dən) *noun, plural* **maidens;** *adjective.*

masthead The top of a mast. From the shore we could see the ship's *masthead* in the distance.
> **mast•head** (mast′hed′) *noun, plural* **mastheads.**

meagre *Also* **meager.** Very little; hardly enough. The sick child ate a *meagre* meal of tea and toast.
> ▲ **Synonyms:** small, scanty
> **mea•gre** (mē′gər) *adjective.*

mildew A kind of fungus that looks like white powder or fuzz. It grows on plants and materials such as cloth, leather, and paper when they are left damp. *Mildew* grows in the shower if the bathroom is always damp.
> **mil•dew** (mil′dü) *noun.*

mongoose A slender animal with a pointed face, a long tail, and rough, shaggy fur. Mongooses live in Africa and Asia, are very quick, and eat rats and mice. On television we saw the quick *mongoose* fight a snake.
> **mon•goose** (mong′güs′) *noun, plural* **mongooses.**

monument 1. A building, statue, or other object made to honor a person or event. The Lincoln Memorial is a *monument* to Abraham Lincoln. **2.** An achievement of lasting importance. The discovery of a polio vaccine was a *monument* in medicine.
> **mon•u•ment** (mon′yə mənt) *noun, plural* **monuments.**

murky Dark and gloomy; cloudy. We couldn't see beneath the surface of the *murky* water in the pond.
> **mur•ky** (mûr′kē) *adjective,* **murkier, murkiest.**

musket A gun with a long barrel, used before modern rifles were invented. The soldiers loaded their *muskets* for battle.
> **mus•ket** (mus′kit) *noun, plural* **muskets.**

mutiny An open rebellion against authority. The sailors who led the *mutiny* were punished. *Noun.*—To take part in an open rebellion. The crew *mutinied* against their captain. *Verb.*
> **mu•ti•ny** (mū′tə nē) *noun, plural* **mutinies;** *verb,* **mutinied, mutinying.**

Nn

naturalist A person who specializes in the study of things in nature, especially animals and plants. The *naturalists* walked through the forest to study the plants and animals unique to the region.
  nat•u•ral•ist (nach′ər ə list) *noun, plural* **naturalists.**

navigate 1. To sail, steer, or direct the course of. They *navigated* the ship through the storm. **2.** To sail on or across. Ships can *navigate* the Atlantic in under a week.
  nav•i•gate (nav′i gāt′) *verb,* **navigated, navigating.**

Word History

The word ***navigate*** comes from two Latin words: *navis,* meaning "ship," and *agere,* meaning "to drive." Sailors *navigate* ships.

nestle To get very close to; snuggle; cuddle. The kittens *nestled* against their mother.
  ▲ **Synonym:** cuddle
  nes•tle (nes′əl) *verb,* **nestled, nestling.**

nightfall The beginning of night; the end of the day. My parents told me to be sure to be home before *nightfall.*
  night•fall (nīt′fôl′) *noun.*

normally 1. Under ordinary circumstances; regularly; usually. Heavy rain *normally* falls at this time of year. **2.** In an accepted or normal manner. In a traffic jam, cars move slower than they *normally* do.
  nor•mal•ly (nôr′mə lē) *adverb.*

nostril One of the two outer openings of the nose. In the cold air, smoke seemed to billow from the mountain climber's *nostrils.*
  nos•tril (nos′trəl) *noun, plural* **nostrils.**

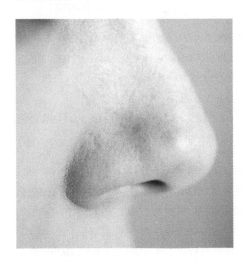

at; āpe; fär; câre; end; mē; it; īce; pîerce; hot; ōld; sông; fôrk; oil; ouᵗ; up; ūse; rüle; pùll; tûrn; chin; sing; shop; thin; this; hw in white; zh in treasure. The symbol ə stands for the unstressed vowel sound in about, taken, pencil, lemon, and circus.

Oo

oblige **1.** To make thankful for a service or favor. We are *obliged* to you for your help. **2.** To make a person do something by law, promise, or sense of duty. My parents were *obliged* to pay for the window I broke.
    o•blige (ə blīj′) *verb,* **obliged, obliging.**

observation **1.** The act or power of noticing. The detective's careful *observation* helped solve the crime. **2.** The condition of being seen; notice. The thief escaped *observation*.
    ob•ser•va•tion (ob′zər vā′shən) *noun, plural* **observations.**

offend To cause resentment, anger, or displeasure. Your rude remark *offended* me.
  ▲ **Synonym:** insult
    of•fend (ə fend′) *verb,* **offended, offending.**

ominous Foretelling trouble or bad luck to come; threatening. There were *ominous* black storm clouds coming in from the sea.
    om•i•nous (om′ə nəs) *adjective.*

onlooker A spectator. The *onlookers* stood on the sidewalk, watching the parade go by.
    on•look•er (on′ lùk′ ər) *noun, plural* **onlookers.**

onlookers

orphanage A place that takes in and cares for children without parents. The *orphanage* finds good homes for children.
    or•phan•age (ôr′fə nij) *noun, plural* **orphanages.**

ozone A form of oxygen. It is formed by lightning or other electricity in the air. Ozone is used to kill germs and freshen the air. A layer of *ozone* in the atmosphere protects the Earth from some of the sun's harmful rays.
    o•zone (ō′zōn′) *noun.*

Pp

parallel Always the same distance apart. The road runs *parallel* to the river. *Adverb.*—Being the same distance apart at all points. If lines are parallel, they never meet or cross each other. The rails of a railroad track are *parallel. Adjective.*
    par•al•lel (par′ə lel′) *adverb, adjective.*

paralyze 1. To take away the power to move or feel in a part of the body. After the accident, my right arm was *paralyzed.* **2.** To make helpless, powerless, or inactive. The bus strike *paralyzed* the city.
>**par•a•lyze** (par′ə līz′) *verb,* **paralyzed, paralyzing.**

parapet A wall or railing built for protection. The rebels retreated to the *parapet* for safety.
>**par•a•pet** (par′ ə pet′) *noun, plural* **parapets.**

peculiar 1. Not usual; strange; queer. It's *peculiar* that the sky is so dark at noon. **2.** Belonging to a certain person, group, place, or thing. The kangaroo is *peculiar* to Australia and New Guinea.
>**pe•cul•iar** (pi kūl′yər) *adjective; adverb,* **peculiarly.**

pelican A large bird that lives near the water and has a pouch under its long bill. The *pelican* flew overhead, carrying a fish in its pouch.
>**pel•i•can** (pel′i kən) *noun, plural* **pelicans.**

pelt To strike over and over with small hard things. Hail *pelted* the roof. *Verb.*—The skin of an animal with its fur or hair still on it. Pelts are used to make clothing and rugs. The trappers traded the animal *pelts* for supplies for their camp. *Noun.*
>**pelt** (pelt) *verb,* **pelted, pelting;** *noun,* **pelts.**

perish To be destroyed; die. Many people *perished* when the ship sank.
>▲ **Synonym:** expire
>**per•ish** (per′ish) *verb,* **perished, perishing.**

permission A consent from someone in authority. You should ask your parents for *permission* to stay overnight at my house.
>**per•mis•sion** (pər mish′ən) *noun.*

persuade To cause to do or believe something by pleading or giving reasons; convince. They *persuaded* me to go with them.
>**per•suade** (pər swād′) *verb,* **persuaded, persuading;** *noun,* **persuasion.**

at; āpe; fär; câre; end; mē; it; īce; pîerce; hot; ōld; sông; fôrk; oil; out; up; ūse; rüle; pùll; tûrn; chin; sing; shop; thin; this; hw in white; zh in treasure. The symbol ə stands for the unstressed vowel sound in about, taken, pencil, lemon, and circus.

783

petition A formal request that is made to a person in authority. All the people on our street signed a *petition* asking the city to put a stop sign on the corner. *Noun.*—To make a formal request to. The students in our school *petitioned* the principal to keep the library open after school. *Verb.*
> **pe•ti•tion** (pə tish′ən) *noun, plural* **petitions;** *verb,* **petitioned, petitioning.**

pier **1.** A structure built out over the water, used as a landing place for boats or ships. We walked to the end of the *pier* and watched the boats. **2.** A pillar or other support used to hold up a bridge. Modern bridges have steel piers to support them. Engineers design *piers* that can hold up bridges during an earthquake.
> ▲ Another word that sounds like this is **peer.**
> **pier** (pîr) *noun, plural* **piers.**

pioneer A person who is among the first to explore and settle a region. *Pioneers* settled the American West. *Noun.*—To be among the first to explore or develop. American scientists *pioneered* in sending human beings to the moon. *Verb.*
> **pi•o•neer** (pī′ə nîr′) *noun, plural* **pioneers;** *verb,* **pioneered, pioneering.**

Word History

Pioneer was first used in the English language in 1523. It is based on the Old French word *peonier,* which means "foot soldier."

---

pneumonia A disease in which the lungs become inflamed and fill with fluid. Pneumonia is caused by a virus. A person with pneumonia might cough or have a hard time breathing. I was relieved when the doctor said I didn't have *pneumonia.*
> **pneu•mo•nia** (nü mōn′yə *or* nū mōn′yə) *noun.*

polio A short form of the word **poliomyelitis.** Polio is a contagious disease that can cause paralysis by attacking the central nervous system. It is caused by a virus. President Franklin Delano Roosevelt was stricken with *polio* and lost the use of his legs.
> **po•li•o** (pō′lē ō) *noun.*

prediction 1. The act of predicting something. The weather forecaster's job is the *prediction* of the weather. **2.** Something predicted. My *prediction* that our team would win has come true.
pre•dic•tion (pri dik'shən) *noun, plural* **predictions.**

presence 1. The fact of being in a place at a certain time. The *presence* of the growling dog at the door made me nervous. **2.** The area around or near a person. The document was signed in the *presence* of a witness.
pres•ence (prez'əns) *noun.*

prosper To be successful; do very well. The town *prospered* when several companies moved their offices there.
▲ **Synonym:** succeed
pros•per (pros'pər) *verb,* **prospered, prospering.**

protective Keeping from harm; protecting. We put a *protective* coating of wax on the floors.
pro•tec•tive (prə tek'tiv) *adjective.*

provision 1. A supply of food. Their ship has *provisions* for one month. **2.** The act of planning ahead for a future need. Has any *provision* been made for the party if it rains?
pro•vi•sion (prə vizh'ən) *noun, plural* **provisions.**

provoke 1. To make angry. Their rudeness *provoked* me. **2.** To stir; excite. Unfair laws *provoked* the people to riot.
pro•voke (prə vōk') *verb,* **provoked, provoking.**

prow The front part of a boat or ship; bow. The *prow* of the ship cut through the waves.
prow (prou) *noun, plural* **prows.**

publicity 1. Information given out to bring a person or thing to the attention of the public. The *publicity* about the band brought a large crowd to hear it perform. **2.** The attention of the public. Most politicians like *publicity.*
pub•lic•i•ty (pu blis'i tē) *noun.*

pulverize To reduce to very small pieces; demolish; grind; crush. We *pulverized* the corn before cooking it.
▲ **Synonym:** crush
pul•ver•ize (pul'və rīz') *verb,* **pulverized, pulverizing.**

at; āpe; fär; câre; end; mē; it; īce; pîerce; hot; ōld; sông; fôrk; oil; out; up; ūse; rüle; pull; tûrn; chin; sing; shop; thin; this; hw in white; zh in treasure. The symbol ə stands for the unstressed vowel sound in about, taken, pencil, lemon, and circus.

785

Qq

quarry A place where stone is cut or blasted out. The crane lifted the blocks of limestone out of the *quarry.* **quar•ry** (kwôr′ē) *noun, plural* **quarries.**

quench 1. To put an end to by satisfying. I *quenched* my thirst with iced tea. **2.** To make something stop burning; put out; extinguish. I *quenched* the fire. **quench** (kwench) *verb,* **quenched, quenching.**

Rr

radar A device used to find and track objects such as aircraft and automobiles. It uses reflected radio waves. The Navy detected the planes with *radar* before they flew over the city. **ra•dar** (rā′där) *noun.*

Word History

The word *radar* is short for *radio detecting and ranging.*

---

rascal 1. A mischievous character. That pup is a real *rascal.* **2.** A dishonest person; rogue. That *rascal* took off with my pocket watch. **ras•cal** (ras′kəl) *noun, plural* **rascals.**

rebuild To build again. After the earthquake in California, the people *rebuilt* what had been destroyed. **re•build** (rē bild′) *verb,* **rebuilt, rebuilding.**

refreshment 1. Food or drink. What *refreshments* will you serve at the party? **2.** A refreshing or being refreshed. I needed *refreshment* after working all day. **re•fresh•ment** (ri fresh′mənt) *noun, plural* **refreshments.**

register To have one's name placed on a list or record. Voters must *register* before they can vote. *Verb.*—An official list or record, or a book used for this. I signed my name in the guest *register. Noun.*
>**reg•is•ter** (rej′ə stər) *verb,*
>**registered, registering;** *noun,*
>*plural* **registers.**

regulation 1. A law, rule, or order. Smoking is against school *regulations.*
2. The act of regulating or the state of being regulated. A thermostat controls the *regulation* of heat in the building.
>**reg•u•la•tion** (reg′yə lā′shən) *noun,*
>*plural* **regulations.**

reject To refuse to accept, allow, or approve. The voters *rejected* the tax plan.
>**re•ject** (ri jekt′) *verb,* **rejected,**
>**rejecting;** *noun,* **rejection.**

reliable Able to be depended on and trusted. We know she will do a good job because she is a *reliable* worker.
>▲ **Synonyms:** dependable, responsible, trustworthy
>**re•li•a•ble** (ri lī′ə bəl) *adjective;*
>*adverb,* **reliably;** *noun,* **reliability.**

reluctant Unwilling. I am *reluctant* to lend you the book because you seldom return what you borrow.
>**re•luc•tant** (ri luk′tənt) *adjective;*
>*adverb,* **reluctantly.**

reserved 1. Set apart for a person or purpose. The only available seats in the theater are *reserved.*
2. Keeping one's thoughts and feelings to oneself. He is a quiet and *reserved* man.
>**re•served** (ri zûrvd′) *adjective.*

reverence A feeling of deep love and respect. Everyone in the town had *reverence* for the old doctor.
>**rev•er•ence** (rev′ər əns) *noun.*

revolt To rebel against a government or other authority. The ill-treated prisoners *revolted. Verb.*—An uprising or rebellion against a government or other authority. The citizens staged a *revolt* against the tyrant. *Noun.*
>**re•volt** (ri vōlt′) *verb,* **revolted,**
>**revolting;** *noun, plural* **revolts;**
>*adjective,* **revolting.**

ruddy Having a healthy redness. She has a *ruddy* complexion.
>**rud•dy** (rud′ē) *adjective,* **ruddier,**
>**ruddiest.**

at; āpe; fär; câre; end; mē; it; īce; pîerce; hot; ōld; sông; fôrk; oil; out; up; ūse; rüle; pu̇ll; tûrn; chin; sing; shop; thin; this; hw in white; zh in treasure. The symbol ə stands for the unstressed vowel sound in about, taken, pencil, lemon, and circus.

Ss

sacred 1. Belonging to God or a god; having to do with religion. Our choir sings *sacred* music. **2.** Regarded as deserving respect. The memory of the dead hero was *sacred* to the town.
sa•cred (sā′krid) *adjective*.

salsa A spicy sauce or relish made mostly with tomatoes and chiles. Many cooks spoon *salsa* on eggs.
sal•sa (säl′sə) *noun*.

satellite 1. A spacecraft that moves in an orbit around the Earth, the moon, or other bodies in space. *Satellites* are used to forecast the weather, to connect radio, telephone, and television communications, and to provide information about conditions in space. **2.** A heavenly body that moves in an orbit around another body larger than itself. The moon is the earth's only natural satellite. All the planets in our solar system are *satellites* that orbit the sun.
sat•el•lite (sat′ə līt′) *noun, plural* **satellites.**

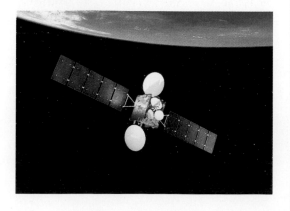

scheme A plan or plot for doing something. The crooks had a *scheme* for robbing the bank. *Noun.*—To plan or plot. The rebels *schemed* to capture the king and queen. *Verb.*
scheme (skēm) *noun, plural* **schemes;** *verb,* **schemed, scheming.**

scholarship 1. Money given to a student to help pay for his or her studies. The university awarded her a *scholarship* for her good grades. **2.** Knowledge or learning. The professor is respected for her *scholarship.*
schol•ar•ship (skol′ər ship′) *noun, plural* **scholarships.**

scorch To burn slightly on the surface. I *scorched* my shirt with the iron. V*erb.*—A slight burn. A necktie will cover that *scorch. Noun.*
scorch (skôrch) *verb,* **scorched, scorching;** *noun, plural* **scorches.**

Word History

The word *scorch* is thought to be of Scandinavian origin, based on the Old Norse word *skorpna,* meaning "to shrivel up."

scratch To scrape or cut with nails, claws, or anything sharp and pointed. The cat *scratched* my arm. *Verb*
scratch (skrach) *verb,* **scratched, scratching.**
▲ **from scratch** From the beginning; with no resources. When their business failed, they had to start again *from scratch. Adverb.*

scroll A roll of paper, parchment, or other material with writing on it, often wound around a rod or rods. The official unrolled the *scroll* and read the message from the king. *Noun.*—To move the text on a computer up or down in order to read it. I *scrolled* through the document to look for words I misspelled. *Verb.*
> **scroll** (skrōl) *noun, plural* **scrolls;** *verb,* **scrolled, scrolling.**

sculpture A figure or design that is usually done by carving stone, wood, or marble, modeling in clay, or casting in bronze or another metal. That statue is a beautiful piece of *sculpture*. *Noun.*—To carve, model, or cast figures or designs in such a way. The artist *sculptured* a lion. *Verb.*
> **sculp•ture** (skulp′chər) *noun, plural* **sculptures;** *verb,* **sculptured, sculpturing.**

settler A person who settles in a new land or country. The first European *settlers* of Florida were from Spain.
> **set•tler** (set′lər) *noun, plural* **settlers.**

severe 1. Very strict; harsh. The dictator established many *severe* laws. 2. Dangerous; serious. The soldier had a *severe* wound. 3. Causing great difficulty or suffering. A *severe* storm is expected.
> **se•vere** (sə vîr′) *adjective.*

shabby 1. Worn-out and faded. The beggar wore a *shabby* coat. 2. Mean or unfair. It's cruel and *shabby* to make fun of other people.
> **shab•by** (shab′ē) *adjective,* **shabbier, shabbiest.**

shoreline The line where a body of water meets the land. We took a helicopter ride up the *shoreline* and saw people swimming in the ocean.
> **shore•line** (shôr′līn′) *noun, plural* **shorelines.**

shrivel To shrink, wrinkle, or wither. The plant *shriveled* because it was too hot in the room.
> **shriv•el** (shriv′əl) *verb,* **shriveled, shriveling;** *adjective,* **shriveled.**

sizzle To make a hissing or sputtering sound. The bacon *sizzled* as it cooked in the frying pan.
> **siz•zle** (siz′əl) *verb,* **sizzled, sizzling.**

> at; āpe; fär; câre; end; mē; it; īce; pîerce; hot; ōld; sông; fôrk; oil; out; up; ūse; rūle; pull; tûrn; chin; sing; shop; thin; this; hw in white; zh in treasure. The symbol ə stands for the unstressed vowel sound in about, taken, pencil, lemon, and circus.

skeleton 1. A framework that supports and protects the body of an animal. Birds, fish, and humans have skeletons made up of bones or cartilage. Many different types of bones make up the human *skeleton.* **2.** Any framework or structure used as a support. The workers built the steel *skeleton* of the building first.
> **skel•e•ton** (skelʹi tən) *noun, plural* **skeletons.**

skeptical Having or showing doubt or disbelief. My classmates were *skeptical* of my plan to get the governor to visit our class.
> **skep•ti•cal** (skepʹti kəl) *adjective.*

sledgehammer A heavy hammer with a long handle that is held with both hands. The workers broke the rocks with their *sledgehammers.*
> **sledge•ham•mer** (slejʹhamʹər) *noun, plural* **sledgehammers.**

snoop One who looks or pries, especially in a sneaky manner. I caught the *snoop* looking through my personal things. *Noun.*—To look or pry in a sneaky manner. *Verb.* The detective *snooped* around the office.
> **snoop** (snüp) *noun; verb,* **snooped, snooping.**

soot A black, greasy powder that forms when such fuels as wood, coal, and oil are burned. The chimney sweep was covered with *soot.*
> **soot** (sut *or* süt) *noun.*

soothe To quiet, calm, or ease. The nurse *soothed* the crying child with a lullaby.
> **soothe** (süth) *verb,* **soothed, soothing.**

speechless 1. Temporarily unable to speak. Her news left me *speechless;* I didn't know what to say. **2.** Not having the power of speech; mute.
> **speech•less** (spēchʹlis) *adjective; adverb,* **speechlessly;** *noun,* **speechlessness.**

spire A tall, narrow structure that tapers to a point, built on the top of a tower. The church *spire* towered above all the other buildings in the town.
> **spire** (spīr) *noun, plural* **spires.**

spiritual A religious folk song, especially one originated by blacks in the southern United States. The group sang beautiful *spirituals. Noun.*—Of or having to do with religion. Priests, ministers, and rabbis are *spiritual* leaders. *Adjective.*
> **spir•i•tu•al** (spirʹi chü əl) *noun, plural* **spirituals;** *adjective.*

sprawl **1.** To lie or sit with the body stretched out in an awkward or careless manner. I *sprawled* in the chair with one leg hooked over the arm. **2.** To spread out in a way that is not regular or organized. New houses *sprawl* across the countryside.
> **sprawl** (sprôl) *verb,* **sprawled, sprawling.**

spurt To pour out suddenly in a stream. Water *spurted* from the broken pipe. *Verb.*—A sudden pouring out or bursting forth. A *spurt* of water came out of the hose. *Noun.*
> **spurt** (spûrt) *verb,* **spurted, spurting;** *noun, plural* **spurts.**

squirm To turn or twist the body. The child *squirmed* in her seat.
> **squirm** (skwûrm) *verb,* **squirmed, squirming.**

stadium A structure made up of rows of seats built around an open field. The crowd filled the *stadium* to watch the soccer match.
> ▲**Synonym:** arena
> **sta•di•um** (stā′dē əm) *noun, plural* **stadiums.**

standard Anything used to set an example or serve as a model. New cars must meet strict safety *standards. Noun.*—Widely used or usual. It's our *standard* practice to send bills on the first day of the month. *Adjective.*
> **stand•ard** (stan′dərd) *noun, plural* **standards;** *adjective.*

starvation The state of suffering from lack of nourishment. Too many people are dying of *starvation.*
> **star•va•tion** (stär vā′shən) *noun.*

statue A likeness of a person or animal, made out of stone, bronze, or clay. The *statue* of the turtle looked so real that you couldn't tell it was made of stone.
> **stat•ue** (stach′ü) *noun, plural* **statues.**

stern The rear part of a boat or ship. The sailor stood at the *stern* of the ship and waved good-bye. *Noun.* —Harsh or strict. Our parents were *stern* when it came to our homework. *Adjective.*
> **stern** (stûrn) *noun, plural* **sterns;** *adjective,* **sterner, sternest;** *adverb,* **sternly.**

at; āpe; fär; câre; **e**nd; mē; it; īce; pîerce; hot; ōld; sông; fôrk; oil; out; up; ūse; rüle; pu̇ll; tûrn; **ch**in; si**ng**; **sh**op; **th**in; **th**is; **hw** in **wh**ite; **zh** in trea**s**ure. The symbol ə stands for the unstressed vowel sound in **a**bout, tak**e**n, penc**i**l, lem**o**n, and circ**u**s.

stifle To smother; suffocate. The smoke was so thick I thought it would *stifle* us.

> **sti•fle** (stī′ fəl) *verb*, **stifled, stifling.**

strict 1. Following or enforcing a rule in a careful, exact way. The teacher is *strict* about spelling. 2. To be followed in a careful, exact way; carefully enforced. That school has *strict* rules.

> **strict** (strikt) *adjective*, **stricter, strictest**; *adverb*, **strictly**; *noun*, **strictness.**

stun 1. To shock. We were *stunned* by the news. 2. To make unconscious. The robin was *stunned* when it flew into the window.

> **stun** (stun) *verb*, **stunned, stunning.**

submit 1. To present. *Submit* your book reports on Monday. 2. To yield to power or authority. The children *submitted* to their parents' wishes

> **sub•mit** (səb mit′) *verb*, **submitted, submitting.**

summon 1. To ask to come. We *summoned* the police to the scene of the accident. 2. To stir up; arouse. I *summoned* my courage and dived off the high diving board.

> **sum•mon** (sum′ən) *verb*, **summoned, summoning.**

superb Very fine; excellent. The actor gave a *superb* performance.

> ▲ **Synonym:** outstanding
> **su•perb** (sü pûrb′) *adjective*; *adverb*, **superbly.**

survey To look at or study in detail. The mayor *surveyed* the damage to the city after the storm. *Verb.*—A detailed study. The company conducted a *survey* to find out who bought its products. *Noun.*

> **sur•vey** (sər vā′ *for verb*; sûr′vā *or* sər vā′ *for noun*) *verb*, **surveyed, surveying**; *noun, plural* **surveys**; *noun*, **surveyor.**

survival 1. The act of surviving. The *survival* of all the bus passengers in the accident seemed a miracle. 2. A thing that survives. The custom of throwing rice at a bride and groom is a *survival* from the past.

> **sur•viv•al** (sər vī′ vəl) *noun.*

swerve To turn aside suddenly. The driver *swerved* to avoid hitting a dog. *Verb.*—The act of swerving. The *swerve* of the car upset the driver's cup of coffee. *Noun.*

> **swerve** (swûrv) *verb*, **swerved, swerving**; *noun, plural* **swerves.**

swollen Made larger by swelling. I can't get the ring off my *swollen* finger.

> **swol•len** (swō′lən) *adjective.*

Tt

tavern A place where travelers stay overnight; inn. The weary travelers stopped to rent a room at the *tavern* for the night.

tav•ern (tav′ərn) *noun, plural* **taverns.**

teem To be full of; swarm. The creek near our house *teems* with fish.

▲ **Synonym:** swarm

teem (tēm) *verb,* **teemed, teeming.**

tempestuous Stormy; turbulent. The *tempestuous* seas tossed the boat around like a toy.

tem•pes•tu•ous (tem pes′chü əs) *adjective.*

tempestuous

thickness 1. The quality of having space between one side or surface and the other. The *thickness* of the walls makes the house quiet. **2.** The distance between two sides or surfaces of something; the measurement other than the length or width. The *thickness* of this board is 1 inch.

thick•ness (thik′nis) *noun, plural* **thicknesses.**

thief A person who steals. The *thief* broke into the house and stole the television.

▲ **Synonym:** robber

thief (thēf) *noun, plural* **thieves.**

thrive To be successful; do well. This plant *thrives* in the sun.

thrive (thrīv) *verb,* **thrived** *or* **throve, thrived** *or* **thriven, thriving.**

at; āpe; fär; câre; end; mē; it; īce; pîerce; hot; ōld; sông; fôrk; oil; out; up; ūse; rüle; pùll; tûrn; chin; sing; shop; thin; **th**is; hw in **wh**ite; **zh** in treasure. The symbol ə stands for the unstressed vowel sound in about, taken, pencil, lemon, and circus.

tiller A bar or handle used to turn the rudder of a boat. The pilot steadied the boat by holding the *tiller.*
　　till•er (til′ər) *noun, plural* **tillers.**

timber 1. A large, heavy piece of wood; beam. The strength of its *timbers* kept the building standing. 2. Wood that is used in building things; lumber. The stack of *timber* was our only clue that they were planning to build something.
　　tim•ber (tim′bər) *noun, plural* **timbers.**

tiresome Exhausting; tedious. It was *tiresome* writing my paper.
　　tire•some (tīr′səm) *adjective.*

tombstone A stone that marks a grave. Tombstones often show the dead person's name and the dates of birth and death. The *tombstones* marked the spot where the old grave-yard was.
　　tomb•stone (tüm′stōn′) *noun, plural* **tombstones.**

tornado A powerful storm with winds that whirl in a dark cloud shaped like a funnel. It can cause great destruc-tion. Luckily, the *tornado* touched down in a field and didn't cause much damage to the houses.
　　tor•na•do (tôr nā′dō) *noun, plural* **tornadoes** *or* **tornados.**

Word History

Tornado first appeared in the English language around 1556. It is a modification of the Spanish word *tronada,* which means "thunderstorm."

---

tortilla A thin, round, flat bread made from water and cornmeal. For lunch I ate rice and beans wrapped in a *tortilla.*
　　tor•til•la (tôr tē′yə) *noun, plural* **tortillas.**

track To follow the marks, path, or course of. The dogs *tracked* the fox. The scientists *tracked* the flight of the missile on their radar. *Verb.*—A mark left by a person, animal, or object as it moves over a surface. We followed the deer *tracks* in the snow. *Noun.*
　　track (trak) *verb,* **tracked, tracking;** *noun, plural* **tracks.**

treacherous 1. Full of danger; hazardous. The waters near the cape were *treacherous.* **2.** Betraying one's country or friends; disloyal. The *treacherous* soldier gave secrets to the enemy.
> **treach•er•ous** (trech′ər əs) *adjective.*

tribute Something done or given to show thanks or respect. The statue was a *tribute* to the soldiers who had died in the war.
> **trib•ute** (trib′ūt) *noun, plural* **tributes.**

trifle To treat something in a careless way. Don't *trifle* with the camera. *Verb.*—Something that is small in amount or importance. One twin is just a *trifle* taller than the other. *Noun.*
> **tri•fle** (trī′fəl) *verb,* **trifled, trifling;** *noun, plural* **trifles.**

tropical Relating to or found in the tropics. In the cold of winter I often wish our weather were more *tropical.*
> **trop•i•cal** (trop′i kəl) *adjective.*

Uu

unbearable Unable to be endured or put up with. Some of us found the singer's voice *unbearable.*
> ▲ **Synonym:** intolerable
> **un•bear•able** (un bâr′ ə bəl) *adjective.*

uneven 1. Not straight, smooth, or regular. The car bounced along the *uneven* road. **2.** Being an odd number. 1, 3, and 5 are *uneven* numbers.
> **un•ev•en** (un ē′vən) *adjective.*

unique Not having an equal; being the only one of its kind. Landing on the moon was a *unique* achievement.
> **u•nique** (ū nēk′) *adjective.*

unpleasant Not pleasing; disagreeable. An *unpleasant* odor came from the sewer.
> **un•pleas•ant** (un plez′ənt) *adjective.*

uproot 1. To tear or pull up by the roots. The bulldozers *uprooted* bushes and trees. **2.** To cause to leave; displace. The flood *uprooted* many families from their homes.
> **up•root** (up rüt′ *or* up rut′) *verb,* **uprooted, uprooting.**

---

at; āpe; fär; câre; end; mē; it; īce; pîerce; hot; ōld; sông; fôrk; oil; out; up; ūse; rüle; pull; tûrn; chin; sing; shop; thin; this; hw in white; zh in treasure. The symbol ə stands for the unstressed vowel sound in about, taken, pencil, lemon, and circus.

usher To act as an usher; lead. The waiter *ushered* us to a table by the window. Verb.—One who leads people to their seats in a church, theater, or other place. We showed the *usher* our ticket stubs. *Noun.*
> **ush•er** (ush′ər) *verb,* **ushered, ushering;** *noun, plural* **ushers.**

Vv

vague 1. Not clearly expressed or understood. The directions to the party were *vague,* so I was unsure where to go. **2.** Not having a precise meaning. To me the meaning of the poem was *vague.*
> **vague** (vāg) *adjective.*
> **vague•ly** (vāg′ le) *adverb.*

variety 1. A number of different things. We bought a *variety* of foods. **2.** Change or difference; lack of sameness. A job that has no *variety* can become boring.
> **va•ri•e•ty** (və rī′i tē) *noun, plural* **varieties.**

violent 1. Acting with or resulting from strong physical force. The falling branch gave the gardener a *violent* blow on the head. **2.** Caused by or showing strong feeling or emotion. My friend has a *violent* temper.
> **vi•o•lent** (vī′ ə lənt) *adjective.*

Ww

waterfall A natural stream of water falling from a high place. The crash of water over the *waterfall* made a thunderous noise.
> **wa•ter•fall** (wô′tər fôl′) *noun, plural* **waterfalls.**

width The distance from one side of something to the other side. The *width* of a football field is 52 1/3 yards.
> **width** (width) *noun, plural* **widths.**

wildlife Wild animals that live naturally in an area. In the forest we saw much of the local *wildlife.*
> **wild•life** (wīld′līf′) *noun.*

woe Great sadness or suffering. The story told of the hunger, sickness, and other *woes* of the settlers of the frontier.
> ▲ **Synonym:** sorrow
> **woe** (wō) *noun, plural* **woes.**

wonderland A place of delicate beauty or magical charm. After the snowstorm the neighborhood looked like a winter *wonderland.*
> **won•der•land** (wun′ dər land′) *noun.*

writhe To twist or contort. The fish *writhed* about when we took it out of the water.
> **writhe** (rīth) *verb,* **writhed, writhing.**

ACKNOWLEDGMENTS

The publisher gratefully acknowledges permission to reprint the following copyrighted material.

AMISTAD RISING by Veronica Chambers, illustrated by Paul Lee. Text copyright © 1998 by Veronica Chambers. Illustrations copyright © 1998 by Paul Lee. Used by permission of Harcourt, Brace & Company.

Poem "Lemon Tree" by Jennifer Clement. Copyright © 1995. Used by permission of the author.

"The Big Storm" by Bruce Hiscock. Copyright © 1993 by Bruce Hiscock. Reprinted with permission of Atheneum Books for Young Readers, Simon & Schuster Children's Publishing Division.

"Breaker's Bridge" from THE RAINBOW PEOPLE by Laurence Yep. Text copyright © 1989 by Laurence Yep. Reprinted by permission of HarperCollins Publishers.

CARLOS AND THE SKUNK by Jan Romero Stevens, illustrated by Jeanne Arnold. Text copyright © 1997 by Jan Romero Stevens. Illustrations copyright © 1997 by Jeanne Arnold. Reprinted by permission of Northland Publishing, Flagstaff, Arizona.

"Dear Mr. Henshaw" from DEAR MR. HENSHAW by Beverly Cleary. Copyright © 1983 by Beverly Cleary. Used by permission of Morrow Junior Books, a division of William Morrow & Company, Inc. Used by permission of HarperCollins Publishers.

"Early Spring" from NAVAJO: VISIONS AND VOICES ACROSS THE MESA by Shonto Begay. Copyright © 1995 by Shonto Begay. Published by Scholastic, Inc. Used by permission.

"First Flight" by Frank Richards from THE PENGUIN BOOK OF LIMERICKS, compiled and edited by E.O. Parrott. Copyright © 1983 by E.O. Parrott.

"Frederick Douglass 1817–1895" from COLLECTED POEMS by Langston Hughes. Copyright © 1994 by the Estate of Langston Hughes. Reprinted by permission of Alfred A. Knopf, Inc.

GOING BACK HOME: AN ARTIST RETURNS TO THE SOUTH interpreted and written by Toyomi Igus, illustrated by Michele Wood. Pictures copyright © 1996 by Michele Wood, story copyright © 1996 by Toyomi Igus. Reprinted with permission of the publisher, Children's Book Press, San Francisco, CA.

"The Gold Coin" from THE GOLD COIN by Alma Flor Ada. Copyright © 1991 by Alma Flor Ada. Illustrations copyright © 1991 by Neil Waldman. Reprinted with permission from Atheneum Books for Young Readers, an imprint of Simon & Schuster Children's Publishing Division.

"Grandma Essie's Covered Wagon" by David Williams, illustrated by Wiktor Sadowski. Text copyright © 1993 by David Williams. Illustrations copyright © 1993 by Wiktor Sadowski. Reprinted by permission.

"How to Think Like a Scientist" by Stephen P. Kramer. Text copyright © 1987 by Stephen P. Kramer. Used by permission of HarperCollins Publishers.

AN ISLAND SCRAPBOOK written and illustrated by Virginia Wright-Frierson. Copyright © 1998 by Virginia Wright-Frierson. Reprinted with permission of Simon & Schuster Books for Young Readers, Simon & Schuster Children's Publishing Division. All rights reserved.

"It's Our World, Too!" from IT'S OUR WORLD TOO! by Phillip Hoose. Copyright © 1993 by Phillip Hoose. Used by permission of Little, Brown and Company.

From JOHN HENRY by Julius Lester. Copyright © 1994 by Julius Lester. Used by permission of Dial Books for Young Readers, a division of Penguin Putnam Inc.

Text of "Knoxville, Tennessee" from BLACK TALK, BLACK FEELING, BLACK JUDGMENT by Nikki Giovanni. Text Copyright © 1968, 1970 by Nikki Giovanni. By permission of William Morrow and Company, Inc. Used by permission of HarperCollins Publishers.

"Life in Flatland" from FLATLAND: A Romance of Many Dimensions written and illustrated by Edwin Abbott. Copyright © 1998 by World Book Publishing. Used by permission.

"The Marble Champ" from BASEBALL IN APRIL AND OTHER STORIES, copyright © 1990 by Gary Soto. Reprinted by permission of Harcourt, Inc.

THE PAPER DRAGON by Marguerite W. Davol, illustrated by Robert Sabuda. Text copyright © 1997 by Marguerite W. Davol. Illustrations copyright © 1997 by Robert Sabuda. Used by permission of Atheneum Books for Young Readers, an imprint of Simon & Schuster Children's Publishing Division.

"Paper I" by Carl Sandburg from THE COMPLETE POEMS OF CARL SANDBURG. Copyright © 1970, 1969 by Lilian Steichen Sandburg, Trustee, reprinted by permission of Harcourt, Inc.

"Philbert Phlurk" from THE SHERIFF OF ROTTENSHOT by Jack Prelutsky. Text copyright © 1982 by the author. Illustration: By permission of Greenwillow Books, a division of William Morrow & Company, Inc. Used by permission of HarperCollins Publishers.

From THE RIDDLE by Adele Vernon. Copyright © 1987 by Adele Vernon. Used by permission of Grosset & Dunlap, Inc., a division of Penguin Putnam Inc.

"Rip Van Winkle" by Washington Irving, adapted by Adele Thane, is reprinted by permission from Plays, Inc., the Drama Magazine for Young People. Copyright © 1966, 1977, 1983 by Plays, Inc. This play may be used for reading purposes only. For permission to produce, write to Plays, Inc., 1 Boylston St., Boston, MA 02116.

THE SEA MAIDENS OF JAPAN by Lili Bell. Used by permission of Ideals Children's Books, an imprint of Hambleton-Hill Publishing, Inc. Text copyright © 1996 by Lili Bell. Illustrations copyright © 1996 by Hambleton-Hill Publishing, Inc.

"The Sidewalk Racer or On the Skateboard" from THE SIDEWALK RACER AND OTHER POEMS OF SPORTS AND MOTION by Lillian Morrison. Copyright © 1977 by Lillian Morrison. Reprinted by permission of the author.

"The Silent Lobby" by Mildred Pitts Walter. Copyright © 1990 by Mildred Pitts Walter. Reprinted by permission of McIntosh & Otis, Inc.

"To Dark Eyes Dreaming" by Zilpha Keatley Snyder. Copyright © 1969. —TODAY IS SATURDAY—Atheneum.

"To Make a Prairie" by Emily Dickinson from CELEBRATE AMERICA IN POETRY AND ART. Collection copyright © 1994. Published by Hyperion Books for Children, in association with the National Museum of American Art, Smithsonian Institution. Used by permission.

"Tonweya and the Eagles" from TONWEYA AND THE EAGLES by Rosebud Yellow Robe, illustrated by Jerry Pinkney. Text copyright © 1979 by Rosebud Yellow Rose Frantz. Illustrations copyright © 1979 by Jerry Pinkney. Used by permission of Viking Penguin, a division of Penguin Putnam Inc.

THE VOYAGE OF THE DAWN TREADER by C. S. Lewis copyright © C.S. Lewis Pte. Ltd. 1952. Extract reprinted by permission.

WILMA UNLIMITED by Kathleen Krull, illustrated by David Diaz. Text copyright © 1996 by Kathleen Krull. Illustrations copyright © 1996 by David Diaz. Used by permission of Harcourt, Brace & Company.

THE WISE OLD WOMAN retold by Yoshiko Uchida, illustrated by Martin Springett. Text copyright © 1994 by The Estate of Yoshiko Uchida. Illustrations copyright © 1994 by Martin Springett. Used by permission of Margaret K. Elderry Books, a division of Simon & Schuster, Inc.

"The Wreck of the Zephyr" from THE WRECK OF THE ZEPHYR by Chris Van Allsburg. Copyright © 1983 by Chris Van Allsburg. Reprinted by permission of Houghton Mifflin Company. All rights reserved.

Cover Illustration
Greg Newbold

Illustration
Lori Lohstoeter, 16; Rose Zgodzinski, 42; Stanford Kay, 64; Stanford Kay, 92; Stanford Kay, 122; Tuko Fujisaki, 123; Cliff Faust, 134–135;

Sally Vitsky, 136; Rose Zgodzinski, 164; Annie Bissett, 198; Adam Gordon, 199; Rose Zgodzinski, 220; Tuko Fujisaki, 221; Rose Zgodzinski, 240; Joe LeMonnier, 250; Rose Zgodzinski, 251; Nancy Stahl, 252–253; Selina Alko, 254; Stanford Kay, 272; Stanford Kay, 306; Stanford Kay, 338; Chuck Gonzales, 339; Annie Bissett, 370; Chris Lensch, 380; Danuta Jarecka, 382–383; Tim Jessell, 384; Rose Zgodzinski, 406; Annie Bissett, 430; Stanford Kay, 462; Rose Zgodzinski, 463; Daniel DelValle, 489; Dave Merrill, 490; Joe LeMonnier, 500; Annie Bissett, 501; Shonto Begay, 502–503; Michael Maydak, 504; Patrick Gnan, 509; Rose Zgodzinski, 530; Wallace Keller, 532–545; Annie Bissett, 552; Stanford Kay, 578; Adam Gordon, 579; Rose Zgodzinski, 600; Chuck Gonzales, 601; Rose Zgodzinski, 610; Bryan Leister, 612–613; Joan Hall, 614; Joe LeMonnier, 646; Annie Bissett, 647; Stanford Kay, 672; Annie Bissett, 696; Annie Bissett 716; Adam Gordon, 717; Annie Bissett, 726; Chuck Gonzales, 727; John Carrozza, 765; Chuck Gonzales, 768, 771, 793; Katie Lee, 777, 783

Photography

5: Don Lloyd/Weatherstock. 7: Association for the Preservation of Virginia Antiquities. 9: Robb Dewall. 13: Matthew McVay/SABA. 15: Paul Edmondson/Tony Stone Images. 18: The British Library, London/The Bridgeman Art Library, London/Superstock. 20: The Bancroft Library, University of California, Berkley, photo by Gordon Honda. 44: National Museum of American Art, Washington, DC/Art Resource, NY. 66: Corbis Images. 68: b. Courtesy, Harcourt Brace and Company/t. Paul Brewer/Courtesy, Harcourt Brace and Company. 70–71 bkgd. PhotoDisc. 72–73 bkgd. PhotoDisc. 74–75: bkgd. PhotoDisc. 76–77: bkgd. PhotoDisc. 78–79: bkgd. PhotoDisc. 80–81: bkgd. PhotoDisc. 84: bkgd. PhotoDisc. 85: bkgd. PhotoDisc. 89: i. AP/Wide World Photos. 91: Express Newspapers/Archive Photos. 94: Collection of Mr and Mrs Paul Mellon, Upperville, VA. 124: Explorer, Paris/Superstock. 130: c. Timothy Marshall/Liasion International. 131: c. Howard Blustein/Photo Researchers. 138: The Granger Collection. 140: Courtesy, Alma Flor Ada. 163: c.r. The Smithsonian Institute. 166: Courtesy of the Westtown School/The Brandywine River Museum. 168: t. Penguin Putnam Books for Young Readers/b. Penguin Putnam, Inc., photo by Myles C Pinkney. 200: n/a Dorothy Zeiman/AXA Financial Inc. 217: Photo courtesy Little Brown & Co. 219: b. David M. Grossman/Photo Researchers Inc. 222–223: © David Hockney/The J. Paul Getty Museum, Los Angeles. 242: Wolfgang Kaehler. 248: b. Sidney E. King/MHSD. 249: t. Association for the Preservation of Virginia Antiquities/b. Association for the Preservation of Virginia Antiquities. 256: Superstock. 271: b. Louis Glanzman/NGS Image Collection. 274: Barnes Foundation, Merion, PA/Superstock. 276: t. Courtesy, Marguerite W. Davol/b. Simon & Schuster Children's Division. 305: c.l. Arne Hodalic/Corbis. 308: Lady Lever Gallery, Port Sunlight, England/Bridgeman Art Library, London/Superstock. 340: National Museum of American Art, Washington, DC/Art Resource, NY. 369: b.r. Corbis. 372: Culver Pictures. 378: Robb Dewall. 379: b.r. Library of Congress/Corbis. 386: Private Collection/Superstock. 388: t. Courtesy, Northland Publishing, Flagstaff, AZ./b. Courtesy, Northland Publishing, Flagstaff, AZ. 405: b.r. Werner Forman Archive/Maxwell Museum of Anthropology/Art Resource, NY. 408: Motion Picture and Television Photo Archive. 429: b.l. The Granger Collection. 432: Hermitage, St Petersburg, Russia/The Bridgeman Art Library International. 464: NOAA/Science Photo Library/Photo Researchers, Inc. 488–89: c. Warren Faidley/International Stock. 492: Julian Baum/Science Photo Library/Photo Researchers, Inc. 499: b.r. The Granger Collection/m.l. Bruce Selyem/Museum of the Rockies/t.l. Bruce Selyem/Museum of the Rockies. 506: The Grand Design, Leeds, England/Superstock. 508: r. Bill Smith Studio. 529: b. Paul Sisul/Tony Stone Images. 532: © 2003 Estate of Pablo Picasso/Artists Rights Society (ARS), New York/Milwaukee Art Museum, Gift of Mrs Harry Lynde Bradley. 554: Musees des Beaux-Arts de Belgique, Brussels/The Bridgeman Art Library International. 580: Werner Forman Archive/Art Resource, NY. 596: b.r. courtesy, Lawrence Yep. 602: Courtesy, Gilbert Elementary School, Gilbert, AZ. 609: i. Phillip Gould/Corbis. 616: Ashley Bryan/Islesford Artists. 644: b. Jacques Jangoux/Photo Researchers. 645: c.l. The Granger Collection/b.r. The Granger Collection. 648: Royal Ontario Museum, Toronto/The Bridgeman Art Library International. 671: t.l. North Wind Pictures. 674: David David Gallery, Philadelphia/Superstock. 695: t.r. Felicia Martinez/Photo Edit. 698: The Smithsonian Institute. 713: Courtesy, Mildred Pitts Walter. 715: t. Matt Heron/Take Star/Black Star. 718: Kathleen Norris Cook. 728: Daniel J. Cox/Natural Exposures. 728: b.r. The Granger Collection. 728–9: Daniel J. Cox/Natural Exposures.

Reading for Information

Table of Contents, pp. 730–731

Chess pieces, tl, Wides + Hall/FPG; Earth, mcl, M. Burns/Picture Perfect; CD's, mcl, Michael Simpson/FPG; Newspapers, bl, Craig Orsini/Index Stock/PictureQuest; Clock, tc, Steve McAlister/The Image Bank; Kids circle, bc, Daniel Pangbourne Media/FPG; Pencils, tr, W. Cody/Corbis; Starfish, tc, Darryl Torckler/Stone; Keys, cr, Randy Faris/Corbis; Cells, br, Spike Walker/Stone; Stamps, tr, Michael W. Thomas/Focus Group/PictureQuest; Books, cr, Siede Preis/PhotoDisc; Sunflower, cr, Jeff LePore/Natural Selection; Mouse, br, Andrew Hall/Stone; Apples, tr, Siede Preis/PhotoDisc; Watermelons, br, Neil Beer/PhotoDisc; Butterfly, br, Stockbyte

All photographs are by Macmillan/McGraw-Hill (MMH); Sidney E. King for MMH; and Richard Hutchings for MMH, except as noted below:

733: b. Ralph A. Clevenger/Corbis. 734: Jack Stein Grove/ProFiles West. 739: b. G Buttner/Naturbild/OKAPIA/Photo Researchers Inc./b. G Buttner/Naturbild/OKAPIA/Photo Researchers Inc; 737: t.l. Andre Jenny/Unicorn Stock Photos/t.r. John Elk/Stock Boston. 740–741: NASA. 748: t.r. Stone/b.r. Corbis/l. Tony Vaccaro/Archive Photos/l. Tony Vaccaro/Archive Photos/t.c. Corbis. 749: b.r. PhotoDisc/bl. Georgia O'Keefe, 1987–1986, White Shell With Red, 1938, pastel on wood pulp laminate board, 54.6x69.8 cm, Alfred Stieglitz Collection, bequest of Georgia O'Keefe, 1987.250.5. Copyright 2000, The Art Institute of Chicago. All rights reserved. 750: l. Tony Vaccaro/Archive Photos/r. Corbis; 750–751: background: Stone; 754: Brown Brothers; 755: National Museum of American History/Smithsonian; 756–7: b PhotoLink/PhotoDisc. 758: bl Tony Freeman/PhotoEdit; 758–9: bkgd S. Solum/PhotoLink/PhotoDisc. 762: L. Newman and A. Flowers. 763: t.r. Francois Gohier/Photo Researchers. 766: bl. Tom Croke/Liaison Agency, Inc. 769: t.l. Francois Gohier/Photo Researchers, Inc. 770: t.r. Thomas Schmitt/Image Bank. 772: William Johnson/Stock Boston. 774: Superstock. 775: Anselm Sring/Image Bank. 776: Chris Close/Image Bank. 779: Jonathan Nourok/Photo Edit. 781: Frederic Jorez/Image Bank. 782: G.M. Cassidy/The Picture Cube/Index Stock Photography. 784: Index Stock Photography. 785: Magnus Rietz/Image Bank. 786: t. Michael Melford/Image Bank/b. Ian O'Leary/Stone. 788: David Ducros/Photo Researchers, Inc. 790: Rafael Macia/Photo Researchers, Inc. 791: Bob Abraham/Corbis-Stock Market. 794: Derik Murray/Image Bank. 795: Pete Seaward/Stone.

Reading Strategy Credits

Craig Spearing, 19–19A; Kevin Beilfuss, 257–257A; Liz Callen, 275–275A; Mike DiGiorgio, 433, 603A, 719A; Luigi Galante, 507–507A; Alexi Natchev, 555–555A; Arvis Stewart, 581–581A; Tom Barrett, 649–649A; The Granger Collection. Pages 45–45a, Grant V. Faint/The Image Bank; pages 67–67a, Jean Lorre/Photo Researchers; page 67a (inset), AP/Wide World Photos; pages 95–95a, Lawson Wood/Corbis; page 95a (inset), PhotoDisc; pages 125–125a, Burton McNeely/The Image Bank; pages 125–125a (inset), Wesley Bocxe/Photo Researchers; page 139, Christopher Cormack/Corbis; pages 139–139a, Randy Duchaine/The Stock Market; pages 167–167a, Corbis/Bettmann; page 201, Courtesy Kids Helping Kids in Crisis; pages 201–201a, AFP/Corbis; pages 223–223a, Copyright Janusz Kawa; page 243, Tim Wright/Corbis; page 243a, David Muench/Corbis; page 309a, Corbis/Bettmann; page 341, AP/Wide World Photos; page 341a, Photograph (c) 2001 The Museum of Modern Art, New York; pages 373–373a, Rafael Macia/Photo Researchers; pages 387–387a, Ed Eckstein/Corbis; page 387a (right), PhotoDisc; pages 409–409a, Reuters NewMedia/Corbis; page 409a (top), Stephen J. Krasemann/Photo Researchers; page 433a (top), Gavriel Jecan/The Stock Market; page 433a (bottom), Superstock; pages 465–465a, The Kobal Collection; page 465a (inset), NOAA; page 493a (left), Georgiana Harbeson/Wood River Gallery/PictureQuest; page 493a (right), Corbis/Bettmann; pages 533–533a, Joseph Sohm/Corbis; page 533a (inset), PhotoDisc; page 603, Craig Hammell/The Stock Market; page 603a, Jon Feingersh/The Stock Market; page 617 (top), Kelly-Mooney/Corbis; pages 617–617a, James P. Blair/Corbis; page 617a (inset), Corbis/Bettmann; page 675, Farrell Grehan/Corbis; page 675 (inset), GK & Vikki Hart/The Image Bank; page 675a, Jeffrey L. Rotman/Corbis; page 675a (inset), Steve Woit/Stock Boston/PictureQuest; page 699a, Corbis/Bettmann; pages 719–719a, Phil Schermeister/Corbis.